Carpet Capital

Economy and Society in the Modern South

edited by Philip Scranton and Douglas Flamming

During the past half century, the American South has undergone dramatic economic and social transformations. Gone is the South of cotton fields and cotton mills, of monocrop agriculture and rudimentary industries, of desperate poverty and stultifying racial segregation. Gone is the South that Franklin Roosevelt saw as "the Nation's Number One economic problem." But if that South is gone, how can we explain the rise of the "Sunbelt," and what has economic change meant to southerners—their daily lives, their attitudes, their culture? This series aims to answer these critical questions through a multidisciplinary analysis of the region's economic and social development since World War II. It seeks to present the best new research by historians, economists, sociologists, and geographers—fresh scholarship that investigates unexplored topics and boldly reinterprets familiar trends.

CARPET

Randall L. Patton WITH DAVID B. PARKER

The Rise of a New South Industry

CAPITAL

THE UNIVERSITY OF GEORGIA PRESS | *Athens & London*

© 1999 by the University of Georgia Press
Athens, Georgia 30602
All rights reserved
Designed by Erin Kirk New
Set in 10 on 14 Sabon by G&S Typesetters, Inc.
Printed and bound by Maple-Vail Book Manufacturing Group
The paper in this book meets the guidelines for
permanence and durability of the Committee on
Production Guidelines for Book Longevity of the
Council on Library Resources.

Printed in the United States of America

03 02 01 00 99   C   5   4   3   2   1

Library of Congress Cataloging in Publication Data

Patton, Randall L., 1958–
    Carpet capital : the rise of a New South industry /
    Randall L. Patton with David B. Parker.
        p. cm.—(Economy and society in the modern South)
    Includes bibliographical references and index.
    ISBN 0-8203-2110-9 (alk. paper)
        1. Rug and carpet industry—Georgia—Dalton—History.
    2. Rug and carpet industry—United States—History.
    I. Parker, David B., 1956– . II. Title.
    HD9937.U53G46   1999
    338.4'7677643'09758324—dc21   98-53802

British Library Cataloging in Publication Data available

For Randall and Matthew

Contents

Preface

This book began as a sponsored research project, funded by a
generous donation from within the carpet industry. As tufted
carpet manufacture neared the half-century mark in the 1990s,
a number of individuals began to express concern over preserving the history of this New South industry. At the outset,
David Parker and I accepted the task of researching and writing a history of the American carpet industry. Our anonymous
donors attached no strings to the grant and have made no effort to exert any editorial control over the project. The only
requirement was that the manuscript reflect the entire history
of the industry, stretching back to the early nineteenth century
and Erastus Bigelow. The history of what we refer to as the
first American carpet industry, associated with the woven process, had already been the subject of two book-length treat-
ments. Cole and Williamson's general *History of the American
Carpet Manufacture* appeared in 1941; Ewing and Norton's
exhaustive treatment of the Bigelow-Sanford company, *Broadlooms and Businessmen* (based on company records), was
published in 1955. Nonetheless, given the time lapse since the
publication of these two works, it appeared logical to us at the
outset to consider giving at least equal treatment to the two
distinct eras of carpet production. Parker, with a specialization in nineteenth-century history, accepted the task of writing
on the early woven industry. My own specialty was in twentieth-century southern and U.S. history, so I naturally was in-
clined to take on the more recent developments associated
with the new technology of tufting.

By the end of the project, it had become clear that the real
story to be told was that of new southern firms in the post–
World War II period. Especially given the nature of the University of Georgia Press's new series Economy and Society in
the Modern South, we decided to reduce slightly the coverage
of the early northern industry and expand my treatment of the

rise of a new southern industry. In order to remain true to our initial commitment, and to provide context and background (especially for those more interested in business history than southern history), we decided to keep an extended prologue that summarizes the early history of the American carpet industry through World War II. Chapter 1, then, begins telling the story of the revolutionary changes that transformed an American industry and the communities of northwest Georgia.

The sections on Georgia's tufted carpet industry were researched and written without the benefit of company records, except for a few scattered references. Oral histories, trade journals, government documents, newspapers, and the records of trade associations were the basic research materials. This book is in many ways only an introduction to this fascinating New South industry. In the future, if companies will open their records, there will be much more to learn about industrialization at the firm level.

Acknowledgments

Any work of this sort embodies the efforts of many. The authors would like to thank all those who participated in the Kennesaw State University Carpet History Project, especially Dorothy Brawley, Virginia Ingram, and Debbie Roebuck. Craig Aronoff and Diane Sears coordinated the grant and took responsibility for reporting to our donor and the administration, allowing us to focus on research and writing. This project could not have been completed without the support of the university's administration, especially President Betty Siegel and deans Donald Forrester and Tim Mescon. KSU's new Center for Regional History and Culture also provided important support.

A number of talented KSU students also helped in the research, by conducting oral history interviews and writing research papers related to the project. Laura Bailey, Kitty Kelley, Jack Melton, Cindy Porter, Bart Threatte, and Linda Williams were especially helpful. Kelley and Threatte delivered papers at professional meetings as a result of their endeavors, a remarkable achievement for these two talented undergraduates. Dorothy Brawley's graduate management classes also aided in the research and deserve special thanks for their hard work. In addition, two graduate students from other institutions participated in the research. James Engstrom of Clark University was particularly instrumental in gathering some of the materials on labor relations and conducted some useful oral histories. We also benefited from numerous conversations with Jim about theories of economic development. Tami Friedmann of Columbia University aided in tracking down some hard-to-find master's theses. Tami also shared freely from her own research into the relocation of the Alexander Smith Company from Yonkers, New York, to Greenville, Mississippi.

Mary Platt, from the KSU library, deserves special recognition. Mary tirelessly tracked down materials related to the carpet industry. Her efforts were largely responsible for the substantial collection of industry-related periodicals, reports, theses, and other documents that the Sturgis Library now holds. Mary also participated fully in ongoing discussions about the research during the course of the project.

The Carpet and Rug Institute opened many of its files for this project, and these sources were immensely valuable. CRI president Ron VanGelderen, Betty Hickman, Catherine Wise, and Brenda Murry of CRI were always gracious and helpful, and their efforts certainly made this a better manuscript. Reg Burnett of RBI Carpet Consultants also gave generously of his time.

A number of colleagues read and critiqued portions of this manuscript in the form of conference papers and articles. John Inscoe of the University of Georgia, Ralph Peters of Floyd College, Mike Cassity of Wyoming, Pamela Ulrich of Auburn, Steven Vallas of Georgia Tech, and Christina Jeffrey offered valuable advice and constructive criticism. Tom Scott and Ann Pullen of Kennesaw State University read the entire manuscript and made a significant contribution to the final product.

Tom Deaton conducted interviews when he began work on a history of the tufting industry in the 1970s. He generously made available his tapes and his expertise, giving sage advice on a variety of matters.

Several faculty members from the Georgia Institute of Technology's School of History, Technology, and Society were particularly instrumental in the process of researching and writing this manuscript, and Randy Patton would like to offer special thanks to them. Gus Giebelhaus made available an extensive collection of papers relating to Dalton Utilities and offered valuable insights into the role of the local utility in industrial development. Robert McMath and Philip Scranton of Georgia Tech offered their own unique perspectives, and the manuscript reflects many of the suggestions they made. Bob and Phil went over much of the manuscript in great detail, suggesting changes that greatly improved both the style and substance of the book.

Doug Flamming of Georgia Tech read an early conference paper based on this research and later critiqued the entire manuscript as well. His critique of the manuscript was particularly helpful at a crucial point in the evolution of this project. Doug was also especially generous with his time and counsel, and Patton cannot thank him enough for all his efforts.

We would also like to thank all those who consented to oral history interviews for this project. Their names are listed in the sources at the end, but they deserve a special thanks. We had virtually no company records to work from with this project, so oral histories were the only sources for some critical events. We should also give special mention to a few individuals from within the industry who were particularly helpful: J. C. Shaw, Charles Bramlett, Bobby Mosteller, Peter Spirer, and Raymond Roach.

We would also like to thank Malcolm Call, Kristine Blakeslee, and all the others from the University of Georgia Press for their help. Malcolm deserves a special thanks for his support in the preliminary stages of the process. Grace Buonocore, our copy editor, also deserves recognition for her extensive work in helping us polish the manuscript.

Glenn Eskew and Brian Wills, Randy Patton's colleagues from graduate school days, have shared, perhaps more than they wished, in this endeavor. Brian read a substantial portion of the manuscript. They are good listeners, and they both made wise suggestions on a variety of matters. Brian and Glenn are model colleagues and, more important, friends.

Numan V. Bartley, Patton's mentor and friend, provided his usual sage advice during the course of this project. He also read the manuscript carefully and thoughtfully (again, as usual). Randy is indebted to him beyond his ability to express it. To him must go a large portion of the credit for anything of value in this manuscript.

David Parker extends a special thanks to Chantal, his wife, and to Gentry and Katie Mae, their children, for their patience and support during this project. He promised them that someday it would be over, and time proved him right. He dedicates his portion of the book to them.

Randy Patton would like to thank his parents, Cliff and Annette, and his sister, April, all of whom have been supportive, on this project and in the past. Most of all, Randy would like to thank his wife, Karen, and his sons, Randall and Matthew. Karen has always been there, and her love, confidence, and support have meant more than she can know. Randall and Matthew are the lights of his life, and to them he dedicates his portion of this book.

Carpet Capital

Introduction

The small northwest Georgia community of Dalton has recently drawn scholarly interest. Douglas Flamming published
a prizewinning study of workers and managers in the cotton
mills of Dalton in 1992. In *Creating the Modern South: Millhands and Managers in Dalton, Georgia, 1884–1984,* Flamming detailed the building of Crown Cotton Mill and its mill
village and eloquently described the birth, life, and demise of
organized labor in this small southern town. He finished by
describing the decline of Dalton's cotton mills and the simul-
taneous rise of a new local industry—tufted carpeting. By the
early 1960s, carpet plants had eclipsed cotton mills as the

largest employers in the Dalton area, and this enterprising New South city had become the "carpet capital" of the world. Flamming's chief focus, however, was clearly on cotton mill managers and workers. As he rightly noted, cotton mills such as the Crown company's represented the South's industrial past; the carpet mill boom was the wave of the future, at least for this southern community. The rapid growth in carpet manufacture in the Dalton area during the 1950s and 1960s, and post–World War II southern industrial development generally, deserve greater scholarly attention.[1]

Small and medium-sized businesses generally deserve more scholarly study as well. In 1991, Mansel Blackford published a survey of the history of small business. He deftly summarized the existing literature and ended with a series of questions designed to stimulate small business research in a variety of areas. In the realm of manufacturing, Blackford asked "just how common were small, flexible firms such as the ones Philip Scranton and John Ingham have written about?" He also called for more research into the role of small business in technological innovation and noted that historians needed to "learn more about how small firms have interacted through their trade associations and other organizations."[2] A study of the carpet industry of Dalton, Georgia, sheds light on all these questions. It can also help expand a new line of inquiry for historians of southern industrialization. Most scholarship on industrial development in the American South has focused on what James C. Cobb has called "the selling of the South": the feverish pursuit of outside investment by southern state and local governments and boosters. This focus has been quite understandable and appropriate. From Henry Grady's New South addresses of the 1880s through Mississippi's Balance Agriculture With Industry program of the 1930s to Alabama's wooing of Mercedes in the 1990s, southern political and economic leaders have tended to look outside the region for solutions to the problems of poverty and underdevelopment. Examples of indigenous southern entrepreneurship, development, and technological innovation have been relatively scarce, and scholars have spent little time on them.[3]

The Dalton carpet district exemplified the advantage of external economies identified by British economist Alfred Marshall. Much economic scholarship has focused on economies of scale that are inherently internal to the individual firm—the efficiencies of the assembly line, vertical integration, mass production, and the consequent rise of "big businesses" such as U.S. Steel and Ford as a way to cut unit costs. Marshall focused on external economies associated with groups of related small and medium firms engaged in decentralized, specialized production. Marshall argued that manufacturing firms often tended to cluster in what he called "localization economies" for three chief reasons. First, "employers are apt to resort to any place where they are likely to find a good choice of workers with the special skill which they require," he observed, "while men seeking employment naturally go to places where there are many employers."[4]

Second, "subsidiary trades grow up in the neighborhood, supplying [the new local industry] with implements and materials." These service firms devote "themselves to one small branch of the process of production," avoiding the risks inherent in overspecialization by spreading their services among the many primary manufacturers. The growth of "subsidiary trades" is both a cause and an effect of localization: the subsidiary firms emerge to meet demand from a growing number of manufacturing companies, then manufacturers multiply as subsidiary industries compete to offer low-cost supplies and services.[5]

Third, and perhaps most important for the Dalton district, "the mysteries of the trade become no mystery," with so many manufacturers of the same product in one area, "but are, as it were, in the air." Technological advancements and improvements in management techniques alike are widely disseminated: "Good work is rightly appreciated, inventions and improvements in machinery, and in processes and the general organisation of the business, have their merits promptly discussed."[6]

Marshall's ideas, out of fashion in economic development circles for several decades, have recently been revived (and much expanded and elaborated) by a number of economic geographers, economists, and historians. The new scholarship of industrialization has taken Marshall's formulation and added a fourth category of external economy: an almost mystical cooperative ethic that emerged from the interplay of the more tangible advantages of industrial clustering. Indeed, the prestigious London *Economist* took note of the resurgence of the concept of localization economies and industrial districts in 1995. The *Economist* even used Dalton as an example of the external economies that could produce economic growth and development. The carpet capital appeared in the same article as, and was favorably compared to, California's Silicon Valley to illustrate the intangible as well as the quantifiable benefits of industrial clustering.[7]

Recent studies of regional industrial agglomerations in other parts of the United States—and the world—have begun to add complexity and nuance to our understanding of industrialization generally, and these studies have important implications for analyses of southern economic development as well. For example, the evolution of California's Silicon Valley, as described recently by Annalee Saxenian, was in some ways comparable to the development of the tufted carpet district of northwest Georgia. Silicon Valley's electronic and computer pioneers created an industrial system much more flexible than that of Boston's Route 128. The system that emerged in California was "organized around the region and its professional and technical networks rather than around the individual firm." Boundaries among firms were porous, and it was common for employees from one firm to strike out on their own and start new companies. The Dalton carpet district evolved in a similar fashion, with a rapid expansion of new firms started by entrepreneurs who had essentially "apprenticed" in older firms. The commitment to craft that characterized Silicon Valley's engineers, on the other hand, was not very significant in the Dalton carpet industry. Certainly, however, the region's culture, like that of Silicon Valley, encouraged risk taking and accepted failure. Cooperation was also a central element in the construction of both districts; Dalton-area mill executives formed an effective regional manufacturers association that helped bind the decentralized industry together. Cooperation between companies and local government also played a significant role in the development of Silicon Valley. In the Dalton district, the main source of public support for the growth of carpet manufacture came from the municipally owned utility company, which consistently adjusted its policies and practices to accommodate a rapidly expanding new industry.[8]

The increasing concentration of carpet manufacture in the Dalton area put great pressure on local resources, especially the water supply. The cooperation among manufacturers also had a darker side. The issue that first, and most effectively, galvanized the cooperative sentiments of Dalton-area mill owners was resistance to labor unions. In spite of the problems associated with Dalton's growth, the northwest Georgia region's industrial growth in the post–World War II period lends at least some credence to Saxenian's argument for economic regionalism. She observed that the experience of Silicon Valley "shows that . . . regions offer an important source of competitive advantage even as production and markets become more global." There were great advantages in regional, rather than national, approaches to industrial development policy, she contended, and the "most effective arena for setting such policies is at the regional level— the level of metropolitan or county government, or even the government of a small state." Saxenian's views on "regionalism" are in some ways reminiscent of an influential school of thought in the American South in the 1930s and 1940s. The southern "regionalists," led by Howard Odum, Rupert Vance, and others, argued that the South was a coherent region bound together by its common problems (chiefly, though not exclusively, economic) and advocated regional planning as a way out of the persistent poverty that afflicted the region.[9]

The Dalton carpet district exhibited characteristics of "industry clusters" identified by Gary Anderson, Michael Porter, and other students of economic development. They defined an industry cluster as "a group of companies that rely on an active set of relationships among themselves for individual efficiency and competitiveness." These sets of relationships can be grouped into three general categories (not mutually exclusive). "Buyer-supplier relationships" are the most common clusters. In these groupings, manufacturers of finished goods establish themselves in close proximity to suppliers of raw materials or other producers of intermediate goods— in textiles, finishing, for example. These relationships certainly existed to a high degree in the Dalton district. "Competitor and collaborator relationships" also characterized the Dalton carpet cluster. This type of clustering relationship is characterized by "companies that produce the same or similar goods and services at a specific level in the value chain." Competitors often "share information (often unintentionally) about product and process innovations and market opportunities." These relationships were found in abundance in the Dalton district. The firms of the Dalton area also participated in "shared-resource relationships." All carpet firms in the district, like firms in Silicon Valley, relied "on the same sources of raw materials, technology, human resources, and information." In the

Dalton area, the Water, Light, & Sinking Fund functioned as a shared re-
source as well, promoting new firm formation.[10]

The rise of northwest Georgia's tufted carpet industry reflects as
much as anything the diversity and contingent nature of industrialization.
Charles Sabel and Jonathan Zeitlin are two of the scholars most responsible for opening the scholarly dialogue on flexible versus mass production. Recently, they have developed the themes of complexity, contin-
gency, and diversity in economic development. Sabel and Zeitlin reject the
assumptions of neoclassical economics that posit human beings as exclusively economic creatures responding more or less blindly to overarching
economic laws. Rather, the story—or, perhaps more appropriately, the
stories—of manufacturing and industrial development are important.
The details of these narratives—iron and steel in Pittsburgh and Birmingham, textiles in Lowell and Philadelphia, for example—reflect more
than the predictable responses of various entrepreneurs and workers to
given stimuli. As Philip Scranton and others have shown, manufacturing
enterprises did not always follow the same trajectory. Human beings, as
enterprising owners and as workers, shaped industrial development in a
variety of ways. In an introduction to a recent volume of essays on this
topic, Sabel and Zeitlin introduced a note of complexity into what had
tended to be a debate between stylized alternatives. Rather than por-
traying the history of industrialization as a contest between flexibility and
mass production, Sabel and Zeitlin concluded in 1997 that the truth was
both less dramatic and more interesting. "Most firms in nineteenth- and
early twentieth-century Europe and the United States . . . carefully
weighed the choices between mass production and what we now call flexible specialization," and whenever feasible, "they developed sophisticated
hedges for reducing their risks by avoiding a definitive choice in favor of
either alternative." The history of industrialization has been marked, then,
by the purposeful calculations of entrepreneurs, managers, and workers.
Mass and flexible production are not necessarily mutually exclusive alternatives, and many economic actors have tried to steer a course that did
not preclude either.[11]

The complex of tufted carpet manufacturers that emerged around Dalton, Georgia, in the mid-twentieth century exemplified this more nuanced
view of industrial development. The Dalton carpet manufacturers were

small firms that shared many of the characteristics of Saxenian's Silicon Valley companies, though certainly not all. These firms developed a flexible method for mass-producing a wide array of slightly different goods. The development of the tufted carpet industry illustrates the attempts of manufacturers to combine flexibility with high throughput and mass-market production. In doing so, the new, mainly southern, entrepreneurs claimed dominance in an important segment of the textile industry during the 1950s.

In 1950, the word *carpet* implied a woven wool construction. By the early 1960s, machine-tufted nylon rugs and carpets dominated the soft floor covering market. A handful of old, established companies in the Northeast controlled carpet manufacturing in the early 1950s; by 1965 the nation's largest producer of soft floor coverings was a new Georgia firm created with a $4,500 investment in 1949. In the early 1950s, U.S. households purchased about two square yards of carpet per year; that rate had changed little since the early years of the twentieth century. By the end of the 1960s, annual household consumption of carpeting had risen to more than ten square yards. New firms—most of them located in and around the small town of Dalton, Georgia, and quite small initially—played the leading role in transforming the carpet industry; such firms were primarily responsible for introducing and refining the new technology of tufting that supplanted weaving.

David B. Parker's prologue opens our story of American carpet manufacture. It summarizes the first American carpet industry, from the early nineteenth century through the 1930s. The scene then shifts to the South as Randall L. Patton begins the story of the transformation of carpet manufacture after World War II. The established carpet industry faced a stagnant demand, especially frustrating in the midst of the consumer spending binge of the 1950s, and chapter 1 traces the efforts of the old woven manufacturers to break out of the slump. The revolution in carpet manufacture wrought by southern entrepreneurs and mechanics is the focus of chapter 2. Labor-management relations are examined in chapters 3 and 4. The Textile Workers Union of America made two vigorous efforts to organize the carpet mill workers of the Dalton district in the 1950s and 1960s. The union's efforts met with mixed success, but carpet mill owners and managers responded to the union campaigns by strengthening their ties to an essentially regional trade organization—the Tufted Textile Manufacturers Association. Chapter 5 traces the rise and fall of the largest and most influential company in the early days of the tufting boom, E. T. Barwick Mills. Barwick Mills exemplified all the strengths and weaknesses of the new industry, usually in larger-than-life fashion. Chapter 6 surveys the wave of new firm creation that characterized the 1960s and 1970s by examining one new company in detail (Galaxy Mills) and several others in brief capsules. Chapter 7 describes the growth of the industry in general terms, concentrating on the changing role of the manufacturers association, local government's role in promoting growth, government regulation, and the fate of small manufacturers. Chapter 8 brings the story into the 1990s with a look at the rise of Shaw Industries, the largest firm in the industry as it neared the end of a half century of rapid growth, and other recent developments. Shaw's story reflected the development of a new atmosphere of intense competition among firms, characterized by Shaw's CEO as a struggle for existence that would result in the "survival of the fittest."

Prologue: The First American Carpet Industry

"Colonial Americans busy carving out a new continent had little time to enjoy such amenities as rugs on the floor," wrote one scholar of American floor coverings.[1] Until the mid-eighteenth century, few Europeans (aside from royalty) had carpets in their homes, and while the colonists were certainly busy people, their lack of rugs and carpets probably reflected more the general European tastes of interior design than their own hectic schedules. The few woven floor coverings in American homes (aside from homemade rag rugs) were imported from England, Scotland, or elsewhere; there was no carpet industry in America and little need for one. The use of carpets in

European homes became more widespread beginning about 1750, and a couple of decades later—ironically, about the time Americans were breaking their political ties to Europe—the trend crossed the Atlantic.

The First American Carpet Manufacturers

William Peter Sprague is generally credited as the first American carpet manufacturer. Sprague, an Englishman who had learned carpet making in Devonshire, brought his family to America toward the end of the Revolutionary War. He first opened a shop in New Jersey, but by 1790 he was located in Philadelphia, capital city of the new Republic, where at his aptly named Philadelphia Carpet Manufactory he made the carpet that graced the Senate chamber of the new Capitol in Philadelphia, the carpet used in the dining room of the house in Philadelphia that George Washington rented during his presidency, and many others.[2]

Sprague's best-known productions were Axminsters, carpets with a luxurious pile, each tiny tuft of which was a separate hand-tied knot. The Axminster process was a tedious one that required not only patience but a tremendous amount of skill. Sprague also produced cheaper carpets, the most common of which were ingrains and Venetians. Ingrains, also known as "Scottish," "English," or "Kidderminster" (from the English city near Birmingham where ingrains were first woven in the early eighteenth century), were quite different from Axminsters. Axminsters were made in one piece and had a pile of hand-tied tufts, while ingrains were flat-woven (that is, they lacked a pile) on narrow looms (usually thirty-six inches). In effect, ingrains were simply a heavy cloth, woven in strips a yard wide and sewn together to produce the desired width to cover a floor. All ingrains in the beginning were "two-ply," meaning that the looms simultaneously wove two pieces of fabric that were connected where the colors in the carpet's pattern changed. Ingrains were therefore reversible, the top and bottom having the same pattern but in opposite colors. In the 1820s, a Scottish weaver developed a "three-ply" carpet that consisted of three rather than two layers of fabric. Americans were weaving three-plies by the 1830s. Venetians, like ingrains, were flat-woven carpets; unlike ingrains, they were made of just one layer and carried the pattern of the carpet in the warp threads (running the length of the fabric) rather than the weft threads (which went across the loom and therefore across the width of the fabric). Venetians, cheaper than ingrains, were especially appropriate for use in hallways and on stairs.[3]

Sprague was just one of many early American carpet manufacturers. William Calverly is reported to have made carpets in Philadelphia as early as 1775. Farther north, Peter Stowell owned "a cotton and carpet manufactory" in Worcester, Massachusetts, in 1794; ten years later, he and his brother, Ebenezer, produced "fine carpets" on six looms "of their own invention and construction." By about 1815, Isaac Macaulay's Philadelphia factory was putting out carpet using yarns produced on site and workers imported from Kidderminster, England. Other early carpet manufacturers included George M. Conradt, an immigrant from Württemberg who produced ingrains in Frederick County, Maryland; James Alexander of Newburgh, New York, who exhibited his prizewinning ingrains at Orange County's agricultural fair in 1819; and John and Nicholas Haight, brothers in New Jersey who in 1821 employed several hundred people in their carpet-weaving mill (in Jersey City) and their yarn-spinning plant (in Little Falls).[4]

The infant American carpet industry grew slowly. As late as 1816, Secretary of the Treasury Alexander James Dallas reported that carpets "have not been the objects of American capital, industry, and enterprise, to any important degree." Dallas placed carpets in his third class of American industries, those "so slightly cultivated as to leave the demand of the country wholly or almost wholly dependent upon foreign sources for a supply."[5] A decade later, however, the carpet industry began a growth spurt that resulted in a significant jump in production and saw the beginnings of some of the most important companies in the industry's history.

In 1825 Alexander Wright, a Scottish immigrant from a family of carpet weavers, secured the backing of a wealthy Boston merchant and converted a woolen mill in Medway, Massachusetts, to carpet production. Philadelphia carpet manufacturers, afraid of losing technological secrets to a potential competitor, refused to let him tour their mills, so Wright returned to his homeland, where he purchased three looms and persuaded some twenty weavers to return with him to Medway. A Boston newspaper advertised Wright's carpets as "equal in every respect, if not superior to the best kidderminster carpetings." In 1828, a group of Boston investors set up the Lowell Manufacturing Company and bought Wright's Medway factory. By 1832 Lowell was running sixty-odd looms and turning out well over 100,000 yards of ingrain a year, in addition to 1,500 hand-tufted rugs and 7,500 yards of Brussels carpet. Brussels, unlike flat-woven ingrains and Venetians, had a pile on one side created by weaving the surface yarn over thin wires. When the wires were removed, they left small loops of yarn that made up the pile. A Wilton carpet was similar to a Brussels except that the wires used in Wilton weaving had small blades on the ends that would cut the loops as the wires were withdrawn; this created a "cut pile" rather than a "loop pile."[6]

About the same time that the Medway mill and the Lowell Manufacturing Company were getting started in Massachusetts, a similar development was under way in Connecticut. In 1825, a group of Hartford investors built the Tariff Woolen Factory to produce woolen broadcloth and carpet in Tariffville (Simsbury), Connecticut. By 1832 carpet had become their main line: the mill produced 114,000 yards that year. But the company somehow fell into financial problems, and through the last few years of the 1830s the firm passed from one set of hands to another, ending up finally under the control of Orrin Thompson and several other investors.

Orrin Thompson, one of the best-known carpet men in America, had started as a merchant, importing carpets from overseas and selling them to retailers. With the boom in domestic production in the 1820s, Thompson switched from carpet importer to carpet producer, forming the Thompsonville Carpet Manufacturing Company in 1828. He arranged with Gregory, Thomson and Company, a Scottish carpet manufacturer and one of his largest suppliers, to contribute capital, as well as technical advice, machinery, and workers, to his proposed carpet factory.

Over the next dozen years the company grew steadily. In 1832 production was about 150,000 yards, mostly ingrain. By the early 1840s, shortly after Thompson bought the Tariffville mill, the plant at Enfield had a hundred looms, several large warehouses, and a worsted spinning mill, where the company produced yarn for its Brussels carpets. Thompson and Company, Orrin Thompson's mercantile and importing business, handled the selling and procurement of raw materials for the manufacturing concern as well as the marketing of its finished product. In the late 1840s Thompsonville went heavily into debt so it could buy new power looms. Unfortunately, the market took a year or two longer to catch up with this new production capability, and in the early 1850s Thompson, strapped for cash, handed over the Thompsonville company to a group of creditors, who reorganized it as the Hartford Carpet Company. At the end of the decade, Hartford bought the Tariffville company, finally uniting Thompson's two Connecticut carpet mills.[7]

Andrew and William McCallum provide another example of the growth of the carpet industry during the boom years of 1825–35. The McCallum brothers emigrated from Scotland in the late 1820s. In 1830 the McCallums purchased a three-story stone mill, previously used for the manufacture of wool cloth, just outside Philadelphia. Because the factory sat in a valley with a very distinct echo, the brothers named their company Glen Echo Mills. The McCallums' company was larger than indicated by the moderate number of workers (twenty-five or thirty) they employed at first, as they contracted out a good bit of their spinning and weaving to other Philadelphia firms. As their physical facilities grew, however, the McCallums transferred all their operations to their own mills. Through much of the nineteenth century, the carpet company started by the McCallums in 1830 was one of the most important in Philadelphia.[8]

These companies and perhaps a dozen others were established in that brief period (mid-1820s to mid-1830s) that Cole and Williamson called "the heyday in the development of the American carpet industry." When Timothy Pitkin compiled *A Statistical View of the Commerce of the United States of America* in 1834, he noted that "the manufacture of carpets has lately increased in this country very rapidly." Pitkin counted twenty American carpet factories that year with an annual production of 1,147,500 yards. (Both these numbers are probably slight undercounts, but they are the first even reasonably complete figures we have for American carpet production.)[9]

Factors Promoting the Growth of the Carpet Industry

While the break in Anglo-American commerce (associated with the Napoleonic Wars and the War of 1812) early in the century played a signifi-

cant role in the development of American cotton- and wool-cloth industries, the real jump in carpet manufacturing came a decade or so later, in
the 1820s. U.S. tariff policy shifted from raising revenue toward the general protection of domestic manufactures, especially textiles, in 1816. But
the real boost to American carpet manufacturing came in 1824, when the
ad valorem (percentage) tax was changed to a specific duty. That year, a
tariff of 50 cents per square yard was placed on Brussels and Wilton carpets; for the cheaper Venetians and ingrains, the specific duty was 25 cents
per square yard. The Tariff of 1828 increased these rates to 70 and 40 cents.
These specific tariffs were important for two reasons. First, they created
a much higher rate, if figured on a percentage scale. Second, the switch to
specific duties was important because the duty was no longer tied to the
value of the goods; if the value of the goods fell, perhaps because of increased efficiency in American manufacturing, the tariff on English imports would remain high, affording even greater protection to the American industrialists. It was perhaps these tariff revisions that convinced
Gregory, Thomson and Company to invest in Orrin Thompson's American mill in 1828 rather than continue to export increasingly expensive
carpets from Scotland. (Incidentally, the tariff on imported carpet wool—
the raw material for the American industry—remained at about its 1824
level.) [10]

An equally important factor in the sudden growth of the American carpet industry was consumer demand. More than half a century ago, Cole
and Williamson advanced this explanation almost intuitively, without any
real support: "The decade of the 1820's, to be sure, is not generally viewed
as a period of economic advance as rapid as that of the 1830's or the
1850's; but advance there was, quite sufficient to permit the introduction of wool floor-coverings of factory manufacture and to induce a broad
consumption in the typical American home, at least in the eastern states."
More recent economic historians have shown that Cole and Williamson's
notion was right on the mark. Paul A. David used various measures to
show that, beginning around 1820 (not in the 1830s, as had previously
been suggested), several factors, most notably the growth of industry, "had
brought about an impressive change in the structure of the U.S. economy."
The decade of the 1820s witnessed more economic growth than any other

decade in the first half of the nineteenth century. This growth, combined with the rise of the American city and an ever increasing population, created a demand for carpets that had simply not existed before.[11]

By the 1830s the American carpet industry was firmly established. In the mid-1780s, practically all American carpet consumption was satisfied by imports. Half a century later, when Pitkin estimated domestic production at 1,147,500 yards, imports averaged just over 600,000 yards; in other words, by the mid-1830s, the domestic industry supplied about two-thirds of American consumption. Imports remained relatively stable over the next dozen or so years, meaning that the American industry itself supplied the tremendous increase in consumer demand. By 1850, domestic production accounted for four-fifths of the carpet sold in the United States.[12] While the total yardage of carpet imported remained stable, the types of carpet imported changed dramatically. Throughout the 1820s and 1830s, about nine-tenths of imports consisted of cheaper ingrains and Venetians; by the mid-1840s, about a third of imports consisted of Brussels, Wiltons, and triple-ply ingrains. Pitkin's statistics for 1834 show the domestic side of these numbers: of a total of 511 carpet looms, 424 were used to produce the cheaper ingrains, and 48 were for Venetians. That is, in 1834, 92 percent of the nation's carpet looms were dedicated to weaving lower-quality carpets, while more and more of the market for higher-quality goods fell to British manufacturers.[13]

Regional Textile Manufacturing: New England and Philadelphia

From its beginnings, firms in the American carpet industry clustered in two main groups: companies in New England and those in Philadelphia. Philadelphia firms grew out of the old handicraft industry that survived through much of the nineteenth century and proved particularly adaptable to carpet production. The system was directed by "manufacturers" who provided the yarn and the specific orders for the weavers, who sometimes contributed the loom as well as their labor. This "putting-out" system, as it was known, had been common in Philadelphia's textile industry before the appearance of carpet manufacturing, and by 1811 "a goodly proportion" of the four thousand hand looms in Philadelphia "were running on

carpets of cheap quality" (meaning ingrain and perhaps rag).[14] Edwin
Freedley, in a midcentury survey of Philadelphia textiles, described the
system:

> The material is furnished by the manufacturers and the weavers are paid by
> the yard. The weaving is done in the houses of the operatives; or in some cases
> a manufacturer, as he may be termed, has ten or twelve looms in a wooden
> building attached to his dwelling, and employs journeymen weavers—the
> employed in some instances boarding or lodging in the same house as their
> employer. Throughout parts of the city, especially that formerly known as
> Kensington [Philadelphia's leading carpet district], the sound of these looms
> may be heard at all hours—in garrets, cellars, and out-houses, as well as in
> the weavers' apartments.[15]

The extension of the old handicraft organization in Philadelphia led to
another distinction: while New England firms tended to be corporations
that built fully integrated carpet factories from the start, Philadelphia companies were usually family firms or partnerships, many of which had been
in other branches of the textile industry for some time. Philadelphia had
more carpet companies—nearly two-thirds of the carpet firms reported in
the 1850 manufacturing census were in Philadelphia—but the Philadelphia firms tended to be smaller than their New England counterparts. Philadelphia's 71 firms employed a total of 1,269 workers (about 18 workers
per firm), but most companies were considerably smaller than that average: 29 employed 5 or fewer workers; another 29 employed 6 to 25 workers; only 2 employed more than 100. (Glen Echo, the largest Philadelphia carpet company in 1850, had grown to 160 workers.) The New England firms started out large: as early as 1832, Thompsonville employed
157 workers, and Lowell was close behind with 153 workers in its carpet
division.[16]

Many of the earliest American carpet companies marketed their own
finished products. William Peter Sprague did his own advertising and selling; his factory probably also served as his store. Other mills had local retail outlets. But early in the industry's history, as carpet companies (especially in New England) began to sell their wares in more distant locales,
they tended to use a selling agent or commission house to handle marketing. These agents generally sold to wholesalers, rather than to retailers or

to the consumer. There was little advertising, aside from showing the company's wares at industrial expositions or inviting wholesalers to visit its offices.[17]

In Philadelphia, the use of commission houses or selling agents was much less common. Instead, according to Philip Scranton, Philadelphia carpet manufacturers tended to stick with the earlier method of direct sale, "bypassing middlemen's commissions and improving thereby both their market sensitivity and their profit position."[18] As a result of these differences, Philadelphia firms tended to be much more flexible and hence better able to cope with changes in demand or business fluctuations. The New England firms, on the other hand, were less flexible, owing in part to their greater capital investment in a particular process or specific products; their absentee form of ownership, which at times fostered conservative management; and their reliance on (and sometimes their indebtedness to) commission agents whose interests did not always exactly match the manufacturers'.

Workers in the Early Carpet Industry

Aside from the setting, little about early American carpet manufacture was American: the styles, the technology, even many of the workers were imported. The first carpets in America were brought from Europe, and the earliest American carpet weavers simply wove the same styles using the same methods. Since those early hand looms required not only a strong back but also a high degree of skill, weavers tended to be men who had learned the craft in Britain. The Boston capitalists who bought the Medway firm "valued Wright's group of skilled Scotsmen even more highly than they valued his machinery," wrote the historians of that pioneering company, "and rightly so, for on the know-how of the workers the business was built." There is no indication that the Lowell Company actively recruited in Britain, but Scottish carpet workers continued to migrate to Lowell, following the first group that Wright had brought over. Other manufacturers did actively recruit, sometimes offering bonuses or passage money.[19]

A second distinctive feature of the workforce in the early carpet mills (aside from the percentage of immigrants) is the large proportion of males.

In his industrial survey of 1832, Louis McLane found that two-thirds of carpet workers were men, about a quarter were women, and the rest were children, mainly boys.[20] The figure for men would be much higher if one counted only the weavers and finishers in carpet production, since most of the women and children were involved in spinning and other preparatory processes. The percentage of women in the early cotton textile industry was nearly 60 percent,[21] so the percentage of men in the carpet industry seems high. There is a good reason for this difference, however: work on wool hand looms was a difficult task, requiring a stronger back than other textiles, and carpets were the largest and heaviest of the woolen goods. Hence, until the advent of the power loom, carpet weavers tended to be men.

Wages fluctuated in the developing U.S. carpet industry but were relatively good. Shortly after the Lowell Company began, weavers made a dollar a day, about 10 percent more than their counterparts in cotton textiles and twice the wage of women and children. In the midst of the depression of the late 1830s and early 1840s, however, the Lowell Board of Directors declared that it was "absolutely necessary from the present depressed prices of our manufactured goods that the wages of the operatives be reduced." By 1842—the first year for which we have reliable wage records from Lowell—rates had fallen to ten cents a yard, which means that the average daily production of eight yards would net the weaver just eighty cents. Wages rose with the end of the depression; in 1844, weavers made as much as fifteen cents per yard, or about six dollars a week, a rate that continued through the decade. Wages at Thompsonville were perhaps a cent more per yard. From the start, workers at Lowell lived in company housing. In Thompsonville, the company originally arranged for workers to stay in local boardinghouses, although later it built its own housing.[22]

Hours in the carpet mills were long—sunup to sundown was fairly common—as was true of all textile production of the period. While there are no industrywide statistics for hours, we know that Lowell began operation with a workweek of seventy-two hours, reduced after a few years to sixty-six (half a day off on Saturday). At this time, most New England woolen mills kept a schedule of thirteen or fourteen hours a day (seventy-eight to eighty-four hours per week), so carpet workers were perhaps somewhat better off. The carpet industry offered little job security, however, even for the most skilled weavers. This was especially true during times of economic depression; in the rough years of the early 1840s, for example, many mills simply closed down for considerable periods. On at least a couple of occasions in those years, Lowell shut down for six or seven months.[23]

Work discipline varied from company to company, but the "Rules & Regulations" posted in New Hampshire's Merrimack Carpet Factory were probably typical:

In order to prevent trouble or misunderstanding between the subscriber and those in his employ, he has established the following *Rules and Regulations,* with which, *all persons* who enter into his employment, as the *Condition* and *Consideration* for the same, *must feel themselves* as much *bound* as they would by a *Written Contract.*

1st. Any one who indulges to excess in the use of *intoxicating* liquors, or who is a frequenter of those places where such are sold, or who shall *bring such liquors* into any Building within the Factory Yard, or who shall smoke in any of said buildings, (the Dye House excepted) *shall be discharged.*

2d. No meeting of the Shop (so called) [the workers' union] allowed to be held within the Mill-yard, the getters up of such meetings (so held) shall be discharged, as also shall those who are guilty of the habitual use of *Profane Language,* of Rapping with their *shuttles,* or who otherwise disturb and annoy their shopmates.

3d. Every Weaver who *commences a Piece* in this Factory, must do so with the express understanding that he thereby *binds himself to finish the same,* in a reasonable time and in a workman-like manner, making good, or paying for all imperfections of his work, and, that in the event of his *leaving* the work, or *joining in a strike, or turn out,* at a time when he has a *Piece in the Loom begun* and *not finished,* he, thereby, *forfeits* all *right* and *claim* to *Payment* for what he may have wove of the *same.*[24]

The Power Loom

Around 1800, Joseph Marie Jacquard invented a device that could automatically adjust a loom to weave a particular pattern. The Jacquard mechanism used thick paper cards, punched with holes (like computer punch cards of a couple of decades ago), to pass coded information through steel needles to the cords that operated the individual harnesses, raising or lowering them as needed to create the desired pattern. The device not only increased the number of practical pattern possibilities; it also decreased the labor requirements of each loom (since the weaver no longer needed an assistant to help maneuver the harnesses). The Jacquard mechanism could function on almost any type of loom, and by the mid-1820s ingrain looms in Philadelphia sported the new Jacquard attachment.

The Jacquard attachment was a tremendous advance in weaving technology, but the carpet looms to which it was attached were all, without exception, hand looms. Power machinery might be used for various ancillary processes (spinning yarn, for example), but for two decades after the carpet industry achieved factory status, the weaving of carpets relied on muscle power. This is not because the early carpet industrialists had a special fondness for traditional ways of doing things; in fact, when Alexander Wright went to Scotland in 1826 to seek resources for his planned carpet mill at Medway, he asked about power looms, only to be told that many efforts had been made along those lines over the previous half century, all of them failures.[25]

The first successful power carpet loom (there had been a number of notable failures) came from the fertile mind of Erastus Brigham Bigelow. As a young man, Bigelow developed a power loom for the manufacture of coach lace (used as a trimming on upholstery in coaches), a machine that lace manufacturers had pronounced an impossibility. With his older brother Horatio, Bigelow then leased a small mill in Lancaster, Massachusetts, incorporated as the Clinton Company, and began successful operations producing coach lace.

Bigelow's reputation quickly spread, and around 1838 Alexander Wright, whose search for power carpet looms in Scotland more than a dozen years earlier had turned up nothing, suggested that Bigelow turn his attentions to producing a power loom for ingrain carpets. Bigelow consented, and within a few weeks he submitted plans and drawings for a loom that showed such potential that the Lowell Manufacturing Company, of which Wright was now a superintendent, agreed to build a model and to finance Bigelow's experimentation and the costs of patenting his inventions, in return for the exclusive use of the loom. By the mid-1840s, Bigelow built a power loom that produced more than twenty-five yards of ingrain a day (hand looms produced just eight), and the Lowell Company had about fifty power looms in operation.[26] Orrin Thompson, impressed by Bigelow's loom, struck a deal with the Lowell Company that allowed his Thompsonville and Tariff factories to use the Bigelow looms in return for a two to three cent per yard royalty payment (which was almost double the royalty Lowell paid Bigelow).[27]

For mill owners, the Bigelow ingrain loom offered greater production combined with more docile labor. For skilled workers, in carpeting as in other industries, technology displaced skills and shifted control over production up the administrative scale. Not only did it triple the production of the hand looms, but it was easier work that did not call for the skills and the strong backs of the hand weavers. Hence, the old labor force, made up largely of skilled immigrant males who often showed a willingness to strike, could be replaced by unskilled women who would work for lower wages and with (managers hoped) fewer labor problems. Furthermore, the quality of the carpet itself was generally better on the power loom: the weaving was more uniform and often contained more body (in the form of "picks"—shots or rows of filling per inch).

But it is easy to overstate the importance of Bigelow's ingrain power loom. It was expensive: the loom itself cost around one thousand dollars, which was eight to ten times the cost of a hand loom, and the user had to pay a substantial royalty for each yard produced. For many of the small companies, the cost was prohibitive. Aside from financial considerations, the loom was more useful for the higher-density ingrains (more picks per inch, which means better quality); for lower-quality carpets, which were produced in greater quantities, the advantage declined and, at the low end, actually disappeared. Perhaps for these reasons, only three firms—Lowell, Thompsonville, and Tariffville—adopted the loom. Within a few years, competing power looms suddenly appeared. A loom developed by the E. S. Higgins Company of New York was a third less productive than the Bigelow loom and hence posed little threat (although Higgins continued to use it for several decades). The "Green" loom, however, turned out almost as much per day as the Bigelow while costing only half as much. In 1860, perhaps a third of the ingrain power looms in operation were not Bigelow's. And by the 1870s and 1880s, newer looms—the Murkland, Crompton, and Knowles—would surpass Bigelow.[28]

Even before he completed his power loom for ingrain carpet, Bigelow began work on a loom for Brussels carpet. Like the ingrain loom, the Brussels loom (first patented in 1846) brought about an immediate increase in production. Weavers on a Brussels hand loom produced three or four yards per day, a figure that could be doubled with the use of a boy to pull the wires that formed the pile. From the beginning, Bigelow's Brussels loom raised production to twenty to twenty-five yards per day without the draw boy, and soon the figure was upwards of fifty yards per day— and this was a better-quality product than that of the hand looms. Bigelow himself claimed that "one woman can weave as much Brussels carpeting by the carpet power loom as 10 men assisted by 10 boys can weave by the hand loom." With a slight modification to the loom, the loop pile of the Brussels carpet could be cut to create Wilton carpet. Bigelow and his brother converted their coach-lace plant in Lancaster to carpet production; by the mid-1850s, the firm of H. N. and E. B. Bigelow, with the newest Bigelow power loom, was producing 200,000 yards of Brussels per year.[29]

A final Bigelow achievement was the introduction of power to the weaving of two new styles of carpet that had been developed in Scotland in the early 1830s: tapestry and velvet. Where Brussels and Wilton carpets have wool yarn buried in the body of the fabric—different colors being brought to the surface with a Jacquard mechanism to produce the pattern—tapestry and velvet carpets contain just one strand of yarn. That single strand is dyed by means of a drum printer to give it a series of colors at intervals along its length that will correspond, when woven, to the colors required by the pattern. Hence tapestry and velvet carpets are in a sense cheap imitations of Brussels and Wiltons. Tapestry carpets, like Brussels, have uncut loops; velvets, like Wiltons, have cut loops.

Tapestry and velvet carpets were apparently first produced in the United States in 1846 by John Johnson, a former employee of the British carpet firm of Crossley. The output of Johnson's twenty-five hand looms in his Newark, New Jersey, factory was apparently the extent of tapestry/velvet production in this country until Bigelow's power loom. Where the hand loom had produced five yards a day, Bigelow's produced sixteen (up to fifty in the 1870s). The E. S. Higgins Company began using Bigelow's tapestry power loom about 1850, the Roxbury Carpet Company shortly thereafter, and by 1860 tapestry was firmly in second place in domestic production, behind ingrain.[30]

During the years when Bigelow was developing his power looms, the tariff on carpets (and indeed on most items) declined significantly from its high of 1828; by 1857 the rate was approximately what it had been with the first protective tariff in 1816. Not surprisingly, imports in the mid-1850s were four times greater than for the 1830s and 1840s.[31] But despite the jump in imports, the domestic industry continued to grow. Where Pitkin had counted 20 carpet mills and just over 1 million square yards in 1834, the manufacturing census of 1850—the first with fairly complete domestic manufacturing statistics—listed 116 firms employing more than 6,200 workers and producing about 8 million square yards of carpet or rugs a year. And the numbers continued to grow: by 1870, the number of firms had risen to 215, the number of workers to 12,000, and the yardage to nearly 20 million. According to tariff historian F. W. Taussig, by mid-century the American carpet industry had "become independent of aid from protective duties."[32]

What made the American industry so strong that it no longer relied on tariff protection? The obvious answer is the introduction of Bigelow's various power looms—but before saying that, we need to look once again at those figures for imports and domestic production, because not only did they increase, the proportions of types of carpets changed. The yardage of two-ply ingrain and Venetian imported into this country actually declined after the 1830s; most of the increase in imports came from higher-grade Brussels and tapestry carpetings (and, to a much smaller degree, Axminster, Wilton, and velvet). At the same time, the increase in the domestic production of ingrain and Venetians far outstripped growth in Brussels or other finer grades.[33]

This makes something of a point against the importance of E. B. Bigelow to the American carpet industry. In that area in which Bigelow's looms seemed to give the United States a decided advantage (the higher grades—Brussels and Wiltons—and the new tapestry style), domestic production increased but still lagged woefully behind imports. In the area of lower-grade goods (two-ply ingrains and Venetians), in which the United States predominated, Bigelow's power looms were scarcely used; as late as 1870 in Philadelphia, the center of American ingrain production, all but sixty-one of its more than three thousand looms were still hand-driven.[34] Ironically, the American industry fared worst in those areas in which Bigelow had been able to apply his inventive genius.

If the Bigelow-benefited sector did not perform as well as it might have, the overall American carpet industry thrived, and it thrived because of growing demand. As Cole and Williamson assessed the situation, by the 1860s "carpeting had come to be a semi-necessity in the United States."[35] Charles P. Dwyer, in *The Economic Cottage Builder* (1856), explained that "as it is customary in this country to carpet every room in the house, flooring need not be laid with a view to appearance." And it is interesting to note that many writers recommended ingrain carpet over Brussels or tapestry. *Godey's Lady's Book* in 1859 suggested to "moderate house-keepers, living within a thousand or twelve hundred a year," that "a bright ingrain or three-ply carpet adds twice as much to the cheerfulness of an ordinary sitting-room as a threadbare Brussels or dingy tapestry."[36] The sisters Catharine Beecher and Harriet Beecher Stowe suggested the same thing in *The American Woman's Home*, a domestic manual published in 1869. They told the story of a woman who on impulse bought a Brussels that was on sale rather than the ingrain she had intended, thinking that, while the Brussels was not especially attractive, it would outlast three or four ingrains. But the Brussels turned out to be no bargain: even on sale it was "one third dearer than the ingrain would have been, and not half so pretty." They concluded that the woman would have to live with "a very homely carpet whose greatest merit it is an affliction to remember— namely, that it will outlast three ordinary carpets."[37]

The 1860s: War and Expansion

The 1860s brought new challenges and opportunities to the American carpet industry. With the onset of the Civil War, demand declined while the opportunities to benefit from government contracts for uniforms, blankets, and so forth increased tremendously. Philadelphia firms, with their greater flexibility, were able to adapt fairly easily to these changed conditions. Much of the nation's spending on textiles for the military already went to Philadelphia—the city's firms had a monopoly on the production of military uniforms, for example—and this helped pave the way for other wartime government contracts. The Quartermaster Corps awarded some twelve million dollars in direct contracts to thirty Philadelphia firms, an impressive figure that does not include the considerable amount of sub-contracted work the firms did for others. A number of those firms were carpet companies that converted to blanket production during the war; the biggest beneficiaries among carpet companies were McCallum, Crease, & Sloan; James Dobson; James Lord, Jr.; and Sevill Schofield.[38] With the notable exceptions of the Lowell Manufacturing Company and the Hartford Company, carpet firms outside Philadelphia did not fare as well, especially at the beginning of the war. New England had 14 carpet companies in 1860; by 1870, the number was down to 9. In New York, the drop was even greater, from 29 to 13.[39]

While much of the nation's carpet industry survived the Civil War, the Philadelphia companies were better able to take advantage of the government's war needs and therefore prospered more. With this government assistance, combined with postwar consumer demand, Philadelphia firms increased both in size and in number; capital invested in the city's carpet sector jumped more than 160 percent in the 1860s, and the number of firms increased from 137 to 184.[40]

Among those new Philadelphia firms was Judge Brothers, begun "on a medium amount of capital" in 1864. William, James, and Robert Judge were natives of Ireland, as was Hugh Nelson, who entered the United States in 1861 and by 1865 had his own carpet mill. James Gilmore, "a native and life-long resident of Philadelphia," also opened a mill in 1865, and a year later another new firm began when Charles H. Masland "returned home from the Civil War, put aside his uniform and sabre, and entered the carpet business." Philip Doerr, who had rented hand looms to weavers in a building beside his home since 1846, decided to expand in the 1860s when his son (Philip Jr.) joined him in the business. They built the first Doerr mill in 1870 and were among Philadelphia's power-loom pioneers.[41] The rise of these and several dozen other firms in Philadelphia in the 1860s, at a time when the New England and New York carpet companies were not enjoying universal success, illustrates the continued vitality of the more flexible Philadelphia textile system.

The Tariff

Carpet manufacturers in the post–Civil War years were of two minds on protective tariffs: they supported high duties on imported carpets but favored lower taxes on raw material imports. There was no domestic production of several imports necessary to carpet production—dyestuffs and jute, for example—hence there was no call for a tariff on these items. There was, however, a considerable amount of domestic wool production, although "in the manufacture of carpets, *no domestic wools are used,* for the reason that they are not only too costly, but too fine to make a serviceable fabric," as a group of carpet manufacturers explained shortly after the Civil War.[42] Instead they used coarser, lower-grade wool from South America, Turkey, and, in later years, Russia and the Orient. But while carpet wool was not produced in the United States, other grades of wool *were* produced domestically, and American wool growers had long insisted on a protective tariff to limit foreign competition.[43]

During the Civil War, with free-trade southern Democrats out of Congress, Republicans were able to raise the tariff significantly. Carpet manufacturers enjoyed the protection offered by the Civil War tariffs, but they wanted relief from the raised duties on raw wool coming into the country. In 1864, Erastus Bigelow and others founded the National Association of Wool Manufacturers "for the purpose of promoting more effectively, by the appropriate means, the advancement and prosperity of the woolen industry."[44] Since the organization included practically all the large carpet firms of the time, the charge was sometimes made that the association was simply a front for the carpet manufacturers (after Bigelow's death in 1879, carpet manufacturers created their own entirely separate organization).[45]

The National Association of Wool Manufacturers met in December 1865 with the National Wool-Growers' Association to draw up a plan that would allow both sides to maintain the high levels of protection of the war tariffs. The Wool and Woolen Act of 1867 embodied the compromise reached by wool manufacturers and growers. This act established an ad valorem duty of 35 percent on imported carpets. U.S. carpet makers accepted a three cent per pound duty on imported wool in exchange for an additional tax on imported carpets based on the amount of wool used in each particular weave.[46] The result of the Wool and Woolen Act of 1867 was a series of rates that did not seem to most Americans to be a significant increase, and that, according to F. W. Taussig, was the whole point. "The truth is," he wrote, "that the wool and woollens schedule . . . was in many ways a sham." The rate schedule was "so complicated" that even manufacturers had difficulty understanding it. "The whole cumbrous and intricate system . . . was adopted largely because it concealed the degree of protection" afforded to manufacturers (between 60 and 80 percent, Taussig concluded).[47]

Shortly after the Wool and Woolen Act passed, the Board of Directors of the National Association of Wool Manufacturers unanimously approved President Bigelow's resolution that the tariff "is as well adapted as any legislation which can now be devised, to promote the growth and development of wool manufacturing and wool growing, and the interests of consumers and the public revenue."[48] At a time when Congress seemed especially determined to help domestic industries through protective tariffs and other devices, carpet and other wool manufacturers benefited as much as anyone. Other industries did the same sort of lobbying for favorable treatment, but in the assessment of Arthur Cole, the National Association of Wool Manufacturers "was better organized than most other industries, its efforts more skillfully directed, and, I think, the results were somewhat in proportion."[49]

The Wool and Woolen Act of 1867, with some slight modifications, set the nation's policy of protection for the carpet industry for the rest of the century. It strictly limited foreign competition so that American manufacturers enjoyed a virtual monopoly on the domestic market. The effect was not immediate; in fact, the peak years of carpet imports during this period came in the early 1870s, when around five million square yards of carpet entered the United States annually. But as its rates increased over the years, the Wool and Woolen Act became very effective at protecting the American carpet industry. As early as 1880 imports were down to less than a million square yards per year, and for the next half century imports were at most a minor concern.

New Products, New Technology, and Instability: 1870–1920

Protective tariffs and rising demand stimulated the growth of the industry. By the mid-1870s, however, the *Carpet Trade* was urging manufacturers to "exercise vigilance for the good of the trade." Overproduction, especially when coupled with the depression that began in 1873, forced carpet prices down during much of the 1870s and 1880s.[50] Production increased from just under 20 million square yards in 1870 to more than 66 million in 1890. Carpet makers faced problems similar to those confronted by Rockefeller, Carnegie, and other industrial giants during the age of industrialization. Productivity increased exponentially with the application of technology, but prices fell and owners feared financial ruin. The increasing integration of the U.S. national marketplace created unprecedented opportunities in the late nineteenth century. The vagaries of the ever expanding national market also created instability and recurrent severe recessions. Carpet makers, like other industrialists, sought relief from a vicious boom-and-bust cycle, with mixed success.[51]

Advances in loom technology played a large role in the industry's growth in the late nineteenth century. Power looms proliferated in the 1870s; by 1880 two-thirds of the carpet produced in the country, and half of the carpet from Philadelphia, was woven on power looms. Hand looms still in active use at the turn of the century probably numbered fewer than a hundred.[52]

Bigelow's ingrain power loom had not been very successful, especially with the lower grades, and the efficiency of competing ingrain looms continued to improve. One of the most successful of the early competitors was invented by John Chester Duckworth, an English immigrant who as a boy had apprenticed in his father's machine shop. The Duckworth ingrain power loom could produce well over twice the daily output of Bigelow's best, and it had the added advantage of taking up just half the space. Duckworth sold the patent to his employer, New York's E. S. Higgins, a company that had built its antebellum ingrain business on a power loom of its own design. Higgins's use of the Duckworth loom lowered its cost considerably and gave the company an advantage over Hartford, Lowell, and other ingrain producers. The Duckworth, a "speedy, but complicated machine," according to a leading trade journal, was itself surpassed by looms from the Crompton Loom Works of Worcester. The Lowell and Hartford companies both replaced their old Bigelow ingrain looms with Cromptons in the early 1890s.[53]

The switch to power looms was most marked in Philadelphia, the center of ingrain carpet production. "Philadelphia was virgin soil for power machinery," one commentator noted, there being no more than a handful of power looms in the city as late as 1870. While the Crompton and the Duckworth were the power ingrain looms of choice in New York and New England, in Philadelphia the Murkland (invented by William Murkland, a Scottish weaver who had been a supervisor at Lowell) led the field. "The strides of the ingrain industry after the Murkland patent became available were something wonderful," wrote woolen textile magnate James Dobson in 1896. "Manufacturers ordered the looms freely and by the year 1880, Philadelphia had more ingrain power looms than all other cities combined." The Murkland loom had "transformed the American industry," a trade journal noted. By the mid-1890s, 3,400 of the nation's 4,800 power ingrain looms were in Philadelphia.[54]

Park Carpet Mills, a family firm run by brothers James and Thomas Gay, was a fairly prosperous company, employing about 300 workers in the mid-1890s. Park ran 87 power looms in 1885, 130 in 1890, and 160 in 1893. These represented a variety of the new ingrain looms, from Babbits (dating from the mid-1870s), Cromptons (an improved model developed in the 1880s), and at least two varieties of Murklands. Another prominent Philadelphia carpet company, Ivins, Dietz and Magee, showed a similar switch from hand to power looms: the firm had 125 hand looms in 1884 and only 50 in 1887, while its number of power looms increased in those three years from 46 to 100.[55]

One of the most significant technical advances during this period was the invention of a power loom for weaving Axminster carpet. In the mid-1850s Alexander Smith, owner of a small ingrain carpet factory in West Farms, New York, asked Halcyon Skinner, a skilled carpenter and mechanic, to help him develop an Axminster power loom. Axminster (or moquette), with its hand-tied tufts, was one of the slowest carpets to produce: two men and a boy could turn out just one and a half yards a day.

The carpet had been very resistant to mechanization, but in 1856 Skinner received a patent for an Axminster power loom. By the end of the decade his loom was producing eleven yards a day with the labor of just one girl.[56]

A few years later Smith left West Farms and bought an old mill in Yonkers. He started again with ingrain, but by 1870 the new Yonkers company—Alexander Smith and Sons—had eighteen of his Axminster looms running. Skinner and Smith spent much of the mid-1870s bringing the Axminster loom to its final "perfected" stage, which they achieved in 1877 with a loom that could produce 20 to 25 yards a day. By the end of the decade the company was producing 1,200 to 1,400 yards a day. In 1879, the Hartford Company agreed to pay Smith $50,000 plus twenty cents a yard for the right to use the looms. Hartford produced 59,000 yards in 1880, and two years later production was up to 273,000 yards.[57]

In the mid-1880s, the Bigelow Carpet Company became interested in Axminster production. Since the Skinner loom was protected by patent, Bigelow had to look for an alternative, one close enough to produce a similar fabric but different enough to satisfy concerns about patent infringement. It happens that Albert and Charles Skinner, Halcyon's sons, "exhibited a predilection for higher mechanical work and several display[ed] remarkable, inventive genius, a splendid natural gift, doubtless, from their talented father," and they developed an Axminster loom for Bigelow. By the end of the decade, Bigelow had seventy-two looms in operation.[58]

Other companies quickly jumped on the Axminster bandwagon. Higgins began production soon after Bigelow. Hartford followed in the mid-1890s when it dumped the Skinner-Smith moquette looms it had acquired earlier and started Axminster production on a loom patented by George Crompton in 1878. Lowell began buying Crompton Axminster looms in 1896. After the Bigelow-Lowell merger in 1899, the reconstituted Bigelow Company replaced its remaining Skinner-Smith looms with Cromptons. Meanwhile, Alexander Smith kept the looms it had developed earlier and remained the Axminster leader, dominating the low-end quality market.[59]

Another late-nineteenth-century development rivaled Axminster in its effect on the carpet industry: the increased popularity of rugs. Rugs had been around since colonial times, but they were for the most part simply small pieces of "roll goods" (the twenty-seven- or thirty-six-inch wide roll of carpet as it came off the loom) that had been sewn on the four sides.

Such a rug would show a section of the repeating pattern of the carpet, but it was impossible to produce by this method a rug with a self-contained design—a feature that Cole and Williamson described as "the outstanding characteristic of the more modern articles which in later decades has been conceived in the trade to constitute a 'rug.'" It was also impossible to produce a rug more than a yard wide. Hence rugs tended to be small and used generally at doorways, by the bed, or in front of the hearth; the larger rugs to which we are accustomed today (six by nine feet or nine by twelve, for example) were not available outside of expensive Oriental imports.[60]

Why the switch in emphasis from wall-to-wall carpet to rugs in the last third of the century? "The so general use of carpets was a necessity some few years ago," wrote a commentator in the early 1870s, "from the fact that the floors of our houses were generally built of such poor material, and in such a shiftless manner, that the floor was too unsightly to be left exposed. Within a short time, however, with greater attention paid to the construction of our floors, having them properly laid in narrow boards, which are accurately fitted, and then stained and oiled, the carpet has become again reduced to its proper position—as a covering for the floor, instead of being a concealer of its defects." This marked the beginning of the modern hardwood floor. Earlier floors had generally been constructed of softwoods and "were never treated to the high-gloss finishes . . . so treasured by owners of old houses today," according to two historians of American floor coverings. The earlier floors were cleaned with sand and water, a practice that "certainly precluded any sort of varnish coat."[61]

There were other reasons for adopting the new improved hardwood floors. Some writers emphasized the fact that wooden floors required less care than carpets, while others stressed their health aspects: "Street soil carried into the house on our shoes, the internal soot and dust, and the soft matters that are occasionally dropped about, such as particles of food," were more "liable to putrefy when subjected to [the] damp and warmth" of a carpet rather than a hardwood floor. Clarence Cook, in *The House Beautiful* (1881), noted that "the advantage of a hard-wood floor . . . is so great on the score of health and labor-saving, that it would seem as if only the prejudice that comes from old associations could long keep up the fashion of carpets."[62]

Carpet makers used three innovations to meet the new demand for rugs: ingrain "art squares" (woven on wide, six- to nine-foot looms equipped with a Jacquard mechanism that produced a self-contained design on each rug); Smyrna rugs (in which a furry yarn called "chenille," from the French word for caterpillar, was inserted into a backing made of jute and cotton thread woven on a broadloom); and seamed rugs (produced by the obvious but technically difficult process of sewing together roll goods to make a large, self-contained pattern). Early in the twentieth century, rugs passed carpet in terms of square yardage.[63]

Ironically, the broad loom for rugs preceded by a few years the broad loom for carpets. The introduction of carpet broad looms varied by style. Brussels and Wilton looms remained narrow (twenty-seven inches), primarily because the thin drawing wires used to create the pile were not practical when lengthened to a yard or longer. Other styles of carpet did not have this problem, and broad looms for tapestry, velvet, and Axminster, six or nine feet wide, were soon developed. By the turn of the century, 3 percent of all carpet looms were broad (more than a yard); by 1909, the percentage had climbed to 8; by 1919, 44; and by 1929, 65.[64]

The American carpet market changed as well: higher-quality goods crowded out cheaper products. Some of this was due to incremental improvements in fibers or loom technology; most, however, can be traced to the relatively rapid decline in the production of lower-quality goods. Ingrain, which had dominated the industry since its beginning—as late as 1870, it accounted for about 90 percent of total production—declined to about 4 percent by 1920. Ingrain came under attack from above and below. Steady advances in loom technology increased the margins of quality that Axminsters, Brussels, and Wiltons had over ingrains, but, more important, those improvements lowered the relative prices of the higher-quality carpets, making them affordable to more middle-class families. By the 1920s, Axminster accounted for a third or more of domestic production. At the same time, cheaper floor coverings grew in popularity: straw matting from the Orient and the so-called wool-and-fiber carpeting, basically an ingrain produced partly of wool, partly of jute (or even paper). Ingrain was therefore squeezed tighter and tighter. When Joseph Taylor & Son's Star Carpet Mills, a Philadelphia company that had been producing ingrain since 1870, closed in 1900, a leading trade journal noted that "ingrain weaving at this time is attended with greater peril than at any former period in the industry." In 1915, the Bigelow-Hartford Company, which by that time included Lowell, announced that it was ceasing all its ingrain production.[65]

The decline of ingrain was felt most heavily in Philadelphia. Some mills, faced with declining ingrain sales, began investing in other carpet styles. A number of factories simply closed. Thomas Bromley, formerly John Bromley and Sons, for years a leading Philadelphia firm, went bankrupt in 1906. Park Mills gradually sold its ingrain looms as production demands declined, and in March 1916 the Gay Brothers recorded the end in their daybook: "After having been in the Ingrain Carpet business since 1868 & which was established by our Father, John Gay, in 1868, & seeing the industry rise & decline & believing it would continue to grow less and less," they signed an agreement to lease their mill building to the Superior Thread and Yarn Company. On May 9, 1916, Park Mills ended its weaving of ingrain carpet. *American Carpet and Upholstery Trade Journal* reported that "about the last Murkland looms in Philadelphia have disappeared with the scrapping of 100 of these worn out veterans by the John Gay's Sons Company . . . and their disappearance virtually brings to an end what once was a thriving branch of the carpet industry in Philadelphia." The last entry in the company's daybook tells of one worker, seventy-five-year-old August Schauble, who had started working for John Gay in 1869 when the mill had been open just one year.[66]

Labor Conditions and Organization

Advances in loom technology had several effects on the workers in the carpet mills. Perhaps the most expected change—a decline in demand for labor, due to the greatly increased productivity of the power looms—never happened, as the expansion of power technology coincided with a rapid increase in consumer demand for carpet. In fact, the number of people employed in the carpet industry grew, from 6,681 in 1859 to 12,098 in 1869, 19,439 in 1879, and 28,736 in 1889, when the numbers stabilized. The nationality of carpet workers also changed less than might be expected. In its early years the American carpet industry had drawn a large number of workers, especially weavers and other skilled positions, from

English, Scottish, Irish, and German immigrants who had mastered their craft before coming to America. Although the proportion of foreign-born carpet workers declined a bit after the Civil War, it remained high, more than 40 percent in most years. American manufacturers obviously continued to value the skilled European immigrant. As late as 1907, the A. and M. Karagheusian Company opened a carpet factory in Freehold, New Jersey, with a skilled labor force it had imported from Kidderminster, England.[67]

The expansion of power-loom technology had an important impact on the sexual division of labor within the industry. In 1850, practically all weavers were male; by 1890, the number of female weavers had increased tremendously. The reason for this change was simple: where manufacturers had tended to see women as too frail to handle the physical requirements of a hand loom, the new power looms emphasized dexterity and patience rather than strength. "Women were poorly adapted to the hand loom," wrote one commentator, "and power was a God-send to them in every respect. For such is the simplicity of the ingrain power loom that women of whatever age are quite capable of attending them." Since the power looms were considerably faster than the older models, weavers (of either gender) on the power looms could be paid less per yard than skilled hand-loom weavers. The difference varied depending on grade and other factors, but typically a power weaver's pay per yard was perhaps a third of the slower hand weaver's.[68]

Hours of labor generally declined in the late nineteenth century in the carpet industry, as was true in practically every industry of the time. The sixty-six hour workweek, typical at midcentury, declined by the 1880s to sixty hours, a figure that remained fairly steady until the turn of the century. But these hours could vary tremendously from one week to the next, usually dependent on changes in orders or the need to prepare a line of carpet for the new season. Philadelphia's Park Carpet Mills provides a good example. In the early months of 1877, the Gay Brothers ran the mill until 8:00 P.M.; in the spring, the mill closed an hour earlier, then at 6:00 P.M. in October; by the following February, hours had again been extended to 8:00 (perhaps to get the spring line ready). Figures given for other years show a similar fluctuation in hours: "Started entire mill on ¾ time" in September 1880, then in December, "Mill commenced running on full time."[69]

Even more frequent than changes in hours were changes in the number of looms in operation. "Business showed a marked falling off so that I stopped off 30 Hand Looms"; "Had 85 Power Looms running to about Sept. 1st then dropped off several looms . . . and run only 12 looms"; "Looms all running full time on Orders & outlook good"; "Very dull— fifty looms stopped"; and so on. And during times of major economic depression, the mills often closed completely, sometimes for months; in 1893, from the last week of July through the second week of August, Park Mills reported the number of looms it had running each day, from 90 (out of 160) on July 24 to 55 on August 4, only 14 on August 9, 2 on the 10th, and just 1 on the morning of the 11th. That afternoon, the Gay Brothers reported: "We this day closed the entire establishment." Park Mills did not reopen for four months, and then on a greatly reduced production schedule.[70] Hence, while the number of work hours declined in the last few decades of the nineteenth century, those hours remained very unsteady in terms of job security: layoffs were a common, even expected, part of the job.

Carpet workers responded to industrialization in the late nineteenth century in the same way as other industrial workers: by trying to organize trade unions. Leadership among carpet workers came mainly from the weavers, as they were the largest group of skilled workers and therefore had considerable bargaining strength. This was augmented by the fact that many weavers were immigrants and brought with them to the United States a tradition of unionism.[71]

Labor organization, and worker unrest in general, often increased in response to certain policies or actions from the employers, which in turn were often responses to larger economic forces. In the spring of 1877, several Philadelphia firms, faced with declining profit margins and growing competition, reduced the wages of their hand-loom weavers by two cents a yard (to thirteen cents). The weavers struck for four weeks, demanding a return to their old rate. The final settlement included a standardized schedule of wages, but it is unclear whether this represented a victory for the weavers.[72]

A year later, in May 1878, Philadelphia's largest power manufacturers formed the Carpet Trade Association with a number of companies in New York to seek cooperative ways to end the continuing crisis. The Philadelphia firms, as they installed and expanded their power-loom capabilities in the 1870s, realized they had more in common with Alexander Smith and Higgins than with the hand-loom manufacturers in Philadelphia. In June, the association decided that each member firm should run its looms only four days a week in order to limit production and eliminate some of the surplus inventory that had been building up. Carpet prices continued to decline through the fall, however, and in November manufacturers decided on a wage reduction, this time for the power-loom weavers. The managers of Park Carpet Mills recorded the result in their daybook: "Power Loom Weavers all struck against a reduction of one [cent sign] per yd made by all the Manufacturers united together." Manufacturers expected a strike with the wage cut, but they figured they could weather a brief shutdown and might in fact benefit from it, as it would allow them to get rid of some of their surplus and to service their equipment. The weavers, almost all female, struck, and the manufacturers closed and locked their factories. In mid-December, with inventory down and the spring season approaching, the manufacturers announced that they would reopen after Christmas. By the end of January, the strike was over: the manufacturers won on the wage reduction, and they had been able to reduce considerably their carpet stockpiles.[73]

Shortly after their success against the power-loom weavers, manufacturers announced a one-cent reduction for the hand-loom weavers. The weavers immediately struck; manufacturers responded by replacing, even faster than before, their old hand looms with new power looms and their assertive skilled male weavers with more docile (it was hoped) unskilled female operatives. "If there had been no strikes there would have been no power looms in Kensington," a manufacturer said of the Philadelphia district in which hand looms had proven most tenacious. "The primary object sought to be gained [by adding power looms] was the better control of weavers and the prevention of strikes," another owner admitted.[74]

By the late 1870s weavers began to attach their local shop organizations to the Knights of Labor, a national union that was experiencing its period of most rapid growth. There were sporadic strikes over the next few years. Power-loom weavers at a few Philadelphia plants struck for higher wages late in 1879. When the Thomas Leedom Company granted a half-cent raise, other manufacturers met to discuss the situation. "Considerable indignation was expressed at [Leedom's] uncalled for actions," wrote one mill owner,[75] but fearing another citywide strike, all manufacturers granted a half-cent raise for their power weavers. New York weavers expressed their dissatisfaction as well. A two-day strike at Higgins brought about a compromise raise for weavers there. At Alexander Smith, shortly after the company's founder died, weavers walked out to protest a 10 percent wage reduction and a general dissatisfaction with the new management; the strike lasted about a month and also ended in compromise.[76]

But these labor conflicts paled in comparison to the strikes of the mid-1880s. It is impossible to say exactly where or when the trouble started, but one of the earliest episodes was on November 19, 1884, when more than thirty Philadelphia power firms posted an announcement of an immediate wage reduction. The reduction came "by order of the Manfr's Assoc.," wrote the owners of Park Carpet Mills, referring to the organization started after the strike of 1878–79. A hundred weavers at Park Mills walked out, as did twenty-five women at Doerr's Philadelphia Carpet Company. They joined a thousand other weavers from other city mills the next afternoon at Liberty Hall, where the decision was made that "no weaver is to go back to work at the reduced rate." When owners offered to pay the old rate to any weaver who would return and renounce the Knights of Labor, weavers refused, implicitly adding another demand to the restoration of the wage cut: recognition of the right of workers to join the Knights. "The employers have their organizations," said one weaver, "why can we not have ours?" Power looms in Philadelphia were almost completely shut down; on some days during the strike as few as a dozen were running in the city.[77] Within a few months, strikes broke out over wage cuts at the Sanford Carpet Company and at Alexander Smith's Yonkers mill.[78]

The American carpet industry seemed on the verge of shutting down in the spring of 1885, but one by one the strikes ended. In Philadelphia, a settlement was announced in April by which the manufacturers agreed to cut the one-cent reduction in half and the weavers agreed "that we will not . . . cause to be introduced into any workshop any system or organization that will in any manner interfere with the conduct or manner in which they shall conduct their business affairs." In other words, the weavers could keep their membership in the Knights of Labor, but "the rules of association shall not apply to the working of the carpet mills or the employing of hands." This wording was probably as unclear in 1885 as it is today, but perhaps that was the intention: by allowing weavers to keep their union membership as long as they kept the union out of the workplace, manufacturers gave the weavers the chance to save face and agree to the arrangement.[79]

The Yonkers strike ended in mid-July with a victory for the strikers: a 10 percent pay raise on top of a restoration of the earlier wage cuts; the rehiring of all union members; a guarantee that future workers would not be dismissed for union membership; an adjustment of the discipline system; and the recognition of a union grievance committee. The union in return agreed not to strike without notice and to try to settle future disputes through arbitration before striking. The wage increase in Yonkers was quickly followed by a similar increase in other New York companies, and within a few months the manufacturers' association in Philadelphia agreed to a half-cent raise.[80]

Labor unrest flared again with the depression of 1893; when the downturn bottomed out in 1894, millions of workers nationwide had lost jobs, and almost 800,000 more were on strike to protest employment conditions. The carpet industry suffered along with other industries: Lowell was shut down for several months in the summer and fall of 1893, Alexander Smith from August 1893 to January 1894, and so on. Carpet workers resented these uncertain conditions. When Park Carpet Mills, closed since August 1893, tried to reopen in November with reduced wages, "many weavers refused to work at cut rates." The mill closed for another two weeks and then offered work at half pay ("on a/c of the exceedingly bad outlook of business"). Just over a year later, in January 1895, Philadelphia carpet manufacturers met, and "all signed a paper agreeing not to grant an advance" on wages. When weavers at C. H. Masland struck on February 18, owners at Park Mills reported that "our weavers (a committee) called on us & asked for the advance like all others have done & after a nice talk we refused to allow & they left for their rooms & nothing more heard of it." But there was a growing unrest among the weavers. A Philadelphia-based trade journal editorialized: "We may say that . . . the manufacturers have met the weavers in the most generous spirit, and whenever a point could be allowed it was done. We may also say that the weavers little comprehend about the present risk of making goods." The citywide strike, involving 2,500 workers at 36 firms, began during the second week in July. A month into the strike, a leading trade journal noted that it had been "a quiet" strike, "saving the gurgle of bad beer, as it goes down the throats of impecunious weavers gathered in near-by saloons to discuss the situation." Manufacturers almost immediately offered the weavers an advance in December, if they would return at the old rate until then, an offer the weavers refused. In August the manufacturers made the same offer, except the advance would come in October; again the strikers refused. Park Mills (and presumably others) began advertising in the newspapers for workers ("*Weavers*—Ingrain Carpet Weavers wanted on Murkland and Crompton Looms"), but "no weavers came." On August 21, manufacturers offered to advance rates in mid-September, and the weavers accepted.[81]

As the strike came to a close, manufacturer William Ivins stated his views of the conflict:

> Ingrain weaving in the future must be recognized as woman's work. It is concededly a class of work which imposes but little strain either on the brain or the body. A bright girl can almost read a dime novel while her loom is turning out the finest of extra super carpet. . . .
>
> Had not the men, who have fastened on to this line of easy weaving, bred disturbance, the girls engaged in it, it is believed, would not have thought of striking, and as men have provoked the strike, the sentiment of several manufacturers is that they must seek work more adapted to their muscles. . . .
>
> The argument of ingrain male weavers that they cannot support their families on $10 and $12 a week is met by the reply that no able-bodied, intelligent man will content himself with a job of the kind, and if they choose to fill a woman's place they must expect a woman's wage. . . .
>
> We do not recommend an iron-clad manufacturer's union . . . but we do suggest . . . THAT ONLY SUCH HELP BE EMPLOYED AS WILL APPRECIATE THEIR POSITIONS AND ACCEPT, AS TRUE AND FAIR, THE STATEMENTS OF MANUFACTURERS AS TO THE WAGES THEY ARE ABLE TO PAY.[82]

Ivins's statement illustrates again the relationship between the power loom and female weavers, the perceived docility of the female workforce, and the manufacturers' perception of the need for employer unity.

Cooperation and Consolidation

Manufacturers, like their workers (and, as we have seen, *against* their workers), also experimented with collective action for their mutual benefit. They had seen the potential of united action with the tariff just after the Civil War and then again in the labor conflicts of the 1870s and 1880s. These organizations, however, tended not to go beyond what Philip Scranton called "crisis associations," groups formed in response to particular short-term problems. The carpet industry seemed unable to develop and maintain "progressive" associations, permanent groups more interested in addressing long-term factors rather than temporary crises. The Carpet Manufacturers' Association, organized by the manufacturers who had united in response to the labor problems of the mid-1870s and who decided after the strike to make their temporary organization a permanent one, is a good example. At its first meeting, the group transacted no business aside from electing officers and voting on the statement that "the object of the Association is to adopt an unanimity of prices." Actually, the association seems to have done little through its brief existence beyond approving that resolution. Similarly, the Carpet Trade Association apparently did not live long after its inception in the late 1870s.[83]

Carpet manufacturers often talked about the possibility of consolidation as a way of dealing with the problems of overproduction and competition in the late nineteenth century. Ingrain and Brussels producers met in 1888 to discuss some sort of consolidation or at least joint action, but when the Lowell Company refused to participate, the plan was dropped. In 1890, several Philadelphia ingrain manufacturers discussed a plan to decrease production, thereby stabilizing the industry and increasing profits. The plan involved limiting hours of operation to forty per week with no increase in loom capacity. Although larger companies apparently liked the plan, smaller companies, aware that such restrictions could destroy their ability to compete, refused to join, and the effort came to naught. In 1892, Hartford directors were told of "an effort . . . to bring about a legal consolidation of the Carpet Company and firms in New England and elsewhere, for the purpose of making the investment in the same more profitable than at present." The directors expressed interest in the plan, but nothing came of it.[84]

Despite the failure of such large-scale efforts, the general trend in carpet manufacture was toward greater consolidation. The 215 carpet companies reported in 1870 were reduced to just over 130 by the turn of the century, and half of those disappeared before 1930. In 1899, the Lowell

Manufacturing Company and the Bigelow Carpet Company merged, keeping the name of the latter. In 1901, the E. S. Higgins Carpet Company merged with the Hartford Carpet Company (itself formed half a century earlier from the Thompsonville and Tariffville mills), again keeping the name of the latter. These two reconstituted firms joined in 1914, creating the Bigelow-Hartford Carpet Company. In October 1929, the merger of Bigelow-Hartford with Stephen Sanford created the Bigelow-Sanford Carpet Company—the largest in the country, accounting for more than a fifth of total production.[85]

Marketing

The marketing of carpet in the last three decades of the nineteenth century followed the pattern set earlier: manufacturers generally assigned their carpet to commission agents, who in turn sold it to large wholesale houses, jobbers, and retail groups. Sometimes the company would use its own agent to move the carpet through these same channels, but for the most part, manufacturers were several steps removed from the consumer.[86]

Many of the major commission agents in the 1870s and later had been around for some time. These firms were so well established that they could almost dictate terms to the manufacturers whose goods they sold. When an agent of the John H. Pray Company called on Philadelphia's Park Carpet Mills in June 1877, the manufacturer had to agree to a provision "that I sell no goods of mine to any other New England House." When an agent for another firm showed up four days later "anxious to put his order in for Fall purchases," the carpet maker had to turn him down; the agent "went away in bad humor."[87] Sometimes the commission house could play competing manufacturers off one another; such was perhaps the case when the Park Carpet Mills agreed to sell to John H. Pray "500 Rolls Extra Super [ingrain], to be delivered . . . at 10¢ less than Lowell list price."[88]

Commission agents exercised substantial control over the manufacturers in other ways—by providing capital and by sitting on the company's board of directors, for example. In the early 1870s, Alexander Smith signed on the firm of A. T. Stewart and Company as selling agent. Stewart, who received a commission of 4 percent, regularly advanced Smith large sums of money. In 1873 Stewart unexpectedly demanded full payment of the outstanding debt (at the time about two hundred thousand dollars). Smith, his money tied up in materials, new machinery, and carpet, could not pay and faced losing his company. Fortunately, William Sloane, of W. & J. Sloane, stepped in and offered the necessary capital. After that, W. & J. Sloane served as Smith's selling agent, and William Sloane himself became a member of the firm of Alexander Smith and Sons.[89] Sometimes the commission agents suggested design or style changes. Given that the agents were able to keep their fingers much more on the pulse of consumer and retailer demand, this is not surprising. The Hartford Company always consulted with Reune Martin, who with his sons handled the sales for the company for several decades in the late nineteenth century, before taking almost any action.[90]

Still, the commission houses lost some of their importance in the last decades of the century. Manufacturers grew tired of paying 2 percent or more of the retail price of carpet to commission agents who seemed to do little more than pass the goods along to wholesalers or large retail groups; after decades in the business, the manufacturers themselves knew who the buyers were and developed a feel for consumer tastes. Carpet mills began hiring their own salesmen and going direct to retailers around the turn of the twentieth century. Alexander Smith took that step in 1901 when it severed its relationship with W. & J. Sloane, the firm that had been in charge of selling Smith carpets for nearly three decades. As company reserves increased and banking facilities improved, the need for financial support (which the commission houses had always offered) was no longer so important. At the same time, several retail establishments were growing large enough that they found it advantageous to deal directly with the manufacturers.[91]

An important step in the move to direct sales to retailers came in the late nineteenth century with the formalization of seasonal openings. Prior to this, the practice had been for a manufacturer to announce new lines in the trade journals and perhaps show them at a New York warehouse or other suitable room. Since the showing of a new line by a large company tended to attract the major buyers, smaller firms would have their own openings at the same time. Gradually these events became more formalized: new carpet lines would be shown in May and November in New

York. In the early 1920s the dates were moved back to January and July, with concurrent shows in New York and Chicago, and in 1940 the July date was dropped altogether.[92]

By the end of the century, manufacturers began to pay more attention to the ultimate consumer. A leading trade journal offered a good example of consumer advertising from a New York firm ("Since Adam stubbed his toe in the Garden of Eden, such bargains as these have never had their equal") and then noted: "Show me a woman who would not read every line of such an announcement as that."[93] The Hartford Company was one of the first to use large-scale consumer advertising. It made good use of national magazines (*House Beautiful, Country Life in America, Good Housekeeping*) as well as its own brochures to promote its high-grade Saxony to the upper middle class. Hartford was one of the first to use slogans: "American Rugs for Private Houses and Public Places"; "Universally imitated but never equalled." Sidewalk tests and exhibitions (one of which went on a national tour) further spread Hartford's name. A remark in a trade journal in 1914 hints at the success of these pioneering advertising efforts: "All of a sudden, as it seemed, two or three years ago, the word 'Saxony' was found to be creeping all over the country."[94]

Other companies followed where Hartford led. By the first decade of the century, Bigelow was putting out lavish catalogs with two hundred color plates; soon it was placing its new trademark (a series of circles with the words "Carpets of Quality") in advertisements in national magazines ("Your carpets like your glasses should be selected to suit you. Through one you see the world, through the other the world sees you"). After the merger of the two companies, Bigelow-Hartford put a large electric sign on a building in New York, made a movie showing how its products were made, and, perhaps most spectacular, began displaying rugs on the sidewalks in front of stores that sold their products. Passersby could walk on the carpet and feel its pile beneath their feet; after a week, the carpet would be picked up, cleaned, and then displayed to show its condition and its wearing qualities. By the 1920s, advertising had itself become a big business. Mohawk Carpet Mills, a new company founded in 1920, was aggressive in its advertising. Companies expanded their efforts from mass-circulation magazines to radio. In 1925 Bigelow-Hartford published a hundred-page book to commemorate the centennial of Alexander Wright's

Medway Mill, the company's earliest forerunner. Advertising was becoming much more important; Bigelow-Hartford spent 1.3 percent of its net sales on publicity in 1926, double its percentage of just two years before.[95]

The Great War and the 1920s

Even before the United States became directly involved in the First World War, American businesses felt the impact of the conflict. For the carpet industry, there were severe shortages of dyestuffs and wool, which made higher prices necessary and led to a sharp decline in sales (from nearly 1.2 million square yards in 1914 to about 800,000 in 1916). Production continued to fall after the American entry into the war in 1917, down to fewer than 500,000 square yards in 1919. Not all of this decline was due to shortages and decreased demand, however; carpet firms, like those in other industries, sought government contracts for various military or wartime supplies, using their looms to turn out cotton duck (for tents) and blankets.[96]

Shortly after the United States entered the war, Alexander Smith began the production of blankets and cotton duck to supply American military needs. The company's tapestry looms could be modified to weave the duck, but Smith also bought a hundred new looms for blanket production. By the end of the war, the firm had produced 4.5 million yards of duck and more than 1.5 million blankets and was said to be the government's biggest supplier of these materials. Meanwhile, it reduced its carpet production to about 15 percent of its prewar totals.[97]

Alexander Smith was not the only company to suspend carpet production to work on government war orders. "No more patriotic class of men can perhaps be found than the floor-covering manufacturers of the country," bragged a leading trade journal in the summer of 1918, noting that a "large number of carpet mills" had devoted 50 to 90 percent of their output to government work. Bigelow-Hartford produced 80,000 blankets and 400,000 yards of duck during the war. Government work could be profitable, of course. Bigelow-Hartford's profits in 1918 were the highest in the company's history, in terms of both dollar amount ($1.78 million) and percentage of sales (nearly 16 percent on sales of $11.2 million).[98]

Involvement in the war effort extended through the industry to the workers. The carpet and rug division of a Liberty Bond campaign in Philadelphia brought in half a million dollars by the spring of 1918; the chairman of the city's War Savings Committee noted that "the carpet industry, from the outset, has shown a willingness to do its full share to bring the Kaiser to his knees."[99] Workers making tent duck in a New York carpet mill threatened a strike when they came upon a batch of material that was defective and therefore especially difficult to process. The mill superintendent told them that the government was probably unaware of the defective material "on account of slack or disloyal inspectors who had passed it. When it was pointed out to the weavers that somebody was evidently trying to put it over on their government, they decided that by striking they would merely be adding to the troubles of the government" and therefore worked through the batch of defective material without further complaint.[100]

The carpet industry at the end of the war, like the American economy as a whole, took some time to recover from the wartime disruptions and reconvert from military production. Even before that recovery was complete, the country was faced with a serious though brief recession, beginning late in 1920; by the spring of 1921, retail carpet prices had declined by about a third from those of a year before (which were already considerably lower than the inflated wartime prices), and only a quarter of the nation's carpet looms were running. The recession ended quickly, however, and carpet companies had good sales figures for the next two years. In fact, the 83.2 million square yards produced in 1923 was a record for the industry.[101]

On the heels of this recovery came a gradual decline in the carpet industry, at a time when the rest of the economy was booming. Renewed sales in 1922 and 1923 convinced companies to expand their manufacturing capabilities; unfortunately, consumer demand for carpet did not rise correspondingly and in fact fell in the mid-1920s. Some placed blame on the indirect competition of other products, such as automobiles and radios, for consumer dollars. Demand stagnated; a third of the carpet companies in existence in 1923 went out of business by the end of the decade. Alexander Smith laid off workers for the first time in a dozen years. While stocks in other industries were doubling and tripling in value, the stock of Bigelow-Hartford fell from $146 in 1924 to $91 in 1928. The company's earnings in the half dozen years from 1924 through 1929 seldom rose much above the earnings for the recession year of 1921.[102]

Faced with these problems in his company and in the industry, John A. Sweetser, president of Bigelow-Hartford, led in the establishment of the Institute of Carpet Manufacturers of America, the first national association in the history of the industry. The goal of the new institute was "to improve production and distributive methods, to prepare for the mobilization of the industry in national emergencies, to co-operate with private and governmental corporations or other agencies involved in similar activities, and to use any and all lawful means for the development of all phases of the carpet industry." The first president of the institute was Irving S. Paull, who had been recommended to the post by Herbert Hoover, secretary of commerce and soon to be president. Paull had worked for Hoover in the Department of Commerce and was author of a book titled *Trade Association Activities.* The institute began with a membership of eighteen companies representing 70 percent of the industry's production; by the end of the decade, it claimed twenty-eight members, representing two-thirds of all carpet companies and 95 percent of production.[103]

The Depression

"During 1929 we enjoyed the most prosperous year of normal business in recent times—until the stock market slump, which temporarily introduced an element of uncertainty into the business situation," according to George McNeir, chairman of the board of Mohawk Carpet Mills. McNeir was writing in the first issue for 1930 of the *Mohawk Rug Retailer,* a magazine published by the company "in the interest of better rug-selling." After urging salesmen to remember their faithful customers and cultivate new markets, McNeir closed with the hopeful statement, "If we all keep a balanced judgment and go about our business determined to take advantage of our opportunities there is no reason why we should not surpass previous records during 1930." [104]

For business leaders, the first few months of the Great Depression were not terribly depressing. In the November 1929 issue of *American Carpet and Upholstery Trade Journal* is the suggestion that "we are still living in a period of unusual prosperity and with the exception of minor setbacks for adjustment purposes the outlook continues good." Such optimism in a prediction written probably no more than a week after the crash is certainly understandable, as was the continued optimism in the *American* (as the journal called itself) over the next few months. The magazine immediately started a regular column, "How Is Business," to describe the economic situation. "A reassuring future," the *American* foresaw in January 1930; "confidence is more widespread" in April; and in June, "by early fall the stage should be set for gradual expansion to normalcy." In the summer the *Journal* urged retailers to advise the public not to put off that new carpet buy hoping that prices would continue to fall. "The bottom has been reached," it said. "Prices cannot go lower without uprooting the economic structure."[105]

Month after month, *American Carpet and Upholstery Trade Journal* asked "How Is Business"? and answered the question in the rosiest possible terms. "There has been greater resistance to any further downward trend" was the best it could say at the end of the year. By the summer of 1931, it reported "little, if any change in business" and "improvement... has been rather disappointing." A year later, the column disappeared, still half a year before the depression reached its lowest point.[106] Bigelow-Sanford recorded its biggest loss ever (more than $600,000) in 1930. Industrywide, sales in 1928 had been $167 million (about 65 million square yards); in 1933, the figure was just $60 million (just over 40 million square yards). During the same period employment slipped from 32,800 to 16,000; for those lucky enough to have jobs, a combination of reduced hours and pay cuts decreased their weekly income from more than $25 to less than $16. Recovery was slow and unsteady, but by 1937 production had risen to more than 60 million yards, with sales of over $137 million, still well below the predepression levels.[107]

The New Deal and Unionization

Early in his first term in office, President Franklin Roosevelt pushed through Congress the National Industrial Recovery Act (NIRA). The act called on each industry to develop its own "code of fair practice" in order to stabilize the industry and protect its workers. Since conditions varied so much from one industry to another, each industry was given the

chance to develop its own code, which would have to follow general guidelines and requirements set forth in the NIRA. One of the most important
parts of the act was Section 7(a), which guaranteed workers' rights to collective bargaining.

In June 1933, the Institute of Carpet Manufacturers of America (ICMA)
met in New York to work out a code of fair practice for the carpet industry. The proposed code was unanimously adopted by the ICMA and
was passed on to government authorities for their approval with the signature of more than nine-tenths of the carpet and rug manufacturers.
Hearings on the code were held in Washington in October, and in January 1934 the code (Number 202) was approved by President Roosevelt.[108]

Hours were limited to forty per week, eight per day (although employees could work up to forty-eight hours, ten per day, during peak periods).
The carpet and rug code called for a minimum wage of 35 cents an hour
in the North and 30 cents an hour in the South ($14 and $12 per week)—
a wage differential seen in the code for every industry.

To satisfy the labor provisions of the NIRA, the carpet and rug code af-
firmed that workers "shall have the right to organize and bargain collec-
tively, through representatives of their own choosing." Employees would
be "free from interference, restraint, or coercion" in the exercise of this
right. The code also pledged that "no employee and no one seeking employment shall be required as a condition of employment to join any company union, or to refrain from joining, organizing, or assisting a labor organization of his own choosing." [109]

In May 1935, the Supreme Court struck down the NIRA as unconstitutional, and with the act's demise, the codes of fair practice and the guarantees for labor under Section 7(a) disappeared as well. A leading trade
journal noted that the passing of the NIRA meant "in general healthier
and sounder economic conditions, such as freedom for management,
greater sense of security, and abatement of hostility toward profits." The
ICMA decided almost immediately to "endorse the principles of fair trade
practice," meaning the regulations concerning marketing and so forth.
The institute stated explicitly that it opposed the restoration of the NIRA,
however.[110]

In July 1935, Congress restored the guarantees for labor with the National Labor Relations Act, also known as the Wagner Act for its cham-

pion in the Senate. The Wagner Act now continued the protections for workers in NIRA Section 7(a) and set up a National Labor Relations Board (NLRB) to hear complaints of workers against their employers, especially those involving employers' antiunion activities.

The 1920s had not been a good decade for unions, in the carpet industry or any other. In an internal report on Bigelow-Hartford's general operations in 1926, the investigator wrote, "The Company, fortunately, is not handicapped by Unions." [111] That statement could have characterized the entire industry before the 1930s. But NIRA Section 7(a) and the Wagner Act changed the prospects for union organizing, in carpets as in other fields. The case of Alexander Smith and Sons has been best documented and serves as an interesting case study. As a result of the "Great Strike of 1885," Alexander Smith began practicing a policy of "practical paternalism" toward its employees as a way of forestalling another series of labor conflicts. In 1889 the company became one of the first in the nation to give its employees a half day off on Saturday with no reduction in pay. In the 1890s the company (or rather a member of the Smith family, which still owned and ran the company) erected a recreation room and clubhouse for workers. When Smith family members died, they often left money in their wills to go to company workers of long standing. One heir, who died in 1909, left a thousand dollars to each employee who had worked for at least twenty years; 381 workers benefited. A similar bequest in 1929 gave a thousand dollars to the 1,100 twenty-year workers the company employed then. The company began a bonus plan in 1911 in which bonuses were paid out twice a year to workers depending on how long they had been with the company. During slack times the company began showing more leniency toward the tenants in company housing. This plan of "practical paternalism" followed "a rather casual and erratic pattern," in the words of one scholar, but it "produced results in the way of worker loyalty and length of service that [were] of definite advantage to the company." [112]

In 1933, with the NIRA, Alexander Smith faced the first serious efforts to unionize the mill in half a century. When workers began organizing meetings to take advantage of the provisions of Section 7(a), Smith officials met with the leaders of the movement and suggested a company union. The company's plan consisted mainly of a set of procedures for allowing employees to air their grievances and make suggestions to management. The plan gave workers no bargaining power. The company financed the union, sent representatives to all meetings of the union, and even provided a stenographer to take the minutes.[113]

A number of workers, realizing that the company union offered no real bargaining power, organized a group called the Carpet Workers Club. In June 1935, this club applied for a charter to become a local of the United Textile Workers of America (UTWA, affiliated with the American Federation of Labor). The UTWA granted the charter, and the new Local 2449 began a campaign for new members in August. When the company fired three of the leaders of the organizing drive, the union used the newly passed Wagner Act to file charges with the National Labor Relations Board alleging that the company had discharged workers for union activities and that it kept a company-dominated union, both of which were illegal. Rather than respond to those charges, the company asked for an injunction against the board, arguing that the Wagner Act, like the NIRA, was unconstitutional and therefore the NLRB had no authority. The company further argued that it had worked hard over the years to build up and maintain the goodwill of its workers and the community and that hearings before the Labor Board would hurt that goodwill. The United States Circuit Court disagreed on the question of the act's constitutionality. Concerning the maintenance of good feelings within the community, the judge wrote that if Alexander Smith's fears were true, "then all that the Company has done for its employees and the community has been a vain effort without appreciative reciprocation." The court refused to grant the injunction, but the company still chose not to put up a defense at the board hearings. In October 1936, the NLRB ordered Alexander Smith to reinstate with back pay the dismissed workers and to dissolve its company union.[114]

By the time the legal proceedings were settled, the American Federation of Labor's Committee for Industrial Organization (CIO) had begun organizing drives in various industries. The CIO had already experienced some success, organizing the automobile and steel industries (as well as Bigelow-Sanford). The CIO's Textile Workers Organizing Committee took over the drive at Alexander Smith in April 1937, the same month in which the Supreme Court upheld the constitutionality of the Wagner Act (in a case involving the steel industry). An Alexander Smith official commented that "ninety-nine per cent of the more than five thousand employees in the mill want no part of this so-called union" and called the organizers "a bunch of Communists," but there was little the company itself could do at this point to stop the organizing drive. In fact, after the Wagner Act was upheld in April, the company took a "hands off" attitude. The biggest threat to the union came not from Alexander Smith but from a group of workers who had belonged to the old company union and who now banded together into a group known as the Independent Smith Workers Union. Most of the support for this new independent group came from older workers who had benefited more from the company's "practical paternalism." The independents were as effective in their campaigning as were the CIO organizers. In June 1937 organizers felt Local 2449 was strong enough to face an election, and they asked the NLRB to conduct a vote to see who would represent Smith workers: the CIO union, an independent union, or no union at all. Local 2449 won by a close vote of 2,755 to 2,440 for the independents.[115]

In the ensuing contract negotiations, the union got practically all of its demands, the major exception being a 7.5 percent increase in pay rather than the 20 percent the union originally demanded. The next year, the union changed when the UTWA decided to leave the CIO and join the American Federation of Labor (which had expelled the CIO). Some of the locals, including Local 2449, refused to go with the union into the AFL, and hence Local 2449 of the UTWA became Local 122 of the Textile Workers Union of America (TWUA), affiliated with the CIO. Local 122 had to face another challenge election from the independent union, which it won handily, 2,682 to 1,474.[116]

Similar stories could be told of the other major carpet companies dealing with the depression and the union movement in the 1930s. Bigelow-Sanford reduced its labor force considerably in 1931, and even more in 1932, and began a series of across-the-board wage and salary cuts. The pay reductions hit everyone equally, "but few weavers would have admitted that [President John A.] Sweetser, whose annual salary fell from $75,000 to $60,750 in 1932, was as severely affected as they were," as the company's historians wryly noted. The company suffered a number of short strikes in the early 1930s and, after the guarantees of the NIRA's Section 7(a), the beginnings of unionism. Some among the Bigelow management were concerned with these developments, while others observed that they felt safe from the threats of organized labor. "Employees are not union-minded," wrote one manager. "If let alone by outsiders, they are not normally individualists and, if not abused, show definitely a conservative and doubtless sympathetic, though inarticulate loyalty to their company." But such statements were overly optimistic. Before the NIRA was nullified, workers at the Thompsonville plant formed a union, at first a local of the American Federation of Labor's United Textile Workers, later an independent union, with a membership of twenty-six hundred. In the spring of 1937, Bigelow recognized the CIO's Textile Workers Organizing Committee as the bargaining agent for workers in its Amsterdam plant, and in Thompsonville, the company agreed to negotiate through the United Textile Workers Union, an independent union that entered the CIO the following year. When the company announced more layoffs and another wage cut in 1938, the two unions called a strike that lasted nearly five months, ending only when an arbitrator recommended that half of the wage cut be restored.[117]

By the mid-1940s, a report distributed to Bigelow-Sanford supervisors starkly summarized organized labor's reversal of fortune within the carpet industry. At the onset of the Great Depression, the industry's workers were completely unorganized. In the spring of 1944, Bigelow executives compiled a chart that detailed the status of unions among the workers of the fifteen biggest carpet companies in the spring of 1944. Twelve of the companies listed the Textile Workers Union of America, CIO, as the exclusive bargaining agent for their workers; two listed what appear to be company unions; and one (Firth) had no union. Workers at virtually all the major carpet-manufacturing firms were now organized, thanks in large part to New Deal policies.[118]

World War II

The Second World War, like the First, affected American industry well before active U.S. involvement. By the end of 1940, carpet companies were losing executives to various government agencies planning war preparations. The industry suffered from shortages in both labor and materials. Wool was in short supply for consumer goods by the end of 1941; fortunately some firms had experimented with various artificial fibers, most notably rayon, and were able to substitute these for part of the wool.[119]

Bigelow-Sanford made an early decision to support the war effort wholeheartedly. Part of this decision was based on President John Sweetser's "intense patriotism," but there were other factors that made the decision easy for the company to accept. With industry experts predicting a huge dislocation of the consumer market, the company wanted to be sure to have something to keep it in business during the war. Anticipated shortages of fuel oil, which the Thompsonville plant burned, as well as the raw materials that went into the carpet itself, led Bigelow to seek war contracts in order to maintain access to those goods. Finally, the company hoped that heavy participation in war production would help it retain skilled workers.[120]

Within a month of the Japanese attack on Pearl Harbor, Bigelow-Sanford created a War Sales Division to solicit government orders for war goods. As before, the carpet industry's greatest contributions would be in blankets and tent duck. The Institute of Carpet Manufacturers of America coordinated the exchange of technical information on war production in general. Under President Sweetser's leadership, Bigelow had been working on the problem of loom conversion (and was in fact the first major carpet company to run blankets for the war), and the company was therefore selected as the industry's guide in that area. The Amsterdam plant alone wove more than five million blankets. Workers at Thompsonville produced cotton duck on modified carpet looms—enough, the company bragged, to make a pathway a yard wide from San Francisco to Hiroshima. Carpet sales continued to decline as the war went on. As late as 1942, military production made up just a quarter of Bigelow-Sanford's output; in 1943 and 1944, however, the figure was in excess of 70 percent.[121]

Labor "was both uncertain and expensive" during the war. The early 1940s, unlike the years of a decade before, were marked by labor shortages, and workers often moved from one company to another, seeking "the easiest and best-paying jobs they could find." With the government anxious to avoid wartime strikes, workers sensed their advantage and pushed for wage increases and other improvements. A threatened strike at Bigelow-Sanford's two plants led the War Production Board to approve raises for weavers in April and June 1942. Other carpet companies also had to grant wage and other union demands during the war, either because of War Labor Board action or to avoid board action.[122]

Postwar Boom and Bust

After almost a quarter century of tough times and unsure carpet sales—the decline through much of the 1920s, the depression decade of the 1930s, and the war years of the 1940s—the industry enjoyed a brief period of prosperity. Pent-up consumer demand and general affluence were the two biggest factors creating a postwar boom. Total sales for the industry reached $430 million in 1948, more than twice the previous peak of 1923. But the boom was actually much less than it appeared. The dollar value of sales was up, but actual production, 89.6 million square yards, was not much higher than the 83.2 million square yards of 1923, and in fact it was not much greater than the previous peak year, 1904, with 82.7 million square yards. Midway through the twentieth century, the industry had seen only negligible growth; when compared with the population increase of the period, the result was actually a decline of about half.[123]

And the boom, such as it was, did not last long. In 1949 Alexander Smith announced a price cut, which other companies soon followed; Bigelow-Sanford's sales fell 20 percent. A temporary but extreme rise in wool prices a year later (occasioned by the beginning of the Korean War) further hurt sales and profits. Bigelow ended 1951 with a loss of $2.3 million, the largest in its history.[124]

At the end of World War II, Bigelow president James D. Wise approached the faculty of the Harvard Graduate School of Business Administration about the possibility of writing a history of his company. He promised to open the company's records to the scholars and to provide free access to the firm's top personnel. Harvard and Bigelow finally agreed to the deal in 1950, and Professors John S. Ewing and Nancy P. Norton were assigned the work of researching and writing the history of the Bigelow-Sanford Carpet Company. Published in 1955 as volume 17 in Harvard's distinguished Studies in Business History series, the book has been widely regarded as a model of corporate history.

Ewing and Norton found themselves writing about a company that had been a leader in its field for 130 years—at a time of serious difficulties and "adversity" (to borrow a word from the book's last chapter). In the last few pages of the book, as they described the current outlook and future prospects for the company, the authors noted that 1953 "witnessed a phenomenal increase in the sale of tufted floor coverings." "The rise of the tufting process," they wrote, "was something the like of which the carpet industry had not seen since axminster leaped forward at the end of the last century to challenge ingrain as the carpet of widest popularity." [125] Perhaps Ewing and Norton realized, but were hesitant to say, that the process they mentioned so briefly in the concluding pages of their lengthy study would bring about the rapid rise of America's second carpet industry, and the end of its first.

Crisis of the Old Order

The established woven carpet industry faced a crisis of stagnating demand and excess capacity after World War II. American carpet manufacturers shifted their operations to the South in the decade of the 1950s. A new technological process threatened the ancient dominance of weaving. Along with the rise of indigenous firms engaged in tufting, woven carpet companies set up shop in Dixie and opened tufting operations. By the end of the 1950s, yet another segment of the textile industry had abandoned the high-wage North for the low-wage South. The crisis of the old order opened a space that new entrepreneurs with new technology rushed to fill.[1]

The crisis of the woven carpet industry mirrored the problems faced by all U.S. textile manufacturers. Textile sectors experienced a brief boom period during and immediately after World War II. The boom faded in the early 1950s as textile manufacture returned to what seemed a permanent state of crisis, which had persisted since the 1920s. Even in the midst of this prolonged state of instability, however, there was room for maneuver by new entrants into the game. Spencer Love established Burlington Mills in the 1920s and guided the firm to the top of U.S. textile manufacturing by the 1950s in spite of the difficulties experienced by the industry generally. Love focused on less expensive, more readily available artificial fibers such as rayon and nylon to build Burlington.[2]

The carpet industry appeared to emerge from World War II solidly positioned to take advantage of pent-up consumer demand. The Textile Workers Union of America, which represented the majority of workers in the woven carpet industry, surveyed the industry's postwar condition in early 1946. The industry made substantial profits during the war, highest in the 1939–41 period. Industry profits rose to an all-time high in 1941 of about $37 million, or almost $1,300 per worker. The union noted that this figure was "only slightly lower than the annual earnings for the average carpet worker" in that year. After-tax profits as a percentage of sales dollars held steady in the 3.1–3.3 percent range in the years 1944–45, down from abnormally high rates in the 1936–42 period averaging more than 6 percent.[3]

The TWUA had successfully pushed up wages for carpet workers during this period as well. Average wages in the industry rose from 56.3 cents per hour in 1936 to 95.3 cents in 1946. The union took most of the credit for these increases, though certainly wages would have risen with increasing profits in any case, though perhaps not as rapidly. The TWUA also noted with pride the "job rationalization program" begun by the union in 1945. This program aimed at standardizing rates of pay for particular jobs and reducing "irrational" wage gaps. Total wages in the industry amounted to about 21.5 percent of net sales.[4]

The prosperity enjoyed by the industry after 1936 contrasted sharply with a bleak performance during the depths of the depression in the early 1930s. Companies were slow to invest in capital expansions until the war ended, in large part because of the unavailability of parts and equipment during the war. In the ten-year period 1936–45, the six public companies in the industry spent a total of about $12 million, or 1 percent of net sales, on capital improvements. The end of the war encouraged carpet manufacturers to consider expansion. In late 1945 and early 1946, two private companies—Firth and Alexander Smith—"put their stock on the market to secure capital for expansion purposes." The Smith firm announced plans to spend $2 million in 1947, while Firth managers planned to raise that company's productive capacity by 16 percent.

Capital investment seemed like a good idea in 1946. TWUA researchers asserted that "the industry faces a period of unprecedented demand for its product with prices which insure a very profitable level of earnings for the next few years." Carpet manufacturers had "no price problem," according to the union. The Office of Price Administration had recently granted rug makers permission to raise prices by almost 10 percent.[5] With the surge of postwar demand, surely consumers would ante up for luxurious soft floor coverings.

Carpet executives moved decisively to try to expand the postwar domestic carpet market with a massive advertising campaign. Individual companies launched their own marketing programs, and the manufacturers' association, reconstituted as the Carpet Institute, mounted an expensive drive of its own. The institute developed the "Home Means More with Carpet on the Floor" marketing strategy (1945–47). This special promotional program included ads in major magazines and joint sponsorship of new displays and marketing techniques by retailers. The Carpet Institute advised retail dealers to market carpets as part of entire home furnishings packages. The institute also provided training seminars and promotional materials to help dealers with the new approach. The manufacturers' association even produced a training film for salesmen and retailers.[6]

Industry and union optimism was reinforced by the performance of the carpet industry in the immediate postwar years. The years 1947–50 represented the "high water mark of production and prosperity" for U.S. woven carpet manufacturers. Production in that period averaged almost eighty million square yards per year, and profits rose accordingly. A financial survey sponsored by the Carpet Institute in 1958 disclosed that twelve companies, accounting for about 85 percent of all woven carpet production, reaped average profits of more than 7 percent of net sales. Profits amounted to more than 14 percent of invested capital in the 1947–50 cycle as well. Total carpet sales nearly doubled in this same time frame.[7]

In the early 1950s, however, the woven carpet industry began to settle into a disturbing new pattern. By the middle of that decade, many large manufacturers were running in the red, and national business periodicals published searching critiques of the industry. At a time when many American consumer products industries were experiencing record growth, established carpet firms struggled. Woven carpet production fell between 1951 and 1956, averaging only sixty million square yards per year.[8] The carpet oligopoly faced at least three substantial challenges in the 1950s. Raw material costs became highly erratic after the war, making planning difficult. Unexpected price spikes and interruptions in the supply of wool in the period 1946–50 shook carpet makers, touching off an intensive search for alternative fibers. Foreign competition also threatened the industry in the 1950s. Japanese, Belgian, French, and Italian Wiltons and velvets took increasing market shares. The Carpet Institute spent much of its time and effort in the mid- to late 1950s trying to convince the U.S. government to raise tariffs on imported woven carpets. Finally, new firms entered carpet manufacturing, firms that employed a new technique— tufting. Southern makers of cotton bedspreads, chenille bathrobes, and bath mats entered the large rug and wall-to-wall carpet market in 1949. Their new technology proved so efficient that by the mid-1950s tufted floor coverings posed a serious threat to the giants' market dominance. Woven carpet companies tried several methods of dealing with this southern threat, with mixed results at best. All of these challenges highlighted the carpet industry's most fundamental problem in the twentieth century: an inability to tap fully the vast middle-class market. The carpet industry had lived with the essential stagnation of demand for a generation or more before the end of World War II. The explosion of the mass consumer market after the war revealed the carpet industry's most glaring weakness.

"It has always been unfortunate," F. H. Masland of C. H. Masland and Sons lamented in November 1950, "that the carpet industry was tied to the back of a sheep. . . . The Creator of man and beast may have had mutton and clothing in mind when He created sheep, but I doubt if He had floor coverings." Masland and other executives accelerated experiments with wool-rayon blends and cotton in an effort to throw off the yoke of woolen oppression.[9] The price and quality of carpet-grade wool had long been a problem for the American carpet industry. High prices for wool, coupled with the limited productivity of the loom, kept woven carpet a luxury item beyond the reach of most consumers.

In the post–World War II era, wool price instability reached crisis proportions for carpet manufacturers. The decolonization of many Third World areas complicated the acquisition of raw materials for U.S. corporations. As in the 1920s, Americans imported 100 percent of the wool needed for carpet manufacture. The best carpet wool came from India, though the largest supplier was Argentina. Between 1945 and 1950, the price of wool rose fivefold, in large part owing to production and export restrictions imposed by the respective governments of India and Argentina. Juan Perón was particularly troublesome for the industry. By April 1950, the dictator had pushed up the price of Argentinean wool to seven times its 1947 average. In December 1950, the U.S. government cut further into the carpet industry's raw material base by prohibiting wool imports from Maoist China, producer of nearly 11 percent of American carpet wool imports.[10]

Carpet executives facing this "new world order" searched for alternatives. A national business publication announced, somewhat prematurely, in the summer of 1951 that "the carpet industry is pretty well emancipated from the sheep." Bigelow-Sanford, Mohawk, Firth, Masland, and James Lees all were experimenting with woven cotton carpets. Tufters already processed a substantial amount of cotton. In addition, all these firms carried an array of wool-rayon blends. The spring 1951 product lines introduced by these companies were illustrative. Twenty-seven percent of Bigelow's spring line that year consisted of wool-rayon blends; by the fall the company hoped to increase that total to 60 percent. Masland already produced 60 percent of its carpets in blends, Mohawk well over half. In the period January–April 1950, the carpet industry used 2.1 million pounds of rayon. In the same period in 1951, rayon use jumped to 10.6 million pounds. *Business Week* reported that industry leaders were "jubilant over the revolution against the unpredictable sheep."[11]

Yet the erratic price and availability of raw materials only exacerbated the carpet industry's other problems in the post–World War II era. Sharply rising wool prices put price pressure on the carpet manufacturer at precisely the time when other consumer goods were becoming more affordable to the American mass market. The dilemma of being a producer of an upper-class product in the midst of a middle-class consumption binge was not new for the industry in the 1950s. During the first half of the twentieth century, per family consumption of carpets actually declined about 60 percent. The American carpet industry had endured several decades of slow growth by the 1950s, earning "the unhappy distinction" of being one of a few industries "where growth has nowhere near matched the potential market—or the growth of the economy generally." [12]

Established carpet manufacturers were keenly aware of the costs of stagnation. Bigelow-Sanford lost more than $170,000 in the first half of 1954. Mohawk's profits in the first six months of 1954 amounted to only $400,000, down from more than $1 million in the same period the previous year. Indeed, by late fall of 1954, the two troubled giants were "weighing the possibilities of pooling their resources," according to *Business Week*. "Like most of the carpet industry," the business journal reported, "the two concerns have had hard going lately." [13]

Carpet firms tried a variety of methods to boost sales in the postwar period, most borrowed from the automobile industry. Bigelow-Sanford experimented with installment buying plans for customers in the mid-1950s. Bigelow also tried to cut costs by introducing new styles only once per year, instead of the traditional twice-yearly product lines, emulating the auto industry's once-a-year style changes. Though *Business Week* editors thought this move seemed to "fly in the face of the trend . . . to build obsolescence in style to create sales," Bigelow executives maintained that "you can carry obsolescence too far." Masland sponsored a study of a proposed "trade-in" program in 1956. Masland executives maintained that there was a market for used carpeting and that the trade-in plan could allow retailers a higher mark-up on carpets. Masland also introduced a leasing plan for customers in 1958. Finally, carpet firms in the late 1950s advocated greater tariff protection to keep out foreign woven carpets. [14]

Carpet manufacturers also tried to cut costs to improve sagging (and occasionally nonexistent) profit margins. Top firms cut "excess capacity" during the 1950s. James D. Wise, president of Bigelow-Sanford, estimated that excess broadloom capacity in 1951 probably stood at 40 percent above sales. In five years, Wise contended in 1956, the industry had cut 35 percent of the looms operating or ready for operation. The ratio had been shaved to about 16 percent capacity over 1955 sales.[15]

Established companies also sought cost efficiencies in cheaper labor and new technology, both of which they found in the South. The new technology was tufting. The machine-tufting process evolved from a local handicraft tradition in the northwest Georgia area in the first half of the twentieth century. Even the early carpet-tufting machines of the 1950s were six to ten times more efficient than looms at producing floor coverings. Small companies emerged in the Dalton area to produce tufted carpet, generally from cotton (later rayon). Georgia Rug Mills, Cabin Crafts, and Barwick Mills among others began tufting area rugs and carpeting between 1946 and 1949.[16]

The woven giants did not merely stand by and watch as their industry was threatened by small-time southern entrepreneurs. Bigelow management quickly recognized at least some of tufting's potential. In 1950, Bigelow became the first woven manufacturer to enter the tufting arena with its purchase of Georgia Rug Mills. James Lees followed Bigelow in 1952, announcing plans to build a tufting facility in Rabun County, Georgia. Mohawk purchased the tufting facilities of Scotland Mills of Laurinburg, North Carolina, in 1954.[17]

James Lees and Sons was perhaps the most effective of the old-line companies in adapting to changing conditions. In 1954, Lees closed its Bridgeport, Pennsylvania, woolen yarn plant. Lees had manufactured the bulk of its yarn at this facility. Though Lees continued to spin some wool elsewhere, the move reflected the company's transition. Lees shifted much of its capacity to tufting in the South. Lees was one of the few relative successes among the old woven oligopolists during the 1950s. In 1954, it was "the industry's only maker to show [even] a slight sales gain." The company attributed this to an investment of three hundred thousand dollars in new tufting equipment devoted to the production of cotton and rayon carpets.[18]

Lees and other manufacturers moved a substantial portion of their weaving operations to the South as well. By 1958, around 60 percent of the nation's woven carpet was made in the old Confederacy. Many of the looms that had not been idled in the cost-cutting wave of the decade were moved south. Lees relocated its principal weaving operations to Virginia. When tufted production was added, American Carpet Institute president Herbert Shuttleworth estimated in late 1958, "areas below the Mason-Dixon line now produce from 75% to 85% of all carpet" in the United States.[19]

The Alexander Smith company followed this industry trend, transferring some of its woven operations to the South. Company president William F. C. Ewing summarized many of the problems facing woven carpet firms in a letter to stockholders in January 1951. Ewing observed that the carpet market had experienced a "pronounced change" since 1945. "First came the greatly increased demand for broadloom widths," the executive informed his stockholders. This was followed by "a swing in popular demand" away from "the floral patterns which had been our bread and butter" and toward "fabrics of a sculptured or textured nature." The shifting tastes of the American consumer had "put a heavy burden on our existing production facilities."[20] These new market challenges made "apparent" the "growing inadequacy of our huge and sprawling carpet mill in Yonkers." Ewing outlined a two-part strategy. Alexander Smith had to "modernize our present plant facilities and increase our total productive capacity." The Smith company had spent more than $9 million on new equipment for the Yonkers plant since 1946. Ewing announced plans in early 1951 to "modernize the plant layout" to increase efficiency in the movement of materials. This was expected to cost "between 7 and 10 million dollars," and Ewing conceded that this would "take a long time." The company's aim, the president maintained, was "to make the Yonkers mill just as modern and efficient as we possibly can." No matter what efforts were expended, though, Ewing cautioned that the Yonkers mill was so outdated that "we may never achieve the efficiency of physical layout of the new mills of some of our competitors."[21]

Alexander Smith did not limit its reform efforts to existing facilities. Smith moved a substantial portion of its Axminster production to Mississippi in 1952. Mississippi, like other southern states, encouraged outside industries to relocate, employing a variety of programs. Mississippi had pioneered the regional effort to "sell the South" with the state's Balance Agriculture With Industry (BAWI) program in the 1930s. Under the

BAWI plan, Mississippi communities could offer five-year exemptions from county taxes and ten-year exemptions from municipal taxes to companies that relocated there. Communities could build factories to company specifications and then lease those buildings to the firm at low rates. Companies could then deduct the entire rental charge as a business expense before taxes. Communities could also offer loans at interest rates below prevailing commercial terms.[22]

The city of Greenville, Mississippi, made such an offer to the Alexander Smith firm in 1951. It offered to build "a $5 million modern, streamlined, air-conditioned, one-floor textile plant for the production of axminster" carpets, covering 15 acres on a 105-acre tract. The city agreed to build the facility strictly according to company specifications, with construction financed by a municipal bond issue.[23] The new facility offered several advantages to the Smith company. The firm's Yonkers facilities were spread out in several buildings, some more than one story. A single large building would cut the time needed to move materials from one processing operation to another and therefore cut costs and improve productivity. Lift trucks could now be more profitably employed to move materials as well, since the building consisted of only one floor. The Greenville site also "had a thirty car siding on the Illinois Central Railroad with facilities for handling six motor trucks simultaneously."[24]

This was literally an offer that Smith management could hardly refuse. The increased efficiency of such a modern facility was crucial for Smith's continued competitiveness. Bigelow, Mohawk, Lees, and other carpet firms had already pioneered in building new facilities with all the advantages of the proposed Greenville site. The Mississippi community also offered Smith the advantage of a location much closer to the growing southwestern market. The company agreed to lease the facility in Greenville. Construction was completed in 1952. By 1954, Smith's Greenville plant operated 114 looms and produced more than three million square yards of Axminster carpeting. President Ewing had maintained in 1951 that he had "confidence" that Smith's old plant in Yonkers could "be made competitive with other newer mills." The "skill and enthusiasm of the thousands of men and women" employed there would be the major ingredients in honing the competitiveness of the old plant. All the "efficient layouts and modern machines" didn't "mean a thing" without "good men and women to run them." To allay workers' fears about the new plant in Mississippi, Ewing announced that the Greenville facility would be "small in comparison to Yonkers" and intended only to provide "added production we badly need."[25] The assertion that the new plant would provide needed additional productive capacity was a bit suspicious in the early 1950s. Indeed, as had been noted, the woven carpet industry went to great lengths to cut "excess capacity" in the 1950s. Alexander Smith needed more efficient, modernized productive capacity, not simply more capacity. Although Ewing extolled the virtues of Alexander Smith's loyal workforce, the company's venture in Mississippi, along with renewed union unrest, would eventually prove the undoing of a century-long relationship between management and labor in Yonkers.

Alexander Smith closed its Yonkers plant in 1954. Faced with financial losses in the early 1950s, the venerable company's management sought all available cost-cutting measures. The city of Greenville had virtually agreed to underwrite the move for the Smith firm, financing construction costs and promising local tax exemptions. The new Mississippi plant was, as one observer noted, "as modern as the Yonkers facility was ancient." It had provided the means for the company to substitute for the production of the Yonkers plant.[26]

Smith's vice president for sales, Robert Bishop, explained the decision to close the Yonkers plant to the company's sales staff and regional managers in July 1954. Bishop acknowledged that the company had indeed decided to "close our Yonkers plant permanently and concentrate our production in our Philadelphia Wilton plant and our super-modern Greenville plant." The Yonkers plant was abandoned, Bishop maintained, because that mill "couldn't be made to compete cost-wise with other plants in the industry—including our other plants in Philadelphia and Greenville." The decision to shutter the Yonkers plant represented an "important step toward making Alexander Smith the most efficient and lowest-cost producer in the carpet industry." The company was "stepping up production schedules in Greenville rapidly." In the future the Mississippi mill would provide Smith customers with "one reliable source for all our Axminster goods, produced in a streamlined beauty of a mill which is the finest in the country, bar none." Bishop tried to reassure Smith's sales force that the company was on sound footing. He specifically mentioned the company's reserve of "carpet-making know-how" and "skilled employees." [27] Such assurances provided cold comfort in the wake of the loss of more than two thousand jobs belonging to Yonkers's skilled production employees.

Smith management must have also welcomed the opportunity to escape from union entanglements. The company had developed a paternalistic relationship with its employees over the decades. Smith "assume[d] a concern for the total welfare of their employees." Wages at Smith were high relative to industry standards. It came as a shock to management when Smith employees followed the trend of the 1930s and voted to organize in 1937. Significantly, though, union contracts at Smith between 1937 and 1945 provided for modest wage increases. The union was content to negotiate shop-floor matters and leave wages to the company's discretion. Union contracts in this period "allowed for a permissive atmosphere, thus affording an opportunity for gradual change and reaching a sensible working solution." According to at least one student of the company, labor-management relations remained flexible and allowed substantial room for maneuver by the firm, even under union agreements. Smith had a remarkably stable workforce. In 1949, one survey found that the company had 157 employees with more than fifty years of service to the company and 9 with sixty years. When the Yonkers facility closed, more than 2,400 workers lost their jobs; 1,100 of them had more than twenty-five years with the company. Sixty percent of those left unemployed were fifty years of age or older.[28]

The earlier pattern of labor-management cooperation had changed after World War II. Alexander Smith employees, like union members in many industries in the postwar era, engaged in strikes in 1951, 1952, and 1954. The decision to close the Yonkers facility was made while workers were in the midst of the 1954 work stoppage. As labor-management harmony eroded, the southern strategy became more attractive. In 1954, the firm decided that the cost advantages of closing these facilities outweighed a century of cooperation with a stable workforce and the community of Yonkers. Thereby, the city lost its largest employer.[29] It is difficult to envision any other outcome, given the changing nature of the carpet industry. This process was repeated often during the 1950s as northern manufacturers shifted to the South.

The *Wall Street Journal* took note of the changes at Alexander Smith in early 1955. The company had "been shrunk" in the past two years "from a half-mile long, 56-acre collection of old four and five story buildings at Yonkers" to one "15-acre, one story mill in Greenville and a three-acre mill at Liberty." The moves had reduced Smith's productive capacity from 20 million square yards per year in Yonkers to about 9 million in the smaller plants. Smith had reached a peak of more than 6,500 employees in 1950; the maximum number of wage-earning production workers in the new plants would be no more than 2,000. Smith's new president, James Elliot, predicted that the firm would save $4 million a year in labor costs alone. This "less is more" strategy reflected a new management plan. No longer burdened by the Yonkers plant and its huge overhead costs, the company now had "much greater flexibility," according to Elliot. Smith could now move away from "the low-end stuff we had to turn out at Yonkers" and begin "trading up in quality." Elliot now expected to "have demand pulling at capacity."[30] This strategy seemed to fly in the face of market trends of the 1950s that indicated a growing demand for inexpensive carpeting.

The *Journal* concurred with Smith management, praising the modern facilities in Greenville. "As you walk into the steamy dye house," business correspondent DeWitt Morrill observed, "a door opens before you, triggered by an electric eye." The door automatically closed, as well, "saving strain on the air conditioning equipment." The electric-eye doors and concrete floor also "permit[ted] lift trucks to pass without halting." The use of lift trucks would have been impossible at the old Yonkers plant, according to Greenville plant manager Jack Potts, where "ancient wooden floors" supported by wooden beams could not safely support motorized lifts.[31]

Potts gave the *Wall Street Journal* reporter a tour of the Greenville plant and a brief lesson in labor relations. Potts explained that at the new facility, each loom tender operated two machines, noting that this "realistic work load" represented a major change from the Yonkers plant, where each loom had its own operator. Potts praised his new Mississippi employees: "The calibre, interest and enthusiasm of these folks is certainly as important as the plant's technical efficiency. I have never seen people pick up the knack [for carpet weaving] so fast." Smith's traditional carpet operation in Yonkers had depended on reliable, skilled, experienced labor. In Mississippi, the company found that others could learn the necessary skills rather quickly. The Mississippi carpet mill workers were apparently fairly docile as well. In the old Yonkers plant, DeWitt Morrill recalled, the walls were covered with red and white signs that read "Cool Off, Don't Pop Off." "Similar signs," he noted, "are conspicuously absent at the gleaming new Southern mills" of Alexander Smith and other carpet firms.[32]

Textile Workers Union of America officials observed the transformation of the carpet industry with great anxiety. The TWUA had successfully organized virtually the entire northern woven carpet industry by 1950. Now the emergence of tufting in the South threatened those gains. The TWUA's Research Department, headed for decades by Solomon Barkin, charted the course of the carpet industry throughout the late 1940s and 1950s. Union officials argued that the successful organization of the woven industry (which *was* the carpet industry before the mid-1950s) could actually benefit the manufacturers by reducing shop-floor conflict and establishing rational personnel procedures.

The TWUA recognized the significance of the new tufting technology as early as September 1954. In its "Economic Notes" for a union conference on the carpet industry, the Research Department cautioned members about the rapid development of tufting. "The story of tufted carpets is changing rapidly," researchers noted, and the TWUA could not ignore the challenge presented to the woven industry by tufting. Obviously identifying with employers in their industry, TWUA officials viewed this new process as a threat. "The problems presented by these [tufted] carpets have been serious." Tufted carpets had already "challenged the lower priced wool products, particularly in the Axminster range." Cotton tufted goods had some drawbacks, however, that prevented their wholesale acceptance at the expense of woven wool. Tufted cotton rugs had lately "been deteriorating in quality and the laundering problems have been serious."[33]

A new and potentially more serious threat had developed by 1954. "The improvement in the quality of rayon staple for carpet purposes" afforded tufters a viable alternative to cotton. Rayon's major selling points as a carpet fiber were "resistance, . . . luxurious appearance, versatility in texture effects and easier removal of soil." Rayon was cheaper than wool and could be used more effectively in tufting rather than in woven carpets.

Rayon's major problems included "difficulties in dyeing" and resilience. Within four months, the TWUA reported that cotton had been "virtually supplanted by rayon staple" in tufted carpets.[34]

The TWUA was also concerned about the level of interest shown by old-line woven companies in the tufting process, and in the South generally. By September 1954, "all of the major carpet companies either [had] a tufted carpet mill of their own or [had] relations with a tufted mill which produce[d] such a carpet for them." Of the three largest companies, Bigelow and Mohawk owned their own tufting subsidiaries. Alexander Smith and Sons contracted with E. T. Barwick Mills of Dalton for its tufted products.[35]

Northern mills continued to shift their attention to the South after 1954. Bigelow-Sanford exemplified the industry trend. The company lost money more than once in the 1950s. Bigelow had rebounded by 1959, though not as strongly as company executives would have preferred. Following a medical analogy, *Forbes* concluded in April 1960 that Bigelow had "benefited from some serious surgery: plant relocations to the South, and switches in key management." *Barron's* offered a similar assessment in 1961. Bigelow's "margins on rugs and carpets have been strengthened by the large-scale relocation to Southern plants." Over a seven-year period, Bigelow shifted "about 85% of its facilities from New England," for a net saving of "between $5 million and $6 million a year in manufacturing costs." The Bigelow family of manufacturing facilities had a distinctly southern accent by 1961. The New England–born company in that year had plants in Summerville, Georgia; Landrum, Calhoun Falls, and Belton, South Carolina; and Bristol, Virginia, in addition to its original facility in Thompson, Connecticut.[36]

The South once again played its traditional role as a haven for a low-wage textile industry trying to cut costs. Carpet manufacturing moved south almost in desperation in the 1950s. Lees and other companies combined new tufting machinery and established woven technology with the South's long-advertised docile and tractable labor force to become "competitive" again. Yet for all their efforts, the old-line carpet makers continued to lose ground to new southern producers.

Elliot Petersen, a vice president at Alexander Smith and Sons, candidly summarized the problems faced by the old woven industry and the attempts to solve them in a 1955 speech before an industry trade group. Petersen listed the various efforts of the past few years to woo consumers. "We have tried direct distribution, distribution through wholesalers, or both at once," he told his audience. "We moved south to cut labor costs. We have sold on price. We have stepped up advertising. We have put carpet on an installment selling basis." Despite all these efforts, the industry still faced a crisis. Petersen argued that "none of [these efforts] has sold enough carpet." [37]

Harry Martin, floor covering columnist for *Retailing Daily*, took special note of Petersen's comments. According to Martin, Petersen had taken on several of the carpet trade's sacred cows. Petersen criticized carpet makers and retailers for excessive emphasis on wall-to-wall carpeting. Martin echoed the executive's sentiments, arguing that "the concentration on wall-to-wall has put floor coverings out of the price range of a great part of the population." Consumers no longer considered area rugs as prized decorative items, Martin maintained. This neglect had led many consumers "to take impossible odds on inferior qualities." Petersen had issued a call for a reorientation of the carpet industry toward products that would be desirable for their aesthetic qualities rather than their price. Petersen's speech was interpreted as a "near post-mortem of the carpet industry," and Martin agreed with the Alexander Smith executive that the problem was not how to produce a cheaper product but how to convince consumers to be satisfied with beauty, quality, and craftsmanship in smaller rugs. Both Petersen and Martin were making thinly veiled criticisms of the trend toward tufted products.[38]

The new marketing and cost-control efforts did not produce adequate results for Petersen's own company, which had slipped badly into the red in 1954. Negotiations with Mohawk were finally consummated in the fall of 1955, and the two old giants became one company, awkwardly renamed "Mohasco." Mohasco's managers set about reassessing their company's competitive position. TWUA organizers correctly cautioned that the effect of this merger would be further "consolidation of resources and a further shift toward the South." TWUA researchers noted that Mohasco would shift most "axminster production to the Southern Smith mills; some velvet production to the Smith Liberty [South Carolina] mill and . . . Philadelphia wilton operations to the [old Mohawk] Amsterdam [New

York] plant. The overall result will be a larger proportion of carpet production in the South," where the TWUA faced tremendous organizing difficulties.[39]

Mohasco followed the Bigelow pattern, with similar success. By 1958, Mohasco had substantially repaired its balance sheets. Despite a 9 percent drop in sales in 1958, it recorded an impressive 88 percent gain in net income over the previous year. Mohasco particularly profited from the sale, and subsequent leaseback, of its Amsterdam facilities. The company sold its Amsterdam property for $8.5 million and paid only about $7 million for a long-term lease on the building and equipment. In addition, Mohasco paid no income taxes on reported profits of $7.6 million in 1958 because of the "carry forward" of old Alexander Smith and Sons losses.[40]

The shift to the South was a large part of the effort by the old woven oligopoly to maintain its control over the soft floor covering industry. Southern workers received 75 percent of the average northeastern wage between 1947 and 1954.[41] Cheap southern labor coupled with the dramatically enhanced productivity offered by the tufting process seemed to offer a way to preserve the dominant position of the northeastern carpet oligopoly. The challenge of the developing South was perhaps the most daunting faced by the old order in the postwar period.

In some ways, the third great challenge to the old order in U.S. carpet manufacture resembled the southern threat. American carpet manufacturers were pressured by foreign competition in the 1950s as well. U.S. carpet weavers had long enjoyed substantial tariff protection against foreign competition, principally British until the postwar period. As late as 1938, average duties on imported carpets stood at 60 percent. As a result of the attempt to establish an open-door global trading system after the war, individual trade agreements and the General Agreement on Tariffs and Trade reduced U.S. carpet duties to 25 percent in June 1951. In 1956, a new GATT agreement lowered carpet tariffs to 22.5 percent, with a further reduction to 21 percent called for in the summer of 1958. As the rest of the world recovered from the Second World War and American trade barriers fell, domestic woven carpets were squeezed by cheaper foreign competition. In June 1958, the Carpet Institute sought protection from the United States Tariff Commission.[42]

Imports of machine-made wool carpets and rugs rose steadily throughout the postwar era. Before the war, imports had never amounted to more than 1.3 percent of the total U.S. production. By 1957, imports amounted to almost 8 percent of domestic output. The problem was worst for two particular weaves: Wiltons and velvets. Imported Wiltons, which had never exceeded 1.8 percent of domestic production before 1948, rose to more than 16 percent of the domestic total. The precise damage to the velvet market, according to the Carpet Institute, was more difficult to calculate, since many foreign products entered the country as "unspecified" weaves. Axminsters and Brussels—the other two major weaves—had "special characteristics" that immunized them from import competition. Axminster carpet required special looms, while Wiltons and velvets could be produced on the same basic loom. To produce a Wilton weave, manufacturers needed only to add a Jacquard harness. This "easy interchangeability of weaves" made possible "a ready shifting of production from one to the other, in response to changing market opportunities." [43]

American consumers had created the opportunity for cheap foreign imports to flood the U.S. market, according to Carpet Institute tariff experts. The U.S. carpet market had changed appreciably since 1945. "The nature of the American market," the institute's spokesmen claimed, "has invited frequent and numerous variations of rug design, color, texture, and qualities." Consumers had increasingly become concerned with the color, feel, and price of carpets. This shift had led to "a consequent lessening interest in the value of basic weave classifications as a factor of market importance." Velvets were "especially susceptible to uncertain, or overlooked weave classification" in import transactions. U.S. tariffs applied to all carpet regardless of weave. The government did specify maximum amounts for imports, which when exceeded should trigger higher tariffs. The hitch, for the carpet industry, was that since most velvets were either misclassified or unspecified, the totals slipped neatly within the import allowance for the entire category of carpets and rugs, while specific imports of velvets and Wiltons hurt makers of those two weaves. [44]

The erosion of U.S. markets by these cheap imports led to dangerous financial practices, and given competition from southern tufting operations, American carpet companies saw their average profits decline throughout the 1950s. Return on invested capital (as a percentage of sales) averaged 14.4 percent in the boom years 1947–50. The rate dropped precipitously to only 4.3 percent in 1951–53; and profits fell further, to 3.8 percent, in the 1954–56 period. This low rate of return for investors and the much slower accumulation of capital implied by reduced profit margins forced firms to borrow more heavily than in the past. All the developments of the 1950s—the rise of the tufting process, the rapidly changing tastes of consumers, the demands for greater advertising to open and help shape new markets, experimentation with new fibers—required capital investments, at a time when profit margins were shrinking substantially. As a consequence, carpet mills shifted to borrowed capital to finance capital improvements. Borrowed capital represented only 6.2 percent of total carpet industry equity in 1948. By 1956, it amounted to more than 42 percent of industry equity. Established carpet firms took on an additional seventy million dollars in debt during the period. Companies that had long resisted public financial markets, such as Alexander Smith and Sons, were forced to sell equity to raise capital.[45]

The Carpet Institute blamed the rising tide of imports for the declining financial health of the soft-flooring oligopoly. Belgian and Japanese manufacturers, especially, took advantage of substantially cheaper labor in their countries to undersell U.S. firms. The average wage for Belgian carpet workers in 1955, according to the U.S. Bureau of Foreign Commerce, was around 40 cents per hour. Their average workweek ran 45–48 hours, with no premium pay for overtime. In contrast, workmen's wages in the U.S. woven carpet trade amounted to more than $1.80 per hour, with, of course, mandatory time and a half for overtime beyond 40 hours.[46] However, the Carpet Institute failed to prove its case to the satisfaction of the U.S. Tariff Commission, which recommended against new punitive duties on imported Wiltons and velvets. The commission implied that the real threat to cheaper woven carpets came not from abroad but from the South, from tufted carpets and rugs.

Woven carpet manufacturers searched for other ways to increase sales and overcome stagnating demand during the late 1950s. In November 1955, the Board of Trustees of the Carpet Institute voted to pursue the possibility of convincing the Federal Housing Administration to include carpeting in FHA-approved mortgages.[47] In other words, the industry wanted the federal government to help finance consumer purchases. Spending several hundred or thousand dollars on carpeting might be an easier decision to make for new homeowners if they could effectively spread the payments out over thirty years. This sort of financing certainly was light-years ahead of the standard manufacturer- or dealer-financed "time payment" purchases introduced in the early 1950s.

The FHA was certain to require some industrywide minimum quality standards in exchange for including carpet in mortgages. ACI member firms debated the merits of a labeling program during the mid-1950s. The establishment of such standards would speed the FHA approval process and also might help bolster the woven industry's sagging fortunes versus southern tufting firms. The decision to seek industrywide standards was thus complex. Many institute members wanted the potential increase in sales FHA approval would certainly bring. Others viewed the setting of industry standards as an internal quality control issue. Efforts to set minimum quality standards included a veiled critique of the tufted industry, whose manufacturers were sometimes accused of trying to sell bedspreads as carpets. The institute approved a set of quality standards in 1956 but decided to refrain from implementing any kind of labeling program until after FHA approval.

The Carpet Institute's proposal to include carpets, accompanied by FHA-approved minimum standards, in mortgages received FHA approval in 1956. The industry faced opposition, however, from its own retailers. Carpet retailers in the mid-1950s expressed growing anxiety over the increasing tendency of carpet manufacturers and wholesale distributors to sell directly to consumers (either commercial or residential). The FHA mortgage proposal appeared to retailers to be one more attempt to cut them out of the profit picture in carpeting. If carpets were included in FHA mortgages, more carpet would inevitably be sold by manufacturers and distributors directly to contractors, cutting out the retailer. The National Retail Furniture Association learned of the Carpet Institute's plan and protested to legislators on the Senate Banking and Currency Committee in March 1956. The Banking Committee responded by pressuring the FHA commissioner, who appeared to back away from prior commitments to the carpet association. In this atmosphere, the legislative committee asked the FHA to devote further time to a study of the matter before making a final determination.[48]

The FHA study of the mortgage issue dragged on into 1957 with no resolution. The furniture association put up a fierce struggle against the measure. In September 1957, John T. Lees, general sales manager for A. & M. Karagheusian carpets, summarized succinctly the attitudes of Carpet Institute members on the whole issue of quality standards and FHA status. Lees began by reminding institute president Paul Jones that quality ratings had already been approved by the woven industry. Lees frankly admitted that there was some opposition to the establishment of standards by those companies that still resented the intrusion of small tufted carpet firms into the trade. "One of the stronger arguments against the establishment of FHA standards," Lees noted, "was that it would automatically improve the status of smaller tufted manufacturers by putting the FHA stamp of approval on their merchandise meeting the minimum standards."[49] While two of the new tufting concerns belonged to the institute (E. T. Barwick Mills and Cabin Crafts), neither qualified as "small," and one of them produced very little "low-end" quality carpeting. They had been admitted to the club, but the dozens of smaller tufted carpet firms were regarded as little more than glorified bedspread makers, churning out shoddy merchandise whose only virtue was low price.

Lees proposed that "members of the Carpet Institute adopt the minimum standards we set up and approved for acceptance by FHA,—only with no tie-in or mention of FHA." He suggested that the association could print and distribute labels that bore the Carpet Institute's "seal of approval." Such a program, Lees argued, would present several advantages. "Carpet Institute members would have a sales advantage over nonmembers and importers," according to the carpet executive, since only institute members would be eligible for the seal. This action would freeze out smaller tufting concerns without the financial reserves to afford the institute's expensive dues. Established concerns would also be "encouraged to manufacture . . . better carpets." Retailers would have an additional weapon with which to convince consumers of the quality of carpets. Most important, "when FHA approval comes, we shall be in business 'overnight' with FHA, as the Carpet Institute Seal of Approval will immediately become FHA standards." Otherwise, Lees feared, "it could be a year before some of our members were set up" to meet the new standards. This "jump ahead" would give institute members a "considerable time advantage over non-members."[50]

The institute moved to implement Lees's suggestions in early 1958. FHA approval, however, remained a prisoner of the turf battle between manufacturers and sellers. In May 1958, the FHA commissioner informed the Carpet Institute that the agency would not include carpet in approved mortgages. The commissioner told the institute's leadership that he had been forced to make this statement "due to the political pressures brought by members of Congress as a result of a letter-writing campaign initiated by some of the retailers." The FHA head also expressed the opinion that the institute "would not be able to get FHA approval for some time" and that the industry should drop the matter for the foreseeable future. The institute's trustees agreed with the FHA commissioner but decided to press ahead even more rapidly with the association's in-house seal-of-approval program.[51]

The Carpet Institute launched a new advertising campaign in the mid-1950s to try to shore up dwindling markets, shape consumer tastes, and counteract the growth of the new, smaller tufted mills. It launched a new "Home Means More with Carpet on the Floor" campaign in 1955 and boosted its annual marketing budget from about $750,000 to $1.25 million per year for three years. This marketing blitz targeted consumers with full-page ads in national magazines and newspapers, television spots, and booklets for consumers. The goal of the new campaign was "to enlarge the total market for soft floor coverings," according to Alexander Smith president James Elliott, by promoting the "functional benefits" of carpeting—"quiet, beauty and warmth."[52]

Individual companies also mounted impressive advertising campaigns as well in the late 1950s. Mohasco and its two main "branches," Mohawk and Alexander Smith, returned to television in 1960 after an absence of more than a decade. Mohawk and Smith each tried to build brand-name identification, sorely lacking in the carpet industry. The Smith division of Mohawk adopted the image of an elderly gentleman dressed in traditional workman's clothes holding a carpet bag as its symbol in new print ads in 1958. Smith's management hoped that consumers would identify with "Mr. Smith, the man behind the loom." The Bigelow company brought back its "a title on the door rates a Bigelow on the floor" campaign and introduced humorous cartoons as print advertisements. James Lees ran a series of ads promoting "best buys" in conjunction with local retailers. These campaigns were aimed primarily at selling brand names.[53]

Firth Carpets developed another theme for a massive marketing drive in 1958. It initiated a series of ads that explained to consumers the dos and don'ts of carpet buying. The company was influenced by a survey conducted by the Carpet Institute that showed that most Americans had little experience shopping for carpets and rugs and were wary of the practice of comparative price advertising that was common in the 1950s. Firth used print ads in 1958 and 1959 to "educate consumers," of course making those consumers aware that Firth was responsible for this new information. In 1960, the company expanded this campaign, sponsoring a half-hour home decorating show called "Spotlighting You." Decorators gave tips on home furnishings, and a panel of consumers asked questions of experts in furniture and carpeting. The show's hosts gave carpet care tips during the broadcast. During the show, local stations participated by doing locally produced commercials for Firth Carpets. The local stations were encouraged to use their own "women's program personalities" in these commercials, and local retailers were encouraged to take out print ads promoting the show in local newspapers. Other manufacturers followed Firth's lead.[54]

The stated goal of the institute's program and the individual campaigns was to promote the idea of carpet in general. *Advertising Age* took note of the ad blitz in March 1959, reporting that in 1958 broadloom carpeting "became the most strongly retail-advertised item in the home furnishings field—usurping the No. 1 spot headed by TV sets . . . since 1948." The advertising journal summarized the results of a study of advertising copy conducted in nine major cities, including New York, Philadelphia, Cleveland, and Chicago. The study revealed that most carpet ads targeted the growing "middle-priced market," or carpets that cost between five and ten dollars per square yard. The established carpet industry was selling for all it was worth by the end of the 1950s.

Herbert Jay, Mohasco's director of public relations and advertising, explained his company's marketing strategy and the company's 1960 return to television. "As the largest company in the industry, we feel that it's our duty to first sell the concept of carpet—the generic of carpet," Jay asserted. If consumers weren't "sold on carpet per se, it doesn't matter how much we advertise the Mohawk line." This sentiment reflected the general strategy of the Carpet Institute and individual large companies within the industry.[55] The established carpet oligopoly evidently assumed that if the public was sufficiently "sold on carpet per se," consumers would obviously turn to firms with the skill and experience of more than a century of carpet craftsmanship. In making this assumption, the established firms were wrong.

In 1955, John S. Ewing and Nancy P. Norton published a history of one of the carpet industry's largest, oldest, and best-known companies, Bigelow, which was synonymous with woven wool carpets and rugs. Ewing and Norton, writing in the midst of the revolutionary changes that swept through carpet manufacturing, noted that the chief "imponderable" with which Bigelow's management had struggled in the postwar period was "the long-range trend of the industry." While Ewing and Norton observed that the Bigelow company had "diversified" by purchasing a tufted rug mill in Georgia in 1950, neither the authors nor Bigelow's managers could have foreseen the virtual replacement of woven wool carpets by tufted constructions made from synthetic fibers, or the rise of a host of small firms in the American South that would dominate the new production process.[56]

William Reynolds, longtime treasurer of the American Carpet Institute, published a study of post–World War II innovations in the carpet industry in 1968. Reynolds examined the demand for carpeting and found a strong correlation between rising per capita income and increases in carpet sales. U.S. carpet sales increased about 1.3 percent for every 1 percent increase in real income in the period 1947–63. Carpeting had long been associated with comfort and luxury in the home. Before World War II, relatively high carpet prices had limited consumption to the upper and upper-middle income strata. The postwar global economic boom, a "golden age" according to Eric Hobsbawm, generated rapid income growth and an unprecedented boom in new housing construction. The general economic boom coincided with the emergence of tufted floor coverings, and consumers freely substituted tufted carpets for woven.[57]

The old woven establishment had long struggled to achieve brand-name recognition and a consumer franchise. These efforts had been less

TABLE 1. Dollar Value of Shipments, Woven and Tufted Carpets and
Rugs, 1951–1959

	1951	1952	1953	1954	1955	1956	1957	1958	1959
Woven	430	388	391	341	390	409	366	319	375
Tufted	19	34	55	97	160	179	230	261	314

Source: U.S. Bureau of the Census, Census of Manufactures, 1958 and 1963.

TABLE 2. Percentage of Households Having Wall-to-Wall Carpeting,
by Room, Selected Years 1955–1964

	1955	1961	1964
Living room	12	25	34
Dining room	12	14	18
Master bedroom	2	8	12

Source: American Carpet Institute, Basic Facts about the Carpet and Rug Industry, 1968.

than successful. In 1961, the American Carpet Institute sponsored a market survey of consumer attitudes toward carpets. The survey's findings confirmed the worst fears of executives within the woven carpet industry. More than 40 percent of consumers who had purchased carpet within the past six months could not hazard a guess as to the brand name for their carpeting. Of those consumers who mentioned a brand name, almost 10 percent mentioned Sears or some other retail chain. Fewer than 40 percent of those surveyed mentioned a manufacturer. Most consumers were unable to differentiate between woven and tufted constructions by sight. The most important factors in consumer purchase decisions were color, style, pattern, price, and durability. Consumers almost never mentioned construction or method of manufacture.[58]

The inability of woven manufacturers to build brand-name recognition combined with another trend to work against increased consumption of woven carpets and in favor of the tufted variety: the decline of ornamental designs that had been popular until the 1920s. From the Great Depression through the 1960s, "demand homogenized steadily in apparel and furnishings textiles." For carpets, this trend favored monocolor constructions rather than the intricate multicolor patterns long associated with high-end woven goods. According to Philip Scranton, this trend was accompanied by a seemingly contradictory demand on the part of home furnishings and apparel buyers for "a wide stylistic variety" within these newly established boundaries.[59] Tufted carpeting made an attractive bargain for floor covering distributors, retail buyers, and consumers. The new tufting machines could make solid color carpeting that closely resembled the most popular woven goods. Tufting machine mechanics worked to create new attachments and designs for tufting machines that could create new styles. Along with an almost endless variety of colors, these variations on the tufting machine helped carpet manufacturers produce an almost "endless novelty," to borrow Scranton's phrase. This novelty was produced within the new homogenized boundaries of the American consumer. A tufted carpet with a simple pattern "sculpted" by cut-and-loop effects, or through a "back-robbing" attachment, was indistinguishable to the average consumer from an Axminster. Indeed, the woven industry's advertising campaigns of the 1950s may have backfired. The marketing blitz extolled the virtues of carpets in general. Most consumers had little knowledge about different constructions or manufacturing methods. Many of the new tufted carpets were indistinguishable from woven carpets at a glance. As per capita incomes rose in the 1950s and 1960s, consumers based their purchases on style (including color) and price. Tufted carpeting was substantially cheaper than woven; Reynolds found that price was, in the final analysis, the key factor in consumer decisions.

The results of all this advertising of soft floor coverings in general were mixed for the members of the elite Carpet Institute. With the industry facing a brand-name identification crisis and rising tufted production by new firms entering the carpet market, all manufacturers benefited from this strategy. Even though almost all of the old-line woven firms had entered tufted production by the end of the 1950s, these companies still had heavy investments in woven carpet facilities and equipment. Cheaper tufted carpets took a larger and larger market share in the 1950s, and that declining market share squeezed woven manufacturers. Mohasco, Bigelow, and other woven giants slashed "excess capacity" and consolidated in the face of a variety of challenges. The American carpet industry, after decades of virtual stagnation, took an a new look by 1960 as southern firms benefited most from the developments of the 1950s.

Tufted Textiles Take the Floor

Jack Turner, a longtime carpet industry executive, insisted in a 1995 interview that in the era of the Great Depression "Dalton and northwest Georgia were still . . . suffering from the after-effects of the Civil War and Reconstruction; a lot of us today have difficulty realizing the degree of economic discrimination against the South" that was prevalent "as late as the Thirties." Turner referred to the colonial economy thesis in explaining the rise of the tufted textile industry in northwest Georgia, which came to dominate carpet manufacturing by the 1960s. Entrepreneurs in Dalton and other small neighboring communities in the long-neglected northwest corner of Georgia created a homegrown industry, helping lift the area into the modern industrial world by its own bootstraps. Turner's remarks underscored the power of the colonial economy thesis as an explanation of the South's economic backwardness; his explanation of the rise of a new industry attested to the vitality of one solution to the vexing problem of southern poverty.[1]

William H. Wilkerson, president of the Auto-Soler Company of Atlanta, Georgia, delivered the following admonition to a group of southern and Georgia business colleagues in 1946: "Dixie . . . Look To Your Bootstraps." Wilkerson detailed his assessment of the South's particular economic predicament to an audience at the annual meeting of the Southern Machinery and Metals Exposition in Atlanta. "It is a fact that we in the South are poor," Wilkerson noted, "and it seems to me, that to overcome our poverty, we need industry." Moreover, Georgia and the South needed "home-grown" industry. There were three kinds of businesses in Georgia, according to the executive. First there were "branch plants" established by "Northern capital." In these plants "the management is absentee," and the "profits are siphoned away to the North." This type of business did Georgia "only partial good." Another category of business was "the type . . . that is owned in Georgia, gets all its income from Georgia and keeps its profit here for the benefit of Georgia." This type of business was "perfectly all right," Wilkerson allowed, but still did not fill Georgia's most pressing need. "The thing that we must have to take our place in the sun," Wilkerson argued, "is the third type of business—our *own* national industry—businesses that are Georgia-owned and Georgia-managed, bringing profits into Georgia from other states and countries." Wilkerson urged Georgia's business leaders to invest in local industry.[2]

Wilkerson's analysis was familiar to southern business and political leaders of the immediate post–World War II era. Georgia governor Ellis Arnall expressed similar sentiments in 1946. The South had for too long operated as a virtual colony of the Northeast, supplying raw materials and cheap labor but reaping few benefits of the American economy's rapid progress. According to Arnall, the South had to break free from its colonial status, not just for the sake of the region but for the economic well-being of the entire nation. Arnall urged government action to spur the development of the southern economy. Vigorous enforcement of antitrust laws and expansion of low-cost credit were the keys. The government should use these policies to help "make free enterprise work," Arnall argued. The governor hoped such policies would contribute to the "decentralization of industry," thus permitting "the development of sections of our country that now have sub-standard incomes, that are underdeveloped, and that are subject to the hazards of a colonial economy."[3]

One of Arnall's most vigorous supporters, *Atlanta Journal* general manager George C. Biggers, made a similar argument to the Southern Governors' Conference in New Orleans in December 1945. Biggers criticized southern business leaders who sat "with hands folded, complacently waiting for the damn Yankee to come down here and build factories and open new businesses." Biggers urged southern business and community leaders to devote more attention to encouraging local industries. Biggers, Arnall, and Wilkerson urged a healthy dose of entrepreneurial capitalism as an antidote for southern poverty.[4]

Southern state governments and community leaders had traditionally followed a different path in attempting to promote economic development: the feverish pursuit of outside investment. The details of this New South strategy, enunciated clearly by *Atlanta Constitution* editor Henry Grady in the 1880s, changed over time, but the central goal remained the same. Advocates of this strategy argued that what the South needed most was capital and that the only reliable sources of investment capital lay outside the region. In order to court outside investors and entice northern corporations to open branch plants in or relocate to the South, southern political and business leaders publicized the region's social stability and favorable business climate—that is, low taxes and no unions. As Numan V. Bartley has observed, it was not until the 1940s that "the southern states established the programs that were to mature during the postwar years into well-staffed, handsomely financed commissions." In *The Selling of the South*, James C. Cobb examined the efforts of these state economic development commissions and the tax subsidies they promoted to attract outside industry. Such programs were "most appealing to industries such as textiles, footwear, hosiery, and furniture where intense competition made all costs, and therefore all savings, significant." The South attracted low-wage industries whose benefits were often outweighed by the subsidies paid to attract them, Cobb argued.[5]

Throughout the South, Bartley noted, the "campaign for locally originated industrial capitalism rapidly dissipated" in the aftermath of World War II. The rising business and professional classes in Atlanta and other southern cities were dominated by real estate developers, lawyers, retailers, and construction companies. These groups were little concerned with the source of business investment and the issue of local ownership. The old southern landlords were openly hostile to substantive changes in the South, such as improved education, that would promote internally generated industrial development. The South lacked a powerful, cohesive group of homegrown entrepreneurs in manufacturing, at least at the regional level. Consequently, southern state governments responded to the prevailing sentiments among their most powerful constituents and "channeled their efforts into cajoling northern corporations to expand into the region." [6]

While the prevailing strategy throughout the South since 1945 has been the courtship of outside industry, small pockets of internally generated industrial development survived and occasionally thrived. The development of the tufted textile industry of northwest Georgia exemplified the approach recommended by advocates of entrepreneurial capitalism. Local entrepreneurs combined a native handicraft tradition with new technology to produce the tufted bedspread industry. As the industry grew, selling agents and merchants from a variety of ethnic backgrounds moved to the northwest Georgia area to take full advantage of this consumer phenomenon.

The tufted textile industry, from which tufted carpeting emerged, evolved as a network of small producers using converted sewing machines to produce a variety of goods: bedspreads, bathrobes, curtains, small rugs, "tank sets," and finally broadloom carpeting. Other companies went into business to launder, dye, and finish tufted textile products. Tufting firms avoided the risks of stockpiling too much inventory of one color or group of colors. Finishers avoided the problems of obtaining raw materials for tufting and captured a larger percentage of the profit from tufting than manufacturers (by most accounts) by adding the crucial style elements (color) and by applying secondary backing to carpeting.

"Like a story-book romance reads the history of the colorful tufted textile industry," the Tufted Textile Manufacturers Association proclaimed in its inaugural *Directory* in 1950. The tale of the origins of northwest Georgia's principal economic institution had already become the stuff of local legend by the mid-twentieth century. "No other industry, no other single business, can boast so phenomenal a growth," the TTMA claimed with a bit of hyperbole, "all within the lifetime of its founder." According to the creation story of the tufted textile industry, Catherine Evans (later Whitener, by marriage), a simple farm girl, revived a handicraft tradition in the late 1890s by tufting patterns onto bedspreads. Evans's first few spreads were made as gifts, but she moved into commercial production in 1900 by selling one of her spreads. Soon Evans "found herself swamped with orders" from potential customers. Evans taught other "mountain women" the art of tufting. Within a few years, a thriving cottage industry had developed.[7]

Catherine Evans was born in 1880 in the small community of Reo, near Dalton, in Whitfield County. As a young girl of twelve, Evans took notice of an old spread on a bed in a relative's home. "I admired it so much," she recalled in later years, and determined that "when I grow older, I'm going to make me one." Evans started her first tufted bedspread in 1895. She took white thread and spun her own thick yarn on the family spinning wheel. "I put it in a bodkin needle and started working," Evans remembered. The finished spread was "like that Irish Chain quilt pattern in squares." Evans then clipped the stitches to produce a fluffy "chenille" effect and boiled the spread several times to shrink the cloth and lock in the tufts.[8]

Evans made her first few spreads for home use and as gifts. In 1900 she gave her brother, Henry, and his bride a tufted spread as a wedding gift. Evans's sister admired the spread so much that she offered to buy one. Evans bought cloth and thread for $1.25, charged the same amount for her labor, and made her first sale for a grand total of $2.50, though she was offered more. Evans "didn't want to charge too much" and felt that $2.50 was a good price considering that "then a man worked for a dollar a day."[9]

Evans's spreads found a ready market, and soon she had to adapt her techniques to keep up with demand. She had originally marked off spread patterns by pencil, but this was difficult and time-consuming. She simplified the process by putting a finished spread on the floor and placing the new material to be tufted over it. Evans then rubbed a pie tin, which had been oiled on a meat skin, over the spreads. This process produced a pattern in black dots.[10]

Evans kept filling orders but soon was unable to keep up with demand. She began to teach friends and neighbors the technique and then employed them to help her keep the business going. Evans stamped the pattern on the spreads and then passed the spreads and yarn on to other women in the community to finish the tufting. After the spreads were tufted, Evans boiled them in a wash pot and hung them out on a line to be bleached and dried in the sun.[11]

After 1910, Evans and her friends sought out broader markets in creative ways. Mrs. J. T. Bates boldly decided to try to sell the spreads to large northern department stores. "We shipped fifteen spreads . . . to John Wannamaker's [department store]," Bates recalled. "On a piece of plain tablet paper I made out a bill for $98.15 and put it in with the spreads. Although there had been no previous contact whatsoever with the store, Wannamaker's sent us a check for $98.15." The store soon ordered more spreads, and this success encouraged Mrs. Bates to continue. She wrote to chambers of commerce around the country asking for the names and addresses of department stores. Legends long maintained that no store ever failed to pay for the initial fifteen spreads, and many bought more.[12]

David Carlton has described the impact of the South's integration into the U.S. national market in the late nineteenth century. As railroads and the telegraph linked southern markets to northern producers, new opportunities and risks appeared. Indigenous North Carolina industries suffered greatly when subjected to competition with more advanced northern producers as "the development of northern markets introduced to southern consumers relatively cheap goods from more efficient firms in the North, sweeping away many local producers previously insulated from outside competition." Numerous important manufacturing sectors lost ground in North Carolina. As small local manufacturers in metalworking, machinery, and transportation equipment fell victim to competition from outside, North Carolina became increasingly specialized in a few extractive and/or low-wage, low-skill industries. Thus, for example, as textiles became a less important feature of the national economy, cotton mills came to dominate the industrial landscape of the South. Southern entrepreneurs lacked expertise in marketing on a national level, so southern enterprise tended to follow a few well-worn grooves of sales and distribution, particularly in textiles, by relying on northern distributors and sales agents.[13]

The gradual evolution of the bedspread industry allowed enterprising individuals to develop experience in dealing with a national marketplace. This unique regional product struck a responsive chord among consumers across the country, and the thousands of small transactions conducted over several decades by bedspread makers and sellers—new designs accepted or rejected by New York, Chicago, or Philadelphia department stores or their customers—taught valuable lessons. By the 1930s, the growing bedspread industry also drew sales and marketing agents from northern department stores and home furnishings wholesale distributors who began coming to northwest Georgia in search of innovative products and designs. These contacts would eventually be instrumental, perhaps crucial, in the creation of the region's carpet industry. Dalton-area entrepreneurs managed to reverse an old trend, then, by innovating and selling a new product to the nation rather than taking over the manufacture of existing products with cheaper labor.

Local men began to realize the profit potential in the tufting business, and by the early 1920s a multitude of "spread houses" had been established. In the spread houses, sheets were stamped with patterns. Then "haulers"—men driving heavily laden trucks, wagons, and mule carts— carried stamped sheets and other supplies over the mountain roads of north Georgia, Tennessee, Alabama, and the Carolinas to as many as ten thousand home tufters. The haulers then made the rounds a second time, collecting the tufted spreads and taking them back to the spread houses for boiling, packaging, and shipping.[14]

Capital requirements were slight, and demand was high; spread houses proliferated. During the 1920s, department store buyers refined the tactic of playing one spread house off against the others, driving prices down. Tufters had earned as much as twenty-five cents per spread in 1910–20; by the late 1920s the average was five to ten cents. Manufacturers began to search for faster, more efficient ways to produce tufted spreads.[15] The origin of the first tufting machine is lost in a mélange of competing claims. A tufting machine may have been in use as early as 1922. The rapidly expanding market for tufted bedspreads and other products encouraged experimentation with machines with the aim of initiating mass production. By the early 1930s, several men laid claim to the invention of a tufting machine. In Dalton, Georgia, local entrepreneurs established Cabin Crafts in 1930, and the tufted bedspread industry moved into factory production.

The move to factory production was made possible by, and in turn encouraged the further development of, a regional machine-making industry.

The early focus of the machine industry in tufting was the conversion of surplus Singer commercial-grade sewing machines. A rocking or oscillating loop hook, designed to pick yarn from the needle, was substituted for the sewing machine's bobbin, and a cooperating blade was added to cut the loops and create the chenille tufts. Most early conversion parts included hand-wrought hooks, or loopers (named for Glenn Looper, the man identified by the Georgia legislature as the originator of the tufting machine), formed painstakingly on a grinding wheel and oil-hardened over open flames. The loopers were then finished flat with a surface grinder to accommodate the cutting action of the interfacing knife, which was a broken section of common hacksaw blade. From quite humble beginnings, these crude adaptations became more sophisticated. A host of machine shops, dealers, and parts makers rose to meet the demand for specialized sewing machine conversion parts, and later tufting machines: Turley Machine Shop; John Peacock of Chickamauga, Georgia; Chatsworth Manufacturing Company; Painter Chenille Supply; and the Hanson Machine Company.[16]

Some converters added additional needles by interposing a steel bar in the place of the traditional needle holder and by mounting the desired number of needles directly into the bar itself. A corresponding number of loop and cut attachments were installed beneath the bed of the machine for each of the needles. The specific throat depth of such open-ended machines, together with the requirement that the needles align precisely with their respective loop and cut mechanisms, limited the number of needles that could effectively be utilized. Nonetheless, with these converted table-top machines, operators could "run a line" or lines of stitching into a backing and with subsequent "passes" create broader patterns over an entire bedspread or rug. The machines, especially those with multiple needles, were notoriously unreliable. As machines came into use, spread houses employed full-time mechanics to maintain the machines. Roy Windham, a mechanic for B. J. Bandy at Southern Craft Company, counseled patience in dealing with an obstinate machine: "Bring machine in the shop and give it a thorough cussing-out, light up a Lucky, and mentally check it over."[17]

TABLE 3. Tufted Textile Products, by Major Group, 1946 and 1953

	1946	1953
Bedspreads	57%	30%
Robes	18	6
Carpets and rugs	25	64

Source: Harry Brandt, "Tufted Textiles," Federal Reserve Bank of Atlanta Economic Studies, no. 2, 1955.

During the 1930s, Cabin Crafts and other companies began using the same machines to produce small rugs for the bath, "chenille" bathrobes, and the ever popular "tank sets"—covers for the toilet lid and tank. The "scatter rugs" first produced for use in the bathroom probably introduced the idea of tufting floor coverings. Backyard mechanics like Mose Painter tinkered with sewing machines to create tufting machines, and with small tufting machines to make bigger ones. Machine tool companies, like Cobble Brothers in nearby Chattanooga, began to patent and produce similar machines.

Dalton-area mechanics and spread house men increasingly turned to nearby Chattanooga, Tennessee, for parts and technical assistance. Chattanooga had long been a center of southern industry. Favorable deposits of iron ore, coal, and timber prompted periodic efforts at iron and steel manufacture, and each successive effort attracted skilled immigrants. Although Chattanooga lost the race to become the South's iron capital to Birmingham, the city developed a substantial iron industry and augmented this heavy industry with textiles. By 1924, the Chattanooga Manufacturers Association could advertise the "Dynamo of Dixie" as the fifth-largest producer of malleable castings in the nation and as "second only to Philadelphia in hosiery output."[18]

By 1937, the industrial climate of Chattanooga with its eighteen iron and steel foundries and sixteen hosiery manufacturers seemed particularly inviting to two hosiery mill mechanics, Albert and Joe Cobble. The two brothers opened a machine shop at 315 West Main Street for the purpose of servicing and reworking hosiery mill knitting equipment. George Muse, among others, began to call upon the Cobbles to manufacture loopers and cutting parts for the converted Singer tufting machines he was maintaining in the family's Muse Spread Company. Response by the Cobbles to this demand soon constituted an adjunct business, and the brothers developed their own unique and effective loop and cut mechanism. They purchased and modified Singer 3115 sewing heads and produced their own tabletop tufting machines with as many as thirty-two needles.[19]

In May 1939, Joe Cobble fulfilled a long-promised offer to provide employment for a favorite nephew, Lewis Card. Lewis, whose family had moved from its native Tennessee in 1931, graduated from high school at Fort Payne, Alabama, in an evening ceremony. He left the next morning for his job at Cobble Brothers and a bed in his bachelor uncle Joe's room at the Chattanooga YMCA. As Lewis began a career as a machinist and the expanding and successful business made its first move to 315 East Main Street, a series of disagreements erupted into a division between the two Cobbles. While the relationship between the brothers was strong, it apparently was not sufficiently elastic to endure the conflicts and compromises of business strains. In 1940, Albert left Cobble Brothers to begin his own enterprise, Tennessee Textile Machinery on Rossville Avenue. Albert's share of the Cobble Brothers firm was purchased by the now familiar patron George Muse.[20]

Joe Cobble produced perhaps the key innovation in tufting in 1940. He conceived and designed a freestanding machine dedicated solely to the process of placing tufted stitches into a full-width backing material. The machine was composed of two end frames and a set of lateral beams that connected the ends. It was a radical departure from the open throat construction of a sewing machine. Cobble's design had three purposes. First, even though the machine was enclosed on each end, he determined that if those ends were spread sufficiently apart and connected rigidly, the entire width of a bedspread backing might be passed between the ends and simultaneously stitched with parallel rows of tufting. Second, if the cloth backing was passed over an ingenious roller that was embossed with helical ribs diverging from its center, a rotation of that roller would spread and hold the cloth taut over its entire width, maintaining the parallel configuration of the stitches. Finally, it would be possible to draw the cloth through the machine automatically by means of discs on which angular teeth were fashioned to engage it. With these concepts fixed, Joe Cobble and shop foreman Sid Manning constructed the machine in the secrecy of a separate building. The frame was constructed entirely of commercially available steel angles and channel. Once completed, the machine was shipped to the Muse family's spread house, where it operated behind closed doors. A password was required to view it. A patent application was filed in January 1941 and granted on November 30, 1943.[21]

The machine was a success from the onset. Its overall open width, determined by the ⅛-inch spacing (gauge) of the one hundred needles, was predicated on a standard spread width. Entire rolls of sheeting could be tufted with a single pass. More important, it assured uniformity in the spacing and parallelism of the tufted rows and precluded errors of judgment inherent in an operator's successive passes under a single head. Beyond these advantages, the machine provided a stable platform fixed on either end from which to mount the tufting needles and their corresponding cut and loop attachments with a heretofore unknown precision. The loop and cut mechanisms were essentially a transfer of existing technology to the new frame in that the intended purpose of the machine was to automate the tufting of bedspreads. Not more than five of the machines were built before the United States' involvement in World War II diverted efforts at Cobble Brothers toward the manufacture of war materials, but the key breakthrough had been made.[22] The development of the "yardage machine," closed on both ends and capable of inserting parallel rows of raised tufts across a wide sheet of backing material, paved the way for the mass production of carpeting with the tufting process. In essence, the tufting machine was an oversized, multi-needle sewing machine.

Lewis Card was also a key figure in the evolution of Cobble Brothers in the 1950s. Joe Cobble gave up the day-to-day control of the company and appointed Card manager of the shop in 1942. Cobble retained majority ownership of the firm but dabbled in other machinery-related pursuits and allowed Card to pursue his own ideas and innovations in the tufting machinery field. Card hired Max Marian Beasley, a boyhood friend, as a draftsman and illustrator, and the two collaborated on a variety of innovations. Card and Beasley developed a differential rate yarn feed system that solved problems of yarn breakage in the operation of large tufting machines. This development also enabled manufacturers to produce patterns on tufted bedspreads and later carpets. Many pattern effects previously only possible on looms or by hand operation were now possible on the highly efficient tufting machines.[23]

Throughout the 1950s, Lewis Card's ingenuity contributed a profusion of ideas and refinements to the tufting machine, including the development of the "universal pattern attachment" that controlled the yarn across the entire width of the tufting machine. The mechanism produced curving effects in accordance with a pattern that was fixed on a pattern drum and, by analogy, operated somewhat like the roll of a player piano. He conceived a means by which to engage and disengage individual needles from the reciprocating needle bar such that a needle could insert a tuft only when required.[24] The technique anticipated some of the refined computer-controlled specialty machines now in use. Machinists developed a variety of cut-pile, loop-pile, and cut-and-loop style machines. By mixing cut and loop piles in the same carpet, the new machines could create simple geometric patterns (though none as elaborate as the old carpet looms). Lewis and Roy Card also developed an attachment that could vary the length of cut or loop tufts by "back-robbing," or pulling back on a few of the yarn strands along the tufting machine's needle bar.[25]

Card's abilities were more than mechanical. By 1952, he had become general manager of Cobble. He presided over the expansion of Cobble's product line including the introduction of a larger machine capable of producing tufted carpets in a seamless twelve-foot width. To stimulate sales, Card shipped machines on an installment sales basis, often keeping the financing in-house, and devised a leasing plan based on a minimum rate with additional charges predicated on yardage actually produced. Leasing imposed strenuous financial demands on Cobble's resources, but it became Card's major marketing strategy to offer tufting equipment to customers who had more ambition than capital.[26] In the 1950s and 1960s, that category would include most of the entrepreneurs entering the field.

Throughout the period, Joe Cobble maintained his room at the Chattanooga YMCA and remained a bachelor. As such, his evening hours were not spoken for, and at day's end, Joe frequently closed his offices at the knitting mill he had established with George Muse and sought company at the Cobble shop. While some evenings were social, they often provided opportunity for Joe to advise and counsel Lewis. For Lewis Card,

Joe was "a shoulder to lean on." His considered advice was often aimed to assuage concern over the considerable responsibility he had entrusted to his nephew. When Card felt the pressures of the business with a particular acuity, Joe could be colorfully conciliatory: "Boy, we came in here with nothing but our ass and a hat, and we can always leave that way." On the other hand, Joe fostered independence. He refused to make personal loans to Cobble Machine for badly needed operating capital during the early years, forcing Lewis to establish banking relationships on his own initiative and solve problems on his own.[27]

By 1954, Cobble Brothers employed eighty-five workers and operated in a satellite system of six buildings spanning thoroughfares and rail lines in downtown Chattanooga. The firm built new quarters on Riverside Drive to bring all operations under one single roof and double floor space to forty-eight thousand square feet. Joe directed the building's construction until January 1955, when he suffered a stroke that rendered him unconscious for six weeks. Lewis was left to manage the transition to the Riverside facility independently.[28]

From 1955, continued success in the mills and development at Cobble yielded steady growth. In 1956 Card opened offices in Blackburn, England, to serve the European tufting industry. In 1959, Cobble bought Super Tufter Machine Company, a formidable competitor that Albert Cobble had founded during the period after he left Cobble Machine. With the 1960 purchase of Southern Machine Company, a smaller tufting equipment manufacturer established by former Cobble employees, Lewis fashioned an environment he considered promising: a market with virtually no competition.[29]

Joe Cobble's health began to decline, however, and he began to consider selling out. George Muse, who had never been actively engaged in the business, was also amiably disposed to the possibilities of a sale. Card was reluctant to sell but did not own enough stock to offset the desires of Cobble and Muse. When Singer, Incorporated, emerged as a potential buyer, Card feared that the company would be sold. Singer's overtures came within a month of the most recent acquisition. Card concluded that attempting to block the sale would be an act of "profound ingratitude to his uncle," and Cobble Brothers became Singer-Cobble in May 1960.[30]

Card found little satisfaction running the company for Singer and resigned in 1963, selling his stock. He entered the jute import business somewhat clumsily during the remainder of a noncompetition agreement with Singer. Lewis Card's brother, Roy, left Singer in 1964 to begin a service business repairing and modifying tufting equipment and maintaining contacts in the industry. By 1965, the two brothers reunited to pursue machine building. In 1969, they merged their interests with Southern Machine Company to form Tuftco. In a series of events remarkably similar to the experience with Singer, Tuftco was acquired September 30, 1972, by a New York holding company. Again chafing at outside control, the brothers left Tuftco and eventually formed their own equipment manufacturing business, CMC, Incorporated. The most up-to-date CMC tufting machines are now capable of producing in excess of one mile of carpet in an eight-hour shift.[31]

The productivity of the tufting machine created an industry and annually threatened to ruin it. Max Beasley recalled that "every year was the last big year for tufting"; it seemed inevitable to many observers during the 1950s and 1960s that the rising demand for tufted carpeting would falter. Lewis Card observed in the early 1950s, "We knew little about the tufting machine and our customers [the manufacturers of carpets and bedspreads] knew less."[32] All the interested parties knew was that year by year demand seemed to exceed supply in the carpet industry. Card and Beasley kept innovating, and new entrepreneurs continued buying faster and faster tufting machines, banking on the future.

Another firm crucial to the evolution of tufting technology was Cabin Crafts. Fred and Lamar Westcott had owned a hosiery mill in Dalton in the 1920s. The Westcott brothers sold out just before the crash of 1929. In 1932, they teamed with Robert McCamy to form Cabin Crafts, the pioneer firm in the factory production of tufted bedspreads. Cabin Crafts quickly developed a reputation as the highest-quality producer of tufted bedspreads. A Cabin Crafts bedspread adorned Scarlett O'Hara's bed in the film *Gone with the Wind*. The company developed its own machines inhouse. Among the most significant innovations developed by Cabin Crafts' machine shop was the needle-punch gun. The gun, weighing about twenty-five pounds, was capable of inserting yarn tufts into cotton sheeting or other backing materials. The needle-punch gun was particularly useful in creating custom-designed area rugs. Cabin Crafts took the basic principle of tufted bedspread manufacture—stamping a pattern on a cotton sheet and then filling it in with raised yarn tufts—and extended it to small rugs. Cabin Crafts workers stamped patterns on heavier backing materials and filled in the pattern using the heavy-duty needle-punch guns. Cabin Crafts area rugs acquired a reputation for quality and style; by the end of the 1950s, Cabin Crafts rugs could be found in a variety of high-profile locations, including the Alabama governor's mansion.[33]

Cabin Crafts was purchased in 1946 by the giant WestPoint textile manufacturing company. WestPoint allowed Cabin Crafts to retain a separate identity and its own management, but the tufting concern benefited from the capital reserves and marketing expertise of the larger firm. The relationship continued until the late 1980s, when Shaw Industries purchased WestPoint's carpet and rug division and Cabin Crafts became part of a new corporate family. The association with WestPoint had an impact on labor-management relations as well. Mary Bell Smith, a lifelong employee of Cabin Crafts, recalled that the Westcotts adopted a paternalistic attitude toward workers. Fred Westcott helped Smith arrange a loan in order to build a house for her parents, and he often gave avuncular advice. The "family atmosphere" continued under WestPoint ownership. The Westcotts remained, and Cabin Crafts employees benefited as the larger company extended higher wages, paid holidays, and other benefits to its Dalton subsidiary.[34]

Cabin Crafts was among the first companies to begin producing broadloom carpeting using the tufting process, along with Painter Carpets, Barwick Mills, and Georgia Rug Company. The idea of producing room-sized rugs and wall-to-wall carpeting seems to have evolved from small rug production by 1949. Cabin Crafts continued to develop its own machines for carpet tufting. Cabin Crafts executives had difficulty in pinpointing a precise date for the production of the first broadloom carpeting. As Travis "Dusty" Rhodes, a longtime designer with the firm, recalled, no one "had the thought of documenting exactly who did what first because we were all so busy doing we didn't have time to be historians."[35]

Cabin Crafts used its internally developed machine-making capabilities and WestPoint's capital to become the acknowledged leader in medium- and high-quality carpeting during the 1950s. The construction and expansion of the company's new Springdale plant in Dalton exemplified the firm's commitment to efficiency and constant modernization. Completed in June 1954, the new facility became the company's fourth manufacturing plant in Dalton. Designed by the company's chief engineer, Bill Sapp, the Springdale plant had all the features needed by tufted manufacturers. The building, occupying an eighty-five-acre plot on the edge of Dalton's city limits, had a single story, making it easier to move large, heavy rolls of carpeting with lift trucks. The floors were concrete, again reducing the problem of carpet weight for storage. New additions in the late 1950s and early 1960s created what Sapp called the best "laid-out tufted carpet mill in this country. Everything is on one floor—no ramps, no stairs. Material flow is virtually in a straight line." Cabin Crafts was one of the first tufting mills to integrate forward to dyeing and finishing, and the Springdale plant included dye becks and latex coaters.[36]

Cabin Crafts focused on the high-end market for carpets and emphasized style, quality, and brand-name recognition. To a greater extent than any other tufted manufacturer, Cabin Crafts was able to build a recognizable consumer franchise. The company produced a wide array of textured carpets, and Cabin Crafts designers constantly experimented with new combinations of cut-and-loop patterns, sculpted designs achieved with shearing machines, and a variety of colors. The firm also pioneered in using artificial fibers. Cabin Crafts was particularly instrumental in introducing rayon into carpeting in the mid-1950s, but rayon proved to be less than satisfactory as a carpet fiber. Cabin Crafts, like most other tufting firms, moved toward nylon, especially after the introduction of a special variety of the fiber by Du Pont in 1958.[37] Other manufacturers, however, especially Barwick Mills, played a greater role in introducing nylon to carpet manufacture on a large scale.

Aside from Cabin Crafts and Joe Cobble, Lewis Card, and their colleagues at Cobble Brothers, perhaps the most influential individual in the early development of the tufted carpet industry's machinery and technology was Mose Painter. Mose Painter was born in Cloverlick, West Virginia, in 1906. Painter's father was a foreman in a local lumbermill. The family moved to Polk County, Tennessee, in 1924, to follow the elder Painter to a better-paying job. Mose went to work for the same lumber company at seventeen, firing the engine for the company's logging train. By 1926, Mose, a quick study, had become an engineer and was running the firm's logging train. Mose absorbed everything he could about the engine and learned to make most repairs himself. He spent his spare time in the shop, watching the mechanics and welders at work.[38]

Painter became shop foreman in 1929, though he admitted that he "didn't know much about the shop": "Here I was surrounded by all these lathes, milling machines, shapers, and a wide assortment of other tools. I thought grimly, 'Well, maybe I can learn it.' I had no teacher. It was up to me and in fact, I was told, 'If you don't learn it, it's not our fault, it's your'n.' " Mose apparently learned well. Within a year, he was keeping the sawmill's train running efficiently and repairing all the firm's equipment. In addition, "people from all over everywhere were bringing broken equipment into the shop for [him] to fix," though Painter received no extra pay for these jobs.[39]

Painter moved to Dalton in December 1940 to begin teaching machine welding extension training courses for the Georgia Department of Education. Painter soon realized that the tufted bedspread industry presented a wealth of opportunity to a talented mechanic. In 1941, Painter and one of his welding students, George Hanson, opened their own shop, Dalton Welding and Machine Company. The company served the local tufting industry almost exclusively. Painter devoted much of his time to the process of adapting sewing machines for the industry, and began to focus particularly on machines to tuft small rugs. In 1943, the partners decided to enter the rug business directly and opened the Hanson Painter Rug Company.[40]

"We decided then that something had to be built in the tufting industry," Painter recalled. Up until the mid-1940s, the machine-tufting industry had been "just sort of a makeshift affair." Painter and Hanson had bigger dreams than the "makeshift" industry could deliver, and "from this line of thinking," Painter modestly insisted, "we went to work and started the carpet industry."[41]

Mose Painter was credited by many with the production of the first carpet larger than four feet by six feet in 1949. Painter and his colleagues in the welding and machine shop (which Hanson and Painter still maintained) set to work, with a little inspiration from a case of rye whiskey, a gift from a visiting salesman. Painter and the other mechanics pieced together a twelve-needle tufting machine from pieces of single-needle machines. Using the new machine, Painter produced several rugs and then pieced them together to make a larger piece of carpeting nine feet by twelve feet.

Painter then had to convince a local bedspread laundry to dye the carpet. Bedspread finishers were reluctant to dye the much heavier carpets, fearing damage to their dye kettles. Painter finally convinced Clarence Shaw, the manager of Cabin Crafts' affiliate, Dalton Spread Laundry, to take the risk. Painter recalled that he promised to fix the dyeing equipment if the carpet damaged it: "Well, if we break the thing, we'll fix it. I've got to fix it every week anyway." Shaw, in return, agreed to pay half the cost of the rug if his equipment ruined it. Shaw dyed the carpet and returned it to Hanson Painter Rug. "That was the most beautiful piece of junk I had ever seen in my life," Painter remembered years later. Tom Carmichael, owner of New York's Stitt and Howell, a major distributor of floor coverings and a regular Hanson Painter customer, "came in the shop the very evening we got the finished carpet from Mr. Shaw. We had it proudly stretched out in our sample room and Tom felt of it and said, 'Oh, that's it! Don't tell anyone about it. Put in about twelve of those machines and we'll sell all the nine by twelves and six by nines you can make!' He sold that first rug to B. Altman Company in New York. . . . I believe we were paid about thirty-five dollars for it and I imagine Tom got about fifty dollars for it." Thus Mose Painter staked his claim as the first to produce tufted carpets larger than four feet by six, a claim backed by his longtime selling agent, Peter Spirer.[42]

Painter sold his interest in the Hanson Painter Rug Company two years later, in 1945, and went on to start numerous tufting-related businesses, from a supply company to his own tufting mill (more than once). Painter continued to experiment and innovate in tufting machinery. He established Painter Carpet Mills in 1953, along with Herbert Rogers and Bill Bowen. They put up sixty thousand dollars to purchase machinery and a lift truck.

Painter and his associates met an immediate obstacle: the ceiling in their rented building was too low to provide space for the creel racks necessary for a carpet-tufting machine. The creel rack was a large frame holding bobbins that fed yarn into each needle in a tufting machine. The small yarn cones are racked on a creel; the typical creel required high ceilings. Painter responded to this challenge by developing a system by which the yarn could first be run onto "beams," large wooden spools that could feed yarn into the machine from a horizontal position. A rack of twelve beams took up much less space, both horizontally and vertically, than a creel rack. A much smaller, shorter creel rack was used to run yarn onto the beams. This added a step to carpet manufacture, but it allowed manufacturers to operate with much less space. It also reduced yarn waste by allowing manufacturers to use a greater portion of any given lot of yarn. This development was especially important for the many small firms that would flourish in the carpet industry in the 1960s and 1970s.[43]

Painter worked closely with V. D. Parrott, manager of the city's municipally owned utility company. Painter went to Parrott in 1954 with a new idea for applying latex backing to carpets that required powerful lights. Painter needed Parrott's help because "the [General Electric] lights were wired up on 440 three phase power." The city of Dalton only had two 440 transformers, and Painter needed three. Parrott listened patiently to Painter's idea and agreed to have the utility purchase a new 440 transformer and set up all three "where you can use them." Soon Painter went into operation with his new drying equipment, complete with a bank of eighteen hundred 500-watt bulbs.[44]

Robert E. Shaw, son of the aforementioned Clarence, remembered other innovations and suggestions from Painter that shaped the carpet industry. Shaw noted in 1982 that "some of my earliest remembrances of the tufting industry started over the back fence at 313 and 315 North Thornton Avenue," where Mose Painter and Clarence Shaw "would discuss some of the problems of our very young industry." One of the most significant conversations Shaw recalled was on the subject of dyeing carpeting in the early 1950s. Existing spread-finishing facilities were set up to dye bedspreads and other chenille goods in small pieces. "How in the world," Bob Shaw recalled his father asking Mose Painter, "can we, as an industry, learn to dye a piece of carpet twelve feet wide and eighty feet long . . . all in one piece?" The discussion ended with Mose's suggestion that an overhead reel be placed over a rough dye tub. The reel could be used to circulate the entire length of a roll of carpet through a dye bath. Though "obvious improvements" had been made, Shaw noted that "this machine was the forerunner of what we now know as dye becks which are still in operation today throughout the industry."[45]

Painter never patented a single innovation. He operated an open shop and rarely even tried to keep his innovations a secret from his competitors. While working on his drier setup in 1954, Painter recalled that a young man from nearby Cabin Crafts regularly crossed the street to observe the work. Charles Bramlett, a future mill owner himself, often joked with his superiors at Cabin Crafts that Painter's equipment couldn't work. Painter essentially offered his expertise to the entire industry, to any who were willing to watch and learn. Painter Carpets became a proving ground for technological innovation in refining and perfecting the tufting machine.[46]

Mose Painter was a crucial figure in bringing many later entrepreneurs into the carpet industry. Among the best and brightest of these was Peter Spirer. Spirer would eventually found Horizon Industries in the late 1970s, a carpet-manufacturing firm that grew rapidly and developed a reputation for high-quality products and imaginative styling. Spirer's story became closely intertwined with that of Mose Painter, and both their stories offer insights into the evolution of the Dalton district.

Peter Spirer was born in Manhattan in 1931, into a "very middle-class family." Spirer's father was an aspiring entrepreneur who had difficulty finding his niche in depression-era New York; Spirer recalled that his father "was in any number of little businesses during the course of the Depression." Spirer went off to college at the University of Miami with dreams of becoming an actor or a lawyer. At the beginning of his senior year, the young man decided that he "really wasn't much of an actor" even though his "heart" was in drama; and he "really had no interest in being a lawyer." So Spirer shifted to the business school at Miami, where he completed the entire two-year program of study in a single year.[47]

Spirer was recruited by R. H. Macy's but left the giant department store after two years to go to work for his father-in-law, Tom Carmichael of Stitt and Howell. Spirer had met Carmichael's daughter at the University of Miami, and the two had been married shortly after graduation. Carmichael asked his son-in-law to join the company as his potential successor (Carmichael's daughter, Anne, was an only child). Stitt and Howell was a major floor covering distributor and the primary selling agent for Mose Painter's rugs and carpets. Spirer joined Stitt and Howell in 1955 and "never looked back on that [decision] with regret." Carmichael took Spirer with him to Dalton often in the mid-1950s, trying to teach the young man the business "as quickly as possible." Spirer recalled that his father-in-law endorsed Painter's claim as the first to manufacture a nine-foot by twelve-foot tufted rug. Carmichael also claimed to be the first to sell such a rug, and Spirer had no reason to doubt his benefactor's claim.[48]

Spirer's recollections of Mose Painter validated many of Painter's claims about innovations in the industry, and his assessment of Painter revealed much about the development of the Dalton district. Spirer credited Painter with a long list of innovations in carpet tufting, though "he never applied for a patent." Painter was "one of these guys that was somewhat more than most men" in that "he really took satisfaction in what he was doing and was happy to contribute" these innovations to the industry "probably for ego recognition."[49]

Spirer wrote a tribute to Painter that was included in Painter's self-published autobiography in 1982. In this essay, Spirer captured the essence of Painter and, in a broader sense, at least one face of the Dalton industrial district in the 1950s. Spirer related the story of one of Mose Painter's innovations. Spirer made one of his regular trips to Dalton in 1958 and found Painter "busting with excitement." Painter had rigged a series of rollers across a normal loop pile tufting machine. Painter had also developed a control mechanism to adjust the yarn feed to the various needles, and this attachment allowed tufted carpeting to be produced with "various kinds of . . . geometric patterns" sculpted into the surface of the carpet. Painter was anxious to show this innovation to his young friend so that Spirer could assess the market potential of new lines of carpeting made with the new pattern attachment. "I was as excited as [Mose] when I saw the carpet," Spirer remembered, "for it added a whole new dimension to what was on the market."[50]

Spirer and Painter went to lunch later that day at the Oakwood Cafe in Dalton, something of a hangout for local businessmen. While at the cafe, Spirer watched in "surprise and anger" as Mose Painter organized a group of a half dozen of his competitors "to show off his new innovation." Spirer "couldn't believe that his pride of invention would extend to such an exploit, but so it did." Spirer also noted that Painter Carpets was "the last carpet mill" in Dalton to "get this New Look into the marketplace."[51]

Mose Painter was, to put it mildly, "not a clever businessman." He did "well enough financially" and provided a good living for his family. But,

Spirer asked rhetorically in 1982, "where were the patents for the dozens of ideas he had turned into functioning machinery for the industry? Where were the sales for his mill which was among the first of the tufted carpet factories? Where was the organization to lead the company to the fore-front of the marketplace?" What made Mose Painter, and probably others in 1950s Dalton, "tick" was "his need to be recognized for his achieve-ments." Painter's desire for recognition "outweighed the normal business-man's fervent pursuit of commercial exchange." Whenever "Mose had done something terrific . . . he wanted to share his excitement with his close friends, who also just happened to be his competitors." [52]

Painter's lack of attention to the details of company management even-tually cost him his company. His misfortune provided his young friend Spirer with an opportunity to enter the carpet business directly in the Dal-ton area. Painter's creditors forced him to surrender his stock in Painter Carpets in 1961, and the company's new owners asked Spirer to become part of the new management team. By this time, Spirer had been divorced from Tom Carmichael's daughter, Anne, for several years. Spirer set up his own floor covering distributorship in the late 1950s and had continued to represent his friend Mose Painter, accounting for about two-thirds of Painter Carpets sales. Spirer received stock in exchange for his agreement to come on board and help manage the company. Spirer and his new wife moved to the Dalton area permanently in 1961. Painter Carpets was sold to Collins and Aikman in 1965, and even the Painter name disappeared from the ranks of the carpet industry for a time.[53]

In addition to the evolution of a local technology, local government also played a large part in the development of the Dalton district, chiefly in the form of the Water, Light, and Sinking Fund (WL&SF), Dalton's munici-pally owned utility company. The bedspreads and later carpets of the dis-trict had to be finished and dyed. These processes required large amounts of water. The spread- and carpet-finishing plants also needed "soft" wa-ter. Individual companies at first tried to install water-softening facilities, but these generally yielded less than satisfactory results and were quite ex-pensive as well. During the late 1930s and early 1940s, the WL&SF used public funds to conduct experiments and then implement a series of ren-ovations at its water purification plant. The WL&SF used community funds to tailor the region's water supply to the needs of industry. The city's utility company added the right mix of water-softening agents and also increased acidity levels in the local water supply to augment the bleaching effect in bedspread laundries.[54]

The relationship between the tufted textile industry and the city's utilities became even closer when V. D. Parrott assumed the leadership of the WL&SF in 1945. Parrott was committed to promoting the interests of indigenous manufacturers and used the public utilities to foster the concentration of tufted textiles in the Dalton area. Parrott immediately initiated plans to expand the city's water supply, anticipating future industrial growth. Parrott "created a series of rural reservoirs" and increased filtration capacity. By 1949, the utility had doubled its plant capacity to more than four million gallons per day, and capacity was doubled again by 1960. Parrott also changed the WL&SF's rate structure "so that increased industrial demand was rewarded by decreased costs for [industrial] consumers." Parrott proved so effective that the mayor and city council gradually ceded total control of the utility to Parrott, making it a government within a government. Parrott's plans called for large capital expenditures, and this also meant changes in utility policy. Before 1949, "Dalton's schools, churches, and the hospital" received free water and power, and the utility regularly turned over surpluses to the city treasury. Parrott's ambitious plans forced him to abandon these policies, as he increasingly invested in expanding the utility's services to industry. Parrott and his policies received near unanimous support from industry leaders.[55]

The experienced pool of labor in the Dalton area also contributed to the evolution of an industrial district. Most workers in the Dalton area were fresh from the farm, and these displaced agrarians were familiar with the tufting handicraft industry and chenille manufacture. Locally developed northwest Georgia carpet companies offered alternative employment, often more attractive and always more remunerative than farm labor. These companies also formed the only potential barrier to the continued hegemony of the northeastern carpet firms. These local companies had the advantages of an earlier entry into tufting, familiarity with the region and the workforce, and a variety of local, small-town "connections." Several industry insiders and observers have noted the importance of the local handicraft tradition in explaining the centrality of northwest Georgia.

Buford Talley, a former president of Barwick Mills, insisted that his company had met limited success in setting up tufting operations outside the Dalton area. Talley believed that local workers had developed a high level of skill in dealing with yarn and fibers from the early hand-tufting days. Bert Lance, a Calhoun, Georgia, banker who helped finance some of the early tufting ventures, also emphasized the skill level of the local population. The people of northwest Georgia had acquired "an aptitude . . . for dealing with yarn and frames," Lance maintained, and many firms had experienced problems when they tried to move their operations out of the area.[56] In addition, these local Dalton-area firms had no existing outmoded capacity to retire. Several Dalton firms had entered the field to take on the giants by the end of the 1950s.

The origin of World Carpets illustrated many of the challenges faced by local entrepreneurs and the combination of ingenuity, luck, and outside intervention that helped tufted carpet makers survive. World's founder, Shaheen Shaheen, came to Dalton to work for his uncle, Said Shaheen. Before World War II, Said worked as an importer of Italian goods. When the war interrupted that trade, Said came South to begin buying and selling the tufted bedspreads and robes of the northwest Georgia region. By the end of World War II, the Palestinian American had decided to remain permanently in Dalton. He and his two older brothers bought a local scatter rug mill and established Katherine Chenilles in 1945. At first, Katherine produced rugs on single-needle machines. By 1948, Said Shaheen invested in a few multineedle machines of the three- to six-foot variety.[57]

Shaheen Shaheen, nephew of Said, went to work for Katherine Chenilles in the summer of 1947, while on break from the Illinois Institute of Technology. The younger Shaheen graduated in 1949 with a B.S. degree in industrial engineering. He went to work selling Katherine's products in the Midwest, traveling about a thousand miles a week. In early 1952, Shaheen Shaheen came to Dalton to oversee manufacturing at Katherine.[58]

Shaheen and Said Shaheen quickly developed different philosophies, perhaps as much a result of the younger man's ambition as any substantive policy differences. This pattern was not uncommon in the family businesses that dominated the early days of the carpet industry. When Katherine Chenilles moved into a new plant (designed by Shaheen Shaheen), the younger Shaheen took advantage of the opportunity to make a break with his uncle. Shaheen Shaheen asked for his 15 percent of the family enterprise. He took it in the form of the old Katherine facility (about fifteen thousand square feet) located on a steep hillside on Green Street near downtown Dalton.[59] Shaheen and his wife of three years, Piera, invested their life savings of about thirty-five hundred dollars in starting their own business.

Shaheen had planned for more than a year to strike out on his own. In the fall of 1953, he scouted the north Georgia area for used tufting and office equipment. Shaheen's World Carpets showed its first sample at the January 1954 Chicago floor covering trade show. The style, Xanadu, was made from cotton yarn. Xanadu proved to be popular, and Shaheen returned from Chicago with more than four thousand dollars in promises to buy. World went into full-scale production in February 1954 with one twelve-foot-wide tufting machine and five employees. Typically for the early carpet industry, Shaheen faced a financial crisis at the outset. The only decent yarn available came from the Bibb Manufacturing Company, but it refused to sell yarn to a fledgling carpet enterprise on credit. Bibb insisted on cash on delivery. "Consequently," Shaheen recalled, "all the cash the company had was paid out to Bibb on Monday morning, February 1st, for their delivery of yarn." World Carpets was as cash-poor as every other carpet enterprise, and credit was difficult to obtain.[60]

Shaheen described the process of creating his first few rolls of broadloom carpeting in his memoirs. The easiest part was the tufting. Shaheen and his five employees creeled the machine's rack and ran the backing material through the machine. To lock in the tufts, the carpet then had to be passed through a coater, which applied a layer of latex to the back of the carpet that acted as glue for yarn tufts and as a thin padding. "Latex coating in those days was a very inexact process," Shaheen noted, as companies experimented endlessly to find the proper mixture. The process was "a messy operation, and a very slow one." The coater was short, and only a small portion of the length of a carpet roll could be dried at a time by the machine's infrared lights. Finally, carpet that had been tufted on Monday was sent off to a finishing company, Dalton Spread Laundry, for dyeing on Thursday. The carpet was returned on Friday, inspected, and shipped the same day to Southwest Wholesale Floor Covering and other customers. At that point, World Carpets had receivables totaling around four thousand dollars.[61]

At this point, World Carpets faced the same problem that confronted most small manufacturing enterprises, and especially those in the Dalton district's carpet industry. Customers had thirty to ninety days to pay receivables. How was the company to purchase raw materials for the next week's work, make payroll, and pay other expenses until these payments were made? World Carpets, like almost all other carpet companies in the 1950s, made these arrangements through factors. Factors advanced money to a company based on the value of its receivables and in return received interest and service charges. Often, factoring agencies also served as de facto credit departments for manufacturers, deciding which potential customers qualified for credit and which did not. If a factor approved a credit risk, the factor paid the manufacturer and assumed the responsibility for collecting the debt and the risk that it might not be recovered. This type of credit was expensive, but it was often the only sort of credit available in the Dalton district.

Shaheen had tried to get a conventional business loan when he founded World Carpets. The newly created Small Business Administration agreed to underwrite a new business loan for Shaheen Shaheen and World in 1954. The federal agency agreed to loan Shaheen sixteen thousand dollars if he could secure a partial matching loan of four thousand from a local bank. Even with SBA backing, Shaheen's loan requests were refused by both major Dalton banks. A historian who interviewed Shaheen recalled that World's founder showed him the letters from the banks and the SBA that confirmed the incident. Shaheen proudly displayed the letters as badges of honor, as proof that he had succeeded with no help from the local banking community. The banks' refusal "taught financial self-reliance," according to Shaheen (and no doubt brought many hours of pleasure in the knowledge that he had proven the bankers wrong).[62]

World Carpets sales reached sixteen thousand dollars in the first month of operation. The company's sales rose rapidly to more than thirty-eight thousand in April 1954. Shaheen noted that World had started operations at an advantageous time during a recession year. "Labor was easy to obtain, the workers were diligent," he recalled, and perhaps most important, "materials were bought at lower prices than [our] competition, who had old contracts at higher prices." World maintained low-cost production, averaging just ten cents per square yard in overhead and labor costs. The decentralized nature of the early carpet industry in Dalton contributed to the low overhead costs. As Shaheen pointed out, the fact that "the dyeing was done outside" certainly "helped World get started." Dalton Spread Laundry had started in business to service the bedspread industry.[63]

By the 1950s, many old bedspread-finishing companies were beginning to dye and finish carpeting as well. The existence of an established dyeing and finishing segment within the old bedspread industry was a crucial element in the success of new companies like World, which were simply too capital-poor to consider in-house dyeing and finishing facilities. Dyeing equipment was more expensive and complex than tufting machinery. The small tufting firms and the finishing companies shared the risk of this new industry. Small firms like World benefited from external economies by being able to maintain inventories of greige goods that could be dyed to a customer's taste within a day, thus reducing the risk of building up too large inventories of unwanted colors. This made the tufted carpet industry remarkably flexible. Likewise, finishing companies spread their services among many tufting firms, diminishing the chances that the failure of any one of them would sink a finishing company. The finishing business generally produced a higher profit margin than tufting, and companies that specialized in dyeing and finishing could devote more money and time to improving and refining their processes.

James Flemming, an employee of a major local bank in Dalton, finished a thesis on the carpet-finishing companies of the Dalton area for the Stonier Graduate School of Banking in 1974. Flemming's analysis of this key segment of the industry was based on his own experiences with firms in the finishing business and interviews with key figures. The Census of Manufactures did not recognize carpet manufacturing and finishing as separate activities; yet in the 1950s and 1960s, few carpet manufacturers had integrated fully through the finishing process. Thus Flemming's work provides crucial insight into the nature of carpet finishing and the relationship between finishers and tufting companies.[64]

Carpet finishing paralleled tufting in its emergence from the process of dyeing and finishing bedspreads and other small tufted items. As tufting companies shifted from small goods to "broadloom" carpeting in the 1950s, many of the bedspread laundries also converted to the dyeing and finishing of the new goods. In the 1950s, finishing companies generally specialized in providing one of two important services: dyeing or the application of a latex coating to lock in yarn tufts. In addition, some cut pile constructions also required shearing to level their surfaces. By the end of the 1950s, a handful of companies provided commission finishing services to tufted carpet makers, led by Dalton Carpet Finishing (successor to Dalton Spread Laundry, an early pioneer in dyeing bedspreads) and Rogers Finishing. In the early 1960s, new companies began to enter the field to take advantage of the explosive growth of the carpet industry. These new companies handled all phases of finishing, thus cutting transportation costs for carpet makers and pressuring older firms to follow suit. By the early 1970s, the half dozen or so firms offering carpet-finishing services had grown to more than twenty and accounted for perhaps one hundred million dollars in sales.[65]

Color was always cited in consumer surveys as a key element in a purchase decision; thus the application of color was perhaps the most significant factor in adding value to tufted carpets. Small manufacturers who produced on a contract basis often used pre-dyed yarns. Manufacturers who competed in the most explosive market in the 1950s and 1960s—the residential housing market—preferred to use uncolored yarns and have their carpets dyed later. This enabled a manufacturer to lower his raw materials inventory (he did not have to stock yarn in multiple colors) and his finished goods inventory (he could dye greige goods as ordered by customers). The undercapitalization of this competitive new industry and the volatility of consumer tastes in color encouraged firms to adopt what might be termed a "flexible mass production" strategy. By withholding the final decision on color until the last possible moment, manufacturers achieved substantial flexibility and ensured a wide arena for consumer choice. Postproduction dyeing allowed manufacturers to focus on other elements of styling, such as pile height and pattern.

Established bedspread laundries in the Dalton area pioneered the chief method of postproduction coloration: beck dyeing. Dye becks were large drums with rollers attached. Finishers used the roller bars to pull the carpet through the dye solution. According to Mose Painter, the first broadloom tufted carpeting was piece-dyed by Clarence Shaw at Dalton Spread Laundry, using small vats designed for bedspread dyeing. By the mid-1950s, local machine and metalworking companies had produced workable dye becks for use in carpet coloration. The Cobble Brothers firm made strategic alliances with dye beck–producing companies like Gowin Machinery of Dalton.

The finishing process required a much greater capital investment than tufting. Tufting machines might sell for $10,000 in the mid-1950s, and Cobble Brothers offered liberal in-house financing to moderate even that expense. By the early 1960s, secondhand tufting machines became available as larger firms modernized with faster equipment. A small entrepreneur could still start a carpet-manufacturing operation on a shoestring well into the 1970s, as Barwick and others had done in the 1950s. Even "a moderate size beck dye[ing] operation, excluding plant facilities," on the other hand, required a capital investment of about $700,000 by the mid-1970s. In addition, finishing companies introduced new, even more expensive continuous dye ranges in the late 1960s and early 1970s. These massive machines could dye large quantities of carpeting more quickly than dye becks by running the carpet in an endless stream under a series of dye jets that sprayed color onto the carpeting. The continuous dye ranges, imported from Europe, raised the stakes even further: one machine might cost more than $800,000.[66]

Tufted carpet manufacture, then, evolved in much the same fashion as the old bedspread industry. By the early 1960s, a handful of finishing companies served a much larger number of tufting concerns. Small, capital-poor manufacturing firms avoided large investments in expensive finishing equipment by contracting for these services. Finishing companies avoided the risks inherent in making stylistic decisions and profited from industrywide success in sales. By the late 1960s, finishing companies were even offering consulting services to their manufacturer customers, advising and cooperating on color choices and developing new color lines.

Carpet finishing was an important source of flexibility. Beck dyeing afforded several advantages, especially to smaller manufacturers. Dye becks could efficiently process relatively small product runs; finishers found that it was cost-effective to dye pieces of carpeting as small as four hundred feet in length. Beck dyeing also produced deeper, richer colors and yielded fewer customer complaints. Especially when producing carpets that would cover large, open floor spaces, manufacturers had to be certain that the dye penetration was even across the entire surface of the piece. The deep penetration of dye achieved with the use of dye becks minimized the "side matching" problem (making sure that the color of a carpet did not vary from one side to the other). Finishers also found ways to use becks to produce multicolor carpets. By applying chemicals to carpet yarns before tufting, manufacturers and finishers could produce "differential yarn affinities," thus making different sections of a carpet accept dyes at a different rate, or causing the same dye to yield different colors when applied to treated yarns.[67]

Continuous dye ranges required larger runs to achieve cost-effectiveness. In the mid-1970s, carpet-finishing managers generally considered fifteen hundred feet the minimum length that could be profitably dyed using the continuous system. Continuous dye ranges had limited applicability, therefore, for small manufacturers who generally operated with wide color lines but limited orders for each shade within the line. Those finishing companies that invested in continuous dye ranges needed customers with long runs of the same color in order to make effective use of their equipment. If long production runs could be guaranteed, however, the continuous dyeing processes offered a much lower cost of production than beck dyeing. A dye beck, operating at peak efficiency, could color about four feet of carpet per minute in 1974. The continuous ranges could dye carpet at the rate of forty-five feet per minute. In that sense, new investments in continuous dyeing represented a step away from flexibility and toward a mass production manufacturing model.[68]

Carpet finishers also applied an adhesive coating—generally latex—to the back of carpets. The adhesives then had to be dried in large ovens. While some small manufacturers (and occasionally larger ones as well) could bypass dyeing by using pre-dyed yarns, all tufted carpets required the latex backing and drying services provided by finishing companies. By the early 1960s, coaters cost as much as $250,000 (by the early 1970s, that figure would be closer to half a million dollars). Flemming noted that executives in the finishing business insisted that small errors in mixing the latex compounds for backing materials could result in operating losses because of poor-quality goods and overuse of raw materials.[69]

Tufting and finishing companies developed in symbiosis, each sector helping the other to reduce risks. The growth of tufted carpet sales in the 1960s led some manufacturers—generally the largest—to pursue forward vertical integration into finishing. The often repeated warning recalled by Cobble Brothers' Max Beasley, though, encouraged caution. Every year throughout the 1950s and 1960s, some pessimistic analysts predicted an end to the carpet boom. For small and medium-sized carpet makers, the benefits of remaining highly specialized in one segment of the new carpet industry outweighed the risks associated with the massive capital expenditures necessary for integration into finishing. In 1962, *Textile World* estimated that Star Finishing, the most up-to-date finishing company in the industry, had required an initial capital investment of more than $750,000 when it opened in 1960.[70]

World Carpets was able to acquire expansion capital because of connections developed through contract work in this decentralized industry. Bob Mathis, owner of a Dalton rug company, dyed and shipped carpet for World. He was impressed with World's ability to hold down costs and make deliveries. When Mathis sold his firm to a larger bedspread company in 1954, he agreed to use a portion of the profits to make a twenty-thousand-dollar loan to Shaheen. Mathis insisted, however, on a rate of interest that was in effect triple the 1954 prime rate of 3 percent.[71]

Shaheen's credit experiences with both banks and industry associates convinced him to follow an ultraconservative financial policy in the future:

> As a result of these early experiences, World operated over the years without borrowing money. It moved ahead doing only as much as it could afford to, using the facilities and resources it had on hand. This meant intensive three-shift activity six and seven days a week. It meant putting off expansion and machinery purchases until absolutely necessary, and only after huge backlogs had developed over a long period of time. It taught very clearly the value and worth of each dollar.[72]

Shaheen's strategy paid off handsomely in the long run. World did not grow as fast or as spectacularly as other firms, but it grew steadily.

If World Carpets stood perhaps at one end of a spectrum of varying strategies and styles in the emerging tufted carpet industry in the 1950s, then standing at the other end, waving his arms, was E. T. Barwick. No other individual, according to the unanimous testimony of his competitors and contemporaries, made a greater contribution to the growth and development of tufted carpeting. E. T. Barwick quickly became the most visible spokesman for the new tufted carpet industry. He succeeded by producing a wide array of products. Few companies in the 1950s and 1960s could match the variety of color, texture, fiber, and style marketed by E. T. Barwick. Barwick also spent more time and money on marketing than other tufting companies. Walter Guinan, longtime CEO of Karastan Rug Mills and later consultant to the carpet industry, lamented that the tufting process in north Georgia was organized and developed by salesmen. Barwick was the quintessential carpet salesman, and his firm would dominate the industry in the 1960s (see chapter 5).[73]

Perhaps the key to the success of the early tufting manufacturers was the emphasis on salesmanship, marketing, and styling. Coronet Industries, another local company, followed a similar marketing-based strategy. The company was founded in 1956 by Jack Bandy, local heir to a tufted bedspread fortune; Guy Henley, an experienced local manufacturing supervisor; and M. B. "Bud" Seretean, a New York–born son of Romanian immigrants. Bud Seretean's experience was similar to Barwick's. He attended Oklahoma State University in the late 1940s after his discharge from the army. Seretean initially tried to make the basketball team but quickly realized that he was out of his league. He remained in school, though, and graduated with honors. While working on a master's degree at New York University, Seretean served as a student trainee with Stern Brothers department store. After receiving his degree, he went to work as an assistant buyer for Abraham and Straus in the floor coverings department. Frustrated with being passed over on the corporate ladder at Abraham and Straus and later at the Allied Stores, Seretean came to Dalton to work as sales manager for Said Shaheen's Katherine Rug Mills. Within three years, Seretean had tripled the firm's sales volume.[74]

While staying in Dalton, Seretean boarded in the home of Mrs. B. J. Bandy. Mrs. Bandy's late husband had been reputed to be the first man to make a million dollars in the tufted bedspread business. In the early 1950s, Bandy's son, Jack, had assumed responsibility for many of the family's continuing business interests. While boarding with Mrs. Bandy, Seretean became friends with Jack Bandy, and over the dinner table during the period 1953–55, Bandy and Seretean quietly made plans to form a partnership and enter the tufted carpet business for themselves. Seretean and Bandy added a partner to supervise manufacturing operations, choosing Chattanooga-born Guy Henley. The three formed Coronet Carpets in 1956.[75]

Seretean, Bandy, and Henley decided that their company should become "the only all-wool tufting company." Coronet adapted the tufting process, which had been perfected on cotton and rayon yarns, to the production of wool carpets. Coronet used the high efficiency of tufting to mitigate the price volatility of wool. Seretean recalled that "the first year we did a little over a million dollars worth of business and made a decent profit." According to *Barron's*, Coronet combined "aggressive merchandising and tight production controls" to produce "uninterrupted gains" since its inception. Coronet's forty-man sales force periodically reported on "retailer and consumer preferences," and the results were "fed into a data processing system." The company combined the versatility and speed of tufting with modern data processing, which "enable[d] the firm to respond quickly to changes in consumer tastes."[76]

These fledgling producers and others in this emerging industry sought security in numbers by forming a manufacturers association. The tufted textile industry tried several times in the 1930s and 1940s to create an effective trade association to help organize first the bedspread, then the growing rug and carpet trade. A manufacturers association emerged in 1945—the Tufted Textile Manufacturers Association (TTMA).[77] It took on new importance in the mid-1950s through its coordination of anti-union activities. Though the association was open to all makers of tufted textile products, it was headquartered in Dalton and was dominated by firms located within a twenty-five-mile radius of the future carpet capital. Initially, the TTMA's main purpose was to negotiate with government on behalf of a group of small manufacturers for scarce raw materials. The organization soon grew into an effective body of medium- to large-sized tufted textile manufacturers. By the mid-1950s, TTMA promoted cooperative research efforts; sponsored workmen's compensation and other insurance plans for tufting companies; compiled statistics on tufted textile sales and shipments for use by members; adopted minimum quality standards for tufted bedspreads; and, perhaps most significantly, advised and trained members in labor-management relations. During the formative decades of the 1950s and 1960s, the TTMA's chief service to manufacturers was in the area of labor relations, in a variety of capacities.[78]

The TTMA elected a president annually from the ranks of executives of leading tufted textile firms. The office of executive vice president, however, was a permanent job, and only two people held that position during the life of TTMA, 1945–68: Henry C. Ball and R. E. Hamilton, who provided the consistent leadership for the organization throughout the period. The TTMA hired Henry Ball in July 1945 to function as a full-time executive director. Ball held degrees from the University of Florida and Northwestern University. He came to TTMA from a government job on the War Manpower Commission. Hamilton served as treasurer at Cabin Crafts before assuming the leadership of TTMA in 1959.

The TTMA took a leading role in helping its members try to organize the tight labor market in the Dalton area. In 1953, the trade association asked the Georgia Department of Labor to develop a comprehensive list of job descriptions for the tufted textile industry. These job descriptions included "job-performance requirements," which the Labor Department defined as those skills and abilities "demanded by the nature of the job," and "employers' requirements," which included "those things that the employer is entitled to require of an applicant but are additional to those things demanded by the nature of the job." The descriptions also listed the "physical demands" of each job. Henry Ball wrote a foreword to the job description list that explained its purpose to TTMA members. The job descriptions would allow tufting manufacturers to use more effectively the state employment service. The local employment office could perform preliminary screening for the tufted industry and weed out obviously unqualified workers. This service could function as a sort of de facto personnel service for capital-starved tufting enterprises. "It is your service and furnished you by the state and federal government," the TTMA's executive vice president reminded the membership; "why not use it?"[79]

Ball outlined another reason for the joint effort with the Department of Labor. He pointed out that *all claimants for unemployment compensation* are required to register with the employment service" (emphasis in the original). Unemployment insurance claimants were "classified on the basis of their experience" and were referred to appropriate job openings listed with the state employment service. "If all employers in our industry place their orders for workers with the employment service," Ball noted, "qualified workers will not continue to draw unemployment benefits." These benefits were charged against the employer's experience rating and contributed to higher costs in the form of increased premiums as well as in the hiring of "less qualified workers . . . at the gate." TTMA members obviously hoped that greater cooperation with the state employment service would lead to a more effective mobilization of the local labor market.[80]

The Georgia Department of Labor job descriptions reveal much about the structure of the industry in its formative years in the early 1950s. Data on wages and benefits for the tufted textile industry of the Dalton district are scanty, but the TTMA conducted wage-and-benefit surveys in 1956 that provide some details. These two sources paint an incomplete but useful picture of an emerging industry. The job descriptions and wage surveys give a clear picture of the nature of work in the new tufted carpet industry and can help explain some the challenges faced by the new entrepreneurs and local workers. These sources also shed light on gender relations in the industry. Women created the original hand-tufting cottage industry, but female workers in the new carpet mills faced substantial wage discrimination.

The heart of a tufted carpet mill was the tufting machine, and one of the highest-paying jobs in the mills was as a "large tufting machine operator." The tufting machine operator took new rolls of backing material (cotton duck, later jute) and sewed the material onto the end of rolls that were almost used up. These operators also started and stopped their machines, watching for broken threads and rethreading needles when necessary. This job required that the operator have "good vision" and be "able-bodied, and quick in all physical movements," but otherwise required "no outstanding or strenuous activities." The typical "employer's requirement" for this job also included a gender and age preference: "male, age 20–40." The TTMA's November 1956 wage survey of twelve reporting tufted carpet mills revealed that the average hourly wage for large machine operators was about $1.58 for loop machines, $1.27 for cut-pile machines, and $1.29 for pattern tufting machines. The reporting mills averaged about ten machine operators per firm. The figures indicated that about 45 percent of machines produced loop piles, 35 percent made cut pile, and 20 percent manufactured patterned carpets and rugs.[81]

The largest single group of employees engaged in carpet manufacture were "creelers." These workers were responsible for maintaining "a full supply of cones of yarn on the rack (creel) from which yarn is drawn by the tufting machine." The creel supplied the yarn that was inserted into the backing material by the tufting machine. Each machine had its own creel rack; large creel racks had two levels. Creelers lifted and mounted (often quite heavy) cones of yarn on the rack's metal prongs in twin series, "tying the finish end of yarn from one cone to the starting end of yarn from the other cone." As one cone ran out, creelers tied another cone on beside the second, full cone. This process assured a continuous yarn feed for the tufting machine. Creeling was crucial in the manufacturing process; it also involved constant, repetitive, and often difficult labor. The job required "moderate . . . walking, climbing, standing, stooping, [and] hearing." "Turning, reaching, lifting, carrying, handling, fingering, and seeing [were] frequent activities" for a creeler. "No one of these activities is strenuous," the Labor Department asserted, "but together they constitute a job of considerable activity." Job performance requirements included a recommended minimum height of five feet, seven inches to enable a worker to "reach up and between cones to mend breaks"; "nimble fingers"; "agility to climb to upper deck"; and a maximum weight of about 150 pounds (presumably related to the necessity for climbing on the creel rack). Employers expressed a clear preference for female workers as creelers. The average wage for creelers in 1956 was around $1.11.[82]

Inspector-menders supervised the output of the tufting machines. Inspectors watched the carpet closely as it passed over a brightly lit frame after it emerged from the tufting machine, and they used hand-held needle-punch guns to mend any missed tufts caused by broken threads. This work required good vision; the inspector was expected to spot flaws in carpeting by sight. The job also included constant standing and close observation, as well as frequent stooping and handling. Employers, again, preferred females for these jobs. Average wages for inspector-menders in 1956 came to about $1.16. Occasionally, this job assignment would be split into two, with one employee inspecting and another mending exclusively. Inspectors' wages were about the same as inspector-menders'; but when a person was employed only as a mender, his or her hourly pay rate fell to about $1.11, equal to that of a creeler.[83]

The mechanics and machinists who maintained and modified the tufting machines were the highest-paid employees in Dalton's carpet mills in the 1950s. Thirty "first class mechanics" or "machinists" averaged $1.87 per hour at a dozen reporting mills; sixty other employees classified as lesser machinists or as "tufting machine mechanics" (large or small) earned more than $1.60 per hour.[84] These mechanics and machinists were often not formally trained, but most were highly skilled. They earned their positions by demonstrating skill.

Tufting represented only one segment in the manufacturing process for carpet and other tufted goods. The Dalton district's tufted textile finishing companies provided essential services for tufters. Carpet finishing involved three basic processes: dyeing, drying, and the application of a latex backing to lock in tufts. Dye weighers, those employees charged with preparing the proper dye solutions, earned about $1.36 per hour in 1956. Dye beck operators received $1.28 per hour on average for overseeing the operations of the dye tanks. These two jobs involved the greatest possibility of error. Flat drier operators ran the large ovens that dried the carpets after dyeing, and their rates averaged about $1.33.

The job category that paid the least and required the most physical effort was that of "loader, puller, or helper." Generally referred to as "beck pullers," these men "loaded articles into washing, bleaching, or dyeing machines" and then pulled washed or dyed goods onto a box truck. Beck pullers then pushed the truck to the extractor and lifted dyed goods into it. These workers also "helped" dye beck operators "load continuous-roll material into machines and to pull it from the machines and fold it onto a flat truck." The only job performance requirement was the "physical ability to perform manual tasks quickly." The job entailed "considerable lifting, pulling, and handling" and required beck pullers to stand in ankle-deep water much of the time in and around dye becks. The average hourly pay for beck pullers in 1956 was $1.11.[85]

Shaheen Shaheen, owner of World Carpet Mills, described work in the dye houses:

> Dyeing carpet this way was not the easiest of jobs. Men had to work in hot, humid conditions, manually loading and unloading the hot, dripping, wet carpet from the dye beck. . . .

[Later] it became very difficult to get anyone to work in a dye house . . . because there were so many jobs available in Dalton that people could choose from. A job in a dye house was the last one that they would pick, unless they were uneducated or unable to do anything else. And it seemed that the sheriff came fairly often after men employed in the dye house, as if that were a good place to hide from the authorities when one had problems in other communities. Many are the tales that were told about this, both at World and at other factories.[86]

Shaheen noted that beck pullers could be hard to find because of a labor shortage in the Dalton district.

The labor shortage influenced every decision made by local entrepreneurs and the TTMA. Indeed, a longtime TTMA officer recalled in a later interview that the greatest challenge facing the carpet industry in the 1950s and 1960s was labor relations.[87] The TTMA devoted most of its time and efforts in this period to helping members cope with the "labor problem." The wage survey and compilation of job descriptions were two early attempts in this direction, but far from the last.

The skills of talented entrepreneurs like Barwick, Shaheen, and Seretean were crucial for the development of tufted carpet manufacture, as was the evolution of a manufacturers association. Perhaps equally important was the development of a new variant of Du Pont's almost infinitely flexible nylon fiber. The emergence of tufting as an alternative to weaving as a method for manufacturing soft floor coverings and the rapid rise of tufted carpet sales during the 1950s prompted Du Pont to speed up its development of new textile fibers. Carpet manufacturers experimented with existing nylon fibers during the early 1950s. Nylon was a continuous filament fiber; nylon yarns for hosiery and other purposes did not require a laborious process of carding and blending to produce long strands. Such continuous filament yarns were more durable than "staple" yarns that consisted of short strands of cotton, wool, or other fibers blended and twisted into longer yarn strands. Especially in "cut pile" carpet constructions, continuous filament nylon yarns were valuable in reducing "fuzzing" and preventing yarn from being pulled away from the carpet backing. Unfortunately for carpet makers, continuous filament nylon had insufficient bulk for use in carpet manufacture. Yarn producers made carpet yarn from nylon by chopping the continuous filaments and baling them like cotton or wool. This "staple" nylon was then processed just like any natural fiber by a process of spinning and crimping to produce the bulk necessary for carpet manufacture.[88]

Du Pont researchers recognized the shortcomings of continuous filament nylon for carpet manufacture and other purposes requiring thicker yarns. Company scientists realized that it would "be far less costly to crimp the original filament yarns as a means of obtaining the bulk of spun staple yarns" in the 1940s. The company sponsored some experimentation with methods of creating bulked continuous filament fibers, but the demand for such fibers was too small to encourage massive investment in such research. In 1951, Du Pont researchers Alvin Breen and Herbert Lauterbach developed a method of using "hot fluid jets to relax yarn continuously." Lauterbach even had a small sample carpet produced with this yarn to illustrate the potential of the new technique. A Du Pont internal history noted, however, that "the business climate of 1951–1952 was not propitious" for such a "carpet development." Demand for carpeting had remained relatively stable for decades, and traditional manufacturers of woven wool carpets were reluctant to make a wholesale move toward synthetic fibers. In addition, the process developed by Breen and Lauterbach needed refining to produce consistently good yarn for carpet manufacture. While working on the bulking process, Breen serendipitously discovered a process for bulking rayon and other nonthermoplastic yarns that became the "Taslan" process. The Taslan process was more commercially viable, and the company diverted personnel and funding to this process and away from the bulking of nylon.[89]

By early 1957, however, "the atmosphere had changed." The carpet tufting process had now "become commercially viable." Indeed, tufting had already supplanted weaving as the primary method of carpet manufacture. Per capita carpet sales increased substantially in the period 1950–57, reversing a decades-old trend toward slow growth or stagnation in the carpet trade; tufted products accounted for *all* of the industry's growth in the 1950s (and beyond as well). The new tufted carpet manufacturers never hesitated to explore alternative fibers and were especially attracted to cheaper synthetic fibers. Working with cotton, rayon, staple nylon, blends of all or some of these, and a few other lesser-used fibers, tufted carpet manufacturers had already revolutionized the manufacture of car-

TABLE 4. Estimated Fiber Consumption in Broadloom Carpets, Tufted and Woven, 1960–1967 (in millions of pounds)

	1960	1961	1962	1963	1964	1965	1966	1967
Nylon filament	18	45	70	90	131	163	170	198
Nylon staple	25	23	25	30	45	53	55	58
Acrylics	15	12	22	45	85	125	140	147
Wool	163	147	149	160	123	112	104	84
Polypropylene	–	–	–	–	–	18	36	33
Polyester	–	–	–	–	–	–	1	6
Cotton and rayon	35	30	25	16	20	9	9	8

Source: American Carpet Institute, *Basic Facts about the Carpet and Rug Industry*, 1968.

peting in the United States. In early 1957, Du Pont researchers "reexamined" the earlier discoveries of Breen and Lauterbach and began an intensive effort to perfect the bulking of continuous filament nylon. In April 1957, Du Pont created a task force to refit some manufacturing facilities to produce bulked continuous filament nylon (BCF). In June 1958, the company announced the new product as Type 501 BCF nylon. Du Pont reached agreements with two large carpet-manufacturing firms to introduce all-nylon tufted carpeting in the fall of 1958—James Lees and Sons and E. T. Barwick Mills.[90]

By 1958 tufted carpeting had replaced woven carpeting as the consumer's choice, owing in part to a marketing blitz put on by Du Pont and Barwick Mills (see chapter 5). The differences between the tufting and weaving processes for carpet production were starkly summarized in the American Carpet Institute's statistical handbook for 1962. Using statistics for 1958 (the most recent year for which complete figures were available), the institute reported that there were 60 companies engaged in the manufacture of woven carpets. These companies operated 69 plants and employed about 15,000. The woven plants produced 82.6 million square yards of carpet in 1958. The woven plants achieved a productivity level of about 1.7 square yards per man-hour of labor. Woven mills paid more than $55 million in total wages that year.[91]

In contrast, 88 companies operated 92 tufting mills. Fewer than 10,000 production workers managed to turn out more than 113 million square yards of tufted carpets and rugs. Even factoring in scatter rugs, which had

TABLE 5. Average Mill Value of Carpet
Shipments, per Square Yard, Selected Years
1950–1965

	All Broadloom	Woven	Tufted
1950	$6.26	$6.26	–
1955	5.30	6.19	3.36
1960	4.50	6.56	3.49
1965	3.76	6.09	3.40

Source: Carpet and Rug Institute Directory and Report, 1970, 126.

lower productivity than broadloom tufting, the entire tufted floor covering industry managed to produce 5.8 square yards per man-hour. Since
figures for man-hours of labor and output for broadloom carpeting were
not kept separately, it is difficult to estimate the productivity of broadloom manufacturing. Certainly, if it were possible to factor out scatter rug
production, the productivity numbers of the tufted industry would be even
higher. Tufting mills paid a total of about $27 million in wages, less than
half the total for the woven mills. The bottom line was painfully obvious
to veterans of the old woven industry: tufting produced more carpet with
fewer workers at lower cost. Tufting plants also outspent woven mills on
capital improvements, $8 million to $5.8 million. If this capital spending
was properly directed, the odds were that the productivity gap would
continue to grow.[92]

Wholesale carpet prices, the consumer's top priority, also demonstrated
the efficiency of the tufting process. Using the 1947–49 average price for
broadloom carpeting as a base, the wholesale price index for wool Axminster carpeting stood at 144.4 in 1956. By 1960, Axminster prices had
risen slightly, to 148.6. Velvets and Wiltons followed a similar pattern in
the late 1950s, both showing modest price gains. These price increases
were quite small in contrast to the immediate post–World War II years
and reflected woven industry efforts to modernize and regain a competitive
posture with tufted carpets and imported wovens. Tufted carpet prices fell
in the same period. The price index for cotton tufted carpets and rugs was
117.1 in 1956; by 1960 it had fallen to 96.0. Tufted products made from
synthetic fibers showed the same pattern of steady price decreases, from
118.4 to 104.1.[93]

If consumers and retailers were convinced by Du Pont–Barwick nylon advertising campaigns launched in the late 1950s that synthetic fibers were equal or superior to wool in color selection and durability, then the battle was over. The question was no longer whether tufting would supplant weaving as the dominant mode of carpet production but who would dominate the tufting industry. The old, established woven firms—tightly organized and better financed—moved into tufting and had many advantages. They were challenged by a growing number of southern firms—loosely organized, poorly capitalized, facing potential labor unrest—that had the advantages of closer connections with and greater confidence in the new technology and no outdated plants and equipment to liquidate. During the 1960s, these two factions competed for dominance within the carpet industry.

The small tufting concerns based in Georgia "prodded the giants in the field into competition," *Business Week* announced in June 1956. The tufting process had "created a man-sized revolution in the hard-pressed carpet industry." The old woven giants now "consider[ed] tufting an integral part of their business." The efficiencies of the tufting process reversed the trend toward declining per family carpet consumption. As the tufting revolution washed over the carpet industry in the late 1950s, *Business Week*'s editors concluded that it was still an open question as to who would dominate the "lower and middle market that has eluded the carpet trade for so many years. . . . But there's no question that tufted has staked out its claim."[94]

A Favorable Business Climate

From the mid-1950s through the mid-1960s, the Textile Workers Union of America made a major effort to organize the mill workers of the tufted textile district, or "Tuftland," as TWUA officials dubbed the northwest Georgia region. The union's efforts to organize Dalton's carpet workers brought the industry's disparate firms together as never before. The union campaign had long-term consequences for the carpet industry and its workers. Carpet manufacturers developed a collective vision of the relationship between industry and the community. Workers had to choose between the social contract put forth by the mill owners and that offered by the TWUA. The mill

owners would counter the union's efforts in part through purposeful organization by forming an effective manufacturers association and in part,
inadvertently, through competition and growth. Manufacturers feared
that an organized labor force might threaten future growth. Twice in the
crucial decade 1955–65, the Textile Workers Union of America made
serious efforts to organize the carpet industry. These union campaigns
were among the most significant developments in the carpet industry in
the 1950s and 1960s.

The TWUA's organizing drive and its outcome revealed the harsh realities of textile organizing in the modern South. While management refined
its techniques, the outcome was often the same: the TWUA had little success in organizing the South. Textile workers in the post–World War II period have received relatively little scholarly attention. Robert Zeiger noted
in his introduction to a group of essays on southern labor history, published in 1994, that "until the 1980s, southern textile workers were the
neglected stepchildren of social and labor historiography." This scholarly
neglect was surely corrected during the 1980s, as "an outpouring of vigorous scholarly literature" addressed the problems of southern textile labor. Most of this scholarship focused on the plight of the South's cotton
mill workers in the period 1880–1945. Historians of southern labor produced a wide array of works that helped rescue the region's cotton mill
people from historical oblivion. A key issue, whether clearly stated or im-
plicit, in most of the new scholarship was an attempt to explain "the repeated failure of union organizing among textile workers." The focus of
almost all these new analyses was the mill village and its attendant cultural baggage, generally embodied in the term "paternalism."[1]

While southern cotton mill workers have received substantial attention
from labor historians, relatively little has been written on southern textile
workers in the post–World War II period. Barbara S. Griffith detailed the
Textile Workers Union of America's participation in the CIO's "Operation Dixie" in the immediate postwar years, and James Hodges is working on a study of the important and highly publicized J. P. Stevens campaign in the 1960s and 1970s. Zeiger observed in 1994 that Hodges's
"emerging work on the J. P. Stevens controversy is one of the few full scholarly historical studies" to examine "post-1960 [textile] workers." Yet the
failure to organize workers in Dixie in the postwar years contributed

mightily to the declining health of the U.S. labor movement, according to both Griffith and Michael Goldfield.[2]

Labor historians have generally advanced a number of explanations for the failure of unionism in the American South, both before and after Operation Dixie. Michael Goldfield has succinctly summarized the prevailing wisdom. He outlined four general explanatory models for the failure of Operation Dixie and southern unionism generally. The weakness of the southern economy was invoked by many to explain southern resistance to unions. In essence, southern workers were accustomed to deprivation, and even the modest level of consumption afforded them by low-wage industrial jobs was superior to the harsh realities of sharecropping and tenant farming. The South's collapsing cotton economy also helped create a labor surplus, forcing industrial workers to consider seriously any activities that might threaten their jobs. The industrial structure of southern textiles encouraged antiunion intransigence among mill owners and also made organizing difficult. The textile industry was "authentically competitive," Griffith observed. Textile firms "lived closer to the margin" and "were perennially short of capital," encouraging owners and managers to adopt "an intransigent anti-labor attitude." Griffith observed that the TWUA often hurt its own cause by accepting stereotypical attitudes toward southern workers based on perceptions of southern culture. TWUA national leaders expressed little faith or trust in southern workers. Southern culture was another staple explanation. Southern culture was so deeply infused with traditions of paternalism and deference, on the one hand, and rural individualism, on the other, that unions seemed dangerous and alien.

Douglas Flamming's pioneering study of cotton mill workers in Dalton has persuasively challenged this "cultural" argument. Flamming has observed that unions rose and fell in Dalton, Georgia, for a variety of reasons, but he identified little in the way of intrinsic cultural barriers to unionization. In a related argument, southern labor historians have cited the "unified opposition to unions" that organizers encountered in the region. The "extremely close integration of economic, social, and cultural power in parts of the South" may have accounted for some of the difficulties encountered by union organizers. Union leadership and strategy have also been roundly criticized. The Textile Workers Union of America has received special attention for its overly cautious, tentative organizing strategies and the failure of union leaders to understand the southern situation or southern workers. The Dalton carpet organizing campaign sheds new light on the role that these factors played in textile organizing in the South after World War II.[3]

The most recent broad explanation for the difficulties of textile organizing in Dixie has emphasized real, if limited, improvements in standards of living and shrewd management strategies. Timothy Minchin has argued that for at least a while during and after World War II, southern textile workers experienced rising wages and rates of home ownership (related to the selling off of mill village housing). In Minchin's schema, "southern culture" played little part in the union defeats of the 1950s and beyond. Likewise, mill owners' crude antiunion tactics—the relatively unfettered use of force and intimidation—gradually gave way to new, somewhat subtler strategies that recognized new realities in the region. The conjunction of out-migration, resulting fears of a southern labor shortage, and a brief textile boom in the immediate postwar years encouraged mill managers and lawyers to experiment with granting wage hikes and other benefits to try to hold workers and discourage union organization.[4]

The Dalton district experienced a social revolution to accompany its industrial revolution in the 1950s. In the four-county area that constituted the heart of the tufted textile industry—Whitfield, Murray, Catoosa, and Gordon—the total rural farm population fell from 27,633 in 1950 to 10,535 in 1960. The total population of the four counties rose in the same period, from 79,176 to 92,885. The percentage of land in farms in this region fell from about 75 percent in 1950 to just 46.5 percent by 1964. At the same time, the average size of farms in the area rose 93 acres to more than 114 during the 1950s and early 1960s.[5] This process of agricultural dislocation was not new. Farmers had been fleeing the land in the South since the 1870s. In Dalton, however, many displaced farmers of earlier generations had found community, organization, a higher standard of living, and respectability. The Crown Cotton Mill and its mill village had offered many victims of the southern enclosure movement a refuge. Crown's workers organized a strong, effective TWUA local during the mid-1930s. Crown's cotton mill people created a community, within the mill village and within the union. A sense of purpose, possibility, and camaraderie sustained the Crown employees, even after the shutdown of the mill in the late 1960s.[6] The existing local cotton mill unions in Dalton gave the TWUA a measure of optimism about organizing prospects in the emerging tufted textile industry in the 1950s. That optimism proved to be misplaced.

The TWUA's organizing efforts in the 1950s and 1960s helped push the disparate elements of the new tufting industry toward more effective organization themselves. The TTMA played a crucial role in crushing a union-organizing campaign aimed at the tufted textile industry during the mid-1950s. The Textile Workers Union of America launched an organizing drive in the industry in 1955. The growth of the carpet sector had decreased somewhat the seasonal character of the industry. Most of the Dalton area's manufacturing, particularly in carpet production, now relied on "a permanent, well-trained group of tufted textile hands." The impetus for the 1955 TWUA campaign came, however, not from the union or local mill workers, according to Douglas Flamming, but from within "the congregation of the Reverend Charlie T. Pratt's Church of God of the Union Assembly." This sect had about five hundred adherents in Dalton (the church's national headquarters) and as many as ten thousand more throughout the South. Pratt's church appealed primarily to poor farmers and mill workers, advocated communal property ownership, and operated several local businesses. The Union Assembly had long been a strong advocate of unionism in the Dalton area and counted a number of local cotton mill workers among its members. Indeed, Dalton was something of a union town in the 1950s with two large, union-organized, traditional textile mills.[7]

Charlie Pratt and others in his congregation decided that the time was right in 1955 to begin an all-out attempt to organize the tufted textile industry. Pratt recruited his friend Don West to help in the effort. Pratt, West, and members of Dalton's existing local unions at the Crown Cotton Mill and the American Thread Company mill (these two mills bookended the town, Crown to the north and the American Thread Company to the south) opened a campaign in early 1955. West began publishing a labor-oriented newspaper, the *Southerner,* to publicize the virtues of unionism and the shortcomings of local employers. West's radical past led to the ultimate defeat of this organizing drive. West was a veteran of radical protest and organizing in the South and had developed contacts with groups including the Communist Party. Local Dalton union leaders had no idea about West's connections; national TWUA leaders did and alerted their local agents. The TWUA had only recently helped lead a fight within the Congress of Industrial Organizations to purge that federation of Communist—and other radical—influence. In the midst of the red scare atmosphere of the 1950s, West's connections to the party and to other supposed front organizations meant trouble.[8]

Dalton Citizen News editor Mark Pace was alerted to West's radical ties by an agent from the Georgia Bureau of Investigation. Pace took the lead in publicizing West's past. The Tufted Textile Manufacturers Association also fought hard against the organizing drive and played the red card along with Pace. Pace wrote editorials accusing West of being a Communist; the TTMA placed full-page ads in the same newspaper proclaiming West's sins as well. In the anti-Communist hysteria of the mid-1950s, this was enough. Pace never criticized unionism in general, nor did he criticize Pratt's church. The TTMA focused on the Communist issue as well, perhaps fearing that a blatant antiunion campaign might not play well in a community with long-standing and influential cotton mill unions.[9]

The strategy worked. The TWUA lost a critical election at Belcraft Chenilles in December 1955 (840 workers voted for "no union," only 625 for the TWUA). The first attempt to organize the tufted textile industry rapidly fell apart in the aftermath of the Belcraft defeat. The TTMA played a role in defeating the union, but members understood that the Communist issue might not work a second time. In 1956, the TTMA established an Industrial Relations Club to encourage member companies to adopt new personnel policies and to educate managers in the field of personnel management. Dalton-area tufted textile manufacturers faced another challenge from the TWUA in the early 1960s, and the union made certain that there would be no hint of Communist influence in that drive.

John Chupka, general secretary-treasurer of the Textile Workers Union of America, visited the Dalton area in early 1962 to assess the prospects for a carpet organizing campaign. Chupka observed that the workers were generally younger than those in other textile industries, perhaps owing to the relative youth of the tufted carpet industry. He also reported that the carpet mill workforce was primarily male. The chenille, or bedspread, industry, still a strong local employer, had a predominantly female work-force. The chenille mills were generally smaller and less profitable by the early 1960s. The tufted carpet mills, on the other hand, had grown at a phenomenal rate since the mid-1950s. Wages remained low despite the rapid growth, Chupka observed. He estimated that average hourly earnings amounted to less than $1.40 in 1961. Workers in the highest-paid category, "Big Machine Operators," averaged only $1.65–1.75 per hour. Chupka caustically commented that "it appears that one must have five years of experience to reach this pinnacle." Fringe benefits were "negligible," chiefly confined to limited vacation pay and minimum group health and life insurance. Workers in the finishing segment of the industry fared somewhat better than their counterparts in carpet manufacturing. Workers in laundries and dye houses earned an average of close to $1.50 per hour. In all segments of the industry, the low wages were supplemented by substantial overtime. Most Dalton-area plants in 1961 operated six days a week, with many departments running only two twelve-hour shifts.[10]

Workers in the carpet industry of northwest Georgia were completely unorganized. The TWUA's initial attempt to penetrate the chenille industry had failed at Belcraft in 1955. Since that election, the TWUA had scaled back its efforts in the area. The union launched a new effort in 1961 and achieved some success. In Calhoun, a small town some twenty miles south of Dalton, TWUA organizers convinced more than 400 out of 650 workers at Dixie Belle Mills to sign union cards. Dixie Belle was owned by Bell Industries, the parent of Belcraft in Dalton. In the 1955 election, all of Bell Industries' Dalton-area operations had been involved in one election. Even though a majority of Bell Industries' employees voted against union representation, a substantial majority at Dixie Belle had voted in favor of the TWUA. Now, seven years later, pro-union sentiment at Dixie Belle was presumably still strong. In those intervening years, Bell Industries had entered the tufted carpet and rug field, and Dixie Belle was its primary plant for tufted floor coverings. Dixie Belle provided the TWUA with a favorable starting point for a Dalton campaign.

Israel Belsky started Bell Textile Company, the precursor to Bell Industries, in 1910 as a textile jobbing company. Belsky moved into textile manufacturing when he purchased Dixie Spread Company, Calhoun, in 1939, and changed the name to Dixie Belle Mills. The Belsky family formed Belcraft Chenilles in Dalton in 1946. Bell Industries was a family business. In 1962, Murray Belsky served as president of the company, and two other family members occupied the positions of treasurer and secretary.[11]

Bell Industries consisted of six subsidiaries in the early 1960s. The company owned a New York textile firm that sold blankets and sheets; the remaining five companies were located in the Dalton area. Belcraft Chenilles produced bedspreads. Dixie Belle Mills included Dixie Belle in Calhoun and the Pride Carpet Mills Division of Bell Industries, located in Dalton. The other companies were real estate companies established to hold titles to the property occupied by the manufacturing plants, and a Dalton laundry used exclusively to dye and finish Belcraft products.[12]

Michael Botelho, veteran TWUA organizer, had conducted a probing operation at Dixie Belle in November 1961. Workers greeted the idea of TWUA organization with such "enthusiasm" that Botelho upgraded Dixie Belle to a full-scale organizing campaign only a month later. After clearing the legal hurdle involving the most appropriate unit for an election, Botelho and the TWUA petitioned for an NLRB election in the fall of 1962. Botelho predicted in September 1962 that if an election was held in the reasonably near future, the TWUA "would emerge as the collective bargaining agent at this plant." Dixie Belle's management, according to TWUA organizers, "continued to operate as though they were back in the dark ages."[13]

Former Dixie Belle employees agreed with the TWUA's analysis of management practices at Dixie Belle and in the carpet industry generally. Raymond Roach, who worked at Dixie Belle for twenty-five years and later served as president of the local union at the Calhoun company, assessed the labor situation in the tufting mills. "They all paid the same," Roach maintained. He also recalled that most mills had similar hiring, promotion, and disciplinary procedures: none. All such decisions were made on the whim of individual supervisors and owners. In the early days of the carpet industry in north Georgia, rapid production was the chief goal. Roach recalled that mill owners liked to identify workers "that they thought the people would be afraid of and they would make him a supervisor" and "pay him a little more." Workers referred to these supervisors as "pushers," because it was their job to "push" the workers into more rapid production.[14]

Roach used a biblical analogy to describe this process. He compared these "pushers" to the "Jewish taskmasters" in ancient Egypt who collaborated with the oppressors of the Jewish people in exchange for "fine homes to live in" and other material benefits. The supervisors at Dixie Belle used their authority to try to terrorize employees into more efficient production, according to Roach. In this environment, workers often "got mad at supervisors" and quit. With industry growing rapidly in the area, jobs were plentiful. Pressure on the local labor market in the 1950s and early 1960s did not lead to substantial upward pressure on wages. Roach and other workers felt that the mills had an informal wage scale and a tacit agreement not to try to lure away workers from a competitor with an offer of substantially higher wages. Workers often complained of the arbitrary behavior of supervisors. Mill employees generally salved wounds to their personal honor by simply quitting and going to work at another mill for roughly the same pay. They remained until another supervisor "insulted" them. Roach and other employees rarely could (or would) recall details of such incidents. The pattern of behavior, though, reinforces the personalized nature of workplace relations in this industry. Workers were hired, disciplined, and fired on the basis of personal whim, hurt feelings, and crude attempts to maximize production through intimidation. Workers responded on an individual basis, by quitting the employment of mills perceived to be oppressive, rather than on a collective basis. The TWUA attempted to channel this frustration among workers in the early 1960s.[15]

The TWUA petitioned for an election at the Dixie Belle plant. The company objected, claiming that the individual plant did not constitute an appropriate unit for purposes of collective bargaining. Bell Industries argued that the 1955 election had settled the issue of union representation unless a majority of workers in all its area mills changed their mind. Chupka believed that if a separate election could be held at the Calhoun mill, the TWUA could establish a beachhead in the tufted carpet industry. Chupka was encouraged by the success of union representatives at Dixie Belle, as well as by the attitudes of the general public in Dalton toward unions. "The community atmosphere in the areas in which these mills are located," the union official informed his colleagues, "is such that we are not apt to meet the same obstacles . . . we normally encounter in other parts of the south." Chupka offered two specific pieces of evidence to support this contention. He described a dinner meeting with Erwin Mitchell and his cousin. Mitchell was a prominent local attorney, Dalton's state senator at the time, and a former congressman from the district. His cousin, Tom Mitchell, was a local businessman. The Mitchells told Chupka that "the business community in Dalton [was] quite concerned" with the general low level of wages in the carpet industry. These community leaders "indicated to [Chupka] that they would give whatever assistance they could if we undertook a real organizational drive in that area." Chupka also noted that the TWUA had two established locals in Dalton, at the Crown Cotton Mill and the American Thread Company. He was confident that the existence of organized labor in the community would help lessen the fear of outside influence that often hampered organizing efforts in the South.[16]

The National Labor Relations Board's Tenth Regional Office denied the petition for an election covering only Dixie Belle's Calhoun plant. The union appealed to the national office, and in June 1962 the previous decision was overturned. The organizing campaign, in the meantime, had started in November 1961 and continued until the election was held in November 1962. The campaign in Dalton continued for months after the election at Dixie Belle. For more than a year, the Dalton area, especially the village of Calhoun, was the center of a massive organizing campaign. By April 1963, the TWUA had spent $111,000 on the "Dalton Campaign," maintaining three permanent and four temporary organizers in the area.[17]

TWUA organizers distributed literature throughout the Dalton area and sent husband-and-wife teams from other TWUA-organized textile mills in Georgia to meet with workers in their homes. The union campaign also included a local radio program that aired on both local radio stations in Dalton, WRCD and WBLJ. The TWUA developed three key themes in its organizing campaign: the charge that the TTMA functioned as a union for employers; the contention that the tufted industry could afford a wage increase; and a promise to curtail arbitrary management practices.

According to TWUA literature, the Tufted Textile Manufacturers Association functioned as an employers' union. TTMA members faced raw materials costs, plant and equipment costs, and so on that were essentially beyond their control. The union argued that manufacturers had control over only one element of cost: labor. "About the only thing a tufted textile employer can 'cut costs' on," TWUA organizers told Dalton area workers, "is YOUR LABOR, YOUR WAGES, YOUR WORKING CONDITIONS, YOUR PAID HOLIDAYS, VACATIONS, INSURANCE, AND WORK LOADS." Manufacturers cooperated through the TTMA, whose program was "to band together and use every effort possible to prevent employees from building a union." The TWUA urged workers to emulate their bosses and join a union to defend their rights.[18]

The TWUA also argued that the tufted industry could afford substantial wage increases. The mill value of tufted products, the union asserted, had risen twenty-two-fold since 1951, yet wages in "Tuftland" hovered "near the bottom of the list" for manufacturing operatives. The union charged that "Coronet, World, Cabin Crafts, E.T. Barwick, among others, are paying wages 75 cents an hour below those paid in organized [textile] plants."[19]

The TWUA's radio broadcasts extolled the virtues of union grievance procedures, promising to give workers a small measure of control over their work environment. The union interspersed brief statements of the virtues of organized labor with musical selections. Labor songs such as "Get on the Union Train" were played often. "The Union Train" caused quite a stir because of its mild profanity: bosses are characterized as "Bastards," company spies at union meetings as "Damn Fool[s]." The program also featured country and popular music tunes with a labor theme. Buck Owens's "Something Better Happen Pretty Soon" was reprinted in its entirety in the broadcast's transcript (it is not clear if these transcripts were produced by the TTMA or TWUA, or the station). Owens moaned that he was "tired of living and a scared of dying, I can't get ahead, there's no use a trying, things had better change, I ain't a lying, something had better happen pretty soon." The singer complained that the man next door "owns a 40-room shack, drives around every day in a big Cadillac, but I'm still walking." Tennessee Ernie Ford's "Sixteen Tons" was another popular favorite on the TWUA broadcast.[20]

At Dixie Belle in Calhoun, the union campaign emphasized the potential material gains workers could expect from TWUA membership. Raymond Roach recalled that during the campaign TWUA organizers often used the United Auto Workers as an example of what workers in the mills could expect. In retrospect, Roach realized that it was unrealistic for workers in the competitive, low-profit-margin carpet industry to expect benefits and wages similar to those enjoyed by UAW members, who worked in a virtual oligopoly. "They didn't tell you you had to crawl before you could walk," Roach lamented. TWUA promises would come back to haunt the organization after the Dixie Belle campaign.[21]

The union campaign of 1962–63 differed significantly from the earlier drive. Dalton had been the scene of a heated organizing drive in the mid-1950s. The campaign at Belcraft Chenille failed, in large measure because of a red-baiting campaign organized and carried out by the Tufted Textile Manufacturers Association, in cooperation with the local Dalton newspaper and the Georgia Bureau of Investigation. The TTMA encouraged the *Dalton Daily News* to publish articles detailing strikes and plant closings in other parts of Georgia and the rest of the country. When local manufacturers learned of renewed TWUA interest in the Dalton area in 1961, the TTMA responded in familiar fashion.[22]

TTMA executive vice president R. E. Hamilton and the association's Industrial Relations Club were the most active elements of the trade organization in the antiunion campaign. The papers of the TTMA's Industrial Relations Club reflect the membership's interest in promoting personnel practices that would help make union organization less likely. The club sponsored several seminars each year, most of them oriented toward promoting greater workforce efficiency and better relations between management and employees.[23] The TTMA's leadership took an active role in the antiunion campaign in Dalton, disseminating information on the union campaign to members, suggesting editorial topics and copy for the Dalton newspapers, and encouraging other local business leaders to join the struggle against the TWUA.

The TTMA also worked hard behind the scenes to prevent union organization. The association circulated a list to members that detailed the Social Security system's pattern for assigning numbers to people entering the workforce. The first three digits of a Social Security number could be used to determine in what state a worker first entered the workforce. The TTMA circulated a guide to using the prefixes, apparently so that local employers could guard against hiring outside agitators. The TTMA also obtained and circulated information from various private "investigative" agencies and brought in experts to instruct TTMA members in the use of polygraph technology.[24]

The manufacturers association's executive vice president helped plant the idea among local merchants and professionals to form a "Dalton Boosters" club. In late April or early May 1962, R. E. Hamilton mailed a letter to "all retail, professional, and other business people in Dalton and Whitfield County." Hamilton may have been writing to counter the mild "pro-union" sentiment among merchants hinted at by Erwin Mitchell. He may also have harbored hopes that local merchants and professionals might be persuaded to join the antiunion campaign. Hamilton warned Dalton's middle-class professionals and merchants that "union organizers may come to you seeking support." These TWUA organizers would promise that greater profits for local merchants, lawyers, doctors, and others would come with union wages for local carpet workers. Hamilton detailed a list of Dalton companies that had scaled back or shut down after union organization, including the Real Silk Hosiery mill (closed) and the American Thread Company (personnel reductions). Although individual wages might have gone up, he implied, total payrolls declined, hurting merchants in the long run: "When jobs and payrolls decrease, there will be *less business for merchants*" (emphasis in the original). This letter may have been the origin of the idea of the Dalton Boosters.[25]

Local businessmen, working in conjunction with manufacturers represented by the TTMA, formed the "Dalton Boosters" in 1962 to spread the gospel about industrial progress in Dalton. The Boosters also cautioned the community against rocking the industrial boat in the area. The Boosters' membership was composed primarily of merchants, doctors, lawyers, and suppliers to the carpet industry. For more than two years, the Boosters regularly placed full-page ads in the Dalton newspaper and sent out mass mailings extolling the virtues of Dalton's economic boom.[26]

The Dalton Boosters claimed to have three primary purposes. First, the organization wanted to "point out the many advantages of living and working in the Whitfield County area." The Boosters also supported "projects for the betterment of the community," such as new recreational facilities. Most important, the Boosters wanted to "encourage the continued growth of industry" and to help "build a climate that will attract new industry" to the Dalton area.[27]

The Boosters were particularly active in pursuing the last goal. A typical Booster newspaper ad explained why Dalton had experienced such rapid industrial growth. "The good, reliable labor supply" was "certainly one of the reasons" for Dalton's economic good fortune. "The most important reason the tufted industry is continuing to expand in this region is simply because of the FAVORABLE BUSINESS CLIMATE that exists here." The Booster ads rarely mentioned the TWUA or unions in general, but in the highly charged atmosphere of a community in the midst of a union-organizing drive, the implication was clear. These ads pointed out that Dalton's textile industry had created more manufacturing jobs in the period 1957–62 than the much more populous counties of Fulton and Dekalb combined. The entire Dalton area was dependent on the nearly twelve thousand manufacturing jobs that supported schools, recreational facilities, hospitals, local merchants. "Common sense and a prudent self-interest," the Boosters offered in a typical conclusion, "tells us that it is to the advantage of all of us to keep industry growing—and in Dalton!"[28]

The Murray-Whitfield Medical Society joined the Dalton Boosters in warning the community to guard against any threat to "a continued favorable economic climate." These doctors expressed appreciation to local industry for its contributions to Dalton's "greatly improved" medical facilities. The Medical Society cautioned that continued improvements in local hospitals and medical services were "directly dependent" upon continued industrial growth.[29]

The Boosters also compared the relative prosperity of Dalton with the seeming chaos that afflicted many other textile communities. One ad showed a central text block circled by smaller blocks. The outer blocks detailed labor problems in other communities. In Tate, Georgia, a "marble workers union" was "on strike . . . violence breaks out. . . . Governor answers request for help by sending in State Patrol to preserve peace and order." Berrien County, Georgia, "desperately need[ed] an additional industry." The Berrien Chamber of Commerce was "in a position to build and rent a building for your company," according to the Boosters. In Cordova, Alabama, six hundred to seven hundred employees "represented by a TWUA union" faced the loss of their jobs as their plant closed. A "costly strike at Combustion Engineering" in Chattanooga had just ended. Chattanooga, despite transportation and infrastructure advantages, found its "industry going elsewhere."[30]

The center of this ad led with the phrases "All around us . . . Strikes . . .

Mills Closing . . . Cities hungry for industry to provide employment and payrolls." "But in Dalton," the Boosters argued, many of these problems happily did not exist. The Boosters claimed that textile wages in Whitfield County had quintupled since 1951. In fact, the area faced "a shortage of trained, experienced help." "Male workers," in particular, were "in demand." The Boosters concluded that "industrial payrolls, regular employment, and good wages make Whitfield County prosperous." [31]

In September 1962, during the North Georgia Fair, the Boosters ran a lengthy message that summarized the major antiunion arguments. Drawings depicted a father, mother, and two small children approaching the fairground. The fairground blended into several scenes representing technological progress: rockets, microscopes, electric power lines, and large buildings. The message encouraged citizens to attend the North Georgia Fair and then began to explain Dalton's prosperity. Dalton was "more fortunate than most communities," enjoying medical services, recreational facilities, and high employment unusual in communities of that size. These advantages, according to the Boosters, "came from the efforts of local people" such as Catherine Evans Whitener.[32]

The Boosters warned Dalton's workers that the progress of the area depended on them. The people of the Dalton area "must be willing to stand up against any group or organization that will halt, hinder, or cripple the continued growth and prosperity of this area." Dalton's carpet workers had a choice. They could "continue to work and support our community [and] our industry," and progress would be assured. "The alternative," the Boosters argued in a clear reference to the textile industry's flight from northern unions, was "to become a dead and blighted town like those in New England when industry moved away."[33]

The Boosters also hailed the triumph of consumer spending in the Dalton area. The organization placed an ad claiming that "Dalton-Whitfield citizens spend $500 more per capita than the state average." Based on state sales tax receipts, the Boosters found that Dalton residents were *making more money . . . spending more money . . .* than most other Georgians for groceries, clothing, furniture, automobiles, etc." (emphasis in the original). Whitfield County citizens spent an average of more than $1,950 in 1962, compared with state per capita spending of $1,453. Again, unions were never specifically mentioned, but the message was clear. According to the Boosters, "industrial payrolls in Dalton provide cash for [a] high standard of living." [34]

Mark Pace, editor of the local *Dalton Daily News*, echoed the Boosters' sentiments in the summer of 1962. Pace's editorials emphasized all the themes of the Boosters campaign. Indeed, some of Pace's editorials are almost identical to TTMA "Newsletters," which supposedly went only to members. The Dalton area's future was "very clearly linked with industry," Pace told his readers. The tufted textile industry continued to grow and expand rapidly. Pace praised organizations such as the local chamber of commerce and the TTMA specifically, organizations that were "doing everything possible to encourage the expansion of present companies and attract new industries and payrolls to Dalton." Pace emphasized that Dalton had competitors—other communities that would love to have Dalton's industry. Pace warned the community that the present union campaign could jeopardize Dalton's economic future. The editor congratulated local companies for continuing to invest in expansion in the midst of the union campaign. These local manufacturers were "betting that Dalton will continue to be fair to industry, . . . that Dalton will remain a good place in which to operate." "All the world admires what Dalton has done in creating and building the tufting industry," Pace wrote with a bit of hyperbole, then added, "We trust that nothing will ever be done to drive that industry out of Dalton, or to wreck it." [35] Pace publicly endorsed the Dalton Boosters and their program in October 1962. The organization was necessary, he argued, because as yet there was "no hard core of progressive people willing to supply the time and energy" to promote growth in Dalton. Pace told his readers, "We are pleased that the Boosters are in operation," and he urged everyone in the community to "Be Boosters!" [36]

Pace emphasized the efforts of the Boosters and the TTMA to attract new industry and expand existing industry. There were persistent rumors, however, that Dalton-area carpet manufacturers were not enthusiastic about attracting new industry and outside investment into the communities of northwest Georgia. Certainly the entry of new industrial employers into the Dalton-area labor market would have put pressure on wage levels. In September 1961, before the union campaign had begun, TTMA vice president R. E. Hamilton publicly denied that members of his organization had a "negative attitude" toward new industries in the Tuft-land. The Dalton newspaper described the TTMA as "devoted to the interest of industrial Whitfield County," a designation that was open to interpretation.[37]

In neighboring Gordon County, home of Dixie Belle Mills, the opposition to the union campaign was organized by the local chamber of commerce. It entered the fray publicly in early October 1962 with a series of newspaper ads placed in the weekly *Calhoun Times*. The Gordon County chamber's campaign was virtually identical to the Dalton Boosters campaign and was doubtless strongly influenced by that organization as well as the TTMA. The chamber informed Gordon County residents that they were "living in one of the MOST HIGHLY INDUSTRIALIZED COUNTIES IN GEORGIA." Five of every eight Gordon County workers were employed in a local plant. This was good, but not good enough, according to the chamber of commerce. Calhoun needed to attract more industry and hold the industry it had. "The best way to attract more industry is to encourage and cooperate with the industry you already have," the business association cautioned Gordon County citizens.[38]

Calhoun Times editor James Hobgood editorialized against the TWUA, closely following chamber of commerce arguments (the same situation was true in Dalton). In the same edition that carried the above ad, Hobgood asked his readers the rhetorical question, "Have you ever thought about what would happen to a town if an industry were lost?" After detailing the disastrous impact of a single hypothetical plant closing on Gordon County, Hobgood reminded his readers of the upcoming Thanksgiving holiday (which was still almost two months away) and urged the people of Calhoun to "pause and think, and give thanks for the industry we do have."[39]

The chamber of commerce intensified its campaign in the next few weeks. In mid-October, its rhetoric changed from cautionary to alarmist. The ad that ran in the October 18, 1962, edition of the local newspaper encapsulated the position of the industrial leaders of the Dalton district:

Gordon County's growth and prosperity have come from the efforts of local people. Enterprising manufacturers and employees have worked together to build a "home-grown" industry for more people than anything that ever happened in this area.

Tufting plants are operating today in Tennessee, Alabama, Arkansas, Virginia, the Carolinas, Indiana, Pennsylvania, California, and other states. Many communities would like to have Gordon County's plants and payrolls. In this North Georgia area we have two-thirds of the tufting industry. We can keep these plants and payrolls here, and growing . . . if we want them. Or we can see our prosperity melt away through community indifference and neglect. Industry thrives where it is wanted and appreciated.

If each of us as citizens of Gordon County continue to work and support our community . . . our industry . . . our retail and other business institutions . . . the future is bright. The alternative is to become a dead and blighted area, such as those in New England when industry moved away. We must be willing to stand up against any line of thinking that would halt, hinder, or cripple the continued growth and prosperity of our community.

The message was clear. The tufting industry's representatives implied that a docile labor force was a crucial element in keeping a homegrown industry at home, and labor peace was a key to progress and prosperity.[40] Henry Grady could hardly have said it better.

TWUA organizers and labor allies responded vigorously to the chamber of commerce ad campaign. On November 5, 1962, members of local unions held a mass meeting to protest the chamber's actions. Members of various unions in the Calhoun area, including plumbers, furniture workers, and barbers, turned out for the meeting. Two unions were dominant: the TWUA, representing Dixie Belle employees; and the International Association of Machinists, representing Gordon County residents who commuted to the giant Lockheed plant in Marietta. Lockheed was one of Gordon County's largest employers. Lockheed workers were organized, and Calhoun natives who commuted daily to Marietta were rewarded with paychecks that were far larger than those of local textile mill employees. The Lockheed example was a powerful one in Gordon County.[41]

Representatives of Gordon County organized labor drafted a resolution that threatened an economic boycott of merchants who supported the chamber's antiunion campaign. AFL-CIO members interpreted the attack made by the chamber of commerce on textile unionism as an attack on all organized labor in the community. The union members declared that they would support Dixie Belle workers "in any way we can economically by withholding our trade from Gordon County merchants who continue to subscribe to the Chamber of Commerce advertisements directed to the Dixie Belle election." This resolution was published as a full-page ad in the Calhoun newspaper, together with an attack on the chamber of commerce for injecting itself into the election at Dixie Belle.[42]

The chamber of commerce responded to the resolution with more ads of its own. Chamber members tried to answer the question posed by other unions in Calhoun: Why had the chamber chosen to intervene in a matter that should have been resolved between Dixie Belle management and employees? The chamber noted that a significant part of its mission was "the fostering of an atmosphere favorable to the continued growth of present industries and the attraction of new industries." Based on a review of "the history of the textile industry," the chamber's board decided "that for the best interests of the workers and the community at large, it should recommend to the employees of Dixie Belle that they vote against the Textile Workers Union of America." A union victory at Dixie Belle would jeopardize a long-standing "local tradition of free and voluntary cooperation between plant owners and their employees."[43]

At this point the union campaign in Calhoun diverged sharply from the pattern emerging in Dalton. In Dalton, the local newspaper and its editor worked closely with the TTMA to publish negative news stories from across the country concerning organized labor, and *Dalton Daily Citizen* editor Mark Pace editorialized extensively against union organization. The editor of the *Calhoun Times* followed the management line as well, but another respectable voice was raised in Gordon County.[44]

J. Roy McGinty, editor emeritus of the *Calhoun Times* and former editor of the *Chatsworth Times* (a weekly paper in neighboring Murray County), wrote a weekly column for the Calhoun paper. The venerable McGinty was, by the early 1960s, a thirty-year veteran of covering community affairs in the smaller towns surrounding Dalton. An old New Dealer, McGinty had served as a panel member and arbitrator on the War Labor Board during World War II. McGinty was troubled by the intervention of the chamber of commerce in the Dixie Belle election campaign. In the same *Calhoun Times* issue in which editor James Hobgood declared the paper's opposition to TWUA representation for Dixie Belle workers, McGinty took issue with his old employers and the chamber of commerce. His column for November 15, 1962, was titled "Declines to Advise Textile

Employees." McGinty commented that "employees of Dixie Belle Mills have had too much unsolicited advice already," and he had "no intention of adding to the plethora." The venerable editor did, however, have "some comments to make, for whatever they may be worth, since the upcoming Nov. 21 NLRB election has set off such a regrettable flare of acrimonious controversy."[45]

McGinty reminded his readers that workers had certain rights under the law, including the right to collective bargaining if they chose. McGinty went on to criticize the "tone" of the advertising campaign on both sides of the issue. He held that it was "especially regrettable" that the chamber of commerce had seen fit to launch "an attack on unionism in general, equating unionism with the destruction of industry, legal strikes with criminal violence." McGinty criticized the chamber for taking sides in "an issue between a local textile mill and its employees." This "intrusion" would "inevitably cripple" the organization as "an effective instrument of community service."[46]

McGinty moved on to the larger issue facing the Dalton industrial district. "There is a choice which this community—and all Northwest Georgia—must make, and which it seems unwilling to face." He argued that "if we want to build an industrial empire in this section, we may as well make up our minds right now to accept organized labor as an attendant circumstance." The longtime observer of northwest Georgia told his readers that "concentrations of industrial power produce concentrations of labor power," and he argued that organized labor was a necessity as a counterbalancing force to organized capital: "We can't have one without the other and remain the free people that we are."[47]

McGinty's column conferred a kind of official sanction on the TWUA. The column neutralized the effect of the official editorial stance of the paper, announced in the same issue (on the same page). In fact, the editor emeritus received letters in the next few weeks that made it apparent that many in the community believed that the paper itself shared McGinty's views on labor, though editor James Hobgood clearly did not. From a tactical point of view, McGinty's words gave substantial aid to union organizers. Dixie Belle employees recalled the column more than thirty years later as a critical turning point in the campaign.[48] McGinty, a familiar, well-respected grandfatherly figure, legitimated the union struggle.

Despite the TTMA, Dalton Booster, and Gordon County Chamber of Commerce campaigns, the TWUA scored a major success in November 1962 when workers at Dixie Belle voted 376–188 in favor of union representation. The union's strategy of targeting a mill outside Dalton, slightly farther away from the day-to-day influence of the TTMA, had paid off. The TWUA also benefited from what apparently had been a particularly oppressive management regime at Dixie Belle extending back to the mid-1950s. Dixie Belle workers contended that management had also engaged in retaliation after the TWUA's loss at Bell Industries (including Dixie Belle) in 1956, creating bitter memories that influenced the second vote.[49]

The difficult matter of negotiating a contract remained. Negotiations were delayed while the company appealed the NLRB's certification election results. TWUA officials claimed that the appeal was frivolous and requested that negotiations begin as early as February 1963. Bell Industries officials and company lawyers held firm, refusing to open negotiations until the NLRB ruled on the appeal. The agency ruled against the company on April 1, 1963.[50] Union leaders expected Bell Industries to remain defiant and try to surrender as little as possible in the contract. Dixie Belle management announced early in 1963 that some two hundred jobs at the Calhoun plant would be eliminated as the company consolidated many of its operations. The timing appeared to indicate that a message about job security was being sent to workers in "Tuftland."

TWUA officials debated alternative strategies for dealing with the Dixie Belle situation. This internal debate reflected the difficulties generally faced by organized labor in southern textiles. Edward Wynne, a national union official, advocated a strike. In a confidential memorandum for union president William Pollock, Wynne acknowledged the dangers inherent in a southern strike. "A strike at Dixie Belle . . . may end in a serious defeat." In virtually all of TWUA's southern strikes, "employers have been able to get large numbers of scabs to cross our picket lines." Southern textile manufacturers had also been successful in securing the cooperation of other employers to maintain production. These other employers had "either sent workers in to help operate the struck mill" or had done work on a "sub-contracted" basis. The local union would have difficulty winning a strike under such conditions. Beyond the immediate danger of losing the strike at Dixie Belle, a failed strike might doom further organizational efforts in the Dalton area. Southern newspapers traditionally gave "enormous play to strikes," and "any strike defeat which we suffer at Dixie Belle would be broadcast throughout the South." [51]

Wynne argued that despite all these dangers, a strike was still a rational alternative. He noted that there was a "reasonable chance" that other carpet manufacturers would not effectively cooperate with Dixie Belle. This was "the busiest season" for tufted carpet makers, and mills that cooperated with Dixie Belle "might well diminish their own production and profit" by doing extensive subcontracting. Wynne observed that carpet manufacturers had cooperated effectively in the past against the unions, but "their efforts so far have not been very costly to them." The tufted carpet industry was not nearly so tightly organized as the airlines or railroads, industries that had typically cooperated most successfully during strikes. "The coordination and sacrifices necessary to fight a strike" would represent a "far greater strain" than anything previously faced by the industry. Dixie Belle was making money, according to recent financial reports, and could afford to pay greater increases. [52]

A successful strike at Dixie Belle could "have very helpful effects" on the TWUA's overall tufted campaign. Wynne argued that tufted carpet workers were interested in the union. If the TWUA could "win a contract that is significantly better than industry rates," the union would enhance its position among other workers in the area. Wynne also pointed out that a strike in this situation could be classified as an unfair labor practice action—that is, the company had refused to bargain in good faith—and striking workers would be eligible for back pay. Scab workers would be subject to discharge as soon as the strike was settled. These factors might make success more likely. [53]

The TWUA's membership in the northern states had been declining for years. The union's "only hope of long-range survival," according to Wynne, was "to promote organization among textile workers in the Southeast." The TWUA could expect to win more elections in the future, "but unless we are able to get decent contracts, these victories will be self-defeating." The TWUA would develop a reputation as a union that could win elections but not contracts. In the long run, that reputation would destroy the union. Wynne predicted that employers could adopt the strategy of "not fighting us during organizing campaigns—but merely refusing to give us decent contract offers if we win." If the TWUA did not strike at Dixie Belle and accepted a less-than-spectacular contract, Wynne warned, "we can be sure that employers will not hesitate to give us a label for ineffectuality." The strike would be a risky proposition, but Wynne maintained that it was a risk worth taking.[54]

Dixie Belle's local workers apparently agreed with Wynne's assessment. They met on April 7 and threatened to strike unless management agreed to open negotiations within two weeks. TWUA organizers had charged during the campaign that Dixie Belle's wages and benefits were fifty cents per hour too low, implying that this might form the basis for opening demands. Local workers took such promises seriously.[55]

Others among TWUA's top brass were more cautious. TWUA leaders such as Solomon Barkin and Paul Swaity resisted the call for a strike. They cautioned that the union had invested sixteen months and almost $120,000 in the Dalton-area campaign by the end of March 1963. "The only success . . . so far has been the winning of the NLRB election at this Dixie Belle plant," Barkin and Swaity concluded. Southern textile strikes had traditionally been marked failures. If a strike was called, it would have to be an unfair labor practices strike to have any chance of success, for reasons summarized by Wynne. Such a strike could be called off in a few weeks if prospects for success diminished, and workers would be reinstated quickly. Such a strike depended on the local workers themselves. An unfair labor practice strike "would mean that we must have a discipline where the workers would take our advice and not revolt." If the workers refused to go back to work when the national office decided to call off the strike, the results could be disastrous. Such revolts among the locals were not uncommon in southern organizing situations.[56]

The risks in such a strike outweighed the possible gains in the eyes of a majority of TWUA national leaders. If the union engaged in an unsuccessful strike, "it means that our organizing in Calhoun and Dalton will be fruitless, and we may as well fold up our tent and move on to some other place." The leadership decided that it "may be wiser to play along in the hopes that we can win some elections in other plants in this region before taking any drastic action." A strike would encourage the tufted carpet

companies "to band together and help Dixie Belle, economically and otherwise, to defeat the Union." TWUA leaders feared doing anything that
might encourage more effective organization among carpet mills.[57]

TWUA leaders decided to "play along." On June 10, 1963, Local 1592
TWUA approved a contract with Dixie Belle management. Dixie Belle
workers got an average 5.5 percent pay increase, or about eight cents per
hour on the average hourly wage of $1.48. Local 1592 also secured sev-
eral paid holidays (a first for Dixie Belle workers), time-and-a-half pay for
working holidays, and increased health benefits. The union compromised
on the issue of seniority and control over promotion. The contract recognized management's ultimate right to make key personnel decisions, requiring only that seniority be taken into account. Although all permanent
vacancies had to be filled from a list of "qualified" applicants on the basis
of seniority, the company retained "the right to make the determination
of qualifications for any job." If the local union objected to a management decision, a grievance could be filed, but "the burden of proving that
the Company's determination was discriminatory or inherently wrong"
rested "at all times" with the union. The low level of the wage increase
and the union's lack of control over hiring and promotions proved to be
public relations problems for the TWUA in the area.[58]

The union's twin victories at Dixie Belle—the election win and the signing of the contract—drew interest from the media in Atlanta. WSB-TV,
an Atlanta television station, produced a thirty-minute documentary on
the labor situation in Calhoun. The program, "A Foot in the Door," narrated by WSB reporter Fred Briggs, aired on July 9, 1963. Dixie Belle officials refused comment, as did other companies in the area, fearing unfair labor practice charges as a result of any perceived antiunion comment,
Briggs noted at the outset. This appears strange given the behavior of several companies and the TTMA during the struggle, but more on that below. Briggs interviewed members of Calhoun's chamber of commerce and
several workers. He gave viewers a look inside the organizing campaign.
Dixie Belle had been an attractive target because of its location in Calhoun. One of Calhoun's largest employers was Lockheed, the Marietta
aerospace giant. Workers in Calhoun certainly wanted higher wages and
benefits. Whether the union could deliver substantial gains for Dixie Belle

workers, though, was an open question. Briggs noted that "every town or community that has a tufted textile mill" would be watching the Dixie Belle situation closely.[59]

The TWUA hoped that achieving a contract at Dixie Belle without a strike would improve the union's image and make the prospect of signing a union card less frightening to carpet mill workers. Some union officials had feared that a strike might provide the galvanizing incident that would lead to greater cooperation among mill owners. As it happened, the election victory and resulting contract at Dixie Belle served that purpose as well, for in the aftermath of the Dixie Belle election, the mill owners organized more effectively than ever before.

A few days before the election at Dixie Belle, the trade association held its interim meeting. TTMA president I. V. Chandler outlined other industry accomplishments and highlights of the previous year and then turned to the ongoing union campaign in the Dalton district. "The tufting industry, and in particular the manufacturers in this area, faces one of its gravest, most serious threats today" in the form of the TWUA's "drive to unionize the industry." Chandler issued a stern warning to his colleagues and competitors:

> As textile mills over the country continue to close—and organized mills operate under a serious handicap—the union continues to lose members and dues. The tufting industry would be a big prize [for TWUA].
>
> Union success in this tufting area would mean the beginning of the end for this area's dominance in tufted production. Employment and production would decline in the Dalton-Chattanooga area as it increased elsewhere. Our advantages of experience, concentration and nearby service industries would be helpful for a short period, but would not be sufficient to enable a unionized industry to compete with large non-union plants in other areas. The implications for small and medium-size manufacturers are particularly serious.

Chandler reiterated the main theme of the antiunion campaign: unionization would lead to the decline of the tufting industry and economic ruin for the Dalton district.[60]

The union had gotten "a foot in the door" in the Dalton district. TWUA leaders hoped that this island of unionism in tufted carpet manufacture could spread its influence gradually and lead workers in the area toward organization. As the union considered ways to use the Dixie Belle example, carpet mill managers began to organize even more vigorously for a renewed antiunion effort. In the aftermath of the Dixie Belle contract, the metaphorical door to union organization, wedged open ever so slightly by the TWUA in 1963, was slammed shut by a well-organized management campaign.

A World of Opportunity within the Tufting Empire

The Tufted Textile Manufacturers Association intensified its efforts to organize mill owners and managers after the union victory at Dixie Belle. Smaller firms responded to the perceived threat of union organization by joining the TTMA and adopting new strategies advocated by the association's general counsel, Frank Constangy. As management shaped new policies to try to prevent workers from organizing more mills in the region, mill hands at Dixie Belle struggled to build an effective union. Even though Local 1592 eventually vanished with the closure of the mill in the 1970s, the existence of a union in a carpet mill in the Dalton district affected the lives of workers beyond Dixie Belle.

The Tufted Textile Manufacturers Association held a mass meeting of owners and managers on July 16, 1963, to discuss the Dixie Belle contract and the industry's response. TTMA executive vice president R. E. Hamilton invited the entire TTMA membership as well as a large number of nonmember tufters to this meeting. He was disappointed that only about a third of the nonmembers responded. Apparently, many smaller manufacturers were not convinced that the TTMA could help them with labor problems. Hamilton chided these mavericks for their reluctance to join the trade association: "We do still have some people in tufting who think that what the rest of the industry does—what you folks do—has no effect upon them and that they can operate anyway they like."

Hamilton then criticized many in the audience for keeping wages too low and engaging in arbitrary personnel practices. "We have too many people who assume that only a few large, major concerns are paying good wages, paid holidays, paid vacations, etc." Hamilton cited the TWUA's charge that the average wage in the tufted industry was around $1.40, noting that while it was in the union's interest to minimize the figure, it was not far from the mark. He appealed to those in the room who paid less than the industry average to boost wages. Hamilton also urged managers to cultivate better relations with employees.[1]

Hamilton then turned the meeting over to Frank Constangy and Lovic Brooks. Constangy and Brooks were Atlanta lawyers who served as counsel to the TTMA and several companies on labor matters. Constangy had substantial experience in southern textile labor relations. Constangy and Brooks had also represented Dixie Belle in its contract negotiations with the TWUA. They came to Dalton to explain the Dixie Belle contract to the rest of the industry and recommend policies designed to keep the union from expanding beyond the Calhoun mill.

Constangy told the assembled owners and managers that the tufted textile environment had changed dramatically in the preceding few months. The companies had "lost one of their major arguments—namely, that TWUA could never get a contract in the tufted industry without a strike." The union had done that. The TWUA's strategy of playing along with management had worked to that extent. The resulting contract, however, had been much weaker than the TWUA had promised during the organizing campaign. This gave the companies a new argument: "that the TWUA's promises are not what they say they are because when it comes time to deliver, they not only get considerably less than what they promised, but in the end the people don't get [any of the things] that they committed themselves to the union to get changed." [2]

"The Dixie Belle contract was painfully and painstakingly negotiated," Constangy noted. The contract "was negotiated," he admitted, "with the realization that when a union is certified you've got to sit down and at least go through the motion of bargaining in good faith. When the union makes demands, you've got to make counter-proposals. Unfortunately, when they accept your counter-proposals, you can't back out of them." Constangy referred to the TWUA's acceptance of contract terms that the company believed were unacceptable to the union. He did not quite say that the company had hoped to provoke a strike, but he allowed that impression to be drawn from his comments. The contract "was designed by management . . . to give the fullest possible freedom of action to the company." Constangy went on to bemoan the loss of managerial freedom inherent in any union contract, but he clearly believed that the TWUA had surrendered control over the workplace to Dixie Belle management. Just after the election, Dixie Belle announced the elimination of certain operations at the plant, with a consequent loss of two hundred jobs. The TWUA protested and promised to get those jobs back, but the company held firm. Constangy recalled that he had participated in numerous contract negotiations over the years, and "if anybody has devised a stronger management rights clause and a greater freedom of action in terms of the elimination of jobs than we got at Dixie Belle I haven't seen it." The company won the right to eliminate jobs at management's discretion, with the union merely winning the right to be notified. [3]

Constangy lectured the tufted textile executives on rudimentary personnel policies. The content of Constangy's remarks and his familiarity with the industry give valuable hints at the nature of labor relations in the carpet industry. Constangy wanted to point out a few elements of the contract "because these are not things Dixie Belle gave away because it was soft-headed or soft-hearted or under the gun." These were policies "that are inherent in any decent relationship between management and its people." Managers of unorganized plants simply had no choice but to adopt these policies "in order to avoid the union [being voted in] simply [to bring] some semblance of order out of the chaos of your industrial relations." Constangy advocated an "industrial relations" strategy similar to that developed by Elton Mayo in the 1940s. Mayo formulated the "human relations" concept of industrial relations, which emphasized the development of better relations between managers and workers as a substitute for unions.[4]

Constangy explained to the carpet executives that "an employee is entitled to know what his weekly period of work is, what his daily period of work is. . . . He is entitled to know when he's going to get paid, and he's entitled to know what his rate of pay is." Employees were also entitled to know the company's procedures for laying off and calling back workers. A worker also had a right to know what his or her specific job assignments were and what opportunities he or she had for moving up into better jobs. Constangy explained that companies should have some rational procedure for determining promotions and job transfers, when a training period has come to an end, what the procedures are for getting a leave of absence, what types of conduct will receive what sort of disciplinary action—a laundry list of "human resources"–oriented personnel practices. The amount of time that Constangy spent explaining the importance of these policies indicated that carpet mill management in the Dalton area was still operating in a crude, informal fashion. Constangy explained the Dixie Belle contract provisions relating to each of these points, implicitly urging owners to adopt modified bidding and seniority practices for layoffs, job transfers, and promotions.[5]

The union had promised, according to Constangy, to produce six paid holidays in the first contract. Local 1592 actually got only three. Constangy strongly implied that many, if not a majority of, local companies still had no paid holidays. The Dixie Belle contract also provided for two (later three) "time-and-a-half" days. On these days, if the plant shut down, no one would be paid; but if the plant was working, employees would receive time-and-a-half pay. The "question of holiday pay has become a pretty serious problem" in the industry. "Up to now," the Atlanta lawyer noted, "the pattern has been in some of the plants in this industry to give a holiday simply by shutting the plant and not letting the people work and having a day off without any pay so that the employee loses by virtue of a holiday." Constangy admitted that, from a management perspective, this was "a good system," but "it simply doesn't work any more." With the specter of union organization looming over the industry now, he told the manufacturers that "it behooves all of you, large and small, to review your situation and begin a program with paid holidays at the plants." Companies could spread out the holidays to minimize the cost "and still leave the union nothing in that field to organize with—if you please."[6]

The carpet industry was highly seasonal and fluctuated widely. Workers often complained about irregular work. It was not uncommon for a worker to report to a mill only to be told that there was no work for him that day. This was the sort of complaint on which the TWUA could capitalize. The Dixie Belle contract required the company to notify employees at least two hours before the beginning of their shift if they were not needed. If employees reported for work and were told, without notice, that they were not needed, they would be guaranteed four hours' work. Constangy told his audience that this was a fair policy and one that should be adopted by the entire industry without a union contract. "There's nothing unreasonable about an employer either telling people the day before that they don't need them the next day, or notifying them before they leave home to come to work," he argued. If workers were not notified, owners should "provide them enough work to have made it worthwhile to make the trip to the job." This policy could be implemented, Constangy maintained, at little or no cost, "yet the employees get a feeling of security out of that sort of provision." Constangy extolled the cost-effectiveness of such a policy. A notification policy had "paper value," but the "monetary cost is little."[7]

Many of the benefits that the union managed to secure were not impressive to observers outside the carpet industry. It is clear, however, that such procedures and practices were nowhere near universal in the Dalton industry. The carpet industry reflected the character of its management. Most operators were flying by the seat of their pants, making crucial decisions on the run. There was little formal planning in many companies, and personnel practices were often arbitrary and nonrational, based on the whim of an owner or supervisor.

The key component of the Dixie Belle contract was, of course, the wage clause. Company management agreed to a general 5.5 percent increase, effective June 10. Constangy informed his listeners that this brought the plant minimum up to $1.275 per hour. This was "a cent and a half lower than [Bell Industries'] Belcraft plant." Dixie Belle's wage scales were complicated. For "big machines," the company's wages were generally above the industry average. "In so far as everything below the big machine is concerned, the Dixie Belle wages are literally lower than prevailing wages in the area," Constangy acknowledged. Before the contract, overall average wages at Dixie Belle amounted to $1.375; the contract raised that to $1.45. This was comparable to a Dalton-area average of $1.48–1.50. He also pointed out that there were "an awful lot of plants" in the Dalton-Calhoun area in which wage rates were "substantially lower than those in effect at Dixie Belle." Constangy urged employers to take a hard look at their wage scales. The Dixie Belle "rates are low, even with the wage increase," he added, "and if the Dixie Belle rates are higher than yours, and if you aren't aware that you're in trouble, you will soon be aware because the union is checking." [8]

Constangy summarized the union's problem in accepting a contract with so few real gains for workers. The TWUA had planned to use the contract at Dixie Belle as an organizing tool. This plan "just fell flat on its face." The union had been "caught in a dilemma." The TWUA did not want to strike, for that would only confirm the worst charges leveled by management. As mentioned above, a strike would have been a great risk. But the TWUA simply "could not get a contract without a strike" except by "agreeing to these freedom of action provisions" on which the company insisted. All this made good fodder for antiunion campaigns.

The veteran union buster urged a preemptive strike against the union movement in Dalton. Once an election was set, employers faced numerous restrictions. In the current period, no elections were set. Organizers were trying to get workers to sign cards, but management was free to campaign against the signing of union cards with few restrictions. Owners should take the offensive in the wake of the Dixie Belle contract, Constangy maintained. "We should open an anti-union campaign in virtually every plant in three or four quick steps." First, the labor lawyer asserted, "we better be sure our house is in order," meaning that the policies and procedures he had outlined should be adopted. Next, supervisors should explain these policies and procedures to the workers. Then management should explain to workers "where these procedures are better than those that the union's been able to accomplish." Finally, management should remind workers that "while the union is around trying to get you to sign a card, the union has demonstrated that it can't do anything better for you, but it has demonstrated that it would like for you to sign that card for $4 a month."

TTMA members had already been practicing what Constangy preached at this meeting. In early March 1963, several large mills had announced a general 5.5 percent wage increase. By late spring 1963, the TTMA's membership had swelled to more than two hundred, an increase of thirty-three new members in an eight-month period beginning in the summer of 1962, when the TWUA organizing drive began to heat up. This increase was touted by the trade organization as the "greatest growth in membership in any similar period since the Association was founded." The new members included a substantial number of smaller mills.[9]

The TWUA attempted to exploit the victory at Dixie Belle immediately following the signing of the contract. The union began distributing leaflets touting the organizational success just down the road in Calhoun. Organizers proudly announced that Dixie Belle workers in Local 1592 would "lead the way to a better day in tufted textiles." New TWUA pamphlets also explained the legal right to organize to Dalton workers and detailed a list of unfair labor tactics that management could not legitimately use. The union reminded workers that plant management could not threaten to close a plant in the event of a union victory, fire pro-union workers, or threaten to reduce benefits in case of union organization.[10]

The union was ultimately unable to turn Dixie Belle into a beachhead of any sort. Management resistance stiffened in the wake of the example of Dixie Belle. As Frank Constangy had suspected, carpet manufacturers in the Dalton area felt less sense of urgency as long as no plants were organized. Once the union got "a foot in the door," owners and managers paid much closer attention to the advice of Constangy and the TTMA's Industrial Relations Club.

The Collins and Aikman company, located in Dalton, became the main battleground for the TWUA's continuing efforts. The union had lost an election at Collins and Aikman in 1962, before the Dixie Belle victory. Collins and Aikman operated a small tufting plant in Dalton. The TWUA targeted Collins and Aikman during the 1962 campaign and petitioned for an election in October 1962. On October 11, a majority of the plant's employees voted against union representation. Collins and Aikman managers had, however, solicited antiunion employees to sign an antiunion petition. The company's plant manager also helped draft the antiunion petition. The National Labor Relations Board found that company officials drafted a written promise to operate the plant on the basis of seniority (especially regarding layoffs) if enough workers signed the antiunion petition. The board found that the company had offered the seniority plan as an inducement to lure workers away from the TWUA.[11]

Collins and Aikman sent a letter to all company employees on October 3, 1962. The letter questioned whether the TWUA could secure greater benefits for Dalton workers than they were already receiving, and it rejected TWUA claims that the union could improve job security. Appended to the letter was a list of nineteen southern textile plants under TWUA contracts that had been closed. All this was permitted under federal regulations, the NLRB determined, but the company went further in this communication. The Collins and Aikman general manager wrote to employees, "You and I have come a long way together. What we have, we got for ourselves. Our record proves that we have better job security than any of the TWUA members at any of the plants named on the attached list. Don't gamble your future security and progress by voting for the TWUA." The board ruled that this last appeal contained "an implied threat of loss of employment" in the event of a TWUA victory and was therefore an unfair labor practice.[12]

Collins and Aikman also used Dalton Boosters' literature in the antiunion campaign. On October 10, company officials distributed to employees a section of the local newspaper that contained a "prominent notice over the signature 'Dalton Boosters.'" In large type, the leaflet declared, "HERE'S WHAT CLOSING ONE MILL DOES FOR A COUNTY," with the phrase "CLOSING ONE MILL" in even larger type. The leaflet warned workers of the dire economic consequences that had followed in nearby Rossville, Georgia, when the Peerless Woolen Mill, a TWUA plant, closed in 1961. The NLRB determined that the wording and timing of the distribution of this leaflet were "calculated to confirm the impression conveyed by the October 3 letter, that a union victory at the polls would lead to the closing of [Collins and Aikman's] Dalton plant."[13] The remedy imposed by the NLRB consisted of forcing the company to cease and desist from all similar conduct in the future and ordering the company to post an apology to its employees. The NLRB refused to order a certification of the union without an election (based on the TWUA having secured a majority of employee signatures on union cards) but later ordered another election.[14]

The second Collins and Aikman election provided the TTMA with an opportunity to try some of the new methods advocated by Constangy, especially the use of the Dixie Belle contract as an example of the TWUA's inability to deliver on its promises. This incident also illustrated the importance of the Dalton Boosters in the antiunion campaign. The company reacted with similar tactics in the second election campaign. During the second election, in September 1963, Collins and Aikman was able to make use of the Dixie Belle contract. The company posted notices comparing pre–Dixie Belle TWUA promises with the actual contract provisions. The leaflets were composed by the Tufted Textile Manufacturers Association and sent out with the TTMA's "Labor Bulletin." Above all, the TTMA claimed, Dixie Belle management had retained "full rights to . . . plan, direct, control, increase, decrease, or *discontinue operations in whole or in part* . . . , to demote, or impose discipline *up to and including discharge* upon any employee . . . , to *move, close, sell, or liquidate* the plant or plants in whole or in part" (emphasis in the original). The trade association reminded workers that Dixie Belle employees had lost some two hundred jobs between the election and the signing of a contract in Calhoun.[15]

Collins and Aikman workers voted 2–1 against union representation on September 6, 1963. The margin was larger than in the first election. The TTMA announced the election results in its September 9 newsletter and wasted no time in drawing a connection with the "failed" contract at Dixie Belle. "The union's 'great victory' and the three-year contract at Dixie Belle in Calhoun is turning out to be considerably less than an asset" in the Dalton organizing campaign, the TTMA told its members. "The surest way for TWUA to lose an election," the TTMA concluded, "is to base its campaign on 'what the union got in the Dixie Belle contract.'"[16] The TWUA organizing drive lost all momentum and never recovered.

The TTMA's Industrial Relations Club continued to instruct member firms in personnel management even after the overt organizing drive by the TWUA collapsed in the wake of the union's Pyrrhic victory at Dixie Belle. The IRC held several meetings each year and in 1968 began a series of annual industrial relations institutes. The IRC spent most of its energy extolling the virtues of enlightened, modern personnel management policies; encouraging the adoption of such policies by members; and instructing members on how to avoid unionization. The Industrial Relations Club advocated a strategy that was often called "personnel preventive maintenance."

The strategy pursued by the TTMA-IRC was summarized by Georgia State College professor Michael Mescon in an address to the organization in October 1964. Mescon emphasized the value of professional training for supervisory personnel. He maintained that the labor movement in the United States had "grown and prospered . . . primarily due to management mistakes." With perfect "20-20 hindsight," many companies in the 1950s had belatedly adopted more liberal fringe benefit packages—insurance programs, pension plans, paid vacations—and instituted rational rules regarding hiring practices, employee termination, promotion, pay raises, and other matters. These programs constituted a part of the personnel preventive maintenance agenda but would not work in the absence of well-trained managers. Management personnel, from top-level executives to line supervisors, needed training. At this same conference, other speakers elaborated on Mescon's call for better management. An industrial psychologist lectured the IRC membership on communication and its importance in management. Another expert detailed the benefits of human relations training for managers.[17]

The IRC also held periodic briefings on the status of organized labor in the carpet industry, usually conducted by Lovic Brooks, an associate of Frank Constangy. These "general discussion[s] of the labor situation in the North Georgia area" were considered to be "matters of the greatest importance" by IRC leadership. At such meetings, the IRC distributed materials from the National Association of Manufacturers and other sources that suggested strategies for discouraging union activity among employees. The organization compiled a list of questions commonly asked of supervisors by workers in the early stages of a union-organizing campaign and suggested standard responses. This list was circulated as "Aids to Supervisors." Supervisors were encouraged to explain in simple terms the workings of the "modern exchange economy," which mitigated against any true job security. While reminding managers that it was illegal to threaten specific job losses in the event of a successful union campaign, the "Aids to Supervisors" document encouraged supervisors to answer questions about potential plant closings forcefully. "The union might force the company to close down this plant," supervisors were asked to reply, "if its demands are such that this would become an unprofitable operation." Although managers could not make specific threats, the IRC told its members that it was acceptable (indeed, desirable) to tell employees that they knew "of other companies who have at times been forced to shut down plants because the rising demands of labor eliminated any possible profit." [18]

Efforts such as this fit well with individual company "educational" efforts, such as the Barwick company newsletter. The monthly *B-Line News* typically contained notices of births and marriages among Barwick workers, safety tips, humorous homespun stories, and a few words from a local clergyman. On the front page of the newsletter, the central story most often concerned labor-management relations. "WE'RE BUILDING OUR JOB SECURITY THROUGH INDIVIDUAL EFFORT," editor Don Sayer proclaimed in a typical headline from October 1963. Sayer explained in the accompanying editorial that building job security involved much more than raw materials, plant, and equipment. It was "the individual effort of each employee" that made the difference, that separated one carpet mill from another. Not only were all carpet mills in competition with one another, Sayer argued, but "each employee of Barwick Mills is engaged in a personal contest for job security. You are competing with every worker in the tufted industry." Sayer and Barwick offered individual achievement as an alternative to the collective security promised by the union.[19]

The *B-Line News* also tried to explain the concept of risk in a capitalist economy. The *News* often ran brief fables like the story of the oyster and the eagle. When God made the oyster, according to the story, he gave him "absolute economic and social security"; all the oyster had to do was open his shell and "food rushes in for him." When God made the eagle, on the other hand, he told him that "the blue sky is your limit. Build your own house." The eagle proceeded to build his house on high mountain tops, "where storms threaten every day." The eagle had to fly "through miles of rain and snow and wind" to find his food. "The eagle, not the oyster, is the emblem of America," the story patriotically concluded.[20]

Other firms also published newsletters with similar messages. Belcraft, the parent company of the Dixie Belle carpet and rug mill in Calhoun, began a newsletter before most other area firms. The company began publishing the *Bell Chimes* in 1955, coinciding with the intense union effort of the mid-1950s described by Flamming. In a typical "economic education" piece from 1961, the newsletter identified profits as "the driving force in the making of jobs." The publication cautioned workers that it was "a serious error" to believe "that declining profits are a result of business slowdowns instead of a cause." The "true function of profits" was "to act as the driving force in the expansion of business and employment." In order to safeguard profits, the newsletter concluded, "increases in the unit cost of production must be avoided." If workers disregarded this fundamental economic law and demanded higher wages, it would be "a mistake which could be fatal to our economic system."[21]

The Barwick newsletter also allotted a great deal of space to stories about the company's unique educational benefits. The *B-Line News* often carried front-page pictures of Barwick scholarship recipients and ran descriptions of the students inside. In September 1963, the newsletter announced that fifty-six students—enrolled in twenty-nine colleges in six different states—would participate in the program that year. Since 1955, more than three hundred students had received Barwick scholarships totaling more than $150,000. The newsletter left no room for employees to doubt the value of this program and the company's general concern for employee well-being: "This is but another instance of our company's interest in the welfare of its employees."[22]

The descriptions of those enrolled in the Barwick scholarship program offer a glimpse into the potential of such a program. Recipients included men like James R. Pope, "a former employee in the Roll-Up Department" in Lafayette. In 1963, Pope entered his fourth consecutive year on a Barwick scholarship, studying veterinary medicine at the University of Georgia. After completing the twelve consecutive month employment requirement, James Parker, from "the Dalton Tufting Department," enrolled at McKenzie College as a first-time scholarship recipient. Glenda

Kay Loughridge, daughter of a Barwick tufting department employee at the Lafayette mill, received a scholarship in 1963 for the first time as well.[23] These scholarships provided educational opportunities for people in an area where those chances had long been scarce.

In the midst of these management efforts, the workers of Local 1592 at Dixie Belle continued to build their local union and negotiate with management for almost twenty years after 1962. If the union played a role in shutting down the plant, it certainly was a slow process. The TWUA, however, was unable to build on the success at Dixie Belle for further organizing gains. The initial contract itself was one factor. Relations between the international union and Local 1592 also contributed to the negative perception of the TWUA among local workers. When the TWUA decided not to strike for a more favorable contract in 1963, the directive to settle at any cost went against the majority sentiment among local workers. Many Dixie Belle workers must have felt vaguely cheated by their own union when the contract failed to provide a more substantial wage increase and greater worker control over personnel practices.

The early days of Local 1592 provide a glimpse into the workings of a tufted carpet mill and into the evolution of a union among people inexperienced with labor organization. In the first two years of the union at Dixie Belle, factional infighting plagued Local 1592. Many workers also apparently were convinced that the existence of a union meant that workers now had some control over the workplace; this mistaken notion led to several disappointing grievance cases.

Edith Langley, the recording secretary of Local 1592, became the center of the most serious factional split within the union. In August 1964, Langley complained to TWUA president William Pollock about her treatment by some officers of Local 1592. Langley had filed several grievances involving suspensions from work for "horseplay," missing work, and being passed over for promotions by less experienced workers. She contended that the leadership of the local union had "passed on," or chosen not to pursue, her grievances in meetings with company management. Langley charged that grievances filed by other workers were handled more seriously by the union. Langley claimed that the local's vice president was fired for not coming to work one night. Following his dismissal, Langley asserted that Michael Botelho, the TWUA's regional director in the area, threatened to "pull our local out on strike to get his [the vice president's] job back." Langley was later fired for missing work, but the local union chose not to take extraordinary actions on her behalf. Langley was now in deep trouble. "No one can get a job in this town," she complained to Pollock, "that has a toe-hold in the Union." She had bills to pay and children to feed. "Don't you think my job is as important as the Vice-President's?" she asked. Langley suspected that her gender was at least partially responsible for her fate. She speculated that male union officers had been "bought out toward my grievance because the company don't like for a woman to have a hand in anything." [24]

Langley's appeal led Pollock to question local union officials and Botelho. All of Langley's complaints were explained away, the national office chose not to intervene, and she remained unemployed. Langley wrote to Pollock again in October 1964 out of desperation. She charged that the present leadership of the union and the regional director resisted all attempts to take grievances to arbitration: "Local 1592 has never had a case [go to] arbitration and as long as we have our [current leadership] we will never." Invariably, Langley complained, "the grievance will be given to the company," unless it involved the union's top officers or their cronies. There is little evidence to dispute Langley's contention. Local 1592 in the first few years of its existence apparently took few or no grievances as far as the arbitration stage. This may have been part of the TWUA's strategy of developing an image as a responsible organization that would not make too many waves. If so, the rationale was lost on workers like Edith Langley: "Why is it we cannot have arbitration? Like our contract calls for? I am not the only one getting hurt." [25]

TWUA representative Paul Swaity went to Calhoun to check out Local 1592. Swaity found that the local was "split into two or three factions." The "most serious factional fight" had grown out of "the Edith Langley case and the Local's refusing to fight her case." Other splits followed from a fight for the office of local president and the general view among some members that the current president "was not servicing the members properly." [26] Swaity met with the membership of Local 1592 on November 29, 1964, to try to change the local's direction. At this meeting, Local 1592's members decided to hire a lawyer and pursue arbitration of the Langley case. Swaity also urged Local 1592 to become more active. Members should begin drawing up "a list of proposals for improving the contract at next negotiations"; consider establishing "a shop paper for information and education of members"; "investigate the feasibility of the local making use of the New York Joint Board Pharmacy so as to obtain drugs for its members at reduced rates"; and hold regular meetings.[27] The subjects of discussion at this meeting suggested that the TWUA had not done the best job of training workers in union leadership. The content of the discussion also hints at a deeper problem. Local 1592's members had not had much autonomy from the beginning. TWUA national leaders effectively took the decision about whether to strike for a better contract out of the hands of local members at the outset in 1963. It was a difficult proposition to ask these workers now to develop a sense of power and competence in directing union affairs.

Not all the grievances processed by Local 1592 were legitimate. The union may have been too conservative early on in pursuing grievances, but admittedly many grievances had little merit. One local union member complained to Pollock in January 1965 that he had been fired. He had "turned in a grievance." The union president had "without my consent [or] a word to the [grievance] committee just drop[ped] my grievance." This disgruntled worker appealed for help to the union's national office. William Pollock replied politely that there was nothing the union could do to help the man. TWUA representatives had informed Pollock that he was "discharged, charged with sleeping on the job." The local union had tried to negotiate with the company to get the man's job back, but the company refused. Consequently, "the membership of the Local voted by a ratio of 3 to 1 not to process your grievance through arbitration since there was not enough evidence to defeat the company's charge that you were sleeping on the job." Pollock advised the former Dixie Belle employee that there were "no further steps the union can take in your behalf."[28]

Dixie Belle Mills was sold to Fulton Industries in 1964. In 1970, a company called Concept Industries bought the mill and changed the subsidiary's name to Venture Carpets. Local 1592 continued to operate, retain and sign new members, and negotiate contracts throughout the ownership changes. Over time, Local 1592 gradually developed a collective sense of power after a rocky start. The membership of Local 1592 often engaged in wildcat strikes. The event that most often precipitated a wildcat strike was the dismissal or severe reprimanding of an employee. Jimmy Walraven, who later served as a TWUA area director, rose from the shop floor at Dixie Belle. Walraven recalled the first "unauthorized work stoppage" at Dixie Belle, about a year after the signing of the contract in April 1963. Walraven contended that management seemed to follow a strategy of trying to undermine the grievance process. Dixie Belle management consistently delayed and stalled in the grievance process, hoping the union would lose interest in grievances. Walraven was convinced that in the early days of the TWUA local in Calhoun, management hoped to show workers that the union could not really deliver on the promises it had made. This came to a head with the firing of John Roland.[29]

Roland was a popular, longtime Dixie Belle employee, about sixty years old. Walraven described Roland as an outgoing person who was always joking around. John Roland was well known throughout the plant as a good-humored man and a hardworking employee. With management's perceived frustration of the grievance process as background, a particularly unpopular supervisor decided to make an example of John Roland. Walraven could not recall what prompted the decision, but, on the spur of the moment, the supervisor fired Roland, an employee with more than ten years' service. In addition, the supervisor made a point of "leading him [Roland] by the arm from the shipping department in the front of the plant all the way to the parking lot in back," passing through nearly the entire length of the establishment. Roland and the supervisor were "jawing at one another" the entire time. Workers left their machines to watch in silence as Roland was publicly humiliated.[30]

The local union leadership did not call for a meeting, but Walraven, then a shop steward, assumed that a grievance would be filed. The next morning, a group of workers greeted Walraven at the plant gate as the first shift was coming to work. These workers were urging their fellows not to enter the plant. Thus began the first "unauthorized work stoppage" at Dixie Belle. The workers effectively shut down Dixie Belle's operations as most workers refused to cross the impromptu picket line. Of course, management protested to the TWUA's national leadership, and TWUA leaders sent telegrams to Local 1592 urging the membership to return to work and end this wildcat strike, which could have legal repercussions for the union. The workers held firm.

Dixie Belle's battle-hardened legal counsel, Frank Constangy, intervened at this point. Constangy was certainly no friend of the union, but he realized that the strike, legal or not, had to be settled soon to avoid serious losses for the company. Constangy negotiated with his own clients in management and a delegation of workers, including Jimmy Walraven. The shop steward recalled that workers and managers sat in separate rooms to avoid the appearance of real negotiations, with Constangy going from room to room carrying proposals and counterproposals. The contesting parties came to an informal agreement. The workers agreed to abandon the picket line and return to work at a specified time the following day. In exchange, management made verbal promises to treat the grievance process with greater respect and to allow John Roland to return to work. In actual practice, management improved only slightly, in Walraven's view, on the grievance process, but Mr. Roland got his job back.[31]

Walraven contended that this was typical of the frequent wildcat strikes at Dixie Belle/Venture. The TWUA national leadership may not have thought much of the small, isolated local in Calhoun, Georgia, but the workers themselves certainly developed a greater sense of autonomy and power. Walraven believed that management deliberately provoked such work stoppages periodically by trying to make examples of workers like John Roland. This was a mistake for the company, in Walraven's view, because the workers almost always won these conflicts. In most cases, Local 1592's members managed to protect the jobs of workers who they felt had been wrongly discharged or disciplined. Dixie Belle's workers challenged the unfettered rights of management to hire and fire in the tufted carpet industry and met with substantial success.[32]

The most serious of these wildcats occurred in 1972. The precise cause is unknown, but on February 23, 1972, Venture personnel director William O'Neill sent a telegram to TWUA international representative Jimmy Walraven protesting an "illegal work stoppage" that had begun the preceding day. The company claimed that officers of the local union were participating in the strike. O'Neill called on the international union to take "prompt actions to terminate" this wildcat strike.[33]

Walraven sent a telegram to the Venture union officers and to the union membership urging them to call off the strike and return to work. O'Neill did not consider this a sufficient response. He informed Walraven that the company was going to post a notice warning that all strikers should return to work immediately or be "subject to discipline including discharge."[34]

Walraven made further efforts to end the strike. He sent a telegram to Local 1592 president Raymond Roach. Walraven directed the officers of the local to "make every effort to stop this work stoppage by leading the workers back in if it is within your power." Walraven noted that Roach had already tried to return to work: "I understand that you and the Officers have tried to go in but have been turned away." Local 1592 officers had been unable to penetrate the picket lines.[35]

Venture management fired eleven workers in the aftermath of the dispute. Eleven others were suspended. All local union officers and stewards "received warnings." The specific background of this strike is unclear. In his preparation for a meeting with the membership of Local 1592 in early March 1972, Walraven prepared notes in which he referred to "the company's policy of harassment leading up the dispute." In the margins, Walraven inserted the names "Smith & Long." Perhaps these were employees who had been singled out for harassment by "management," at least in the eyes of Local 1592's members. Walraven and other union officials considered Venture's management practices to be arbitrary, capricious, and outdated. The local's papers, as well as interviews with union members, leave few clues as to the specific issues involved. Raymond Roach maintained that all the illegal strikes grew out of disputes with supervisors over treatment of workers. Arbitrary firings were the most durable source of these disputes.[36]

Shortly after the conclusion of the illegal strike, Walraven met with Local 1592 to propose changes in the local's structural relationship with the TWUA. Walraven urged the membership in Calhoun to join other TWUA locals in the regional "joint board," headquartered in Chattanooga. Membership in the joint board would mean raising dues, but Walraven pointed out the necessity for and advantages of the change. As late as March 1972, Local 1592 did not participate in state or national TWUA conferences or conventions. The small Calhoun local acted almost as an independent union. This left members greater freedom to engage in strikes that violated the union contract (the TWUA apparently paid little attention to Local 1592 by the early 1970s), but members also could count on little support from the national office. Walraven urged the members to

take a more active role in national union affairs. Walraven feared that Local 1592 would be overwhelmed if members did not make a stronger financial and organizational commitment. Carpet companies, including
Venture, had become much more "sophisticated in labor relations and
management" since the TWUA's victory at Dixie Belle in 1962. Carpet
mills "no longer have just 1 personnel worker," he told the Calhoun
union; "most have 3–4 or even 5, plus their high-priced attorneys." Carpet mill owners and their personnel managers no longer "isolate[d] themselves in several different offices," and they received "all their labor relations information from [the law firm of] Constangy and Powell."
Walraven told Local 1592 members that more than 80 percent of TWUA
locals belonged to joint boards. These locals had easier access to the
TWUA's legal defense fund and enjoyed greater support from the international union. The membership heeded Walraven's advice and voted to
join the TWUA's area joint board.[37] Walraven moved on to discuss the
union's contract with Venture Carpets, which was due to expire soon.
The union had only thirty-four days to give notice of contract termination. Walraven urged the union to move quickly to terminate the contract
and open negotiations for a new deal. Perhaps swayed by Walraven's assurances that joint board membership would strengthen the local and improve its bargaining position, Local 1592 voted to terminate the current
agreement.[38]

The union and the company entered into negotiations, which produced
little agreement. The negotiations broke down on June 15, and Local
1592 went out on strike. This was the first and only legal strike, involving the entire membership, conducted by the Calhoun union. The strike
dragged on for approximately one month before the two sides agreed to
end hostilities and sign a new contract. The local newspaper gave little
coverage to the union situation in Calhoun, the editors apparently hoping it would go away. TWUA records hold no clues as to the specific
events leading the workers to strike. Interviews with workers produced
no concrete details. Notes taken by Jimmy Walraven at a July meeting of
Local 1592, at which the union accepted the company's final contract
offer, give only a hint of the underlying tension that the strike evidenced.

Venture's final contract offer, dated July 21, 1972, was identical to
the company's offer of June 15, which had precipitated the strike. The

workers essentially accepted the economic offer that the company had been willing to accept a month earlier. The contract provisions included wage increases over a three-year period that would boost average rates by about 55 cents per hour at the end of the contract. This would bring average wages in the plant to around $2.60 per hour. Increases in insurance and an additional holiday represented a hidden gain of another 25 cents per hour, Walraven claimed.[39] Again, though, all this was included in the company's offer of June 15. Why did the union membership decide to strike, and why did they accept the offer later?

Walraven hinted at the roots of the unrest at Venture. After detailing the economic package, he continued, "But the strike was not over wages & benefits, it was over local management trying to be dictators." Walraven told Local 1592 that he had spoken with William O'Neill personally and had been "assured . . . that starting Monday, there was a new Venture Carpet to work at." Because the local had "made it so costly on the owners," Venture management had made several unprecedented promises, unprecedented at least for the South. The strike had led to scattered violence, with several union members facing legal charges. The company, Walraven noted, had signed a separate agreement stipulating that all workers participating in the strike could return to work. In addition, the company had agreed to drop all outstanding charges against union members and refrain from pressing any new charges in the future that might arise from the strike situation. Walraven admitted that there were times during a strike, this one included, "where the strikers must get tough to maintain their picket lines." In the South and other "right-to-work" states, this almost always led to the union having to accept that a number of workers would be dismissed when the strike ended. "We have beat this tradition," he announced to the membership.[40]

Walraven may have been simply trying to put the best face on a strike that failed to win any increase in material benefits. But perhaps the strike had been over other matters, as the earlier wildcat strikes had been over noneconomic matters. Dixie Belle workers, then Venture workers, consistently demanded and fought for greater control over their work environment and greater respect from management. Local 1592 rarely won grievances against the company that involved job promotions, filling job vacancies, or workload. The original contract, and those that followed, ceded substantial control over the workplace, including virtually the sole right to judge workers' qualifications, to management. Many of the details have been lost, but the consistent testimony of workers attests to the arbitrary nature of management practices in many carpet mills of the 1950s and 1960s. The concern expressed by Frank Constangy, the TTMA's chief antiunion legal gunslinger, in 1963 and the TTMA's continuing emphasis on improving members' management practices through the Industrial Relations Club lend credence to the basic perception of many carpet mill workers that they were often treated with less respect than they expected.

The workers also expressed some discontent with the TWUA in the aftermath of the 1972 strike. Many workers felt that Walraven had left the impression that joint board membership would mean unlimited strike relief funds and legal support. Many were dissatisfied with the level of support they received from the national union. Walraven reminded workers that the union could only pay those bills that had come after the strike started, and it could not help with those who had gotten behind in their payments before the strike. Apparently, several union members faced the repossession of their cars. Walraven tried to convince the membership that "strikes are not easy. Workers must suffer some economically." Walraven estimated that the joint board and the TWUA together had already spent more than thirty-one thousand dollars on the strike. Walraven reminded the workers that the union had made two commitments at the outset of the strike: "1) that all would be fed. 2) That bills which could not be put off, would be paid." So far, he noted, the union had kept these commitments. As a result of these commitments and the resolve of the workers, Walraven boldly asserted that "you have the wages and benefits to help organize the other workers here in this area." [41]

Despite these brave words, Local 1592 had no capacity to organize the rest of the tufted carpet industry in the Dalton area. TWUA national leaders had made crucial decisions early on that diminished the power of the Dixie Belle/Venture example. The TWUA had also counted too much on the example of stable, Dalton-area unions such as the Crown Mill local to provide an example. The only long-lasting textile unions in Dalton were those that had grown in the mill villages. The mill village provided a crucial community setting in which mutual bonds of respect, familiarity, and concern could foster collective action. Ironically, textile unions had worked best, in the long run, in precisely those environments that had been constructed to prevent labor organization. Carpet mill workers were quintessential commuters; most lived many miles from the mills. As a sociological study of the late 1970s found, most carpet mill workers in the Dalton area knew few or none of their neighbors and changed jobs frequently. Indeed, a survey of Whitfield County workers in the early 1990s found that more than 40 percent of those employed in the county commuted from other Georgia counties or Tennessee. There was little or no sense of community left among these workers.[42]

The increasing concentration of the tufted carpet industry in northwest Georgia also discouraged the evolution of a community in the workplace. In 1958, 92 establishments manufactured tufted carpets and rugs. By 1963 the number had almost doubled, to 181. One hundred and one of these establishments were located in Georgia, employing more than 12,000 production workers. The number of tufting establishments in Georgia rose to 132 in 1967 and climbed to 220 by 1972. A decade later, the numbers stood at 285 Georgia establishments, employing about 24,000 production workers.[43] This explosion in the number of tufting establishments matched the increasing demand for carpets. As tufted carpet sales set new records annually during the 1960s and early 1970s, new entrepreneurs entered the field in search of opportunity. The relatively low costs associated with entry into the tufting industry, combined with the almost complete absence of brand-name identification and a rapidly expanding market, inevitably led to an ever increasing number of firms, large and small. The expansion of carpet-manufacturing firms in a relatively small area produced a steady competition for experienced workers in the Dalton district.

The competition for workers was reflected in carpet industry turnover rates. The carpet industry's monthly quit rate began to diverge significantly from the average rate for durable goods manufacturing after 1961. The gap rose until the quit rate for carpet doubled that of all durable goods in the years 1971–73. A research report on personnel in the carpet industry prepared for the Wharton School succinctly summarized the situation in the Dalton district. "A large portion" of the carpet industry's "almost continual growth" since the early 1950s had been "concentrated in a small corner of northern Georgia, greatly magnifying its impact on personnel practices." From the management perspective, the labor situation in the Dalton area was "best characterized as undergoing severe shortages accompanied by a cutthroat competition among firms for trained personnel." From a worker's perspective, the situation looked quite different. "A world of opportunity . . . existed within the tufting empire," according to the Wharton School report. With experienced labor increasingly in demand, it was relatively easy for workers to choose their job. If an employee was dissatisfied with his or her employer, it was easy to move. Even if a worker became disenchanted with the entire lot of existing firms in the area, "there was always a new plant opening down the street." [44]

The Dalton district's mills were small compared with the average for Georgia's textile industry, especially the giant cotton mills. Tufted carpet mills employed an average of 134 people while the average Georgia textile mill provided 255 jobs. The carpet mills provided more bang for the buck, however, producing an average of $8.05 in value added per production worker hour while the state's textile industry as a whole averaged $4.78. In this category, tufting outperformed the average of all manufacturing establishments in Georgia ($6.84). Production workers in tufted carpets and rugs took home in the form of wages only half the percentage of value added (23 percent) that Georgia workers in textiles (46 percent) received, and significantly less than the average for all manufacturing workers in Georgia (33 percent) or the United States (32 percent). [45]

The tufting process demonstrated its efficiency in the statistics cited above. Mill owners and managers were justifiably proud of the performance of this homegrown industry. For workers in Georgia's booming carpet industry, the statistics for 1963 tell a slightly different story. Hourly wages for Georgia's carpet workers ($1.58) lagged behind textile industry wages ($1.65) and average earnings for all Georgia manufacturing workers ($1.84) and fell far short of the national average for manufacturing workers ($2.53). In Dalton, carpet wages ($1.64) were a bit higher than the state average, virtually equaling the state textile industry norm. The wage situation was complicated in Dalton, however, by the existence of unions in the Crown Cotton Mill and the American Thread Company mill. Overall textile wages in Whitfield County, excluding floor coverings, stood at $1.76. [46]

TABLE 6. Hourly Wages, 1963–1967

	1963	1967	% Change
Ga. tufting mills	$1.58	2.05	30
All Ga. textiles	1.65	2.03	23
All Ga. mfg.	1.84	2.22	21
All U.S. mfg.	2.53	2.92	15

Source: U.S. Bureau of the Census, Census of Manufactures, 1963 and 1967.

TABLE 7. Value Added per Hour, 1963–1967

	1963	1967	% Change
Ga. tufting mills	6.94	8.05	16
All Ga. textiles	3.57	4.78	34
All Ga. mfg.	5.59	6.84	22
All U.S. mfg.	7.84	9.41	20

Source: U.S. Bureau of the Census, Census of Manufactures, 1963 and 1967.

TABLE 8. Wages as Percentage of Value Added, 1963 and 1967

	1963	1967
Ga. tufting mills	23	25
All Ga. textiles	46	42
All Ga. mfg.	33	32
All U.S. mfg.	32	31

Source: U.S. Bureau of the Census, Census of Manufactures, 1963 and 1967.

High worker turnover rates and the explosion of new firms in the Dalton area exerted upward pressure on wages in the district. Production workers' hourly wages in Georgia's carpet tufting plants rose from $1.58 in 1963 to $2.05 in 1967, an increase of almost 30 percent. In contrast, hourly wages for all textile workers in the same period went up by just over 20 percent, and the average increase for all manufacturing workers nationwide was just 15 percent.[47] Managers in the Dalton district in 1963 were in the midst of a struggle with the TWUA to prevent unionization of the carpet mills. The wage increases in Georgia's tufting plants outpaced those in other industries perhaps in part as a way to "buy" the loyalty of local workers. Certainly the substantial growth in carpet sales made a difference; the high wage increases were in part the result of record performances in the marketplace. The wage gains also indicated a process of "bidding up" the prevailing wage in the Dalton district.

The Wharton School report cited a private 1974 wage survey of two tufting mills in the Dalton area and two tufting mills located in south-central Georgia. Dalton workers in most job categories were better paid than those in south Georgia. The highest and most consistent wage differentials were at the bottom of the wage scale, for job categories such as tufting inspector, creeler, and materials handler. Apparently the chief distinction between Dalton-area tufting concerns and those located elsewhere in Georgia was that Dalton-based firms had to pay higher wages for unskilled and inexperienced labor.[48]

The Wharton study also revealed small differentials between job classifications and an absence of pension plans. Although mill managers claimed to be committed to a "promote-from-within" policy, the nature of the labor market mitigated against long-term workforce stability in the absence of wage promotion incentives to remain at one establishment. The quickest way to get a raise was to find a job at a new or relatively new mill and simply quit the old one. Most mills didn't offer traditional pension plans. Managers told the author that workers preferred higher wages in the here and now to a promise of a better standard of living during their retirement. Managers argued that the failure to develop a comprehensive benefit package was a result of the high rate of labor turnover. Some manufacturers began experimenting with profit-sharing plans in the 1960s in an attempt to build worker loyalty. The carpet industry's profit-sharing schemes had the virtue of not requiring an employer contribution in years in which a company failed to show a profit. The lack of a specific commitment to make an annual contribution at a particular level made such programs especially attractive to executives in a poorly capitalized industry with low profit margins.[49]

Were the high quit rates noted earlier a result or a cause of miserly and poorly planned personnel practices? Anecdotal evidence and some contemporary professional analyses indicated that management skills were less than adequate in the Dalton district. Yet low barriers to entry—no brand-name identification, low startup costs—made it easy to start new companies, and expanding demand made it difficult to fail in the short run. The large number of relatively small companies and the youth of the industry tended to reinforce a personal style of management.

In this atmosphere, the refusal of workers to risk joining the TWUA cannot be interpreted as irrational or motivated by some slavish devotion to southern ideals of individualism, though that individualism existed (see the actions of Local 1592 above). Workers likely saw some real promise for individual improvement in changing jobs. The union's strategy was also partially responsible for the failure of the campaign. Perhaps a strike over wages at Dixie Belle in 1963 could have made a difference. The workers themselves were willing to take that chance. In the absence of any evidence that organizing could produce substantial gains, workers were left with little confidence in the TWUA's promises. Yet the existence of a local union in the industry exerted upward pressure on wages, benefits, and personnel practices industrywide. Raymond Roach described the process by which local workers at other mills used Local 1592 to get better deals from their own employers. Workers dissatisfied with a particular employer would attend a few meetings at the union hall in Calhoun and ask for a few leaflets to be distributed at their establishment. Within days, a paid holiday would be granted, a ten-cent-per-hour wage increase would be announced, or a particularly obnoxious supervisor would be fired. The disgruntled workers would stop attending meetings and lose interest in further organizing efforts. Small victories counted for much among workers accustomed to long hours and low wages.[50]

The cynicism of the TTMA's approach, represented by the advice of Frank Constangy, was obvious. The text of his remarks hinted at the weak management skills and poor personnel practices in this emerging industry. Constangy's advice to his clients also fit into a larger pattern that emerged in southern textiles in the 1950s. Labor historians have only recently begun the project of examining southern workers in the post–World War II era, continuing the investigation into the question of why southern workers have proven so resistant to unionization. Traditional explanations have emphasized southern culture, paternalism, and the hostility of state and local governments. Timothy Minchin has recently argued that real material improvements in the standard of living for southern workers, and the manipulation of those advancements by shrewd management, may be the real key to the failure of mass unionization in Dixie. Minchin noted that in the immediate postwar decade, 1945–55, the intensely competitive southern textile industry faced an expanding market along with the out-migration of increasing numbers of southern workers, black and white, and the breakdown of the mill village system. Mill owners responded to the more mobile labor force by trying to hold on to workers with regular wage increases. The vast majority of unorganized textile mills matched or came close to matching the wage gains of the few unionized mills in the region. Many mills also made a concerted effort to improve personnel policies (or at least to institute *some* rational practices). For a decade or so, southern textile workers made some progress in closing the regional wage gap. Minchin argued that this explains, at least in part, the failure of the 1951 general strike in particular and the failure of unions generally in the region. After the early 1950s, the situation changed as the union threat subsided. Indeed, Minchin argued that the noneconomic benefits of unionization provided more fertile ground for organizing than material benefits, especially in the South. Workers wanted not just higher wages but to be treated with greater respect in the workplace. The union's excessive emphasis on undeliverable material gains damaged the TWUA's reputation.[51] Minchin noted that even though southern textile workers chose not to join the TWUA, the union deserved much of the credit for improving the standard of living throughout the region. The threat of union organization prodded southern textile firms to raise wages and improve management practices. This appeared to be the case in the Dalton carpet district a decade later.

Though the TWUA's attempt to organize the tufted carpet industry fell apart in the mid-1960s, the union considered a renewed effort in 1973. The TWUA's Research Department made a proposal to the union's executive council for a renewed carpet drive. Researchers argued that the carpet industry met one of the most important criteria for a successful organizing campaign: a positive "long-term economic outlook." The writers noted a recent Chase Manhattan Bank study that had predicted that "carpet and rug manufacturing will continue to be one of our nation's outstanding growth industries in the next decade." Employment in the industry was rising, from 36,000 in 1967 to more than 49,000 in 1972.[52]

The TWUA's executive council declined to make a major new effort in the carpet industry. The same problems had been faced before, unsuccessfully. By the early 1970s, the industry's version of the social contract between business and labor was unchallenged in the Dalton area, the center of the industry. The only local established during the 1962–63 drive was barely surviving. Carpet manufacturers continued to refine their personnel practices and announced occasional general wage increases to mitigate the worst complaints of workers. In addition, the labor shortage and consequent high turnover rate among carpet workers had a double impact. High personnel turnover minimized the close contact and camaraderie necessary for union organization, and the labor shortage gave workers a measure of individual bargaining power. As late as the early 1970s, the practice of "body-snatching" was commonplace; that is, mill managers often hired away good workers from competing firms by offering better wages or working conditions.[53]

Paradoxically, in the midst of competition for the best and most experienced workers, a majority of carpet mill employees faced the prospect of long hours and overwork, reminiscent of the infamous "stretchouts" of cotton mill days. The "undermanned labor force" was part of a "vicious circle which plagues this industry," as William T. Deyo of the First National Bank of Atlanta put it in 1970. "From this problem," Deyo continued, "springs the additional problem of overworking the existing labor force." Deyo acknowledged that "this is undesirable not only from an efficiency and morale standpoint, but also for economic reasons." The labor shortage forced mills to require excessive overtime work, thus "greatly increas[ing] the labor cost." Ten-hour shifts were commonplace and twelve-hour shifts not uncommon.[54]

The labor shortage was real enough to reach into Dalton-area secondary schools. Whitfield County school superintendent Charles Bowen found in a 1973 survey that Dalton's schools had one of the highest dropout rates in the nation. There were plenty of jobs available for people without high school diplomas in the carpet mills. Bowen reported that students who dropped out of school in Dalton earned almost as much as those who had completed high school.[55] Young people in their late teens could find gainful employment at incomes that must have seemed, to them, princely. A steady job in a carpet mill could provide a young person with the means to buy a car (probably used), rent an apartment, and set up his or her own household. Indeed, one study concluded that "the carpet industry [has for decades] made Dalton a mecca for job-seekers, who came to fill jobs which only required low skills but paid decent wages." Whitfield County carpet mills employed about twenty-five thousand carpet mill workers in 1990; an estimated 40 percent of those lacked a high school diploma.[56] The prospect of sharply curtailed future earnings must have seemed too remote to consider for many teenagers and young adults in the midst of the possibility of so much independent consumption.

Carpet mill workers, whether high school dropouts or not, enjoyed higher incomes than most Georgians outside the metropolitan Atlanta area. Per capita income in Whitfield County, for example, rose from 81.7 percent of the national average in 1959 to 91.2 percent in 1984. Of Georgia's 159 counties, only the 5 that made up the core of metropolitan Atlanta had a per capita income higher than the national average. Whitfield was one of only 9 other counties with per capita incomes above the state average. These income statistics reveal the impact of the concentration of the carpet industry in the Dalton area. The United States as a whole garnered 23.8 percent of its income from manufacturing employment in 1984; the state of Georgia was a little behind the national rate at 22.1 percent. Whitfield Countians received more than 55 percent of their earnings from manufacturing. In Gordon County, home of Dixie Belle Mills, 53 percent of total earnings came from manufacturing, though per capita income (at about 85 percent of the U.S. average) lagged behind that of the neighboring "core" of the carpet industry, Whitfield. The low-skill manufacturing economy of the region made it possible for people with little education and few skills to enter the consumer economy.[57]

The rapid industrialization of the Dalton area took its social toll in other ways, as well. The Reverend George Sparks of St. Mark's Episcopal Church, and a past president of the Whitfield County Mental Health Association, described for the *Atlanta Journal and Constitution* in 1972 the new services needed in the area. Sparks detailed Dalton's (and surrounding communities') high rates of alcoholism, abandonment, juvenile delinquency, and divorce. Dalton, in fact, had a divorce rate significantly higher than the state and national averages. Sparks saw a direct relationship between the rapid industrialization of the Dalton area (within a single generation) and increased social and psychological problems. These problems were caused in part by "uprooting people from agricultural life and moving to an industrial setting." The Episcopal minister related a series of recent initiatives from city, county, state, and federal governments and private donors to deal with the increasing level of "anomie" in "Tuftland": a $200,000 mental health outpatient clinic in the works; a twenty-five-bed in-patient mental health ward under construction at the local hospital; a large private donation from the estate of Ben Winkler, a former executive at Belcraft Chenilles, to fund a health education center for practical nurses and paramedics.[58]

Certainly there were other causes for the explosion of mental health services in the Dalton area in the early 1970s. The social dislocation of industrialization no doubt played a part as well, as local observers recognized. The social cohesion that the former Crown mill workers found first in their mill village and later in their union did not develop among the larger group of carpet mill workers. Carpet mill workers found greater access to the consumer economy through cash wages, and greater personal freedom through the choices that cash incomes provided. They also lost contact with their neighbors and turned inward, losing touch with a broader vision of community.

The material benefits gained by workers in the carpet industry should not be minimized. Raymond Roach remembered with great pride the paid holidays, rational personnel procedures, and higher wages his union won at Dixie Belle. Those benefits were small compared with those achieved by steel and auto workers. For workers in the carpet industry, those gains were real and substantial. Roach was convinced that the progress made by Local 1592, halting though it may have been, helped pressure other carpet firms into improving wages, benefits, and working conditions.[59] Local 1592 also fought successfully for greater respect in the workplace for its members. The local's most notable successes came in the form of small victories—winning back jobs for workers unjustly fired, for example. These small victories proved more difficult to spread to unorganized mills.

By the early 1970s, the prospect of general organization among carpet mill workers had receded. Had the organization of Dixie Belle, and the efforts at other mills, been a failure? The record suggests that general wages, benefits, and personnel practices improved during the 1960s at least in part as a result of the organizing campaign and the existence of a

union at Dixie Belle. Workers did experience some tangible material benefits from the union campaign in the Dalton area. The rising demand for
workers led to a labor shortage that, ironically, did not serve so much to
drive up wages as to entice teens to drop out of school and allow great
freedom of movement to experienced mill workers. Cash incomes associated with carpet mill jobs allowed many northwest Georgians to enter the
consumer economy, albeit in a limited fashion, for the first time.

The Calhoun newspaper's editor emeritus, J. Roy McGinty, had been
wrong: union organization was not inevitable in the Dalton district despite the increasing concentration of the carpet industry in the region.
TWUA strategy robbed the Dixie Belle victory of much of its symbolic
power as an example. Well-organized management opposition took full
advantage of the union's failure of nerve. In a broader sense, the TTMA's
and the Gordon County Chamber of Commerce's antiunion campaign
also outlined the social compact in the Dalton area between management
and workers. Carpet firms promised continued employment and growth.
Dalton-area mill owners made highly publicized gifts to fund expansion
at the local recreation center in the summer of 1962. Carpet companies
promoted their image as good "corporate citizens," investing in the community. At the same time, these companies asked for complete freedom of
action, with no interference from organized workers. The new manufacturers promised that growth would continue, but only so long as workers
resisted the temptation of organization. The community got the message.

New South Boom

The Dalton district was the home of a diverse array of tufting enterprises in the 1940s and 1950s. These companies manufactured a wide range of tufted textile products, including bedspreads, robes, scatter rugs, bath sets, area rugs, and broadloom carpeting. By the mid-1960s, the Dalton district had drifted toward almost complete dependence on broadloom carpet manufacture. The market for spreads and other small products was saturated, whereas the demand for tufted carpeting appeared to be insatiable. New money for innovation and experimentation flowed into carpet, not bedspreads and other chenilles.

The decline of the bedspread and robe markets encouraged manufacturers to specialize in carpeting. The total dollar value of all tufted bedspread shipments steadily declined from 1952 through 1964, from $52 million to about $48 million. The value of tufted robe shipments fell even more precipitously, from a high of almost $11 million in 1952 to just over $4 million in 1964. The unit value of bedspreads fell from $4.43 in 1951 to $3.38 in 1964. The value of each individual robe rose, but volume shipments dropped so dramatically that the increase was doubtless cold comfort to manufacturers.[1]

Carpet production entered a period of even more rapid growth, however, and much more than made up for the decline of other tufted products. The story of the carpet industry in its boom period, 1958–73, was in many ways the story of E. T. Barwick Mills. Barwick and his company exhibited all the industry's strengths and weaknesses in larger-than-life fashion. Barwick sought feverishly to become, and then to remain, the world's largest manufacturer of carpet. The company's growth strategy reflected some prevailing trends in the industry and ran directly opposite to others. Gene Barwick helped create the tufted carpet industry, and for a time his firm defined carpet manufacture, but in the end his ambition cost him his company.

No other individual, according to the unanimous testimony of his competitors and contemporaries, made a greater contribution to the growth and development of tufted carpeting. He was certainly the most flamboyant "outsider" to enter the tufted textile business in the Dalton district. Born in Lake City, Florida, in 1914, Eugene T. Barwick came from a self-described modest background. The young athlete attended the University of North Carolina at Chapel Hill on a football scholarship. In 1961, *Sports Illustrated* named Barwick as a member of its silver anniversary college football team.[2]

Barwick Industries was the early leader among local Dalton-area carpet manufacturers. Gene Barwick began buying and selling tufted goods for Sears in the late 1940s. He bought out one of his chief suppliers, McCarty Chenille of Chatsworth, Georgia, in 1949, and formed his own company. Barwick hired former owner Frank McCarty to continue to run the production end of the business while he himself concentrated on sales. Barwick risked his entire life savings—$4,500—on the venture. He logged more than 100,000 miles traveling to hawk his carpet in 1949 and returned with orders totaling $998,000. Barwick's sales doubled in 1950, and he began expanding his facilities. The small company that had started with "one superannuated tufting machine in an old grocery store in the backcountry town of Chatsworth, Ga." grew into a firm that claimed to produce 25 percent of all tufted floor coverings in 1954. Barwick Mills' revenues topped $26 million that year. In addition to price advantages, tufted floor coverings offered color and styling variety. The cotton and synthetic carpets produced in Barwick's mills brought new choices to consumers, according to the owner. Woven wool carpets were limited to dark, murky colors. Postwar consumers wanted something brighter, "more modern," Barwick argued, and cotton and synthetic tufted carpets offered a much broader, and brighter, range of colors.[3]

"It didn't take a genius to figure out after the war that tufted textiles were the coming thing in floor coverings," Barwick told *Business Week* in 1955. "They offer more in color, styling, and materials. Besides, you can turn out as good or better product a lot faster and cheaper by using the tufted process than you can get on the most up-to-date looms now available." No one was more adept at selling the new product than Gene Barwick. By 1955, he had twenty-two distributors scattered throughout the country and salesrooms in New York, Dallas, San Francisco, and Chicago. Barwick continued to travel extensively, showing up unexpectedly at all these facilities. *Business Week* concluded: "Most competing salesmen shudder when they hear that Barwick is calling on customers. Chief reason is that he carries with him the authority to shave or cut prices and conclude a contract on the spot. He'll spend as much time, money, and effort to sell a small department store as he will a chain. And, if the competition gets tight, he'll send one of his planes to pick up the buyer and bring him to the plant to see how Barwick rugs are made."[4]

Throughout the 1950s, Barwick remained a vigorous spokesman for the flexibility of the tufting process. In an address to the Tufted Textile Manufacturers Association meeting in New York in October 1954, he outlined his own bright view of the industry's future. Barwick observed that workers could change creels on a tufting machine in an hour and be ready to produce carpet of an entirely different color and style. Such a change-over might take days on an old Jacquard loom, he argued. "Our machines," Barwick contended, "producing a room size rug every 30 seconds, have accomplished miracles never believed possible with heavy fabrics in the textile field." These developments led to "a better product at lower cost to the consumer."[5]

Barwick's strategy had three essential elements. E. T. Barwick firmly believed that marketing was the key to any company's success. He worked harder, and more creatively, to sell tufted carpeting than any other individual or company. Innovation formed another key element in the rise of Barwick Mills. The firm pioneered in developing new processes and products and in experimenting with new fibers. Finally, Barwick recognized the value of a loyal, well-trained workforce long before most of his southern colleagues and competitors. Barwick Mills initiated an ambitious, inventive, long-range educational program that Barwick hoped would be emulated throughout the industry.

Barwick used a variety of methods to market tufted floor coverings. The primary targets of his promotional efforts were retailers and distributors, though the firm went direct to consumers with ads in the late 1950s. Symbolic of Barwick's personal energy and salesmanship was the DC-3 airplane that the company purchased in 1955. *Retailing Daily* reported in April 1955 that Barwick had flown a group of Detroit floor covering retailers down to Lafayette, Georgia, for a tour of a Barwick manufacturing plant. Barwick escorted another group of midwestern floor covering dealers to Lafayette and Dalton in June 1955.[6] These junkets became a Barwick trademark.

Barwick combined marketing with product innovation. Barwick Mills introduced several all-nylon lines of carpeting in 1956, along with new rayon styles. The company worked with Du Pont and American Viscose to promote the new products. G. Fox & Company, a fashionable Hartford, Connecticut, department store, hosted the first retail showing of Barwick's new nylon and rayon lines in April 1956. Barwick, the fiber companies, and the department store used the occasion to present "the full story of manmade fibers in floor fashion," a trade journal noted. G. Fox carried carpet-related displays in its "full bank of windows," with one window devoted entirely to carpet. The department store launched the promotion at a YMCA luncheon. The lunch meeting featured the editor of *Guide for Brides* delivering a talk called "Around the Clock in Home Fashions," which emphasized the new nylon carpeting by Barwick Mills. The promotional campaign was set to last for five days and included a fashion show that incorporated Barwick nylon carpets. Local television and radio ads promoted the entire affair.[7] A Fox store executive described the campaign as "by far the most successful rug promotion in our 109 years." More than 5,000 people visited the floor covering department on the eighth floor of the department store. Barwick Mills offered 100 "room-size" rugs, each 9 feet by 12 feet, at $99.50–155.50, in daily specials. On the opening day of the promotion, April 7, the first 100 rugs were sold in less than 100 minutes.[8] Barwick combined promotion of his own lines of carpeting with an attempt to educate consumers about artificial fibers.

Barwick later explained the evolution of his special relationship with Fox. The store's buyers were originally reluctant to move into synthetic products like nylon. New Englanders, store officials told Barwick, "don't particularly take to new things like synthetic yarns." Barwick made the store an offer it couldn't refuse. Barwick maintained that the reason Fox had trouble selling synthetic carpets was that store managers and salesmen themselves had "not been enlightened." Barwick asked Fox executives to pick out "the worst week in the year" and "give us that week." He offered to take back any merchandise that did not sell, but he insisted on "the whole cooperation of the store. I'll pay for the ads, . . . and I will talk on the radio or television or whatever." Barwick's nylon campaign "drew 5,000 people in that store with the carpet in five days. It was the biggest week of the year."[9]

By the end of the 1950s, Barwick Mills had settled on nylon as its principal fiber. Barwick announced in March 1958 that 95 percent of Barwick carpets were currently being made of nylon. Nylon's chief synthetic competitor, rayon, had too many problems, including poor durability. Barwick admitted to a meeting of distributors that 70 percent of the consumer complaints his company fielded were on the issue of durability. Barwick Mills had handled more than seven hundred thousand dollars annually in "adjustments," or refunds to consumers to cover complaints about quality, on rayon carpeting alone in the period 1953–57. The industry was moving rapidly away from rayon by 1958. In 1954, three manufacturers offered a grand total of six carpet styles in nylon. Barwick noted that by January 1958 twenty-three producers offered seventy-seven styles of nylon carpeting.[10]

Barwick and G. Fox collaborated on a succession of impressive marketing drives for the new nylon carpeting. In April 1958, the carpet maker and the retailer decided to "torture test" Barwick nylon carpeting at the store to kick off a new promotion. Store management placed two carpets at the main entrance to G. Fox. A third strip of nylon carpeting was placed in the G. Fox garage at the package pickup counter. This latter carpet would be subjected to both foot and automobile traffic. After a few weeks, half of each carpet strip was to be cleaned to demonstrate both durability and cleanability. Du Pont and Barwick sent representatives to Hartford to be available for customer questions during the promotion.[11]

At about the same time, Barwick began a similar test in San Antonio in conjunction with a distributor, the Alamo Carpet Showroom. Alamo carpeted the driveway of a busy San Antonio service station with a "frosted light green" nylon carpet supplied by Barwick and advertised as selling for $9.95 per square yard. This test was just as successful as the G. Fox demonstration. After two weeks of heavy automobile traffic, most of the carpeting was still in good condition, except for "a couple of rips at one edge due, in one instance, to an irate motorist 'spinning his wheels,'" according to *Home Furnishings Daily.* Later that same month, Barwick laid a strip of nylon carpet across San Antonio's Houston Street. Barwick Mills cosponsored about three hundred similar "torture test" promotions in 1958 during an all-out marketing offensive to sell consumers on nylon.[12]

Barwick also set about educating retailers and distributors on the advantages of nylon. The tufted carpet innovator conducted a series of fifty-one seminars on nylon carpeting in various important market cities between August 1957 and April 1958. Barwick advertising chief John Hoff told *Home Furnishings Daily* that carpet dealers and distributors were much more willing to accept nylon carpeting at the end of the seminar series than before. "We were flooded with questions for the first few months after each seminar," Hoff noted. But "after the first of the year (1958), we started to notice that the number of questions dealers were asking us was getting smaller and smaller." In fact, at the final nylon seminar, in Bridgeport, Connecticut, "only three questions were asked." For Hoff, this was evidence that "the dealers today no longer have any doubts as to the product." The nylon seminars were so successful that Barwick decided to repeat the series beginning in the summer of 1958.[13]

Georgia's carpet salesman par excellence took the nylon story to television in the fall of 1959. *Home Furnishings Daily* characterized an upcoming Barwick television campaign as "the biggest promotional assist yet" for "retailers of the E.T. Barwick Mills' line of nylon carpeting." Gene Barwick announced in September 1959 plans for a joint advertising campaign to be shared with Du Pont. The campaign called for Barwick and Du Pont to tell "the manufacturer's story" in a series of ads on NBC's "Today Show" on three successive days, September 29–October 1. The ads would "name personally more than 200 Barwick dealers." In addition, similar ads would air during the Du Pont–sponsored "June Allyson Show" on CBS. Barwick claimed that "never before has a carpet promotion been scheduled to so big an audience." Tufted carpeting's top manufacturer and marketer predicted that "more customers than ever before will learn what the Du Pont label means to them in the purchase of carpet for their home. Our dealers can expect their biggest selling push this fall." [14]

Barwick developed a close relationship with Du Pont, which was crucial to this marketing blitz. Barwick Mills, with about $30 million in sales in 1958, could not hope to finance a national television advertising campaign of this magnitude. Huge fiber companies like Du Pont could, and the tufted carpet industry needed help in national marketing and advertising. Du Pont needed to expand the potential market for its nylon fibers. It was a marketing marriage made in heaven, much to the chagrin of the old established woven companies.

Smaller, more flexible tufted carpet manufacturers used a new production process to win market share from established woven manufacturers, but it was the development of better synthetic fibers by chemical companies that completed the tufting revolution in the late 1950s. As Du Pont and Monsanto introduced filament nylon and Acrilan, the quality of tufted carpets rose. The low profit margins associated with traditional textile industries, however, made advertising and marketing a luxury that many tufting companies could not afford. Tufters sidestepped this problem by allowing the fiber producers to bear the brunt of the advertising burden. As more and more tufting operations turned to synthetic fibers such as Du Pont's "501" nylon, the fiber producers saw the obvious advantage in promoting increased carpet sales.

In the late 1950s, Chemstrand, Du Pont, Monsanto, and other synthetic fiber producers began labeling carpets produced by various manufacturers. Masland introduced the first carpets made from Chemstrand's "Acrilan" acrylic fiber in 1957. Du Pont began "franchising" the use of its synthetic products in 1958. The cheapness and availability of the synthetic fibers, however, served to level the playing field for small-time tufters and long-established carpet giants. When consumers read the "Du Pont" label, they usually did not inquire as to which company had actually attached the yarn to a backing. Brand-name loyalties to particular established carpet firms declined, while new firms traded potential brand-name recognition for initial sales and immediate respectability in the association with Du Pont and other fiber companies. By 1964, Du Pont had permitted fifty companies to become franchised manufacturers of its 501 nylon. "By virtue of these agreements," a major business publication concluded in 1964, carpet manufacturers "benefit[ed] from the fiber producers' extensive research and advertising programs." [15]

Du Pont and other companies established themselves as the primary marketers of synthetic fiber carpets in the early 1960s. In August 1960, E. I. Du Pont de Nemours and Company announced a new television advertising campaign. The campaign would "increase television emphasis on Du Pont carpet nylon and promote Orlon acrylic fibers for carpet applications for the first time on tv" in the fall of 1960, according to *Advertising Age*. The company would promote 501 nylon and other fibers "heavily" on such programs as "Today" and "June Allyson," while "carpets containing Orlon will be seen on the [Jack] Paar Show." [16] The fiber manufacturers, financial giants compared even with the largest carpet firm, used their clout to finish the reshaping of the carpet market.

Woven manufacturers and the Carpet Wool Council fought back with an ad campaign designed to sell the virtues of wool carpeting and, by implication, woven carpets. Several woven manufacturers formed Wool Carpets of America to run the campaign. Wool Carpets of America placed ads in *Life*, the *New Yorker*, and the *New York Times Magazine*, among other publications. These print advertisements disputed the claims of Du Pont and Monsanto about the quality of synthetic fibers. "Wool trades on its own virtues," asserted the wool floor covering group, granting human qualities to inanimate objects. "It does not claim to be like other fibers. It is what other fibers are trying hard to be." The organization continued in this vein when comparing (unfavorably, of course) wool with the popular synthetic fibers: "Nylon boasts of durability. Acrylics claim resiliency. Rayon stresses uniform colors. Polypropylene talks up abrasion resistance. But wool carpet has all these advantages—and more." [17]

Jack Warwick, president of the Carpet Wool Council, charged that "certain synthetics campaigns tend to confuse rather than help the consumer." An advertising journal speculated that Warwick was referring specifically to a Monsanto television ad for carpets made of its Acrilan. "Every woman wants a wool carpet," according to the Monsanto commercials, "but Acrilan has the same qualities and is cheaper." [18] This one sentence speaks volumes about the difficulties of the traditional woven wool carpet trade in the 1950s.

Southern firms led a textile revolution in the 1950s. In 1951, tufted carpets made up only 6,076,000 square yards shipped out of a total industry production of 73,000,000 yards. By 1960, tufting had dwarfed weaving as the primary production process. In that year, tufted carpet shipments amounted to more than double the woven shipments, 113,764,000 to 52,044,000. By 1963, tufted manufacturers shipped more than 250,000,000 yards of carpet, while woven goods shipments had slipped to about 41,000,000 yards. [19]

Perhaps more important, total industry production more than tripled between 1951 and 1963 as the more efficient tufting companies opened new markets for carpeting. James Lees and Sons estimated in 1960 that the company's tufting operations produced 6.68 square yards of carpet per man-hour, as compared with 1.76 square yards per man-hour in the weaving operation. This cost saving made it possible to sell tufted carpet for less than half the price of woven goods. [20] The rise in tufted carpet shipments in the 1950s far exceeded the decline in woven production. The tufting process had made it possible for carpet manufacturers to accomplish the goal that had eluded them for decades: the penetration (and eventually, the saturation) of the growing middle-class mass market. This market penetration, however, favored new producers over old and came with a high price tag for established firms. Barwick was the most successful of those new firms in the 1960s.

In addition to marketing and innovation, Barwick focused on building employee loyalty and improving employee skills. Evidence suggests that Barwick's wages established the upper end of the Dalton district's pay scale. As of December 1953, no Barwick employee earned less than $1.00 per hour, this more than a year before the $1.00 minimum wage took effect. A March 1955 wage increase brought the firm's average hourly wage for trained workers to $1.10.[21]

Barwick's most innovative attempt to improve employee relations and improve the skill level of his workforce was the college scholarship program initiated in 1955. Barwick originally offered 25 partial scholarships annually to employees or their children who could graduate high school and gain acceptance into any accredited college in the seven southeastern states. By the early 1960s, Barwick had increased the annual number of scholarships to 56 to meet increasing demand among his workers. During the first six years of the program, Barwick Mills provided 180 scholarships of approximately $500 per student per year. Over time, Barwick added features to the program. For example, the firm also guaranteed summer employment to scholarship recipients to enable them to earn the remainder of the money needed for their education. Mill employees who took advantage of the scholarships were under no obligation to return to Barwick Mills, though by 1961 fifteen had done so. These scholarships were awarded on a noncompetitive, first-come, first-serve basis to any qualified applicant.[22]

Barwick characterized the program as both a community service effort and an attempt to help the carpet industry build a better, more skilled workforce for the future. Barwick had been shocked at the number of simple mistakes being made in his plants in the early 1950s. He investigated and found that many of his employees were either functionally or completely illiterate, victims of Georgia's generally poor public school system and the lack of emphasis on education in rural farming communities in particular. Many of the employees had not finished high school. He found that many of his employees "just couldn't read." Barwick initiated the program to give area students an incentive to finish high school and go on to college. Barwick recalled that he was deeply affected by the plight of the typical southern textile worker. The program was intended to benefit the company and the industry generally, but it was "more than that; textile workers had never been highly paid. . . . They wanted their kids to go to college like anybody else but they couldn't afford it." In 1961, Barwick expressed a great deal of hope for the future as a result of this program and hoped that other companies would emulate it. "I like to think," the carpet executive proudly proclaimed, "that we will have made the community a better place—a condition that could not have happened had we not been here." [23]

There were pragmatic benefits to the program as well. Barwick envisioned the entire Dalton-area carpet industry cooperating in this effort to build a more skilled and competent workforce and a greater pool from which to draw trained managerial talent. The improved level of education would have innumerable spin-off benefits for the community as well, not the least of which might have been the encouragement of some economic diversification for the area. These college graduates would have experience in the industry, having been either employees before going to college or employed during the summer while in college.

Barwick was bitterly disappointed later in life that the rest of the industry in the Dalton district did not follow his lead. "I was hoping the whole industry" would launch similar programs, he noted, "because it didn't cost a whole lot." But none followed his lead. "If the whole industry could have done that for their employees, what a hell of a deal it would have been," Barwick wistfully remembered. "But not a damn single one of them would follow." [24]

E. T. Barwick built a remarkably successful tufted carpet company during the 1950s. He used his own blend of persuasive salesmanship, an eye for the right innovation, and a set of perhaps paternalistic but nonetheless enlightened personnel policies to establish a unique formula for success in the tufted industry. Barwick was as responsible as anyone for putting the Dalton district on the industrial map by the end of the 1950s.

Barwick's visibility had helped him become a director of the National Association of Manufacturers (NAM) by 1959. In that capacity, he clashed with the congressional representative of the Dalton industrial district, Erwin Mitchell. Mitchell and Barwick debated the relative merits of pending labor legislation in 1959. The specific issue of contention was the Landrum-Griffin bill, but the disagreement between Barwick and Mitchell hinted at deeper divisions within the social elite of the district.

Erwin Mitchell was a Dalton native. After graduating from the University of Georgia's law school, he set up a practice in his hometown. Mitchell, in his early thirties, was elected to Congress from the north Georgia district that contained Dalton in 1958. He received backing from Barwick and other tufted textile mill owners. Mitchell also developed good relations with organized labor in his district. He was on friendly terms with both the textile locals in Dalton itself, at Crown and American Thread. In 1958, Dalton was in the same congressional district as Marietta, home of the South's largest industrial establishment, Lockheed, and the company's well-organized machinists. Mitchell walked a fine line in appealing to small and medium-sized manufacturing firms such as Barwick Mills and organized labor. He had the bad fortune to enter Congress at a particularly difficult time to try to maintain such a balanced constituency.

In the summer of 1959, Georgia congressman Phil Landrum cosponsored a bill that would curtail the power of labor unions. In the wake of the labor racketeering hearings of the mid-1950s, Landrum and other conservative Democrats allied with Republicans to advocate further changes in the nation's labor laws. Erwin Mitchell, already an admirer of the junior senator from Massachusetts, initially sided with Kennedy and the liberal Democrats. Mitchell publicly expressed serious reservations about the Griffin-Landrum bill and support for Kennedy's efforts to produce a weaker bill that would be less objectionable to organized labor. As a showdown vote neared, Gene Barwick, acting as a director of the National Association of Manufacturers and a leader of the business community in Mitchell's district, sought to persuade his congressman to support the tougher Griffin-Landrum bill.

Barwick characterized the Kennedy substitute bill as an "incredibly weak and ridiculous" attempt at labor reform. The tufting magnate was convinced that the "Griffin-Landrum Labor Bill is the best that has been proposed," and he urged Mitchell to stop vacillating and support this legislation as well. "I hear through the Chamber of Commerce," Barwick wrote to Mitchell, "that you are wavering as to whether or not to support the Griffin-Landrum Bill" or the Kennedy substitute. Barwick was "at a loss to understand" Mitchell's difficulty in staking out a clear position. He warned Mitchell that "in the future you will be chosen [either] by the voters in your district, or by a bunch of hoodlums in the labor rackets." [25]

Mitchell responded to Barwick's criticisms a few days after receiving the last and most vehement correspondence from the manufacturer. Mitchell tried to maintain maneuvering room, writing that he would support "the most effective bill which can become law." He claimed that he shared Barwick's concern about the abuses of organized labor over the past decade, but he maintained that an overreaction by Congress in the other direction would be just as bad. Mitchell implied that the Kennedy bill might be the strongest bill likely to pass the full House and Senate. Holding out for a tougher bill would be both futile and unnecessary, the young congressman averred. Mitchell took a considerable political risk near the close of this communication to Barwick. If Barwick and his colleagues at the NAM were "interested in genuine labor reform," Mitchell urged them to support the Kennedy bill. If Barwick and his allies were, however, like the Republicans, interested only in trying to "create an issue," then they should support Griffin-Landrum.[26]

Barwick exploded with anger upon receiving Mitchell's response. He shot back immediately, charging that Mitchell was either "the most naive legislator the country has ever seen" or he had "succumbed to gangster and hoodlum controlled labor leader money." Barwick was "equally unimpressed by the naive, inexperienced, fumbling, labor leader sell-out artistry of Senator John Kennedy for the selfish purpose of being nominated for the presidency." Barwick reminded his representative that President Eisenhower had come out in support of Griffin-Landrum and that there had been "an avalanche of support from United States citizens. . . . Who are you to go against the President's and the people's request?" Barwick closed with a deadly serious warning to Mitchell: "I personally spent time, money, and energy getting you elected. . . . I can assure you that I will devote one hundred fold more energy, time and money to getting you out if you support the kind of legislation you announce in your letter."[27] Barwick left Mitchell with a difficult choice. Mitchell had some ties with organized labor in his own district, a desire to remain loyal to the Democratic Party, and a deep personal admiration for JFK. On the other hand, Mitchell wanted a political future of some sort within northwest Georgia. The young politician could hardly afford to alienate the tufted textile manufacturers of his district or their money.

Mitchell ultimately voted for the more restrictive Landrum-Griffin bill on August 13, 1959. Predictably, he began receiving angry letters from organized labor leaders within days. James B. Carey, longtime CIO and AFL-CIO representative in the Deep South, threatened to try to unseat

Mitchell in 1960. Carey heaped abuse on Mitchell because the congressman had "yielded to the pressures of the Chamber of Commerce and the National Association of Manufacturers." [28]

When the Textile Workers Union of America attempted to organize Dalton district workers in the early 1960s, Barwick worked individually and with the TTMA to discourage union sentiment among his own workers. Barwick Mills established a company newsletter in 1962, the same year that the union campaign began in earnest. The Barwick newsletter emphasized two major themes: the virtues of individualism and an unfettered free enterprise system; and the corporate welfare work advocated by Barwick.

Gene Barwick developed a vision for both the tufted carpet industry and the community that sustained it. The industry consisted of (literally) hundreds of firms competing for markets. Each firm had similar plants, equipment, and technological know-how. Barwick projected the idea that management skill and dependable, efficient labor were the crucial components, the key factors in separating one mill from another. In this sense, not only did the mills and owners compete with one another, but workers competed among themselves, as well, either building their own job security through hard work and determination or (implicitly) squandering their opportunities by accepting the pie-in-the-sky promises of collective security offered by the TWUA. Barwick's vision offered the sky as the limit for the Dalton district's owners and workers.

Barwick Mills became the largest producer in the Dalton district by the mid-1960s, and eventually the largest in the world, in large measure owing to Barwick's emphasis on marketing. Barwick constantly chided competitors for not being sufficiently responsive to consumer demand. A Wharton School study of the carpet industry prepared in the late 1960s neatly characterized the dominant orientation of the industry and the nature of Barwick's challenge:

> Commitment to the "marketing concept" . . . is not a widespread practice in the industry and the product development efforts of most firms remain rooted to production orientation. The reasons for this unfortunate situation are obvious. In their role as textile converters, the carpet manufacturers have been naturally orientated toward getting the product out, solving the problems of raw material supply, minimizing the risks of equipment obsolescence,

and adapting new process technology. Their marketing organizations existed mainly to move the finished goods, often with price as a major tool, not to search for new market areas for which no product existed.

Even firms that had "gravitated closer to the marketplace" had done so not out of a response to a competitive imperative but because "they have been pushed there by such strong-willed individuals as Eugene Barwick."[29]

Barwick continued to lead the tufted carpet industry through the 1960s with his emphasis on new product development, style, and salesmanship. As the industry neared the end of the decade, he reached the zenith of his influence within the carpet industry. Barwick served as the keynote speaker for the annual TTMA convention in 1968. With carpet sales setting new records annually during the 1960s, TTMA members had begun the practice of holding leisurely annual meetings in resort areas like the Bahamas. More attention was paid to golf than serious business issues. In Freeport, Grand Bahamas, in May 1968, Gene Barwick jolted the TTMA with an address described as a "scold[ing]" by an *Atlanta Constitution* business writer.

Just as the prosperous carpet executives from the largest mills were getting comfortable in their tropical surroundings, Barwick delivered an address designed to shake attendees from their self-congratulatory reverie. He chastised the tufted carpet industry for resting on its laurels. The industry leader was "not one bit impressed" by statistics that showed a dramatic increase over the past decade in per capita carpet sales. These figures may well have been "enormously better than figures of ten or twenty years ago, but it's still a pretty rotten performance, considering the general affluence of the country." There was "a vast untapped market" for carpet that manufacturers were missing, he maintained, including schools, hospitals, and other institutional settings in the contract field and kitchens in the residential market.[30]

The ever ambitious Barwick predicted that the industry could triple its output and value of production in fifteen years if it accepted "the real opportunity and challenge." The challenge lay in duplicating "what the automobile industry did many years ago—persuade the consumer that its product was not a luxury but a necessity." Marketing, advertising, product innovation, and salesmanship were the keys to virtually unlimited growth.[31]

Barwick matched his words with actions two months later. The carpet mogul filed a registration statement with the Securities and Exchange
Commission and offered 400,000 shares of common stock for sale. Barwick went public in an effort to raise capital to fulfill his vision for his
own firm. One year later, the company named Buford Talley as its new
president. Barwick remained as chairman of the board and chief executive officer. The move allowed the chairman to "concentrate on policy
matters and be more active in promoting sales, while leaving day-to-day
administrative tasks to Talley." [32]

Barwick continued to advocate a consumer-centered focus for the carpet industry. In an address to the Philadelphia Carpet Club, Barwick lectured the assembled carpet merchants on strategies for adjusting to the
"new consumer." He observed that "a growing trend to individualism"
was transforming home furnishings into "a form of expression for people
in their homes." This had long been true for the affluent but only since
World War II for the working class. "The delicate job of the retailer is to
analyze the directions in which his consumer group is moving and antic-
ipate them with proper selection," Barwick noted. Consumers in the late
1960s could "afford to indulge themselves," and creative merchants could
influence consumer choices. Housewives, the typical consumer of carpeting according to carpet executives for a century, had ideas when they entered home furnishings stores, but they could "be guided by the availability and proper marketing of new products." Retailers and manufacturers
still had a role to play in shaping consumer demand. Retailers had to stand
ready with "a range of new possibilities your creative customer might not
have considered." Barwick pointed to kitchen carpeting as an idea that had
to be sold "and wouldn't have occurred to most of your customers to even
consider it . . . yet they are accepting it in droves." [33]

Barwick cut against the grain among carpet executives in the late 1960s
by advocating an expanded market system. Since the 1950s, Bigelow and
other large firms had tried to push the carpet industry toward fewer market shows, thus cutting down on the number of new product lines that
companies had to create to maintain the appearance of industry leadership. Barwick, of course, had long sponsored his own markets: road
shows, designed to take Barwick carpets to dealers across the country.
The industry leader advocated more markets in the late 1960s. This po-

sition was consistent with his emphasis on style, marketing, and expansion of consumer options. In May 1968, Barwick called for an expansion of the current two-market system to a four-market seasonal series of trade shows. Barwick's call came at a time when the debate within the industry was between the "stick-to-two" group and a variety of manufacturers trying to convince the industry to scale back to one market per year. Barwick argued that more yearly markets would encourage "a more consistent flow of new ideas," creating closer contact between manufacturers and retailers and allowing for the introduction of new styles gradually rather than in gluts twice per year.[34]

Barwick expanded his consumer-first crusade to Europe in late 1968. In November of that year, he traveled to Oss, the Netherlands, to dedicate a four-million-dollar tufting plant. Barwick purchased a Dutch weaving mill and converted it for tufting. In his address to assembled dignitaries, he summarized the previous two decades of carpet history in the United States. In the past twenty years, Barwick observed, the American carpet industry had undergone a "dramatic shift" from the weaving process to tufting. He detailed his own company's strategy for success. Barwick Industries had become "the world's largest carpet manufacturer" because of the organization's commitment to building an "effective distribution system" and a "zeal for service." Barwick believed that service and styling would "combine to form the foundation on which future progress will be built." He extolled the virtues of free trade and detailed the advantages his firm would derive from having a manufacturing facility in Europe. But Barwick returned, at the end of his speech, to his main theme. "Let us not forget," he reminded his audience, "the person to whom this plant is really dedicated—the consumer." Barwick asserted that his firm had from its inception been dedicated to consumer satisfaction. He finished with a pledge "to conduct our business in a way that will benefit Netherlanders and all Europeans both as citizens and as consumers."[35]

Barwick's product innovation strategy, pursued vigorously in the 1960s, produced mixed results for his firm. Barwick Industries' sales for the years 1967 and 1968 led the industry (when Mohasco's furniture sales were factored out), at $104 million and $127 million, respectively. Profits, though, remained under 4%. Barwick's innovations in carpet printing typefied his approach. Barwick became the first U.S. producer to purchase carpet printing equipment in 1963. The firm acquired screen printing machinery from Maschinenfabrik P. Zimmer Company, a German company. The printing machines allowed for the duplication in tufted goods of intricate, multicolored patterns that had previously been exclusively associated with weaving. At an initial cost probably in excess of $1.5 million, Barwick began to experiment with printed tufted carpeting, attempting to anticipate and later create markets for new products. Initial efforts in printing met with mixed results at best; it took several years of fine-tuning to overcome "poor pattern definition" and produce salable goods. Barwick introduced a relatively successful line of printed carpeting aimed at a new market—kitchens—in 1967.[36]

Barwick later recalled the introduction of printed carpets as one of his company's most significant innovations. The machinery was complex, and it took some time to get the printers into operation, but "we had it going by 1965." Barwick held his first showing of printed carpets in New York the following year. "It was supposed to be a small gathering" of distributors and retailers, "but more than 5,000 people attended. We shipped $43 million the first year while everyone was saying 'it won't sell, it won't sell.' We proved them wrong." The highly successful printed "Kitchen Classics" line was introduced shortly afterward.[37]

Barwick's "Kitchen Classics" line was the latest in a string of innovations that resulted from a "prodigious . . . capital investment." Barwick and a few other carpet firms went against the prevailing trend within the textile industry generally by investing relatively heavily in new plants and equipment in the early 1960s, while most firms waited until the second half of the decade to begin increasing such investment.[38]

The market for tufted carpeting expanded so rapidly in the 1960s that such product innovation, capital expenditures, and growth in general could be supported only by massive borrowing. Rising indebtedness did not seem a problem to entrepreneurs like Barwick who continued to bank on limitless expansion and growth in demand for their products. The growth curve of the tufted carpet and rug industry in the 1960s was little short of miraculous. The industry shipped 71 million square yards of carpet in 1958; in 1968, tufted manufacturers shipped 395 million square yards. This dizzying pace was surpassed by only three other product classes in the same period—computers, television picture tubes, and aircraft—out of more than four hundred industrial groupings ranked by the U.S. government. The tufted segment of the industry continued to outgain woven carpets by a wide margin. Woven shipments fell from 51 million square yards in 1958 to only 40 million a decade later. Tufted goods represented about 91 percent of the total carpet and rug industry by 1968, completely reversing the relative market shares the two industry segments had held in 1951. Tufted goods were primarily responsible for the industry exceeding $1 billion in shipments for the first time in 1964; by the end of the decade the mill value of industry shipments had almost doubled and stood on the verge of surpassing the $2 billion mark.[39]

This rapid growth in carpet sales masked underlying weaknesses in the industry. Kurt Salmon Associates, a management consulting firm based in Atlanta, published an analysis of the industry's cost and profit structure in *Textile Industries* in 1969. Salmon Associates created a hypothetical "Model Tufting Company" and compared it with industry averages. The article was a thinly veiled critique of the management of most tufting firms. Most carpet companies in the late 1960s were "underachievers," Salmon's team charged. The industry's rapid growth in the previous two decades "hasn't automatically resulted in a corresponding growth in profits." The tufted carpet industry had grown significantly faster than the general textile industry in the 1960s, yet carpet profits were almost identical to those in the textile sector. Between 1963 and 1967, textile firms earned an average after-tax profit on sales of 3.1 percent; these companies returned an average of 8.6 percent on stockholder equity. Publicly owned carpet companies during the same period averaged a return of 3.3 percent on sales and 8.7 percent on equity. Many observers claimed that low returns were the price to be paid for rapid growth, but Salmon Associates rejected this notion and argued that the carpet industry suffered from poor planning, bad management, and less-than-ideal personnel relations.[40] It was in many respects an industry growing in spite of itself.

The tufted carpet industry's impressive sales and cash flow attracted outside investors. Beginning in the early 1960s, many of the new tufting concerns began to tap the public capital markets by selling equity. E & B, Coronet, Barwick, Trend Mills, and more than a dozen others began going public in 1963. Reflecting the management style of the period, most of these firms went public "to make the principals rich," according to a veteran carpet executive. In essence, the wave of public stock sales in the 1960s represented a "cashing out" process for many of the original entrepreneurs of the tufted industry. Max Beasley of Cobble Brothers recalled that in the 1960s there were widespread fears that each year would be the last "big year" for tufting.[41] Most managers within the industry realized that the growth rates of the 1960s could not be sustained indefinitely. As it happened, the entrepreneurs who cashed out did not miss the mark by very much. By the mid-1970s, growth had slowed substantially.

At about the same time that many Dalton-district firms were going public, tufting concerns also became attractive to larger conglomerates. Many of the district's entrepreneurial firms were bought by larger, more diversified national corporations. Floor covering giant Armstrong purchased E & B, expanding into the carpet field for the first time. The Armstrong venture was a logical move; other mergers and acquisitions made strange bedfellows. S & H Greenstamps bought Trend Mills (as well as the old Bigelow-Sanford Company), and the electronics giant RCA acquired Coronet Carpets. In most of these mergers, the original entrepreneurs were retained as managers, and the carpet divisions functioned relatively autonomously, at least in the beginning. Carpet company founders made small fortunes in going public and usually made much larger fortunes in these buyouts.[42]

The mergers and acquisitions of the late 1960s led many observers to conclude that the carpet industry was reaching its peak and that the number of firms would inevitably decline as a number of large, well-adapted companies and/or conglomerates exploited economies of scale to dominate the industry. Such judgments were a bit premature. The carpet industry had indeed become more concentrated in the mid-1960s. The relative market shares of the top four, eight, twenty, and fifty firms all declined between 1958 and 1963 and then recovered by 1967 according to that year's Census of Manufactures. After 1967, however, the trend reversed itself again, and by 1972 the market share for the top twenty firms in tufting had dropped to 57 percent, down from 67 percent in 1967. As late as 1977, the top twenty firms held only a 60 percent market share and did not approach the 1967 level until 1982. The top four, eight, twenty, and fifty companies all had smaller market shares in 1982 than in 1958.[43]

New players continued to enter the field in the late 1960s and through-

TABLE 9. Number of Tufting Machines in Place, Selected Years
1963–1968

Machine Width	1963	1964	1966	1967	1968
9 feet	76	72	131	148	114
12 feet	81	76	121	96	89
15 feet	335	356	494	532	670
Over 15 feet	46	64	40	64	46
Total	538	568	786	840	919

Source: Robert W. Kirk, "The Carpet Industry: Present Status and Future Prospects," Wharton School of Finance and Commerce, Industrial research report no. 17, University of Pennsylvania, 1970, 54.

out the early and mid-1970s. Moreover, these new players were not simply carving up a stagnant or shrinking market share; the larger firms, as noted above, lost market share between 1967 and 1972 and gained little until the late 1970s. The number of tufted carpet manufacturers almost doubled from 1958 (88) to 1963 (167). New firm creation slowed in the mid-1960s. The number of tufted manufacturers rose by only 43 (or about 26 percent) in the period 1963–67. A new wave of entrepreneurs flooded the industry after 1967, however, as more than 120 new tufting companies were created by 1972, an increase of almost 60 percent. The rate of firm creation slowed again after 1972 to a 19 percent gain, but new entrants continued to outnumber losers at least until 1977, as the ranks of tufted carpet companies swelled by 64 to almost 397.[44]

Despite all the new entrants into the tufted carpet industry, the Barwick firm ended the 1960s as the largest producer and the acknowledged leader in new product development. Its CEO was the most visible and dynamic executive in the industry. Stockholders could point to a two-decade history of rapidly rising sales, product innovation, and effective, if flamboyant, marketing and salesmanship. Barwick was the only firm that recorded carpet sales in excess of $100 million. The chief executive's recent decisions to take the firm public and relinquish some control of daily operations seemed appropriate responses to the company's growth, but Gene Barwick would soon come to regret both decisions.

Barwick had always been more interested in generating sales and cash flow, innovation and experimentation, than in the company's profit margin. For many years, the expanding carpet market made close attention to debt ratios a matter of less-than-pressing concern to Barwick. His withdrawal from daily management chores only exacerbated the problem. By the mid-1970s, the firm was in deep financial trouble. Rising raw material prices caused by the oil crisis of 1973, rising interest rates, and the recession of 1974–75 and consequent slowdown in the construction industry exposed the fatal weakness of Barwick's sales, credit, and style strategy.

Barwick had, according to *Business Week,* promoted his company's growth by employing "as much financial leverage as possible, depending heavily on short-term debt and expensive factoring agreements." Barwick Mills had "historically" maintained a debt-to-equity ratio of "more than 2-to-1, relatively high for a manufacturing company." Barwick's approach worked well enough as long as sales rose steadily and interest rates remained relatively low. His public offering of 1968 had raised about $8 million in new capital. None of the proceeds from that offering went toward retiring existing short-term debt. A large portion of this new cash went toward the purchase of new plant and equipment. The firm invested more than $14 million in capital expansion in 1969 alone.[45]

Barwick's actions expressed a faith that the low interest rates and rising consumer demand of the 1960s would continue. Rather than use the new infusion of capital from the public offering to reduce the company's debt-to-equity ratio, Barwick chose to continue with his own expansion plans. When carpet sales began to slide, he was hit hard. In the fall of 1973, the CEO negotiated a huge loan of $12 million with the Walter E. Heller factoring firm, Barwick's old reliable source of credit, to meet cash-flow shortfalls. This short-term loan violated a long-term loan agreement Barwick Industries had made with Metropolitan Life, which limited such loans from factors to no more than $1 million, and eventually led Met Life to boost its interest rates on Barwick's long-term notes substantially in 1974. The financial squeeze forced Barwick into default on much of its short-term debt. All these financial manipulations drew the attention of the Securities and Exchange Commission, which asked to see the company's books in July 1975.[46]

In the midst of the financial chaos, Gene Barwick was forced out as CEO of Barwick Industries by pressure from creditors. The company's creditors were willing to allow Barwick Industries to continue to operate on a month-to-month basis if the chairman stepped down. Barwick agreed, and Charles Selecman, a former president of U.S. Industries, became the company's new CEO in May 1975. Selecman instituted drastic reforms in Barwick's management and fiscal practices in an effort to keep the firm's creditors at bay. In his first day on the job, Selecman slashed salaries for all executives earning more than $25,000 by 20 percent. He cut other wages by 10 percent. Selecman also sold the company's British-made jetliner (the equivalent of a DC-9). The plane had long been a symbol of Barwick's personal style and approach to marketing and dealer relations. Selecman refused to criticize Gene Barwick's management style specifically but told *Business Week* that "the largest companies were built by certain people with tremendous talents in certain areas, and at some point in time the business got big and more and different talents were required." [47]

Selecman continued his austerity program, slashing expenses and selling unused assets. Over the next year, he sold a 260,000-square-foot Dalton warehouse and shut down two Dalton manufacturing plants. Selecman put the two plants and a small office building on the market. Barwick Industries recorded net earnings of more than $600,000 for the quarter ending in November 1976, the first time the company had shown a profit since the fall of 1973. The new CEO also dumped Barwick's Dutch subsidiaries, selling to local management. Selecman's performance enabled him to renegotiate some of the company's outstanding debt, cutting average interest rates by about 2.5 percent, encouraging company officials to issue optimistic predictions about the firm's future. [48]

Eugene Barwick spent this time alternately fighting with Selecman over the latter's austerity program and defending himself against allegations of lying to the SEC. In November 1977, Barwick resigned himself to the inevitable and entered a guilty plea, admitting to misleading government authorities about his knowledge of financial improprieties in the late 1960s and early 1970s. He acknowledged that some of his employees had inflated inventory figures for the purpose of overvaluing Barwick Industries' public stock offering in 1968 and that he had discovered the problem in 1973. When questioned by SEC investigators in November 1975, Barwick denied any knowledge of these activities because, as he told the judge, "I just couldn't bring myself to acknowledge it." Barwick justified his actions by claiming that he was defending his company and its workers: "I did it to protect the company, the 4,000 people working for the company, to protect myself and the company's reputation." [49]

Barwick obtained new financing and managed to regain control of his company in the fall of 1978, but his return was anticlimactic. The company was too far in debt and had lost too many customers as a result of the protracted legal entanglements and the well-publicized internal struggle between Barwick and Selecman. On the eve of Barwick's return to power at the company, Barwick Industries' book value was −0.82 per share, reflecting the dangerous debt load. In typical Barwick fashion, just after regaining control of his company, the once and would-be-future carpet king turned his attention to "revamping the [company's] entire product line," with which "Barwick was displeased," according to an *Atlanta Constitution* business writer. The sixty-four-year-old Barwick remained as optimistic as ever about the future and immediately began planning to resume his company's commercial carpeting lines, another victim of Selecman's budget ax. [50]

By the end of 1979, Barwick Industries was bankrupt, the founder's recovery plans were in ruins, and the firm ceased operations. The company was much too far gone when Barwick resumed control. It is doubtful that Selecman's program of retrenchment would have done more than prolong the death agony of this former industry giant. Barwick's more ambitious scheme, at least, put the firm out of its misery fairly quickly.

Barwick later blamed the company's financial disaster on stealing by some of his executives. He charged that, under the cover of an employee stock option plan, certain company officials used the occasion of the public stock offering of 1968 to enrich themselves and then to misrepresent inventory values to try to cover their tracks. Barwick was particularly miffed because one of the suspects was "a preacher-turned-businessman." The carpet pioneer bitterly recalled a warning given to him by Walter Heller in the early 1960s: "Beware of hymn-singing sons of bitches." [51]

Certainly unscrupulous managers were not uncommon in the Dalton district in the 1960s and 1970s, but Barwick's problems were in all likelihood deeper than simple corruption. A Barwick officer noted in the midst of the creditor takeover of 1975 that the company had bought two new continuous dyeing machines in 1967 for about $450,000 each. As of May 1975, "one of them [was] still in the crate. It just seemed like the way we did everything back then," recalled Barwick president A. J. Paton. Barwick Industries had the capacity "to make approximately $300 million in domestic carpet sales a year," Paton observed, yet "the best year we ever had was $192 million." Charles Selecman agreed, claiming that "we [had] huge facilities not being fully utilized."[52]

Barwick never did anything in a small way. He developed an expansive vision of the role of the tufted carpet industry in the northwest Georgia area. The industry had the capacity to produce deep, fundamental change in these communities, and Barwick viewed his company's participation and leadership in such efforts as a civic duty. He also tried to shift the carpet industry's focus away from producing ever cheaper carpeting and toward greater attention to new product development and consumer satisfaction. Barwick admitted that his management style was nontraditional: "We ran a loose ship." Barwick recalled with pride that he had always allowed employees ample opportunity to display their "creative ability" and maintained that "we'd go along with them almost every time. Whether there was a mistake or not, there wasn't any squelching [of new ideas]."

Barwick's energy and enthusiasm for sales was crucial to the early development of the industry. He was without question the tufted carpet industry's number one salesman. Barwick's talents were not so well suited to the task of managing a mature firm in a maturing industry. As long as total industry sales were rising dramatically, during the 1950s and 1960s, Barwick's high-risk, try-everything-and-see-what-works strategy was viable. The Barwick style, however, was not popular among the other large producers within the industry. The financial problems of Barwick Industries in the 1970s severely damaged the tufted carpet industry's reputation with Wall Street investors. Barwick Industries, only a decade earlier the largest and apparently most successful firm in tufting, had ceased to exist by 1980. The task of restoring—indeed, establishing—the industry's standing with potential investors fell to other companies.

Barwick reflected the often contradictory impulses that energized the entrepreneurs of the Dalton district. He sought relief from the low prices and low-quality goods he feared were ruining the industry. He pursued "bigness" with a passion, borrowing money at an alarming rate to finance expansion. The very flexibility that gave birth to the tufted textile industry was sacrificed bit by bit with every advance from the Heller company.

Barwick Mills became the world's largest carpet producer, but at a tremendous cost. Barwick's love affair with large-scale production financed by credit created a dependence on ever increasing sales. Barwick's very size, at least in the manner in which it was achieved, curtailed the firm's flexibility. The carpet industry's top salesman refused to accept commodity status for his products, yet consumers consistently refused to take note of efforts to create name-brand recognition. Barwick preached specialized production, product differentiation, and an expanding product line. His methods forced him to accept the mass-production mentality or reject it at his peril.

A World of Opportunity II

The rapid pace of growth in the Dalton district led to competition for workers among manufacturers. This competition in turn led to high turnover rates, wage gains, and rising expectations among workers in the Dalton area. As the carpet industry experienced unparalleled growth in the 1960s, workers sought to improve their wages and working conditions as well. For a time in the early 1960s, it appeared that the district's workers might choose to organize under the auspices of the Textile Workers Union of America. By the end of the decade, the threat of unionization had receded for the manufacturers, in part because of effective management resistance and a rising standard of living and intensified competition among new firms for workers. The explosion of demand for tufted floor coverings created new opportunities for enterprising individuals in the Dalton district. The low barriers to entry into tufting, rapidly rising demand for tufted products, and the existence of finishing companies in the area encouraged the creation of new enterprises in the Dalton district. The carpet market changed significantly in the late 1970s, and a new slow-growth environment had settled in by the early 1980s. The manufacturers association attempted to manage conflict between large and small firms and deal with government regulation from the late 1960s through the 1980s but met with limited success.

The carpet industry had virtually completed its southward drift by the early 1960s. Tufted carpets and rugs dominated the marketplace, accounting for $2.56 in shipments for every $1.00 in woven shipments. More than 70 percent (130 of 181) of the firms engaged in tufting carpets were located in the South. Among southern states, Georgia was far ahead of any other in tufting carpets and rugs. Georgia tufted carpet mills represented 56 percent of the establishments in the industry and accounted for 63 percent of the dollar value of tufted carpet shipments and 64 percent of total value added. The hub of all this manufacturing activity was Dalton. Sixty-seven floor covering mills in Whitfield County alone produced 56 percent of the value added for the entire tufted carpet and rug industry in 1963. The value added by Whitfield County's floor covering mills more than doubled in the years 1958–63, from just under $29 million to almost $61 million.[1]

The Dalton district of the 1960s exemplified the hopes of those southern leaders who had advocated entrepreneurial capitalism as a development strategy in the 1940s. Enterprising businessmen and workers took risks, developed new stylistic innovations, and created new companies and jobs. The new firms that came to characterize the Dalton district bore little resemblance to the old textile institutions that had dominated Dalton before the tufting revolution. The Crown and American Thread Company mills were large, traditional, paternalistic, and stable. The new carpet mills were small and innovative; they originated from and in turn encouraged a greater sense of economic individualism; and they were anything but stable.

TABLE 10. New Firm Creation in the Tufted Carpet Industry, Selected
Years 1958–1982

	Number of Companies	Number of Establishments	Number of Small Establishments[a]
1958	88	92	20
1963	167	181	60
1967	210	244	91
1972	333	381	145
1977	397	449	198
1982	324	367	140

[a]Establishments with fewer than 20 employees.

Source: U.S. Bureau of the Census, Census of Manufactures, 1963 and 1992.

Evans-Black, or E & B, Carpet Company was an excellent example of the fluidity of the Dalton district. Eddie Evans and Art Black met in Dallas, Texas, in 1950. Black was in Dallas as a sales representative for a home furnishings distributor. Evans, a Fort Worth native, was the southwestern sales representative for Barwick Mills. The two became friends, and soon after, Black went to work for Barwick Mills as a sales manager in Atlanta. Black recalled that "we both had this burning desire to be in the carpet business for ourselves, so we left Barwick in 1957 and opened Evans-Black Carpet Company, a wholesale distributor," in Dallas. Evans and Black used the contacts and connections (especially in the Southwest) developed in their years with Barwick to start their own firm. Initially, Evans-Black was a sales-only company, buying carpet from Dalton-area manufacturers and selling to home furnishings retailers. Within two years, the new company was facing stiff competition from manufacturers who had decided to begin selling direct to retailers. "Competition got so rough," Black recalled, "that we formed E & B Carpet Mills in 1959" as a commission seller for direct mill shipments. By the end of 1959, Evans and Black had decided that the company must begin manufacturing its own products. They convinced their silent third partner—Frank McCarty, a former vice president for manufacturing at Barwick Mills and one of the most capable manufacturing managers in the tufting industry—to become an active participant in the business. McCarty came on board to oversee manufacturing operations in Dalton, while Evans and Black remained in the Southwest to manage the firm's sales.[2]

E & B was immediately successful, in large part as a result of the contacts of Evans and Black and the manufacturing expertise of Frank McCarty. E & B began with 1 tufting machine in 1960; by 1966 the company operated 12 tufting machines, and its mill covered more than 140,000 square feet in Dalton. E & B turned out more than 650,000 square yards of carpet per month in 1966. Unusual for a medium-sized carpet mill, E & B was fully integrated from yarn spinning through dyeing and finishing. The company, which manufactured carpet exclusively from synthetic fibers, focused on selling groups of similar carpet fabrics, rather than individual products. E & B achieved great success with American Cyanamid's acrylic fiber, Creslan. E & B successfully marketed to retailers a Creslan "collection" called "Governor's Row," which included five quality grades and a wide selection of colors. E & B also emphasized training for its sales force to a greater extent than most other manufacturers. By 1966, E & B employed more than 650, with 450 working in manufacturing in Dalton and the rest engaging in sales and administrative work.[3] E & B also spawned new mills, created by former employees, such as Galaxy Mills.

The story of the origins, rise, and eventual sale of Galaxy Carpet Mills illustrates almost all the major trends in the district from the late 1950s to the end of the 1980s. Galaxy was a prime example of the way new firms were created in Tuftland, particularly in the "second wave" of the carpet industry's growth after 1967. Galaxy's CEO, Irv Harvey, also played a key role in reforms that reshaped the industry's trade association in the 1970s and early 1980s. By the end of the 1980s, the Dalton district was a much less hospitable environment for new players and small firms.

Dalton was not the only small town in northwest Georgia transformed by the rise of the carpet industry. Chatsworth, Calhoun, Ringgold, and other small communities participated in the tufted carpet boom as well. Galaxy Carpet Mills, formed in 1968, was a Chatsworth success story. The company's main facilities were located in Chatsworth, and one of the four partners who initially founded the company was a Murray County native. Galaxy's founders learned the business in some of the pioneer companies of the 1950s and early 1960s—Cabin Crafts, Barwick Mills, Katherine Chenilles, and E & B. Galaxy rose to become a "top ten" company within the carpet industry before a buyout in 1989.

Bobby Mosteller was born and raised in Murray County, Georgia. His father worked as a sawmiller before acquiring the Chevrolet auto dealership in the county seat of Chatsworth. Mosteller's mother encouraged her son to finish high school and attend college if he wanted to avoid working in the sawmill. Bobby took her advice. With help from his family, he graduated from Lincoln Memorial University in 1953. After spending two years in military service, Mosteller returned to Chatsworth in search of a livelihood. He worked as a bookkeeper for his father's car dealership for a year. He then turned to teaching and spent a few years as a math teacher at Murray County High School. In 1958, Mosteller entered the carpet industry. A friend at Katherine Chenilles suggested that Bobby apply for a job there. He initially worked in production but moved quickly into customer service.[4]

Katherine Chenilles was a seedbed for the industry in the late 1950s. The company was owned by the Arab American Shaheen family. Said Shaheen had moved to Dalton from Chicago to establish the company. His nephews worked with him in the business, while other relatives in the Midwest marketed Katherine products. Mosteller went to work at Katherine just after Said's nephew, Shaheen, had left Katherine to form his own company, World Carpets. While at Katherine, Mosteller worked with Bud Seretean and Guy Henley, who later founded Coronet Carpets, and Willis Mashburn, an industry technological innovator who was later a key player in Painter Carpets. All these industry pioneers passed through Katherine Chenilles in the 1950s.[5]

Mosteller left Katherine in 1961 to become customer service manager at Pride Carpet Mills in Calhoun, Georgia. Mosteller left Pride abruptly in 1962. Workers at Pride Mills and Dixie Belle Mills, a division of Bell Industries, voted in favor of union representation. The workers joined the Textile Workers Union of America and negotiated the first union contract in the tufted carpet and rug industry, signed in 1963. Though workers' wages and benefits rose under the union contract, Mosteller was suspicious of the union and uncomfortable working in a union mill. As soon as the union was voted in, Mosteller began looking for employment elsewhere.[6]

Mosteller quickly found an alternative. He got a job as tufting room supervisor at the Dalton plant of E & B Carpet Mills. Mosteller moved up quickly at E & B. He organized and managed the company's sample department in Dallas, Texas. He was appointed assistant to the president (then Art Black) in charge of market research and development a year later. By 1964, Mosteller was a stockholder and vice president at E & B.[7]

While moving up the ladder at E & B, Mosteller encountered a group of men who would later help him found Galaxy Carpet Mills. Irv Harvey and Irv Pomerantz, E & B salesmen in the Chicago area, impressed Mosteller with their ability to move the merchandise. Harvey would later serve as president of Galaxy, and Pomerantz would serve as marketing director.[8]

Mosteller also became friends with another Dalton-area native while at E & B, Charles Bramlett. Bramlett grew up "poor," in his estimation, in Dalton. He was a star football player at Dalton High School, blocking for teammate Bob Shaw, later CEO of Shaw Industries. Bramlett turned down a college football scholarship, opting instead to marry and start a family just after graduation from high school. Bramlett's résumé was a virtual who's who in the carpet industry in the 1950s and 1960s. He worked for Frank McCarty at McCarty Chenilles. He and McCarty stayed on with the company after it was purchased by Gene Barwick. Bramlett was thus present at the creation of Barwick Mills, the largest company in the industry in the late 1950s and 1960s, as well as the most colorful. Bramlett moved to Cabin Crafts in 1955 as assistant plant manager. During a six-year apprenticeship there, Bramlett proved to be an outstanding production organizer. He was hired away by Frank McCarty to work with E & B in 1960. By 1964, Bramlett had become McCarty's assistant plant manager, a stockholder, and a vice president of the company. When McCarty retired in 1965, Bramlett took over as general manager in charge of production at E & B.[9]

Mosteller and Bramlett began discussing the possibility of forming their own company while working at E & B in the mid-1960s. After the workday was over, around 5:00 P.M., Mosteller recalled, "Charlie and I would . . . go into the office, sit down, and put our feet up and talk about going into business for ourselves someday." Then in 1967, Armstrong World Industries acquired E & B, and Mosteller and Bramlett had an opportunity to sell their stock. Mosteller saw Bramlett "walking through the plant one day and Charlie says, 'If we're ever going to do anything, now's the time to do it.' " The two production-oriented Georgians decided that they needed help in sales and marketing. They contacted Irv Harvey, E & B's director of marketing. Harvey agreed to come on board and suggested Irv Pomerantz, then E & B's sales manager for the Midwest, as another partner.[10]

The choice of the name "Galaxy," according to Mosteller and Bramlett, was a conscious effort to associate the new company with the idea of "space-age" design and technology. Formed in 1968, the company came into prominence at the height of the Apollo moon program. Many of the company's initial styles had space-based labels and names associated with the space program, such as "Schirra Shag," named for one of the Apollo astronauts.[11]

The partners made an interesting foursome. Harvey and Pomerantz were Jews from Chicago and New York, respectively; Bramlett and Mosteller were Southern Baptists from the heart of the Bible Belt. Bramlett remembered his initial trip to New York in the early 1970s, when Galaxy went public, as culture shock: he said that he almost "broke [his] neck looking up at the buildings." Harvey, for his part, had never been happy living in Dallas during his time with E & B. He and his wife much preferred their native Chicago.[12]

The new company's unique organization afforded Harvey a chance to go back to Chicago. The partners decided to split Galaxy's functions between two main locations. The company would be officially headquartered in Elk Grove Village, Illinois, just outside Chicago. Harvey and Pomerantz would be based there, and they would run the sales and marketing operations from Elk Grove. Harvey and Pomerantz had extensive contacts in the Midwest, based on years of selling carpet and other products in the region. Galaxy initially limited its marketing and sales efforts to the Midwest, trying to maximize the advantages of those contacts and avoid stretching the new company's production facilities.

Bramlett and Mosteller took charge of organizing and managing the company's production facilities. Galaxy's management chose to locate in the Dalton area, taking advantage of Mosteller's and Bramlett's knowledge of the area and the existing carpet expertise of the area's workforce.[13] More specifically, Galaxy located in Chatsworth, which in itself was moderately unusual. Carpet, or other industry for that matter, had never quite "taken off" in Chatsworth and surrounding Murray County.

Galaxy's founders had their own view on Chatsworth's relative lack of development compared with Dalton. Chatsworth native Mosteller was convinced that Chatsworth lacked the farsighted leadership that Dalton had in men like V. D. Parrott. Mosteller told the story of McCarty Chenilles as a way of illustrating Murray County's long-standing ambivalence toward economic development. In 1940, Frank McCarty had started his chenille company in Tennga, a tiny community in Murray County situated right on the Tennessee-Georgia state line, hence the town's name. A few years later, he moved into the relative metropolis of Chatsworth. As Mosteller told the story, McCarty had two ways of shipping his goods out of town: the L & N Railroad and the Mason-Dixon rail company. Around 1946, George Murdock decided to start a new freight company in Dalton, Murdock Freight Lines. Murdock wanted to extend his service into Murray County and provide competition for the two established lines, thus exerting some downward pressure on freight rates. Murdock needed government approval for such a move. The new freight line owner asked Frank McCarty, one of the largest employers in Murray County, to go with him to testify on behalf of Murdock Freight Lines before the state public service commission in Atlanta. To McCarty's surprise, J. Roy McGinty, the editor of the *Chatsworth Times,* appeared at the hearing to testify *against* allowing Murdock Freight Lines into Murray County, arguing that Murray County didn't need another carrier. Mosteller recalled that McCarty believed that McGinty had probably been contacted by Mason-Dixon. Whether that was true or not, McGinty evidently had the support of other community leaders in Murray County. The commission turned down Murdock's request. The day after the hearing, McCarty began looking for property in Dalton. Within a few months, McCarty Chenilles had moved to Dalton.[14]

Despite that history, Bramlett and Mosteller were convinced that Chatsworth was an ideal location for Galaxy. Many people in Murray County worked in the carpet industry but had to commute to Dalton.

Mosteller believed that many people would stay home to work for Galaxy. Indeed, Bramlett and Mosteller already had lists of experienced Chatsworth workers who were employed by Dalton manufacturers. Galaxy hired away many of these, causing some ill feelings between the new company's owners and old friends in Dalton.[15]

Another factor in the decision to build in Murray County was a seemingly new attitude on the part of the community's leadership. Irv Harvey detailed the contributions of a group of "community-minded businessmen" known as Chatsworth Enterprises. This group "made available a package of land [seventeen acres]" and financing for the new company. Galaxy would construct a 30,000-square-foot manufacturing facility. The total cost for land and building was projected to be about $140,000. The Chatsworth-based Cohutta Banking Company held a first mortgage of $57,500, and Chatsworth Enterprises held a second mortgage of a similar amount. The average interest rate on the two loans was roughly 7 percent. The remaining initial investment came from money raised from the sale of E & B stock owned by the partners.[16] Galaxy would begin production on a contract basis at leased facilities in Tennga while the plant was under construction. The new building would house two tufting machines, with a capacity for two more. The company's initial plans called for the addition of a dye house on the same site in Chatsworth within two to three years, beginning a process of vertical integration.[17] Company officials were assured by Chatsworth leaders that the city would have adequate water supplies and treatment facilities by that time. As Mosteller and Bramlett recall, however, the city of Chatsworth never did deliver on that promise of new water facilities. When Galaxy built its dyeing facility in 1972, the company had to locate it in Dalton in order to get adequate water. This separation of the dye and tufting plants did not eliminate, but certainly cut into, the anticipated cost savings from integrating the two processes within the same company. As Bramlett said, every time a roll of carpet is loaded onto and unloaded from a truck, there is another opportunity for damage. Despite the problems with the lack of "vision" among Chatsworth's leadership, Bramlett and Mosteller expressed no regrets about locating in Chatsworth. The labor force, according to them, made up for other difficulties.[18]

In his prospectus for the new company, Harvey laid out Galaxy's strategy. The company would concentrate on building sales in the Midwest first and then spread out from there. Harvey wanted to build a system of regional distribution centers and avoid distributors. "Future growth of this industry," Harvey predicted, "lies in direct sales, and only with service centers strategically located can a company give the service necessary." But he wanted to move slowly. Other companies, he warned, had tried to "go national" too quickly and spread themselves "too thin." Harvey believed that the company should not expand beyond the Midwest until it established a five-million-dollar annual sales level, which he projected at two to four years. Galaxy would open with a "short line" of about ten carpet styles concentrated in the "low-medium category."[19]

Harvey contended that mills in the 1960s had followed one of two marketing strategies. There were "mill operations," which shipped direct from the mill to retailers. These mills carried short product lines and made sales based on price rather than service. The problem with these mills was inventory control, which could sink a highly leveraged company. Then there were "distributing-oriented operations," which sold mainly through independent distributors or company-owned service centers. These companies usually carried longer lines "in an effort to have every type of carpet a dealer might want." These companies, particularly the majority who sold through wholesale distributors, Harvey argued, "spread themselves too thin from an efficiency standpoint." Galaxy officials hoped to "combine the best features of both philosophies."[20]

Despite Harvey's elaborate plan of action, the company struggled. By early 1970, Galaxy was on the verge of going under. Mosteller recalled getting a frantic phone call from Irv Harvey. "You guys come to Chicago," Harvey told him. "We've got to turn this thing around." Charlie Bramlett suggested that he and Mosteller go in style: "Let's go first class; it might be our last flight." Luckily, Mosteller and Bramlett took with them samples of a new style, Caravelle. Harvey and Pomerantz "hit the road selling." According to Mosteller, "that one product probably saved the company."[21]

Small-town relationships also helped bail out Galaxy. Bramlett recalled that early on, Galaxy was strapped for cash to finish a plant expansion. The company managed to get a $1 million loan from Bert Lance's Calhoun First National Bank. Bramlett signed a note putting up his $25,000 home as collateral. As he knew at the time, this was basically a character loan. Lance approved the loan on the basis of Bramlett's and Mosteller's standing in the community and Lance's estimation that they could make the company work with a little more capital. By December 1970, Galaxy was boldly celebrating "a quarter-decade of progress," led by "'Caravelle' carpet, 1970's big winner." In January 1971, the company announced the opening of the first of its regional warehouses in Dallas.[22]

Galaxy's strategy appeared to be working. By mid-1971, the company had survived the early crisis and began to establish itself in the community in Chatsworth. The company employed about three hundred people, most in Murray County, running ten tufting machines. The company was in the midst of its second plant expansion in less than a year. Galaxy had increased its product line to twenty-five. Galaxy stayed in the low-medium price range. As the company slogan put it, Galaxy made "very rich carpet that not so rich people can afford."[23]

Company management made the decision to go public shortly, in December 1971. A company prospectus released at that time demonstrated Galaxy's quick progress. Company sales were up 87.7 percent in fiscal 1971, to more than $15.5 million. Profits rose a phenomenal 400 percent, from $151,525 (or 0.17 per share) in 1970 to $725,405 (or 0.76 per share). According to plan, 85 percent of total sales were direct to retailers through the virtually brand-new regional warehouses, with no single customer accounting for more than 2 percent of sales.[24]

Galaxy's rapid rise led to industrywide interest in the company's leadership. *Home Furnishings Daily* profiled the company's top management in April 1972. Irv Pomerantz gave his own interpretation of Galaxy's management strategy. "A lot of mills are R&D-oriented, but thank God we didn't choose that route," Pomerantz told *HFD*. Pomerantz identified two paths for carpet companies: "that of design leader with smaller profits, or that of following the market closely and bringing out popular styles and price points." Galaxy "chose the latter." Pomerantz acknowledged that "we don't want to be leaders. We'd rather jump in on good big selling numbers." Galaxy wanted "the volume items." Bluntly, Galaxy to an extent typified the "copycat" strategy often employed in carpet manufacture. Styles and colors were difficult to protect in this industry. Galaxy's market strategy reflected this philosophy. The company typically started a carpet market with five or six new styles of carpet, and if any were not immediately accepted, they were pulled. "None of this 'it's a slow starter' stuff," Pomerantz said. "If it's not moving by, say, midmarket, we'll pull it and could end up with [only] four new items." [25]

Company president Irv Harvey echoed his partner's sentiments. When asked about Galaxy's position on plant expansion, Harvey responded, "We believe in expanding—catch up with sales rather than building a huge plant, then going out to fight for orders to fill it. And it looks a lot better on your P&L statement, which is what we're interested in." Harvey and Pomerantz agreed that the regional warehouse, though not a new idea, was the key to Galaxy's success. [26]

Another key event in Galaxy's evolution was the company's cosponsorship with Dow Chemical of urethane backing for carpets. The venture, completed in 1975, gave Galaxy a one-year head start on other companies in using this new backing material. "For that time, it was a proprietary product for us," Harvey noted. [27] The risk involved was perhaps uncharacteristic of the company, but it paid off handsomely.

Galaxy continued to expand through the mid-1970s. Sales and profits generally rose. The conservative approach worked fairly well for the company. The only major disappointment in the first half of the seventies was the failure of Galaxy's initial limited foray into commercial contract carpets. Galaxy moved to integrate the company's operations further with the purchase of a yarn-spinning mill in 1974. The company continued to open new regional warehouses. [28]

In 1977, Galaxy tried to jump on another emerging trend. The company signed a contract with the famous fashion designer Oleg Cassini. Galaxy wanted Cassini to create a line of original designer carpets. Irv Harvey announced that Cassini was selected after extensive market research, which indicated that Cassini was one of the most widely recognized fashion designers in the world. After all, Galaxy was not the type of company to risk much on a nobody. Cassini was quoted as saying that he was looking forward to this new endeavor like "Aladdin on his Magic Carpet. I see carpet taking on new dimensions in the home, covering walls and furniture as well as the floor. There is no telling where these inspirations will lead us." [29]

Harvey announced that Galaxy would be installing new equipment to open up a broader spectrum of colors for Cassini. "The entire palette is open," Cassini said, "but I hope to emphasize the Old Masters of the Italian Renaissance. Their soft tones, as well as the inherent qualities of carpet, should provide the family with warmth—psychological as well as physical." Galaxy introduced the Cassini line in the spring of 1978. Harvey reported that "interest [among dealers] has exceeded our expectations."[30]

Galaxy launched a television ad campaign for the Cassini line in the summer of 1978, targeting fifteen major markets. The line also received significant attention as the subject of articles in more than 350 newspapers. Store placement for the Cassini line was characterized as "fabulous" by Harvey in June 1978. Macy's carried the carpets exclusively among New York department stores. Harvey made it clear that though the Cassini line was a high-end product, Galaxy was still primarily a company interested in high-volume, low to medium-priced carpets.[31]

At the time the Cassini line was introduced, Galaxy was riding high. The company had risen to become the thirteenth- or fourteenth-largest volume seller in the industry by 1978, quite an accomplishment in the firm's first ten years in a crowded field. Galaxy's fiscal 1977 sales stood at $74 million, producing a net income of roughly $2.2 million. Galaxy had effectively integrated its operations, with thirteen hundred employees in Georgia and Tennessee handling yarn spinning, tufting, dyeing, cutting, and finishing. Galaxy's technological jump on the competition with urethane backing, coupled with its well-publicized association with Oleg Cassini, came close to giving Galaxy something so rare as to be almost nonexistent in the carpet industry: a brand name that could sell products.[32]

Galaxy's management proved able to cope with and profit from recession, something unusual in the carpet industry. The company did it by following an aggressive strategy that would later be perfected by Shaw Industries. Just before the recession of 1973–75, Galaxy had gone through a major expansion in warehouses. "Instead of closing them down" when the recession hit, however, Irv Harvey noted that "we continued opening new warehouses." Galaxy thus took some inventory pressure off small retailers and thereby enhanced the company's competitiveness with those stores. Galaxy kept its machines running and its regional warehouses stocked. "During the recession," Harvey said, "retailers kept their inventories lower; they needed steady, quick shipments." Galaxy also profited during that recession because of its commitment to styling. The company installed new dye equipment in late 1975 and increased its margins on certain products. The company held firm on these prices, counting on color and style to sell the goods. "Some companies got into trouble by dumping goods, which we did not do," according to Harvey.[33]

Similarly, Galaxy seemed to emerge from the 1981–82 recession stronger than ever. According to a Chicago business publication, Galaxy was "flying high on the magic carpet of merchandising" in 1981 while its competitors suffered "sluggish sales and pinched margins." Galaxy's sales were up 40 percent in the previous year—this in a year when the total dollar value of U.S. carpet shipments rose only 13.9 percent. The company attributed about half its increase to higher volume and about half to price increases.[34]

Galaxy's strategy was the same as it had been in the earlier recession. "Paramount" in that strategy was attention to retailers' concerns. The firm increased its warehouse inventory and eased the "burden on dealers facing low demand and high interest rates." While all mills promise customer service, Galaxy "distinguished itself by making good on the promise." Carpet dealers were particularly impressed by Galaxy's commitment to new styles aimed at the "higher-income consumer." Galaxy introduced two new "velvety carpets" at the January trade shows, "Biarritz" and "Deville." These carpets sold wholesale for fifteen to twenty dollars per square yard. These "high-end" products tended to be less recession-sensitive than low- and medium-end carpets.[35]

The good times continued to roll for Galaxy in 1982. In July, Kurt Salmon Associates, management consultants, published its eleventh annual "Performance Profile of Textile Companies." Galaxy ranked first among the eight publicly owned companies producing only carpet products. The competition included Shaw Industries, Peerless of Canada, Masland, Salem, and several others. Galaxy posted higher numbers than Shaw in nine of eleven categories of analysis. Shaw had higher gross sales ($250 million) than Galaxy ($144 million), as well as a greater net income ($8.4 million to $5.8 million). In other important respects, as the analysis moved away from primarily size-related criteria, Galaxy outperformed Shaw. Galaxy's net income as a percentage of sales was slightly higher than Shaw's (4 percent to 3.36 percent). Galaxy's return on total assets was 8.78 percent to Shaw's 5.94 percent. In terms of gross profit margin, Galaxy bested Shaw as well, 26.43 percent to 16.78 percent. Galaxy's performance was good enough to place the firm in *Fortune*'s "Second 500" list for 1982, at number 929.[36]

Galaxy's earnings and sales did dip in fiscal 1982 because of the recession, but not as low as many manufacturers'. Galaxy rebounded strongly in 1983. After sales and income each fell in 1982 from 1981 levels, by 1983 both were up substantially above 1981 marks. Sales were over $200 million and income topped $7.8 million. In a cutthroat market, *Crain's Chicago Business* asserted, Galaxy had "managed to emerge as a solid winner." Galaxy's policy of maintaining inventories and production during recessions was paying off, according to industry analysts: "Galaxy was willing to do less well in a recession, and their customers remembered the good service later. This is how they've picked up marketshare all along."[37]

Galaxy also launched "an aggressive advertising campaign—unusual within the carpet industry" in an effort to build a brand name for its products. Ads appeared in magazines such as *Architectural Digest, House & Garden,* and *Woman's Day.* With increased advertising, Galaxy also added plant and equipment to match anticipated new sales, as much as $20 million between 1981 and 1983. The company boldly announced plans to spend an additional $30 million over the next three years. Galaxy also announced plans to enter the commercial carpet business, probably by buying an existing manufacturer. In early 1984, the company's future appeared bright.[38]

Less than a year after these glowing assessments based on record earnings, Galaxy experienced a severe reversal of fortune. A price war swept the industry in 1984, and Galaxy's earnings fell 20 percent in the second quarter. E. F. Hutton, only a few months before "a Galaxy cheerleader," drastically "scaled back bullish earnings forecasts" for the year. Galaxy's attempts to buy an existing commercial carpet company did not pan out. President Irv Harvey indicated that the company might start up a commercial line with existing equipment and sales force, contrary to previously stated policy. Most industry insiders knew that commercial and residential carpets were two different animals that did not mix well; this move may have reflected frustration.[39]

Harvey also admitted that the company would not spend all of the planned $30 million on capital improvements within three years. Indeed, the company would spend less than $7 million of a planned $10 million in 1984. Most of this money had been targeted for plant modernization and new capacity. The decision to cut capital spending did not sit well with Wall Street observers. "Textile companies are becoming more automated all the time, and companies that don't update their equipment won't be around too long," one analyst warned.[40]

Over the next year, Galaxy was able to acquire a commercial carpet company, Hartford Carpet Mill in Chattanooga, Tennessee. Harvey cautioned that it would take some time, perhaps a few years, to get Galaxy's commercial line in full operation, so the company could expect no quick returns on this investment. Falling prices continued to plague Galaxy's, and the industry's, balance sheets, as well. The company had a record $222 million in sales in 1984 but saw net income fall 11 percent for the year. Harvey also reversed his position on capital spending again, announcing in March 1985 that the company was on target for its original three-year, $30 million plan.[41]

The company continued to struggle in the mid-1980s. Earnings were off in 1985 and 1986. Throughout these difficult times, Galaxy refused to make wholesale price cuts, as many competitors had. Galaxy sacrificed volume for price, the opposite of the industry's historical trend. The company did lower some prices, but not as dramatically as competitors. Harvey admitted in 1986 that "we probably stuck to our guns a little too strongly" in the price war.[42]

Galaxy's management turned the company's sagging fortunes around in late 1986 and 1987. Two major moves highlighted Galaxy's comeback. First, Harvey and company restructured Galaxy's marketing strategy, which had been described as "aimless" by analysts. The company pulled off a major marketing coup by reaching an agreement with Sears in late 1986 to become a major carpet supplier for the retail chain. Galaxy would manufacture "private label" carpets that would bear the Sears label in stores. Second, Galaxy was among the first companies to embrace enthusiastically Du Pont's new stain-resistant fibers in 1986–87 (see chapter 8). Galaxy committed more resources than most companies to production of carpets using the new fibers. By early 1988, about 75 percent of Galaxy's product line was stain-resistant, "substantially higher than most competitors' mix," according to industry observers. The increased consumer demand for the new fibers meshed with Galaxy's philosophy of holding prices steady. People were willing to pay more for the new stain-resistant carpets, and smaller competitors could not as readily slash prices on such capital-intensive products. In 1987, Galaxy's broadloom carpet line sold at an average of $7.17, compared with an industry average of $6.16.[43]

These new strategies led to a turnaround for the company. Galaxy's sales for fiscal 1988 were up 29 percent to more than $260 million. Earnings rose fivefold over those of 1986, to almost $6 million. Galaxy was again characterized by stock market analysts as a well-run company that was undervalued. Galaxy stock traded at about $12 per share, only two-thirds of its book value. One analyst projected that if Galaxy were sold, the stock would not go for $12; an opening bid of $24 per share was more likely.[44]

Rumors circulated that Galaxy's management was open to a buyout offer. Bobby Mosteller recalled that he and his original partners, still the top management of the company, had decided that the industry was changing rapidly and they were unsure that they wanted to do what it took to compete. Galaxy had reached a crisis point in 1987–88. As a high-volume residential carpet producer, either the company had to get much bigger to compete with the likes of Shaw Industries, or it had to sell out. It was "acquire or be acquired," according to Mosteller. So the company began to put out the word that, for the right price, Galaxy was on the market.[45]

Mosteller and Charles Bramlett candidly recalled the problems faced by Galaxy in the late 1980s. Facing Shaw Industries' withering onslaught (see chapter 8), many companies were caught short. Shaw was a merciless competitor and the undisputed low-cost producer in the industry. If Galaxy management wanted to compete with this cost-cutting giant, the company would have to get lean and mean. Mosteller admitted that by the late eighties, Galaxy had "layered itself to death" with too many managers with "fancy titles." Charles Bramlett recalled that the company became too enamored of complexity and bureaucracy for its own sake. He remembered getting daily reports from several departments that were often several inches thick. Bramlett became so frustrated with the volume of useless paper and unmanageable data that one morning he picked up the report and walked all over Galaxy's corporate offices in Chatsworth with the report trailing behind him. By the time it was unraveled, it covered most of the floors in Galaxy's offices. He told his staff to condense the reports down to one page in the future.[46]

Both Mosteller and Bramlett also expressed genuine reluctance to engage in the personnel cuts and "downsizing" that would have been necessary for Galaxy to run at the pace Shaw Industries was setting. The two area natives had known many of their managers personally for years, attended the same churches, sent their children to the same schools, cheered at the same high school football games. Bramlett also expressed anxiety over the responsibility the company's owners had toward the community, with Galaxy providing several thousand jobs. By 1988, it was time to get out.[47]

Galaxy's financial turnaround proved temporary, adding pressure on top management to sell. By early 1989, though Galaxy was ranked ninth on the latest carpet industry "Top 25" list, analysts doubted the company's long-term survivability. Galaxy posted a $600,000 pretax loss for the year ending in September 1988 (though onetime accounting changes transformed that into a $1.5 million net profit). The roof collapsed on Galaxy's Dalton dye house in 1988, and insurance payoffs did not come close to meeting company costs for repairs and lost production, according to Galaxy officials. No sooner had the roof been repaired than the Dalton area was struck by floods, again interrupting production and necessitating extensive repairs. Order cancellations forced customers to switch to companies able to make deliveries. The company rebounded slightly in the first quarter of 1989 but slumped even lower in the second quarter: Galaxy lost $1.4 million in the three-month period.[48]

Galaxy announced on May 1, 1989, that the company had accepted a buyout offer from Peerless Carpet Corporation, a Canadian firm. Peerless acquired Galaxy at $14 per share, or $46 million. This was substantially below the estimates of a year earlier but left the original partners well fixed for retirement income. Peerless also agreed to assume $74 million of Galaxy's debt. The company sold at only a slight premium over the $12.37 current market value of its stock. The purchase price amounted to 15 percent of Galaxy's sales volume and 75 percent of the company's book value.[49]

Galaxy succeeded in bursts, with longer periods of struggle. The Chatsworth-Chicago company could not really sustain or take full advantage of these advances. Galaxy integrated backward, trying to produce its own yarn supply and thus gain freedom from dependence on yarn suppliers. Galaxy also made substantial investments in technology and capital improvements. The company teamed with Dow Chemical to develop urethane backing in the mid-1970s. Galaxy also was quick to invest in continuous dye equipment and experimented with a variety of color systems. The company acquired a reputation as a style leader—or, more properly, a very quick and inexpensive follower, though this reputation began to slip in the 1980s.

Diamond Mills offered a quite different example of new firm creation. The force behind Diamond was Ed Weaver, described by *Carpet & Rug Industry* magazine as "a flamboyant entrepreneur." Weaver, a native of Murray County, Georgia, differed significantly from the founders of Galaxy Mills. Weaver had little formal education or training. A friend recalled that in the mid- and late 1960s, a young Ed Weaver got his start by picking up scraps from larger mills such as Coronet. Weaver and his wife, Linda, then worked at home cutting the scraps into small scatter rugs. Weaver's Diamond Rug Mills of the late 1960s was a small family operation. In 1969, Weaver bought three tufting machines, hired a dozen workers, changed the company's name to Diamond Rug and Carpet Mill, Incorporated, and began manufacturing broadloom carpeting. In the early 1970s, Weaver began applying an extra-thick foam backing, aptly called "Fatback," to some of his lines. Diamond's founder recalled that the backing was a key to much of the company's early success; the backing was popular with dealers, who promoted the plush comfort offered by Fatback.[50]

In 1978, with sales nearing $100 million, Diamond moved toward vertical integration by buying its first dyeing facilities. Until then, Diamond had contracted out all of its dyeing, though some finishing was done in-house (the application of Fatback). Diamond acquired two of the most modern dyeing facilities in the industry in 1978 (Crusader Carpets' Chatsworth dye house) and 1980 (Venture Carpets' Calhoun, Georgia, facility). Weaver also installed an oven for making its own urethane backings in 1980, making Diamond the first tufting company in the industry with such a capacity. Diamond scored another industry first in 1982 with the installation of two machines capable of extruding polyester olefin yarn for the manufacture of indoor-outdoor and artificial grass carpets. Weaver attributed much of Diamond's success in the early and mid-1980s to the company's introduction of a line of grass carpeting. "We're probably the largest manufacturers of . . . grass carpet for the do-it-yourself market," he observed in a 1986 interview. Diamond also experimented profitably with new thermal dyeing systems in the mid-1980s, enhancing color clarity.[51]

Diamond followed a product innovation strategy. The diversity of the company's product lines (along with low prices), Weaver contended, was the strength of the company. Diamond was "different from most mills," the founder argued, because the company offered "everything from indoor/outdoor carpet, . . . to contract lines, . . . to a complete line of residential carpets. We're not locked into any part of the manufacturing process." By 1986, Weaver's seemingly scattershot approach had proven successful. The company's sales exceeded $210 million, and Diamond employed more than eleven hundred in five tufting, finishing, and yarn extrusion or spinning facilities.[52]

Weaver also became one of the more colorful characters of the Dalton district. The mill owner became most famous locally for his conspicuous consumption. The poor-boy-made-good enjoyed his money; Weaver began collecting classic automobiles as his personal fortune grew in the late 1970s and early 1980s. By 1986, Weaver had 175 classic cars stored in a large air-conditioned warehouse near the firm's original manufacturing facility in Eton, Georgia (near Chatsworth). Weaver enjoyed choosing his car of the day from among several Jaguars, Mercedes, Lamborghinis, and Rolls Royces, as well as a complete collection of Corvettes representing every model year since the car's introduction in 1953.[53] Weaver's attachment to consumption seemed in a sense to mirror the tendency of the area's workers to trade benefits for higher cash wages in the short run and job security for the ability to change employers frequently. Many in the Dalton carpet district apparently wanted to enjoy the material benefits of industrial progress in the here and now.

The Ed Weaver story merged in the public consciousness with many less spectacular stories. For every Ed Weaver who went from outhouse to penthouse, there were literally dozens of Dalton-area natives who managed to achieve a degree of independence. The number of tufted carpet and rug manufacturing establishments employing fewer than 20 persons grew from 26 in 1963 to 112 by 1982. The market share of these small firms rose as well, from about 1.5 percent of industry shipments in 1963 to nearly 3 percent by the time of the 1981–82 recession. Obviously, market share did not rise as fast as new small firms multiplied, but neither were these very small companies merely subdividing a stagnant or dwindling share of industry sales.[54]

These very small establishments typically were started on a shoestring, sometimes by employees or former employees of existing larger mills. An enterprising worker might invest several years' savings—perhaps a couple of thousand dollars—in what Tuftland natives called a "pass machine." A pass machine was simply an older tufting machine that had two, four, or eight needles. These smaller, less expensive machines were no longer used by large firms but were still serviceable in the late 1960s. With a pass machine, an operator had to make several passes over a piece of backing material to produce a piece of carpeting twelve feet in width. The work was time-consuming and tedious and required a steady hand. With a pass machine and perhaps some yarn seconds or leftovers purchased at bargain-basement prices, a single individual or family might produce a few dozen square yards of carpeting that an enterprising salesman might be convinced to hawk. The proceeds from many such small sales eventually might allow a small entrepreneur to purchase a larger, standard twelve- or fifteen-foot-wide used tufting machine. An older, used machine might be slower but nonetheless was still capable of turning out a substantial volume of product. In the late 1960s and early 1970s, new commercial markets opened for cheap carpeting—mainly new office construction, motel chains, and moderately priced housing developments. A small operator with connections and contacts built up over years of working in and around the industry might be able to acquire contracts to supply carpet for new motels or replace worn-out carpet. It was difficult to turn such an operation into a Diamond Carpet Mills; such a leap only rarely occurred. The continued vitality of very small firms such as the one described above, however, also held out the promise of social mobility, if in a more modest form. A large number of such firms operated on the fringes and in the interstices of the tufted textile economy of northwest Georgia. The opportunity to become one's own boss was a reality within the Dalton district, at least for a time.[55]

Commission tufting was another outlet for small and medium manufacturers. Production scheduling was an imprecise science at best in Tuftland, and during the boom years from 1958 through the late 1970s demand often put pressure on production capacity. Small firms often took subcontracts from larger mills, filling orders that exceeded the capacity of the large mill. As the practice became more widespread, some small firms specialized in commission tufting just as many better-capitalized entrepreneurs specialized in carpet finishing. Julian Saul of Queen Carpets recalled that the first broadloom carpeting marketed by his company was actually manufactured by other companies. Saul's father and longtime Queen CEO Harry Saul long resisted his son's requests that the family business enter the tufted carpet market. Harry Saul made a substantial fortune making and marketing bathrobes and other small tufted goods. Julian was "very allergic" to the cotton lint that permeated the air at the plant, and he urged his father to shift toward tufted carpeting and artificial fibers. The elder Saul reluctantly allowed his son to experiment with the idea in 1963. Queen's first carpet was "commission-tufted, commission-dyed, commission-backed"; though it carried a Queen label, the carpet was entirely produced by subcontractors. Queen continued with the commission system of carpet production until 1969, when Julian and Harry Saul decided it was time for the company to take control of its own manufacturing processes.[56] The commission tufting system helped firms spread the risk inherent in introducing new products; commission tufters had other contracts, and Queen had other product lines. Queen benefited, at least initially, from the external economy of subcontracting.

Such contract and commission tufting offered opportunities to enterprising middle managers, salesmen, and, occasionally, workers. Browning Tufters was a good example of a successful commission tufting firm. Tom Browning began his association with the carpet industry in 1962, when he went to work for machine maker Singer Cobble. Browning learned to make parts for tufting machines, build yarn creels, and install tufting machines at plant sites. Browning later worked as a sales representative for Southern Machine Company, another Chattanooga-area tufting machine producer. In this capacity, Browning developed extensive contacts with carpet mill owners. He gradually became aware of the opportunities that existed in commission tufting.[57]

Large mills regularly received orders on short notice that exceeded their own capacity. Particularly during and after the recession of 1974–75, medium and large mills were reluctant to invest too much capital in expanding manufacturing capacity. It seemed prudent for large mills to maintain productive capacities that could be efficiently used even in slack times and to rely on subcontractors to fill the gap in good times. Floor covering distributors also represented a substantial market for contract tufting. Browning decided to begin his own contract tufting business in 1974. Within two years, Browning Tufters operated five tufting machines and two eight-hour shifts daily, producing more than four million square yards of carpeting in 1976. In addition to turning out duplicates of merchandise produced by large mills, Browning also experimented with new designs, often convincing a customer to add a Browning design to its collection. Although Browning Tufters produced a substantial amount of carpet, the company did not manufacture anything that bore a Browning label. All merchandise carried the brand label of a larger mill or distributor.[58]

Other firms grew by focusing on specialized markets. J. Rollins Jolly formed J&J Rugs in 1957, and he was joined by partner Thomas Jones a year later. J&J Rugs started out as a jack-of-all-trades company, making small scatter rugs and processing odd lots of pre-dyed yarn (various colors left over from larger runs, "seconds," etc.). J&J was successful, as were a number of small firms in the 1960s and 1970s, in using leftover yarn purchased at bargain-basement prices to produce what came to be called "candy stripe" carpet. Candy stripe became popular for many commercial applications, such as inexpensive new office space and motel chains. It was cheap, and observers had a difficult time determining whether such carpet was stained or soiled (a stain might simply blend into the random multicolored background—thus low maintenance costs).

The company became J&J Industries in 1966, and the new name signaled a new strategy. J&J began specializing in the emerging commercial contract market. The company aggressively pursued emerging high-end markets in major corporate office space, schools, hospitals, retail stores, airports, and other public facilities. J&J invested the profits of its low-end market success with candy stripe in the latest technology, including printing machines. The company faced considerable risks in purchasing expensive equipment, and other firms (most notably industry leader Barwick) suffered from overinvestment in such areas in the 1970s. Rather than using printing and other expensive technologies to enter the mass consumer market, though, J&J focused on a smaller, specific market with high profit margins. J&J quickly developed a reputation for imaginative styling, and by the early 1990s, the company had sales in excess of $150 million. The company remained a private, family-owned enterprise. According to President Jim Jolly, "public companies had an obsession with short-term results." Jolly contended that such pressures often resulted in sacrificing long-term viability for short-term profits, and he refused to take his company in that direction. As the acquisition fever peaked in the carpet industry in the late 1980s, Jolly and his other top managers met with their employees to discuss the company's position. Jolly reassured nervous workers that "we have no plans to be acquired." A decade later, J&J had continued to chart an independent course.[59]

By focusing on extremely high-end, high-margin goods, J&J staked out a market position that was difficult for high-volume producers to attack. Other small and medium-sized producers faced a different challenge in the 1980s. For those smaller firms that tried to compete with the largest producers in the mass residential carpet, it became increasingly difficult to survive. The promise of wealth became more difficult for newcomers to realize as the national economy shifted gears.

Mechanics and inventors perfected the machine-tufting process for bedspread and carpet manufacture in the Dalton area, and the early concentration on the new tufted carpet industry in the Dalton area could be explained by this alone. Carpet manufacture became even more densely concentrated in the northwest corner of Georgia, however, in the 1960s, well after the technology had been refined. The clustering effect seemed to gain momentum in the severe recession of the early 1980s and again during the downturn of the early 1990s. By the mid-1980s, about two-thirds of all U.S. carpet mills were located in Georgia (most in the Dalton district). Two-thirds of the carpet sold by Georgia mills was shipped more than five hundred miles. The tufted carpet industry exemplified the virtues of export-led growth as espoused by William Wilkerson and other spokesmen for southern entrepreneurial capitalism.[60]

Geographers surveyed executives in carpet manufacturing to try to explain this regional manufacturing agglomeration in 1984. The results of the survey revealed clear differences between Georgia and non-Georgia mills on a variety of issues and explained much about the continuing, and increasing, concentration of carpet manufacture in the Dalton district. Mill executives both within Georgia and from elsewhere identified "good service from suppliers of raw materials" as the chief factor in their firms' success. Georgia mill executives, however, valued "proximity to machinery manufacturers" much more highly than those outside the state. Georgia mills also ranked "proximity to the center of the textile industry," and therefore major yarn suppliers (the Carolinas), as an important advantage. Georgia mill owners also clearly believed that "location near other carpet mills" was an important factor in their success, while executives in other sections ranked this variable significantly lower. Even more revealing were the numerical rankings assigned by executives to certain variables. Owners and managers were asked to rate a variety of factors from "1" (essential to success) to "5" (unimportant). Only one variable— service from suppliers of raw materials—received an average score below 2 from executives outside Georgia. Georgia managers gave such scores to four factors, including "lack of unionization." The absence of unions was ranked as the fourth most important variable by Georgia carpet executives, very close behind proximity to machine manufacturers. While mill owners and managers in the Dalton area opposed organization among their workers, the same management personnel apparently placed somewhat less importance on "favorable labor-management relations," a factor they ranked nearer the middle of the twenty-six variables considered (eleventh).[61]

As long as consumer demand grew, the decentralized nature of the Dalton carpet district made it possible for smaller firms to compete effectively, subcontracting with commission finishers to spread the risks associated with new colors and styles. Market conditions changed during the late 1970s. The new conditions favored a vigorous strategy of vertical integration and relentless efforts to cut production costs.

New firms proliferated in the boom years of the 1960s. As demand for tufted carpets rose, so, too, did the dreams of enterprising salesmen, managers, and (occasionally) workers in the Dalton district. In the early 1970s, Dalton had more millionaires per capita than any other city in the nation. The booming carpet industry created wealth and opportunities for accumulation in the communities of northwest Georgia. Peter Spirer, the enterprising young man who came to Dalton to work with his father-in-law and Mose Painter in the late 1950s, clearly expressed the emerging ethos of the Dalton district. Spirer recalled that when Tom Carmichael had asked him to come along on a carpet-buying trip to Dalton in late 1956, he "pictured a small town whose energetic citizens were creating a whole new industry. And, that's exactly what I found." On that initial visit, Spirer noted, "I made up my mind—this is where I will come to seek my fortune." [62] Many shared Spirer's dreams, and for a time tufted carpet manufacture fulfilled that promise of social mobility. The boom in this new industry, however, was intimately connected to broader trends in consumer demand and general economic growth. As the postwar economic golden age tarnished in the late 1970s and 1980s, the economic landscape of the Dalton carpet district changed as well.

Managing Growth

Both the Water, Light, and Sinking Fund (WL&SF) and the trade association struggled to keep pace with the growth of the carpet industry throughout the 1960s and beyond. New mills opened regularly, and the demand of the new production facilities for electricity and water at times threatened to overwhelm the municipal utility. The trade association also encountered increasing difficulty in holding together large, medium, and small firms in a changing marketplace. The WL&SF and the industry's trade association had to deal with government regulation of, respectively, water pollution and product safety and quality. By the mid-1980s, the atmosphere of growth and optimism that had characterized the first two decades of the industry's history had faded.

V. D. Parrott made it his chief goal, however, to accommodate the needs of this burgeoning local industry. The local utility pioneered in using natural gas in the 1950s to offset electricity costs. Parrott convinced the WL&SF commission and the city government to fund the construction of a pipeline to connect with the Southern Natural Gas Company's main line, and construction was completed in 1955. By the early 1980s, Dalton led all Georgia's municipally owned utilities (there were eighty-nine) in natural gas sales; industry accounted for 85 percent of natural gas usage in Dalton. Dalton Utilities and the WL&SF also entered several joint ventures with the Georgia Power Company to help reduce electricity costs. The utility even invested in Georgia Power's controversial nuclear facility, Plant Vogtle.[1]

It was, however, water—quantity and quality—that caused the greatest concern for both the utility and the carpet industry in the 1960s and 1970s. V. D. Parrott devoted his full energy to facilitating the growth of carpet manufacture in the Dalton area. He constantly sought new sources of water—needed in ever increasing amounts by the finishing segment of the carpet industry. The Dalton district was favorably situated near abundant water resources, but the carpet industry's appetite for water overran even the generous natural endowments of the region. Parrott and the WL&SF built a sewage filtration test facility in 1959 to deal with carpet plant waste water.[2]

The region's mills often faced water shortages. The dry summer of 1963 combined with rapid production growth to force many finishing plants to dig their own wells and build pumping stations to access nearby streams. Parrott and the city utility began construction that year on yet another new water treatment facility. Dalton's utility chief observed that until the completion of the new treatment plant, shortages would continue. The carpet industry was "so important" to "the local economy" that Parrott urged all citizens to conserve water. The utility continued building new treatment facilities throughout the 1960s. By the end of that decade, Dalton ranked second only to Atlanta in statewide daily water usage.[3]

As the tufted carpet industry neared the peak of its remarkable rise in the late 1960s, V. D. Parrott began receiving recognition throughout Georgia and the South for his management of the local utility company. The *Atlanta Journal* labeled Parrott a "one-man chamber of commerce" in a positive 1967 profile. The *Journal* noted that executives in the carpet industry gave much of the credit for the industry's growth to the municipal WL&SF and Parrott personally. Parrott himself identified two key factors in the success of the utility's policies. The first was "complete cooperation from industry." Second, Parrott contended that the utility had been successful because it had been "allowed to function without political pressures." Parrott referred to the virtual insulation of the WL&SF from local politics. Parrott was given free rein to operate the utility with no interference from city government, except the members of the WL&SF commission. Membership on that commission was, however, remarkably stable, and Parrott was the acknowledged sole authority on most decisions made by the WL&SF.[4]

Just two years later, the *Atlanta Journal* reported a quite different kind of story from Dalton. In December 1969, the paper referred to Dalton's Mill Creek as "an open sewer." Dalton-area mills and homes were dumping an estimated six million gallons of raw domestic and industrial waste into a small creek that fed Mill Creek daily. The Conasauga River also was reported to be seriously polluted. The water needs of the carpet industry had run directly afoul of the increasing public concern over environmental degradation. Despite the WL&SF's efforts, industry growth had outpaced the ability of the utility to cope.[5]

The election of Jimmy Carter as Georgia's governor in 1970 would eventually force Dalton-area authorities to deal more effectively with the water problem. Carter made environmental protection one of his chief goals, and Dalton quickly became one of the governor's favorite targets. Carter came to Dalton in October 1971 as part of what local officials believed to be a simple goodwill visit. Dalton had recently been designated by the state legislature as "capital for a day." Carter's visit was anything but routine. Carter used the occasion to attack publicly the pollution problem in Dalton. Carter contended that Dalton-area industries were creating one of the worst pollution problems in the state. He threatened a halt to all further construction unless substantial measures were taken to clean up the local rivers and streams. "Dalton is polluting the water to such an extent," the governor observed, "that as far down as Rome people can't swim or fish in the water. As governor, I have no alternative but to see that the laws [on water quality] are enforced." Industry and civic leaders in Dalton expressed shock that Carter would raise the issue on a good-will visit. The governor's sharp remarks may have had an effect. Within six weeks, the WL&SF and the State Water Quality Control Board had reached agreement on a plan to curtail waste water dumping in the short run and improve treatment facilities to clean up the Conasauga River.[6]

As new federal and state regulations in the 1970s assigned to corporations the responsibility for cleaning the wastes they dumped into the nation's waterways, Parrott and Dalton Utilities subsidized local carpet manufacturers by accepting the task of removing dangerous chemicals from the local water supply. State authorities regularly chastised Dalton Utilities, however, for encouraging too rapid growth and pushing local water treatment facilities past their limits.[7]

In the late 1970s, the water problem reached crisis proportions. Dalton-area carpet mill owners, especially newer entrants into the field, showed little concern for water quality. Indeed, many new entrepreneurs felt constrained by Dalton Utilities' minimal restraints on growth, and those mills located outside the jurisdiction of Dalton's WL&SF especially chafed under the limited water resources provided by surrounding counties. The mills sometimes engaged in outrageous actions that only exacerbated the problem. The files of the Georgia Environmental Protection Agency reflect the difficulties between local authorities and manufacturers in Dalton and state and federal environmental protection agencies. In April 1979, for example, a Dalton Utilities water treatment plant operator reported "a dark gray color in the Conasauga River." The utility's operations manager, Marshall Painter, investigated, and by midnight that evening he reported that "we had found a small stream about ½ mile upstream from the [water] plant running bright red into the river from the east side." An hour later, Painter "found the source of the color" at a major carpet mill in "an industrial park north of Chatsworth," Georgia. The company had started running a new continuous dye range the previous evening. Frustrated with the inability of local government officials to produce on promises of improved water treatment facilities, the company's management had improvised a solution. "A ditch had been dug," Painter observed, "away from the plant several hundred feet to a small surface stream and the dye waste was running into the ditch." This small stream carried the dye "into Mill Creek and then into Conasauga River." The company shut down the dye range temporarily but presumably resumed operations soon after.[8]

By the end of the 1970s, Parrott was searching for new alternatives to traditional water treatment facilities. New Environmental Protection Agency regulations demanded total elimination of chemical wastes, and existing equipment simply could not sufficiently clean carpet waste water. To meet the new EPA guidelines, Parrott investigated new technologies. After several international tours, he decided that the only economically feasible method for industry would be an experimental "spray irrigation project." In such a system, "the waste water [was] put through a secondary treatment plant, then sprayed over the land, where it filters through the earth, leaching out any impurities that weren't filtered out in the treatment plant, ultimately returning the water to the rivers in a near-pure condition," according to *Carpet & Rug Industry* magazine. Dalton Utilities acquired some thirteen thousand acres, extending from Whitfield into neighboring Murray County, for the massive land application project. Because it was classed as an innovative program, the EPA covered 85 percent of the estimated $70 million cost of the project. The new facility went into operation in 1985.[9] By the mid-1980s, it appeared that Dalton Utilities had moved close to a solution to the waste water problem, allowing free rein to local entrepreneurs. The growth agenda of local civic and business leaders, focused on serving the needs of indigenous industry, remained intact.

Local entrepreneurs continued to form new companies at a rapid pace throughout the 1960s and 1970s, testing the limits of the market for tufted floor coverings (as noted in the previous chapter) as well as local natural resources. These new firms entered the market to take advantage of certain new government regulations and survived in spite of others. The Tufted Textile Manufacturers Association, representing the new tufted textile manufacturers, and the American Carpet Institute, representing primarily the old woven establishment, merged in 1969 to form the Carpet and Rug Institute (CRI). The merger had been proposed and debated earlier in the decade, but the initial proposal failed. Members of both associations tired of paying dues to two organizations and continued to pressure the ACI and TTMA to merge as an efficiency measure. Under the merger agreement, the venerable American Carpet Institute surrendered its charter and ceased all operations. The Tufted Textile Manufacturers Association (which had recently changed its official title to Tufted Carpet and Rug Institute) changed its corporate name to the Carpet and Rug Institute and agreed to take over the marketing functions of the ACI.[10]

The new trade association elected to establish its headquarters in Dalton, Georgia, home of the TTMA and more than half the nation's carpet production in 1969. The new trade association and its location signified the new reality within the American carpet industry. An industry that had been exclusively northern less than a quarter of a century earlier had become overwhelmingly a southern affair, and the entrepreneurs who created the tufted carpet business succeeded in shifting the focus of power for the entire carpet industry to the small town of Dalton, Georgia.

Almost immediately the new trade association was faced with a crisis that pushed marketing and other concerns to the background. A nursing home fire in Marietta, Ohio, in January 1970 marked a change in focus for the carpet industry and its trade association. Thirty-two patients died in the fire, and federal investigators determined that a hallway carpet was chiefly responsible for the rapid spread of the fire and the smoke that killed most of the victims. Government relations quickly became the primary focus of the new Carpet and Rug Institute.[11]

The Marietta nursing home fire touched off a running battle between the industry and various federal agencies. Carpeting had come under a minimum of federal regulation in 1967 shortly after the inclusion of carpeting in FHA mortgages. The government had no accepted guidelines on flammability for carpeting, but the Commerce Department informally adopted the Methenamine Pill Test, or simply "pill test," for FHA carpeting and carpets for most government buildings. During a pill test, a Methenamine tablet was placed on a sample of carpeting in a draft-free box. If the material burned more than three inches in any direction, the carpet failed the test.[12]

The carpeting in the Marietta nursing home corridor had been subjected to the pill test and passed. The carpet in the institution had been manufactured by Dan River Mills in Cartersville, Georgia, in 1965, prior to any federal involvement. Dan River therefore had no legal liability, but the incident ignited a wave of regulatory scrutiny of carpeting. In February 1970, the Social Security Administration proposed new regulations for carpeting used in nursing homes. The SSA regulations required the Steiner Tunnel test. The tunnel test was developed in 1941 for measuring the surface burning characteristics of ceilings, walls, floor units, and other building materials. The subject material was mounted on the ceiling of a test tunnel and then subjected to a flame and a draft. Temperatures reached 1,200 degrees Fahrenheit. Materials were then rated for their burning characteristics compared with three-fourths-inch red oak flooring. Red oak was rated at 100, nonflammable materials rated zero, and other materials were rated as being more or less flammable on this scale.[13]

Investigators ran tunnel tests on samples of the carpet from Marietta. The carpet burned less than an inch from the spot of the Methenamine tablet in the pill test, but the tunnel test yielded shocking results. Carpet samples with no padding (sponge rubber in this case) earned ratings of 105–140, while a sample with padding rated 275. The sample with padding produced three-and-a-half times as much smoke in ten minutes as red oak flooring. The Department of Health, Education, and Welfare had established guidelines based on the tunnel test for hospitals. HEW set a limit of a 25 rating for exits and 75 for patient rooms. Results such as these prompted the SSA's action.[14]

Although the SSA's action did not directly affect a large volume of carpet sales, the potential ripple effect was ominous from the point of view of carpet manufacturers. Many in Congress began calling on federal agencies to adopt the tunnel test for all government buildings and FHA-grade carpet. A federal advisory committee on textile flammability publicly criticized the proposed tunnel test in April 1970. The Carpet and Rug Institute agreed with the advisory committee, pointing out that the test position of carpets in the tunnel test was "unnatural." Observers questioned the credibility of a seventeen-member advisory committee with nine members representing manufacturers or retailers. An independent laboratory prepared a report on flammability testing for the old American Carpet Institute in the late 1960s in anticipation of such problems. The *New York Times* revealed that Southwest Research Institute of San Antonio, Texas, had done a battery of tests for the ACI. The lab concluded that the pill test was "a very mild test" that did not reflect real-life conditions.

"Many factors, such as draft, fire loading, thermal radiation, or preheat from sunlight, heaters, or fireplaces that affect flammability," the institute noted, were "ruled out." [15]

In September 1970, the Social Security Administration officially published its new regulations, including the tunnel test. The Commerce Department announced that the pill test would be the standard for all other government buildings, and FHA followed suit by adopting the pill test for its purposes. Official adoption of the standards by Commerce and FHA was set for April 1971. The Commerce Department also announced, however, that while it accepted some of the industry's criticisms of the tunnel test, the agency would continue to search for a new test to replace the pill test. [16]

The shuffling of responsibility for carpet flammability standards worked to the advantage of manufacturers. First the FHA, then the Social Security Administration, then HUD, and eventually the new consumer protection agency all took turns with the regulatory responsibility. While the SSA did retain the tunnel test for nursing homes and hospitals, other federal agencies settled for the pill test in most applications. Regulatory agencies did not set any more stringent requirements for FHA-grade and general residential carpet, and the federal government adopted a new industry-friendly test—the radiant panel—for carpeting in corridors and exits in government buildings in the mid-1970s. The Carpet and Rug Institute developed a large-scale public relations campaign aimed at convincing the public that carpet was safe, and the institute worked with government to develop the radiant panel test. Carpet industry executives adroitly played the political game. During the 1972 presidential campaign, the Nixon reelection committee put the squeeze on numerous industries for large contributions. A carpet industry delegation met with former Commerce secretary Maurice Stans in July 1972 to discuss the possibility of delaying any new stringent carpet flammability requirements. Two weeks later, prominent industry executives E. T. Barwick and Bud Seretean began making substantial contributions to the Nixon campaign. The two donated a total of about one hundred thousand dollars each to various Republican campaign committees nationwide. The Consumer Product Safety Commission eventually retained the pill test as the standard for FHA and other residential carpeting. [17]

The trade association played an important role in the development of the radiant panel test for corridors and exits in government buildings. Barry Torrance, a longtime CRI hand in dealing with government on product safety issues, recalled that the new flammability regulations put pressure on manufacturers. According to a CRI study conducted in 1970, the pill test alone eliminated about 25 percent of all the styles then offered by member firms. A wider application of the tunnel test would have eliminated a majority of carpet styles then on the market. Industry insiders understood that the pill test was not sufficient for all applications, particularly corridors. During the early 1970s, "we were . . . fighting the tunnel test" and conducting research on alternative tests, Torrance remembered. The CRI cooperated with the National Bureau of Standards to develop a new procedure that the association was able to sell to government regulators: the flooring radiant panel test. The radiant panel test evaluated the tendency of a floor system to spread flame when mounted on the floor of a test chamber and exposed to heat produced by a gas-fired radiant panel. The test produced a rating in terms of watts per square centimeter that was used to classify carpeting for particular uses.[18]

Torrance "spent the better part of seven years out on the road," visiting "state fire marshals for every state" and trying to convince them to adopt the radiant panel standard, as opposed to the tunnel test, in their local building codes. Many more carpet styles were able to pass the radiant panel test, and the cost impact of meeting this standard was much less severe than that which would have been required to meet the tunnel test. In addition, various state authorities were beginning to engage in "one-upsmanship" in the safety arena using the tunnel test ratings. The CRI and member manufacturers were concerned about the proliferation of different standards in each state. Torrance and the CRI were successful in this campaign, and in the mid-1990s the pill test remained the standard for most carpeting, with the radiant panel test covering a few specific applications in almost every jurisdiction in the United States.[19]

Tufted carpet manufacturers encountered significant government regulation for the first time in the late 1960s. The industry benefited from the inclusion of carpeting in Federal Housing Administration–backed mortgages in 1967; it provided a boost in carpet sales, helping the industry to penetrate the growing market in new apartment and tract housing developments. Shaheen Shaheen of World Carpets attributed most of the industry's doubling of sales between 1967 and 1972 to the new FHA policy. The FHA policy also revealed less-than-scrupulous observance of basic business ethics among many manufacturers and exposed long-standing management weaknesses that threatened the reputation of the entire industry. And as a consequence of FHA mortgage inclusion, the federal agency established minimum requirements, including safety standards, that created a new set of challenges for the carpet industry.[20]

The old woven oligopoly had sought FHA approval for the inclusion of carpeting in mortgages in the 1950s. Those early efforts had foundered against the opposition of the furniture retailers, who feared losing business to contractors. The popularity of tufted carpeting prodded the federal agency to reevaluate its stand in the mid-1960s. The FHA approved carpeting for mortgage inclusion on November 18, 1966. Working with the TTMA, the federal agency set a minimum standard for quality: twenty ounces of face yarn per square yard of carpet. Theoretically, less dense carpet would not be eligible for inclusion in FHA mortgages.[21]

The carpet industry's chronic management problems surfaced quickly in the FHA program. Shaheen Shaheen recalled that almost immediately many manufacturers began selling carpet that they claimed met the FHA's minimum standard but that in reality contained substantially less than twenty ounces of yarn per yard. The FHA had established no inspection procedure, and unscrupulous or sloppy manufacturers merely supplied distributors and contractors with a letter certifying that the carpets met FHA standards. This covered the legal backsides of the purchasers and left consumers buying low-quality carpet with their new homes. Consumer complaints began piling up in the late 1960s, and by 1970 the FHA began to demand that the Carpet and Rug Institute do something about the situation.[22]

Shaheen and World Carpets had already raised the issue of compliance. Shaheen convinced the old TTMA to meet to discuss the problem as early as November 1967, though the membership voted against taking any action. Shaheen joined the FHA in asking the trade association to take action to ensure compliance with the FHA's minimum quality standards in 1970. Shaheen estimated that before FHA standards were introduced, World Carpets had about 15–20 percent of the contractors' market.

Builders traded with reliable, reputable suppliers in the absence of official standards. After the introduction of FHA standards, World lost business to unscrupulous manufacturers willing to produce shoddy goods and certify that the carpet met the FHA minimum. By 1970, World's share of the now rapidly growing contractors' market had dipped to 5 percent. Shaheen began to demand industry action.[23]

CRI president George Paules presented Shaheen's request to the association's executive committee in July 1970. The CRI's executive committee voted against taking any action to establish standards and a voluntary compliance program; the sense of the committee was that "such action by CRI would be inappropriate, if not illegal." The CRI's legal counsel, Frank Constangy, was directed to study the legalities of such a program.[24]

Shaheen developed a close relationship with the staff at the FHA and prodded the agency into action. Shaheen recalled that FHA officials were "not so concerned with carpet meeting the standards" until the complaints from consumers and builders accelerated in 1969 and 1970. Whether from Shaheen's prodding, a response to complaints, or a combination of both, the FHA issued an ultimatum to the industry and its trade association in the fall of 1970: the standards had to be met or the FHA would rescind its approval of carpeting in agency-backed mortgages.[25]

President Paules informed the CRI's executive committee in December 1970 that the "FHA has become extremely cold on the inclusion of carpet in FHA mortgages, unless some immediate action could be taken to correct the product deficiencies." The FHA clearly wanted the industry to regulate itself in this regard. The committee voted to solicit suggestions from all CRI manufacturer members and to continue work on a certification program for presentation to the association's board of directors in March 1971.[26]

The CRI's board decided against instituting an association-sponsored certification program at the March 1971 meeting. This placed the institute and the industry in a precarious position with the federal agency. Paules again spoke with FHA officials and relayed the agency's position. The FHA continued to hold on to the notion that the industry might be convinced to police itself. Paules told his executive committee that the FHA would have only two choices if the industry refused to do so. The agency could either institute and police a certification program of its own or simply eliminate carpet from FHA mortgages. FHA officials were clearly reluctant to impose an agency-policed solution; Paules noted that the FHA's Porter Driscoll had "stressed the point that FHA was not staffed with adequate manpower to police" such regulations.[27]

Certain members of the CRI's executive committee were clearly uncomfortable with the industry's lack of resolve in this matter. The venerable Walter Guinan of Karastan told his colleagues that he had met with FHA representatives personally and that the main impression he received was that "what they really wanted was for the carpet and rug industry to exhibit responsibility for producing a good product." Most members of the executive committee agreed that new standards would be introduced by the FHA at some point and that the only real question was that of policing. The CRI's leaders "agreed that the industry did not want the government to do the policing" and that "it was unrealistic to charge CRI with that responsibility." The committee voted to instruct the Government Affairs committee to study the question of policing and "recommend back to the Executive Committee what independent agency should act as auditors for FHA standards."[28]

The FHA continued to press the trade association for action, and the association continued to confer with its membership. In May 1971, the executive committee assembled to review responses to a survey of CRI members on the FHA matter. Seventy-seven of the CRI's ninety-seven members responded. The overwhelming majority (sixty-six) of responding firms concurred with the CRI's current stance of refusing to agree to self-regulation. Three companies were in favor of establishing the voluntary program, and eight companies wanted to "get completely out of covering carpet in FHA mortgages." The dominant sentiment was summarized by Arthur Lauman: most members "preferred to leave the discussion with FHA open" and wanted the association to "do more research on the consequences of closing the door with FHA." Lauman expressed his own concern about closing the FHA door. He estimated that the FHA market "might comprise as much as 25% of the entire industry output," though others put the figure closer to 10–12 percent.[29]

CRI chairman J. C. Shaw summarized the sentiments of the CRI membership in a telegram to the FHA. He presented the telegram to the executive committee for discussion and approval. Shaw explained to the committee that the CRI was "definitely leaving the door open for continued dialogue with FHA." His telegram would "merely place the issue back into the hands of the FHA, with the industry declining the offer to regulate itself." Shaw noted that FHA officials with whom he had spoken had not yet decided what action to take if the industry continued to refuse the self-regulation option. Walter Guinan noted that he had spoken with several industry insiders who believed that "there would be little or no enforcement by the government" because of the lack of personnel. Guinan was adamant that these regulations should be enforced if they were enacted.[30]

The FHA standards controversy dragged on for several years, with the carpet industry continuing to pursue "dialogue" with the federal agency, and the agency refraining from either imposing government-enforced regulations or removing carpet from FHA mortgages. In the meantime, Shaheen Shaheen continued to press for some form of industrywide FHA standards. Shaheen pulled World Carpets out of the CRI in the early 1970s in protest over the association's refusal to move on standards, and he cooperated with the FHA independently in developing new standards and an enforcement procedure.

In February 1975, Shaheen's persistence paid off. Officials from the FHA and the Department of Housing and Urban Development met with industry leaders in Washington to discuss new government proposals. Shaheen recalled that "the carpet industry did not want standards and came to oppose" the government's new measures. World's founder described the meeting vividly:

> All the top industry executives were there, Roger Milliken, Gene Barwick, Walter Guinan, Mike Masland, Frank Greenberg, Bud Shaw, Bud Seretean, and others, for a total of more than 20. Also present were representatives from the offices of more than 20 Senators and Representatives. Senator Strom Thurmond of South Carolina came in and opened the meeting with a five-minute discourse on the importance of not going ahead with the FHA program. Arrayed against this vast group was World, represented by Shaheen, and Armstrong. . . .
>
> James Lynn, who was appointed that day by Richard Nixon to be the head of the Office of Management and Budget, sat next to Shaheen. . . . He threatened to drop all carpet from inclusion in government mortgages. The CRI position was that 90 days more be given for them to come up with a

proposal. However, upon questioning, it was very apparent that there was not even the outline of a proposal to present then.

Shaheen "felt very sorry for the poor presentation of the industry" and regretted that he "had to be involved in opposing them." The FHA and HUD imposed new standards on the industry and set up enforcement procedures.[31]

The government had been prodded into action by studies that seemed to show that the quality of carpeting—both for government-backed mortgage housing and the broader market—was going down. A 1970 study found that about one-third of one hundred randomly selected samples failed to meet some FHA guidelines, though almost all met the minimum yarn-weight requirement. Half of the carpet samples tested in a 1974 study failed to meet the minimum weight standard. Individual firms could not police themselves, and the trade association refused to do so. The FHA announced a series of new regulations after the aforementioned meeting. The plan raised the minimum weight for nylon carpeting from twenty to twenty-four ounces and gave carpet manufacturers an option in enforcement. Manufacturers could have carpet styles pretested by independent FHA-approved laboratories; these styles would then be certified as meeting FHA guidelines. These carpets would be "spot-checked" for the next two years by HUD to monitor compliance. If they chose, manufacturers might test and certify carpets in their own labs—provided those labs were inspected and approved by the FHA—and then spot-checked for three years. An FHA official admitted that there were no realistic performance standards for carpet: "It is generally conceded that increased weight and density of the fibers mean a better product." The FHA also acknowledged that the new regulations would raise manufacturers' costs by twelve to twenty-five dollars per one hundred square yards on the most expensive lines, less on others. Shaheen estimated that the new regulations would involve no more than two cents per yard in increased costs in most FHA-grade styles.[32]

The FHA standards became de facto industrywide minimum standards, though they technically applied only to a specific segment of the market. The inclusion of carpet in FHA mortgages boosted sales and opened new markets for the industry but also brought internal conflict and revealed the industry's penchant for buccaneering management. A decade later, Shaheen concluded that the industry's affiliation with the FHA had been beneficial because it forced the industry toward better, not to mention more ethical, management practices. The "prime beneficiary" of the new regulations "has been the consumer who gets better quality carpet for his money." [33]

The flammability crisis presented the new industry with a significant challenge. Individual firms cooperated, through the trade association, in the struggle to shape federal safety regulations in the direction most favorable to the industry. Such cooperation, while serving the interests of carpet manufacturers, did not necessarily serve the interests of consumers. The image of small and medium-sized companies working together to create new products, jobs, and economic growth called forth positive connotations. Whether the defeat of tougher flammability standards indicated a return to reason or a retreat from consumer safety, manufacturers closed ranks to resist.

The struggle over FHA quality standards, on the other hand, illustrated the fragility of the Dalton district's cooperative spirit. The trade association had a difficult time coming to terms with the idea of industrywide, minimum quality standards. In an industry characterized by small, new firms frequently entering the marketplace and a lack of brand-name recognition, the temptation to cut quality in the interest of short-term profits was great. Obviously, a number of firms, large and small, succumbed to that temptation. That the CRI had such difficulty in formulating a response satisfactory to all its members indicated the severity of the problem. Opportunism threatened to devalue or destroy the social capital that had accumulated among tufting firms since old bedspread days. The trade association's task of mediating among the competing interests of its members became increasingly difficult in the 1970s and 1980s as growth slowed.

The Carpet and Rug Institute helped guide the industry through the flammability and FHA controversies in the early and mid-1970s and helped craft the industry's testing procedures. By the late 1970s the CRI faced a severe challenge from within. The strains of industry consolidation and the slowdown of growth after 1973 combined to push different segments of the industry into opposing camps on a variety of issues. In the end, the CRI accepted the leadership of a particular segment of the carpet industry, and the institute's choice revealed much about the changing nature of the Dalton district.

The Carpet and Rug Institute surveyed its membership and selected nonmember firms in 1979 to try to gauge the sense of the industry about its future. The CRI's Long-Range Planning Committee used the results of this "Opinionnaire" as a basis for discussion. The survey was "subjective in nature"; the CRI was as interested in "feelings" as in facts in considering changes in its operations. Thirty-six companies, or one-third of the CRI's more than one hundred members, responded to the survey, which may have suggested a certain lack of enthusiasm for the organization. The firms were asked, among other questions, to assess the state of the industry as of 1979. Sixteen respondents "felt the industry was in fair to good shape," while three responded that "the industry was floundering." Two company officials complained that "twenty companies dominate[d]" the trade, squeezing out the smaller firms.[34]

The survey also asked executives to identify "the single biggest problem facing the industry." Surprisingly enough, considering the quite recent experience of the carpet industry with government during the flammability crisis, only two respondents listed government regulation as the industry's "biggest problem." "Far and away," according to the CRI's Richard Eldredge, "profitability led the problem parade." This problem was expressed in a variety of ways, from "overcapacity" to "bad price structure." Profitability was mentioned again as the most likely "area of potential trouble for the industry for the next three years." When asked to name the "single greatest blessing to the industry," four companies responded with dark humor that the best thing that could happen to carpet manufacture would be "for two-thirds of the companies in the industry to go out of business."[35]

The executives who sought relief from low profits in the failure of a majority of carpet companies were probably quite serious. The boom of the late 1950s and 1960s had run out by the mid-1970s. The "golden age" of U.S. and Western economic growth, spurred by government policies to boost consumption, had begun to tarnish. After an unbroken string of annual increases in both square yards shipped and dollar value of shipments, the bottom fell out for the carpet industry in 1974. Shipments fell by more than 6 percent in 1974 from the previous year; the mill value of those shipments dropped by about 1 percent (rising prices cushioned some of the shock). Shipments declined by almost 11 percent in 1975, and the value of shipments fell by nearly 8 percent. Employment figures told the same story from another perspective. Total production worker employment in carpets and rugs reached an all-time high in 1973 of more than 66,000. Employment in the industry dropped to about 62,000 in 1974 and fell below 60,000 in 1975. In the two decades since, the industry's employment totals have not again reached the 1973 level.[36]

The CRI's Richard Eldredge circulated another copy of the "Opinionnaire" in early March 1979, along with his own analysis of the ills facing the CRI and the industry. Eldredge framed the crucial question for the trade association's future. The CRI had lost members in the past few years, many of them textile conglomerates for whom carpet was only a portion of their business. Many of these firms preferred membership in the American Textile Manufacturers Institute, which had lower dues. As textile conglomerates bought large tufting mills and large carpet manufacturers began to acquire relatively large competitors, "the visible trend toward consolidation through acquisition" put the CRI in a difficult position. "In an ideal world," Eldredge noted, the association would "represent both the highest possible number of companies which in turn would represent the clear majority of industry volume." This "ideal world" clearly did not exist in 1979, and the institute had to make a difficult choice. "Is it possible to represent both numbers of companies and volume," or "if both are not possible, which is the more significant factor—numbers or volume?" Eldredge suggested that it might become necessary for the institute to "discourage participation by smaller companies" in order "to attract volume producers."

By the end of the 1970s, many of the medium and small carpet mills of the Dalton district began to feel the pressure of a maturing market. The smaller mills responded first by pressuring the Carpet and Rug Institute to launch a marketing campaign. At about the same time, of course, the CRI was assessing the results of its "Opinionnaire," which indicated a strong sentiment that there were too many mills competing for shares in a market approaching saturation. As smaller and midsize mills tried to push the CRI in one direction, the larger mills pulled in the other. The result was growing dissatisfaction with the trade association in the late 1970s among members of both groups. The association made critical decisions in 1979 and 1980 that recognized the changing conditions within the industry.

Peter Spirer, then owner of Horizon Carpets, a rapidly rising new star in the industry, served as chairman of the CRI's board of directors in 1980; he was an active board member for several years before and after. Spirer recalled three major difficulties that faced the institute at the time. Large manufacturers were upset about the influence of small firms in the association. "The big players, guys like Shaw, terribly resented the involvement of all the small companies." The CRI, like its predecessor, the TTMA, operated on the "one man [company], one vote" principle.[37]

Dissatisfaction with this principle perhaps was a reflection of a deeper division between small and large firms in the industry. Spirer noted the contradictory attitudes held by some of the CRI's board members. Many companies favored a new structure that weighted voting on policy matters within the institute toward the large firms. "On the other hand," Spirer remembered, other executives and owners reminded the board that "the industry was spawned by little guys, and you never knew who the next big guy would be, because the Shaw of the 1980s was a piss ant in the 1970s; he was barely known. But if he hadn't had the chance to flex his muscles on the way up he might have been squelched." Spirer noted that this difficulty was resolved by giving larger mills greater clout on the executive council of the CRI and giving the executive council a clear role as the primary formulator of future association policy.[38]

The CRI's dues structure also caused controversy within the association. The institute had counted more than a hundred companies as manufacturing members in 1975; by 1979 nearly fifty firms had dropped their memberships. The institute maintained a graduated schedule of dues based on company sales, so that larger firms paid much more than smaller firms. The rate was 0.43 per thousand dollars in sales, with a $1,000 minimum and a $30,000 maximum. In 1979, thirty of the CRI's remaining sixty-six members (45 percent) were in the minimum dues category. Only six members qualified for the maximum dues rate. The thirty companies in the minimum category accounted for only about 6 percent of total CRI dues; the six firms at the top paid more than 45 percent. Of the forty-six companies that had left the CRI since 1976, only twelve were in the minimum dues range, "with a fairly even spread upward." Eight defectors, each of which paid more than $12,000 annually in dues, represented more than half the association's dues losses.[39]

The withdrawal of large firms from the CRI caused consternation within the organization. Many companies had become so large and the market so crowded that the disadvantages of cooperating with smaller firms began to outweigh the advantages. The issue that crystallized this conflict was marketing. Smaller and medium-sized companies within the CRI increased the intensity of their calls for an expanded CRI marketing program aimed at promoting the idea of carpeting, similar to the old Carpet Institute campaigns of the late 1940s and late 1950s.

These suggestions from smaller companies provoked intense opposition from certain quarters, and the matter was finally settled in late 1979 and early 1980. Peter Spirer recalled that advocates of a marketing program for the CRI argued that the institute should develop an advertising campaign to "raise the consciousness of the public" about carpet in "the [same] way that the cotton council" promoted all manner of cotton goods. Many of the larger manufacturers opposed the idea, especially Robert Shaw of Shaw Industries, a rapidly growing company that began as a commission finishing business: "Bob Shaw was the guy who really gunned down that whole thing." Spirer paraphrased Shaw's position: "He said: 'I am leaving any association that I would pay dues to . . . that caused my competitor to prosper. I'm not doing it period. I will not support an organization that's into marketing. We'll [Shaw Industries] do our own marketing; we'll create our own brand name; we'll create our [own] consciousness among consumers; we will not do that [support a CRI marketing campaign].' " Shaw's colleagues "had to calm him down at that point," and "ultimately" Shaw's position "prevailed."[40] The CRI had lost several large firms as members already; it could not afford to lose any more, especially Shaw Industries. Shaw had for years been perhaps the CRI's most loyal supporter among the large manufacturers. Bob Shaw had long served as the organization's treasurer, and his brother, J. C. Shaw, was a past president of the organization and board member.

Small and medium-sized carpet companies formed the Carpet Manufacturers Marketing Association in 1979 to press ahead with cooperative marketing plans. Rejected by the CRI, the smaller firms tried to pool their own resources in an effort to increase sales in a narrowing market. The chief goal of the newly formed CMMA was to put together a small trade show, a "mini-market," in Dalton about two weeks prior to the annual major market show at the Atlanta Merchandise Mart. By 1979, many major mills had established their own showrooms and distribution centers and often lined up customers prior to the major trade shows. The carpet industry's reliance on trade shows diminished throughout the late 1970s and 1980s. Smaller mills first sought aid from the CRI in the form of a carpet advertising campaign. When that effort failed, they turned to self-help.

Whitecrest Carpet Mills typified the membership of the CMMA. A former CPA for a Dalton accounting firm and a carpet company controller, Ken White started his own mill, like so many other managers in the Dalton district. Whitecrest Carpet Mills went into operation in 1973 in a small leased facility with two employees. For almost a year, Whitecrest relied on commission tufting to manufacture its products. Ken White added tufting machines after several months, and Whitecrest gradually moved toward production of its own merchandise. Whitecrest focused on the residential market initially but after 1979 moved toward the commercial arena. The company proved especially adept at designing styles specifically suited for schools (with extrastrength adhesives to prevent tufts from pulling away from the backing under heavy use), health care facilities (complete with an antimicrobial treatment), and country clubs (spike-proof carpets) and other similar specialty applications. The company prospered by emphasizing product development. Although most of Whitecrest's sales fell into the high-end, specialty market, the company still maintained a significant presence in the ultracompetitive residential market. One-quarter of the firm's sales in 1990 went into this largest of carpet market segments. It was Whitecrest's "split personality" that attracted owner Ken White to the new CMMA. White was a key player in the formation of the association and served several terms as president of the CMMA in the 1980s.[41]

The Carpet Manufacturers Marketing Association held its first trade show in December 1979 at the local Holiday Inn in Dalton. It was a makeshift affair, with motel rooms turned into product showrooms. The

CMMA moved the furniture out of the Holiday Inn's rooms, stored it in trucks in the parking lot, and then replaced the furniture when the show ended. The association chose the Holiday Inn as a site because Dalton lacked a trade and convention center, and there were few viable alternatives for a legitimate trade show. Nonetheless, the CMMA's first show was a success, and the CMMA market quickly became an annual event. The CMMA's first show attracted eighty-one exhibitors, the vast majority small mills whose names were hardly household words even within the small world of floor covering sales. Most of these firms became members of the new association.[42]

By 1983, CMMA members were talking about the possibility of making the Dalton market a permanent affair, and the search was on for a new site. Small manufacturers realized that the Holiday Inn simply was not suitable for a major trade show. CMMA members and community supporters investigated several possibilities, including an old Crown Cotton Mill building. CMMA president Ken White of Whitecrest Carpets, Crown America president David Hamilton, and Jack Turner of Cabin Crafts proposed renovating the 1907 structure to serve as a convention center for the city. The group estimated that the renovation would cost about $4 million. Turner, White, and Hamilton proposed that the project be funded in part ($300,000) by a grant from the Appalachian Regional Commission, with the rest coming from the city of Dalton, Whitfield County, and private contributions in equal measures. The fledgling association's plan fell through when Dalton's First National Bank denied a "sizable loan" to the new trade center's developers. The CMMA moved its trade show to nearby Chattanooga's trade center in 1986 but remained committed to establishing a Dalton facility.[43] By the mid-1980s, CMMA members and Dalton boosters had turned their attention to another potential source of funding for a local trade center—state government.

Dalton-area carpet manufacturers and their state representatives floated a plan in the Georgia legislature that would have financed construction of a $12 million trade center with state funds. The *Atlanta Constitution* noted that the proposal "created a political storm," drawing opposition from representatives of other areas of Georgia. For carpet manufacturers, the controversy revealed the industry's "lack of recognition" around Georgia. Dalton state representative Tom Ramsey testily observed in 1986 that the carpet industry in Georgia was "three times as big as the citrus industry in Florida, which everybody hears about when their crop gets in trouble. But you never hear anything about us." The carpet industry in the mid-1980s was the economic lifeblood of northwest Georgia, especially Dalton and Whitfield County. Georgia was home to more than 220 of the nation's roughly 340 carpet mills. Georgia's carpet mills employed 25,000 of the industry's 35,000 workers and paid more than 70 percent of industry payroll. Whitfield County alone accounted for 125 carpet mills that were responsible for almost 15,000 jobs. "Nobody ever thought that we would have to promote ourselves in South Georgia," said CRI president Ron VanGelderen.[44]

The Dalton trade center proposal bounced around the legislature for almost a year. Support for the center from Governor Joe Frank Harris waxed and waned, and the criticisms from state representatives from south of Atlanta mounted. "I just don't think the state should get in the business of building civic centers," complained state senator Al Holloway of Albany. "A lot of communities like mine have busted their belts to build their own." Holloway charged that "the best information we could get was that the [CMMA] carpet market would use the center only twice a year. To me it's more of a civic center [rather than a trade mart]." Nonetheless, Dalton representatives had the support of powerful Georgia House Speaker Tom Murphy, and Murphy introduced a bill in early 1987 to fund construction of the center at $14 million. Lieutenant Governor Zell Miller blasted the proposal, citing a feasibility study that predicted that the center would lose money and become a drain on public resources. Murphy responded by reminding Miller and Holloway that the legislature had spent state funds to assist both Atlanta, through the World Congress Center, and Savannah, through improvements to port facilities. Murphy concluded that it was time for the state to do something to help the carpet industry.[45]

Ultimately, a compromise was reached. The state legislature voted to spend $8.2 million on the Dalton Trade and Convention Center. The rest of the funding would have to come from local sources. The city of Dalton committed $2 million, Whitfield County another $2 million. Dalton city officials chose a site donated by Jack Bandy, one of the founders of local Coronet Carpets. Construction was completed in 1991, and the Dalton

Floor Covering Marketing Association (the CMMA's new title) held its first market in the new facility in October of that year.[46]

By the early 1990s, the Dalton district's small and midsize carpet manufacturers had formed what amounted to an alternative trade association. This association provided a group workers' compensation insurance plan for members, held trade shows, introduced small firms to new technology through equipment and machinery exhibitions, and generally coordinated the efforts of smaller firms to survive in an increasingly competitive environment. The split between the CRI, which now explicitly focused on the larger manufacturers, and the CMMA-DFCMA had existed for decades. Reforms in one trade association and the formation of a new one only offered formal recognition of the increasing segmentation of the carpet industry. Small firms, cooperation, and decentralization had once characterized the tufted carpet industry. By the end of the 1980s, integration, consolidation, and concentration were the major trends.

By the time the trade center was completed, many of the larger firms in the industry had abandoned the idea of attending trade shows altogether, leaving the field to the smaller firms. Growth was no longer free; the carpet industry's period of rapid sales increases was over, and a trend toward slower growth emerged in the 1980s. The complex web of relationships that held together Dalton's version of an industrial district began to fray and tear. Survival was no longer possible for the merely ambitious. For the survivors in this increasingly competitive industry, ambition had to be combined with other virtues: relentless attention to cost; either the development of economies of scale and vertical integration or the carving out of a distinctive market niche; the purchase of market shares through acquisitions; the judicious use of debt; and wise, not merely extensive, investment in plant and equipment. Mistakes and sloppy management were no longer minor annoyances within the industry by the 1980s; they were now fatal flaws. The industry's emerging pacesetter, Shaw Industries, made certain of that.

Survival of the Fittest

The age of expansive growth for the U.S. carpet industry, which began with the introduction of tufting in the early 1950s, ended with the recession of 1981–82. The golden age of postwar prosperity expired, followed by an era of stagnating incomes for middle-income Americans and the increasing segmentation of the U.S. mass consumer market. For three decades, new and old firms in the industry used the dual innovations of tufting and bulked continuous filament (BCF) nylon to penetrate the long-elusive (for carpets) mass consumer market. By the early 1980s, that market had been fairly saturated; most current homeowners who wanted carpet had it. The conditions that had permitted the multiplication of new firms no longer prevailed. The rapid growth of consumer demand in the postwar period had created opportunity for virtually all firms in the tufted carpet industry. Consumer tastes changed as well. Carpet's share of consumer spending in the overall floor covering market rose from under a third in the early 1950s to more than 80 percent by the early 1980s. That trend in demand reversed itself by the mid-1980s, and carpet's share of consumer floor covering dollars declined to just 58 percent by the late 1990s. As the *Wall Street Journal* noted succinctly in 1998, carpet manufacturers were faced with an unpleasant truth: "The American Dream no longer requires wall-to-wall carpeting."[1] The severe recession of the early 1980s combined with these long-term trends to produce a seemingly permanent state of slow growth for the industry. At the end of the difficult decade of the 1980s, Shaw Industries—the creation of Robert and J. C. Shaw—emerged as the leading company in the industry. Indeed, Shaw had become by 1990 the most dominant single firm in the carpet industry since the pretufting era.

"He was a fine competitor, and you saw something in him that you did not see in every kid. You could see that something special lay ahead for him," recalled Alf "Snake" Anderson, Robert E. Shaw's high school football coach. Indeed, Bob Shaw, by all accounts, took the competitive spirit he exhibited in high school sports into the business world. Shaw's fierce competitive nature helped him to build Shaw Industries, the largest carpet-manufacturing company in the world in 1990.[2]

Shaw's father, Clarence, was born and raised on a farm in Bartow County, Georgia, and "worked hard all his life," according to the carpet magnate. Clarence Shaw's parents were involved in a number of classic southern businesses in the early twentieth century: cotton gins, lumber mills, and "primarily" cotton planting. J. C. Shaw, Clarence's eldest son, recalled that "the family went broke" because "cotton went to a nickel a pound in '22." Clarence Shaw joined the speculative fever of the 1920s by moving south to participate in the Florida land rush. Clarence went "down [to Florida] with nothing and he came back with nothing," according to J. C. Shaw. Clarence Shaw had received an education in textile engineering at Georgia Tech, and after the collapse of the Florida land bubble, he decided to apply the skills he had learned. He went to work for Lamar Westcott's hosiery mill in Dalton in 1929, working in the dye-

TABLE 11. Carpet Shipments per Household (Square Yards)
and Mill Value per Square Yard, Selected Years 1950–1990

	1950	1960	1970	1980	1990
Sq. yds.	1.97	2.81	8.46	11.12	12.34
Mill value	$6.24	$4.50	$3.56	$4.82	$6.46

Source: Carpet and Rug Institute, Carpet and Rug Industry Review, 1993, 13.

ing department. Westcott soon sold out to Real Silk Hosiery, and Real Silk closed the Dalton plant in a consolidation move associated with the depression in 1930.[3]

Clarence Shaw then moved his family to Nashville, Tennessee, where he worked as a dyer for Washington Hosiery Mill. Shaw also began to do some extra work at night dyeing tufted bedspreads for Tennessee Tufting Company. In the fall of 1941, the Shaw family returned to Dalton. Clarence went to work for Dalton Spread Laundry, managing the dyeing of tufted products: scatter rugs, tank sets, and the like. Shaw had been recruited by Dalton Spread Laundry's biggest customer, Cabin Crafts, and one of its owners, Lamar Westcott. Though Dalton Spread Laundry was independently owned, Cabin Crafts' management was upset about the quality of dyeing work on their products and urged the firm to bring in Shaw. The spread laundries of Dalton were accustomed to washing, bleaching, drying, and finishing white goods but had little experience in dyeing. Shaw brought his Georgia Tech education back to Dalton in 1941 and participated in the tufting revolution.[4] The elder Shaw was quite successful, acquired a reputation as a skillful dyer, and, typically for the Dalton district, soon struck out on his own. Shaw and John McCarty formed Star Dye Company in 1944. Clarence Shaw and John McCarty formed the company to dye the "scatter rugs" that were in many ways precursors to the tufted carpets of the 1950s.[5]

After graduation from high school, Bob Shaw tried college but eventually settled into working as a salesman for a chemical company. His brother, J. C. "Bud" Shaw, graduated from Georgia Tech, like his father, and worked for J. P. Stevens. By the late 1950s, J. C. Shaw was running a yarn mill for Stevens. Upon their father's death in 1958, the brothers inherited their father's dye company. Bob became the new chief executive

officer of Star Dye. By 1960, Bob Shaw had formed a new company, Star
Finishing Company, to replace Star Dye, which became a dormant corporation. Star Finishing became the largest commission finisher in the carpet industry within seven years.[6]

Clarence Shaw had managed Star Dye quite conservatively. J. C. Shaw
remembered that his father's business philosophy had been shaped by the
experience of being burned in the Florida land rush and the depression.
Clarence Shaw was always a bit wary of new developments and trends,
particularly the trend toward tufted carpeting in the 1950s. Throughout
the 1950s, Clarence Shaw continued to focus primarily on dyeing "traditional" tufted goods and small scatter rugs, with only occasional and limited forays into dyeing and finishing tufted broadloom carpeting. Shaw's
sons, J. C. and Bob, often urged their father to expand Star Dye's operations and tried to convince their father that broadloom carpeting represented the future of the tufted industry. The disagreements between father
and sons were apparently quite heated at times, but J. C. Shaw came to
respect his father's position. During the 1950s, the elder Shaw "had three
other children to educate," and he had just "gotten his stake, Star Dye
Company, and he ran that on a very, very conservative basis." Even though
J. C. Shaw tried to convince his father "to expand a whole heck of a lot,"
the elder Shaw steadfastly refused. In retrospect, J. C. Shaw noted, "I look
back on it I think he was very wise to do it."[7]

Star Finishing quickly acquired a reputation for efficiency and quality.
Textile World profiled Star Finishing in October 1962, almost two years
after the firm's January 1961 start-up date. Star Finishing's growth in this
brief period presaged later developments at Shaw Industries. "Efficiency"
was the "byword" for the Shaws, and the desire for efficiency was evidenced by the "spare-no-legitimate-expense" strategy implemented by
Bob Shaw. Star Finishing was a state-of-the-art carpet dye house, representing an initial capital investment of three-quarters of a million dollars,
far in excess of the requirements for establishing even a fairly large tufting operation. Star Finishing had already enlarged its receiving warehouse
twice since January 1961 and had almost doubled the number of dye
becks in use. Star's dye becks and drying ovens were manufactured by the
local Gowin Machinery Company.[8] Bob Shaw expressed his confidence in
the continued growth of the carpet industry by making the capital investment necessary to create a highly efficient carpet-finishing establishment.

In 1967, Bob and J. C. Shaw moved to include tufting in their operations. Star Finishing's "backward" vertical integration mirrored a trend among manufacturers toward establishing their own dye houses. As the Galaxy story in chapter 6 revealed, the integration of the industry disrupted old relationships but led to greater efficiency. Bob and J. C. Shaw implicitly recognized this, establishing a holding company to hold Star Finishing's stock as well as the stock of newly acquired tufting and yarn-spinning facilities. Thus Shaw Industries began its corporate life as the Philadelphia Holding Company and kept a low profile for more than a decade. The Shaws did not advertise Star Finishing's move into tufting, in part because it might have even further encouraged the trend toward vertical integration among tufting mills. Shaw Industries evolved in its early years as something of a "stealth" company and appeared to many observers to spring from nowhere as a major player in the industry in the late 1970s.[9] The Philadelphia Holding Company represented the merger of Bob Shaw's Star Finishing, Bud Shaw's new Sabre Carpets, and the dormant Rocky Creek Mills and Star Dye corporations. Bud Shaw became chairman and CEO of the new company, with Bob Shaw serving as president. The Shaws' main purpose in merging their separate companies was to make it feasible for the new, larger company to purchase Philadelphia Carpet Company.[10]

The Philadelphia Carpet Company was an old and respected name in carpeting. The company had been founded in 1846 by Philip Doerr, and the business remained a family concern until its purchase by the Shaws. For more than eighty years, Philadelphia produced only narrow-width woven carpets. In 1929 the company began producing broadloom carpets. The Doerrs acquired a tufted carpet mill in Cartersville, Georgia, in 1958. Two years later, Philadelphia merged with the tufting operation. By February 1963, Philadelphia had stopped the production of woven carpet for retail sale. Later that year, Philadelphia moved its general offices to Cartersville. The company sold its Philadelphia plant in 1964; Philadelphia remained active only on a limited contract basis in the woven industry, leasing space in its old building. The tufting process had overwhelmed the woven side of Philadelphia's business.[11]

Philadelphia Carpet had been known historically as a producer of medium- to high-quality woven wool carpets. Though the company had by the mid-1960s shifted almost exclusively to the manufacture of tufted carpets, Philadelphia products were still sold on the basis of quality, style, and design rather than price. Market analysts believed that Philadelphia had made a mistake by remaining exclusively a "high-end" producer. The company missed "the dynamic growth in popular priced carpets made possible by the efficiencies of the tufting process." The "high-end" market was estimated at only around $150 million, or 10 percent of the total carpet market. Philadelphia's strong history as a quality producer could not offset the need for volume sales, which, according to a J. C. Bradford analyst, were "so important to a profitable tufting operation." The acquisition of Philadelphia immediately gave the Shaw interests a strong foothold in the upper-end quality market. To maintain continuity of sales and take advantage of the Philadelphia brand name, the new owners continued to market Philadelphia Carpets under that label through the existing sales organization. Within five years, the Shaws had redirected some of Philadelphia's resources toward the medium-range market and had doubled Philadelphia's sales volume.[12]

Soon after the acquisition of Philadelphia Carpet, effective in December 1967, the Shaws moved to expand the company's product lines. The commercial finishing division, still known as Star Finishing, acquired a flatbed Zimmer printing machine in October 1968. Barwick had pioneered in printing with his "Kitchen Classics," and the Shaws believed there was a future for printed carpets. The Zimmer machine could print designs on carpet at high speeds in up to six colors. It took the company more than eight months to get the new machine up and running. The Shaws purchased another Zimmer machine, this one capable of printing in up to eight colors, in July 1970, though, again, production was long delayed.[13]

The Philadelphia Holding Company went public in 1971 as Shaw Industries, listing on the American Stock Exchange. The decision to go public was chiefly motivated by the Shaws' desire to gain greater access to capital. "We saw the Barwicks and Coronets able to raise money on the public market and that gave us the confidence to do the same," Bob Shaw recalled. Unlike many of their competitors, the Shaws plowed a substantial portion of the proceeds from this initial stock sale back into the business, reserving about five million dollars for construction and working capital. The Shaws recognized earlier than most that the carpet industry had to move away from the high-cost credit associated with factors like the Heller Company. The company also got a boost in 1971 from a six-million-dollar loan from the Prudential Life Insurance Company.[14]

In March of that year, the company asked Drexel Firestone to evaluate the company and estimate the fair market value of its stock, in preparation for the public offering. The Drexel report included an evaluation not just of the Shaws' company but of the entire industry. Drexel concluded that the carpet industry was "highly competitive" and that "the number of carpet mills in operation has increased with the growth in sales of tufted carpet." Though Drexel noted that the industry had seen a wave of consolidation in the years 1968–70, "no single company enjoy[ed] a dominant position in the industry." The Philadelphia Holding Company was in a "unique position" within the industry, according to Drexel's analyst, because the company derived 26 percent of its revenues from finishing services provided to other carpet manufacturers. For that reason, the company's stock could only be evaluated within the context of the total carpet industry. If other companies' sales went down, Shaw's finishing operation would not produce as much revenue. Even if the company's carpet sales held their own during a recession, losses in the commission finishing operation could still bring down total earnings.[15]

The industry was just emerging from such a downturn in 1971. The consolidation mentioned by Drexel at the end of the 1960s had come "in a business climate that has not been favorable for the carpet manufacturers in 1969 and 1970." In examining the performance of eight other publicly held carpet companies during this period, Drexel found that all had experienced a decline in net income, and four—including Barwick Mills, the largest company in the industry—were operating at a loss. It was in such an environment that several independent carpet companies had been acquired by "significantly larger, more diversified companies," including RCA's purchase of Coronet Carpets, a top five company within the industry.[16]

That was the "downside" to Star Finishing's position as the leading commission finisher in the industry. The "upside," at least on the surface, appeared to outweigh any disadvantages. The bottom line was that the Shaws were large producers of tufted carpets. They achieved substantial cost savings by being able to finish Philadelphia and Sabre carpets "in-house," giving them an advantage over producers who could not finish their own goods. In addition, not only did the Shaw interests experience cost savings, but they also made a profit on finishing the goods of many of their competitors. In the long run, Shaw accumulated working capital from its competitors, which was later used to invest in new equipment and technology that enabled Shaw to surpass those same competitors. In the next wave of consolidation, Shaw would be a major player.

In August 1972, five months after Shaw Industries' stock first traded on the AMEX, Drexel Firestone prepared a progress report for the company. The report provided a glimpse into the makeup of the future industry leader shortly after its inception. Shaw's product lines and sources of revenue were already diversified. "Philadelphia" label products, essentially higher-end goods, accounted for 42 percent of company sales in fiscal 1972. Philadelphia carpets were marketed by thirty-six full-time salesmen to more than twenty-five hundred retailers in the United States and Canada. "Private labels," or Shaw carpet sold with someone else's label on it, represented 26 percent of the company's sales. Sabre Carpet lines accounted for around 20 percent of company sales. Sabre's tufted products were geared toward the low to medium end of the price and quality spectrum. These products made up the bulk of Shaw's carpet sales. The company maintained a presence in the woven industry with a not insubstantial 10 percent of company sales coming from custom-made woven carpets. Around 2 percent of Shaw's sales came from custom-designed, wide-width (up to twenty-five feet) carpets. Shaw ranked fifteenth among U.S. carpet manufacturers in 1972, but in terms of profitability, the new company was already an industry leader. In 1970, while the industrywide dollar value of carpet shipments rose only 2.5 percent, Shaw's total revenues climbed 14 percent, and the company's net income doubled. Shaw earned a return of almost 21 percent on equity in fiscal 1972. The company achieved cost efficiencies by keeping a tight control on inventories and achieving a high rate of inventory turnover. Going public in 1972 gave the company greater access to capital that "substantially reduce[d] costs associated with factoring" (the chief source of credit for most carpet manufacturers in the Dalton area).[17]

Shaw Industries had become a successful, growing concern by the mid-1970s. The Shaw family changed the company's management structure and philosophy in 1977, and the company experienced a period of even faster growth. In December 1977, Bob Shaw replaced J. C. Shaw as CEO of the company. J. C. remained chairman of the board but took a less active role in the day-to-day operations of the company. Bob Shaw denied reports that there was a power struggle between the two brothers. "Bud and I have never been in disagreement," he maintained.[18] Whether or not there was a power struggle, Shaw changed its corporate strategy following the shift in top management. The company announced plans to shift its marketing emphasis away from reliance on Philadelphia and other subsidiaries' brand names, marketing Philadelphia as a division of Shaw Industries. This would help build the overall company reputation. The company also redirected its efforts to concentrate more on integrating backward toward suppliers and better access to raw materials.[19]

By early 1982, Shaw Industries had moved up to become the fifth-largest carpet manufacturer in the United States, trailing only Burlington, World, Mohasco, and WestPoint Pepperell (i.e., Cabin Crafts). Shaw's sales reached $250 million in fiscal 1981, and the company produced the highest return on investment of any publicly held firm in the industry. At that point, the entire carpet industry entered an economic chamber of horrors, and Shaw Industries did not escape unscathed. Bob Shaw learned some hard lessons, though, and his company profited in the long run from the experience.[20]

The 1982 recession hit the industry and Shaw hard. Shaw's sales fell by $18 million in one year, reaching only $232 million in 1982. Shaw's international sales, a relatively new growth area that accounted for 5.5 percent of company sales, fell by 27 percent. Despite the temporary tough times, investment advisers continued to express confidence in Shaw Industries. Shaw earnings had rebounded by 1983, and analysts expected further growth in the future. In December 1983, Merrill Lynch projected Shaw earnings per share to jump more than 100 percent in fiscal 1984. The investment firm praised Shaw's "vertical integration" and "state-of-the-art production equipment," which enabled the company to derive the maximum benefit from improving consumer demand. Shaw also had demonstrated a strong commitment to capital improvements, which would ensure that the company would continue to enjoy the maximum return on any increase in sales volume.[21]

Shaw's continued strength and quick recovery may in part be attributed to "bold moves" made by Bob Shaw in the midst of the 1982 recession. Shaw insiders met in 1982 to map out a new company strategy. The Shaw team set out to become the lowest-cost producer in the carpet industry. In later years, Shaw spoke of "low-cost production as if it is—or ought to be—the holy grail of all business people." In an industry that had traditionally operated on high volume and low profit margins, this was perhaps the only logical strategy for a company the size of Shaw Industries. Unlike many of Shaw's competitors, however, the company did *have* a strategy. Bob Shaw and his management team confidently set a new goal for the company: one billion dollars in annual sales. Word of the goal leaked out within the industry, and many business insiders scoffed at the very notion of a billion-dollar carpet company. The Shaw team simply went about implementing its new directives.[22]

First, Shaw took advantage of the recession to buy six yarn-spinning mills at roughly twenty-five cents on the dollar, including a portion of the Comer family's Avondale Mills in Alabama. Even at bargain-basement prices, this represented a tremendous capital outlay at a time when most companies were cutting back. Shaw's goal, of course, was to achieve long-term cuts in materials costs through vertical integration. Yarn spinning was the most logical place to look for cost savings: face yarn made up about 65 percent of the cost of producing carpet. By 1985, Shaw senior vice president William C. Lusk could boast that "we have control over virtually 100% of our yarn supply in-house. . . . It's very comforting."[23]

After the acquisition of the yarn mills, Shaw implemented a new production strategy. Shaw Industries continued to produce yarn and carpet in spite of economic conditions. In recessionary periods, Shaw cut prices to maintain sales and increase market share. When the economy picked up again, Shaw maintained a portion of the market share gained by price cuts and bumped prices up a bit. The consistent market Shaw provided for the chemical companies helped cut the company's raw materials costs.[24] Shaw's acquisition of the yarn mills was an example of the company's continuing commitment to capital expenditures for expanding and improving plant and equipment. Since the company's inception, Shaw typically spent about twice the industry average on capital improvements, measured as a percentage of total sales. Shaw management understood that the carpet industry was "a capital intensive business and financing is an ongoing process. It's not hard to keep all of your funds fully employed." Shaw Industries' financial managers had long exhibited a talent for finding the longest debt at the lowest interest rate available.[25]

At around the same time, Shaw began to shift its marketing strategy away from reliance on carpet distributors. The entire industry had become dependent on wholesale distributors for marketing carpet; by the early 1980s, distributors marketed around 80 percent of total carpet production in the United States. According to some analysts, the power inherent in this dominance led many distributors to try to force mills to sell at lower and lower costs. Industry consultant Reg Burnett contended that "wholesalers . . . have been holding the mills' feet to the fire, so to speak, by trying to use their muscle to buy low cost." In 1982, 55 percent of Shaw's sales were to distributors, national accounts, and overseas accounts; only 45 percent of company sales were direct to retailers. By 1985, Shaw had dramatically altered the mix: 80 percent of Shaw's sales that year went straight to retailers. By going directly to retailers, Shaw was able to bypass the 22 percent average distributor markup, sell cheaper to retailers, and still increase his profit margins.[26]

The decision to move away from the distributors proved expensive. In order to have facilities to provide inventory storage and prompt service to customers nationwide, Shaw increased its number of regional warehouse facilities from two to ten. This move nearly doubled overhead costs. Shaw also invested in new telephone and computer systems to keep up with the dizzying increase in the number of customer accounts: up from 3,400 to more than 14,000 within two years of the changes. The company decided to expand its sales force and put all its salesmen on salary rather than commission, in hopes that this would help to shift their loyalty from the customers to the company, and began an intensive training program.[27]

These changes helped the company grow even faster than before. The company's annual sales doubled from 1982–85, and Shaw became the first carpet company with more than $500 million in U.S. sales in a single year. Company earnings for 1985 were estimated at $28 million, a 20 percent increase over the previous year. Employment at Shaw Industries rose by 1,300 in 1984–85 to 4,700. In May 1985, Shaw Industries made its first appearance among the *Fortune* 500, ranking 480th.[28] Though some were still skeptical, Shaw's billion-dollar goal was no longer a laughing

TABLE 12. The Growth of Shaw Industries, Selected Years 1980–1992

	1980	1986	1992
Carpet shipments (billion sq. yds.)	1.1	1.2	1.4
Number of mills	285	170	100
% Carpet sold by distributors	55	25	13
% Yarn produced by carpet mills	20	80	80
% Market share, Shaw Industries	4	8	23

Source: RBI Carpet Consultants, Dalton, Georgia.

matter. Albert Wahnon, editor of the trade journal *Floor Covering Weekly*, expressed confidence in the company's ability to deliver on its promise: "I believe it when Bob Shaw says he'll be selling a billion dollars worth of carpet a year soon." Wahnon also compared Bob Shaw to the man who rescued Chrysler and prodded the entire U.S. auto industry toward a better competitive posture: "He's our Iacocca." [29]

Shaw moved to make maximum use of its decreasing costs in April 1985. Bob Shaw had long been angered by what he perceived as a "sloppy market with prices" nationwide in the carpet industry, as well as the numerous special "deals" cut by many competitors with distributors, according to an anonymous "mill man," quoted by *Floor Covering Weekly*. "Rather than pick away one by one" at such deals, Shaw announced broad price cuts on selected carpet lines of 3–8 percent. Now Shaw was holding many of his competitors' "feet to the fire." Shaw was now in a position to undercut virtually any specific deal cut by a competitor and was offering the new low prices with no strings attached. [30]

Shaw tried to use its own newfound muscle to change the industry's marketing practices as well. The highest cost associated with carpet marketing was sampling. The industry turned over approximately a third of its product line every year. The success ratio for new products was under 50 percent. The industry also traditionally held several large regional "markets," or trade shows, every year: in Dallas, Atlanta, Chicago, and San Francisco, in January and June. Each show required samples. In the mid-1980s, Shaw began cutting back on its participation in the markets. "We have taken the position," Bob Shaw said, "that we will participate in only one market—January." Shaw contended that there were "more efficient ways to serve our customers than by spending millions of dollars annually at markets which are attended by only a small percentage of dealers." Instead, Shaw Industries would hold private and semiprivate showings at its own regional warehouses, each of which included showroom facilities. "In the decade of the '80s, this industry spent in excess of $2 billion sampling new styles," Shaw explained in a 1989 interview. "And of that $2 billion, we have only $½ billion still working. . . . We spent four times as much on samples as the industry made. Does it make sense for us to proliferate new styles? It is not practical for us to be at market." Shaw's main goal was to escape the development schedule and seasonality of the industry. Industry analysts projected that if Shaw was successful, the company "will have come a long way toward eliminating fixed costs . . . , [which] trip up manufacturers in a recession economy."[31] Shaw had essentially the same goal sought by John D. Rockefeller more than a century earlier in the oil industry: to overcome the "boom-and-bust" business cycle and eliminate "ruinous competition."

Shaw Industries climbed over a few more competitors in 1985, scrambling to the top of the industry's sales ladder, only to be displaced the following year, ending 1986 as the nation's number two carpet manufacturer. Shaw's sales for fiscal 1986 topped $624 million, second to Burlington Industries' $651 million. Shaw's U.S. sales actually exceeded those of Burlington's, making Shaw the top seller of carpet to the American market. Shaw strengthened its position in a year in which other large manufacturers were engaging in restructuring and buying out competitors. Burlington, for example, became the top producer with its purchase of Masland. WestPoint Pepperell, another top five company, bought Stratton Industries, enlarging its business significantly.[32]

Fiber producers introduced a new generation of stain-resistant nylon in the final quarter of 1986 with a massive advertising campaign. In essence the fiber companies forced the carpet manufacturers to accept the new fiber and frantically rush to get it into production by going straight to the consumer. This development was almost as significant as the mergers and acquisitions of 1986. Companies faced substantial new costs in establishing production of the new Stainmaster carpets. The carpet manufacturers were buying virtually all the Stainmaster fiber that Du Pont could produce, with plants in the fiber industry running at 95 percent of capacity.

The carpet industry, however, had long been plagued with excess capacity. The mills were running at around 40 percent of capacity. While there was demand for all the fiber Du Pont and other chemical companies could produce, the carpet producers faced a tougher market. The chemical companies naturally took advantage, raising their prices to their best customers—the carpet mills. Carpet prices remained relatively steady even with the introduction of a popular new product; competition mixed with excess capacity ensured that. Many carpet firms blamed the chemical companies for squeezing them.[33]

The tufted carpet industry had functioned as a converter for the chemical industry since the introduction of Du Pont's "501" nylon in 1958. The introduction of reliable, high-quality artificial fibers for carpet manufacture combined with the simple efficiency of the tufting machine to revolutionize the floor covering trade in the United States. Nylon replaced cotton and wool as the principal fiber for carpets and rugs by the early 1960s. As one consequence of that shift, the carpet industry ceded much of its consumer advertising to Du Pont and the other chemical companies. In the pre-nylon 501 days, the woven carpet manufacturers had sponsored lavish advertising campaigns. The smaller, less well capitalized tufted carpet firms took advantage of the deep pockets of the chemical companies, allowing those firms to shoulder the bulk of the expense of promoting nylon tufted carpeting to the mass media. Low-margin tufting concerns lost whatever opportunity might have existed to develop brand-name recognition for individual mills; those same mills avoided the expense of television and national magazine advertising. The deal was mutually beneficial.

The lack of a consumer franchise was of little consequence so long as the industry grew at the dizzying pace of the 1960s. The rising tide of demand for economical soft floor coverings lifted almost all entrepreneurial boats. After the industry's rapid growth phase petered out in the mid-1970s, carpet manufacturers became increasingly concerned about the low prices and anemic profit margins that accompanied commodity status. By the end of the 1970s, the tufted carpet industry seemed to have peaked. The recession of the early 1980s began a "weeding out" process, clearing out many less-than-healthy competitors, but prices and profits remained low even after the recovery began. The chemical companies intervened in the late 1980s, as they had in the late 1950s, to reinvigorate the industry and their own textile fiber profits. Du Pont took the lead in researching the problems of the carpet trade and introducing a potential antidote to the industry's slow-growth malaise.

Du Pont suffered from its own malaise in the 1970s and early 1980s. For most of the twentieth century, the company had been the largest chemical producer in the United States. By 1970, Du Pont was the sixth-largest corporation in the country. At the end of the decade, however, Du Pont had declined to the thirteenth spot in the *Fortune* 500. Many observers claimed that the old giant had become complacent. Du Pont was jolted from its complacency by the acquisition of the Conoco oil company in 1981. This acquisition represented a bold new strategy for Du Pont. Du Pont had for years been the classic example of what John Kenneth Galbraith labeled "the technocracy." Du Pont managers were skilled in the technical aspects of the chemical business, in the proper approach to research and development, and in developing new products, often over long periods of time. Du Pont had never been particularly proficient, or even interested, in marketing.

The new company officials who managed the takeover of Conoco were charged with the mission of invigorating the old firm's marketing strategies. As a result of the complicated wrangling over Conoco's fate, the Bronfman family of Seagram's became the chief stockholders in Du Pont. The Bronfmans reinforced the company's new direction, insisting on a market-oriented strategy for the firm. Du Pont pursued new directions in many areas, including the textile fiber department, which produced staple and BCF nylon for the carpet industry.[34]

Du Pont's fibers division had suffered from the same problem as the general textile and carpet industries in the early 1980s—stagnation. Broadloom carpet shipments surpassed 1.2 billion square yards in 1979; industry shipments declined during the recession of the early 1980s to about 885 million square yards in 1982. The industry's yardage shipments jumped by 23 percent in 1983 as the general economy began to recover, but growth flattened quickly to an average rate of about 3 percent for 1984 and 1985. The dollar value of mill shipments mirrored the decline of the early 1980s, falling from a high of almost $5.1 billion in 1979 to $4.9 billion in 1980. Dollar sales recovered more quickly than yardage sales owing to substantial price increases (almost 10 percent in 1980, followed by a hike of more than 14 percent in 1981), and carpet makers' total sales of $5.2 billion in 1981 barely exceeded the 1979 level. Sales dipped again in 1982, though, falling back to $4.9 billion, before jumping almost 22 percent in 1983. The roller coaster ride slowed through the mid-1980s as sales gains matched yardage gains at about 3 percent in 1984 and 1985.[35]

Du Pont saw the stagnating carpet industry as a threat to the continued profitability of the textile fibers division. Indeed, the company's fibers department saw its sales revenue decline throughout the early and mid-1980s. In early 1985, Du Pont's traditional emphasis on research and development produced a breakthrough that promised to rescue at least the flooring systems section of the textile fiber department. While conducting research into the feasibility of developing a nylon fiber dyeable at room temperature, Du Pont chemist Armand Zinnato discovered that "certain dye-resist agents previously used to improve wash-fastness" in carpet fibers "would also impart stain-resistance." By January 1985, Zinnato had confirmed his suspicion that these chemicals could make carpeting "nearly impossible to stain."[36]

Bruce Koepcke, long-range strategist for Du Pont's flooring systems division, advocated an aggressive marketing strategy for the new process as a way to boost carpet fiber sales. Koepcke's approach fit in well with the company's new marketing orientation, and upper management agreed to his proposal for a fifty-million-dollar promotional program for the new product, now referred to as "Stainmaster." Du Pont's allocation for this campaign constituted "the largest consumer product marketing effort ever staged" by the company.[37]

Koepcke and the flooring systems division originally planned to introduce Stainmaster at the January 1987 carpet trade shows. News leaked to the trade press in the spring of 1986 that Monsanto was also working on a stain-resistant fiber process, and Du Pont management decided to speed up the timetable. The company began presentations to carpet mill management teams in May 1986, and the first carpets made with the Du Pont Stainmaster chemicals were certified in September 1986. The consumer advertising campaign began in October 1986.[38]

Du Pont's television campaign was indeed massive. The company placed ads on eight of the top ten prime-time television programs in the first week of January 1987 and set as its target 1.7 billion "gross impressions" by the end of the year, or 6 for every citizen of the United States. The American public was inundated with images of red-haired "little Ricky" spilling all manner of messy foods and beverages on white carpet touted as stain-proof. The ads achieved their purpose, according to a marketing research firm that tracked the effectiveness of consumer advertising through surveys. The Du Pont Stainmaster ads were ranked in the top ten in effectiveness for 1987 by Campaign Monitor. Stainmaster commercials made a strong impression on more than 79 percent of the 7,000 consumers interviewed by Campaign Monitor. The initial Du Pont Stainmaster ad won praise for quality as well, taking a prestigious Clio award for excellence in advertising in 1987.[39]

By October 1987, some observers were touting the Stainmaster consumer advertising campaign mounted by Du Pont as an "important turning point for the modern carpet industry." "Two years ago," *Carpet and Rug Industry* editor Frank O'Neill observed, "no one in the carpet industry would have dreamed that one company could change the industry's fortunes from six years of no growth to a projected real growth rate around 5%," but that seemed to be what Du Pont had done. O'Neill noted that the industry achieved record sales of more than $7.3 billion in 1986, and he traced that success in large part to the boost provided by the early introduction of Stainmaster. The industry also experienced healthy growth in 1987, and the mill value of carpet shipments cracked the $8 billion plateau in 1988. Mill sales grew at an average of 9 percent per year for three consecutive years. O'Neill admitted that some of the growth in 1987 was accounted for by a 6 percent increase in sales of existing homes, but he contended that "the biggest consumer advertising in the history of the carpet industry almost certainly prompted a lot more of those new home owners to tear out old carpets and put in new ones." Du Pont was obviously the "big winner" in the Stainmaster campaign; according to one executive, "the payoff was fantastic. It nearly doubled our expectations."[40]

Carpet manufacturers were considerably less sanguine in their appraisal of the Stainmaster phenomenon. The costs involved with starting a new product line were enormous, despite Du Pont's help in providing the Stainmaster chemicals free of charge. The ad campaign was so successful that carpet mills were forced to accelerate their changeover from traditional products to new stain-resistant lines. Most firms had anticipated being able to convert slowly to stain-resistant carpets, spreading the cost out over a year or two. Consumer demand was so ferocious that the mills were forced to bear this increased cost over a few months instead. In addition, samples of the new stain-resistant carpets had to be produced or purchased by the mills. Competition within the still overcrowded field of tufted carpet manufacture compounded these cost problems. Intense competition prevented manufacturers from recouping the increased costs in the form of higher prices on stain-resistant products. One industry consultant estimated that the new process had added about fifteen cents per pound to the cost of carpet production, but "the volume-oriented mills have not increased prices to compensate for the higher costs." Stainmaster also made existing inventories difficult to sell except at bargain-basement prices. Thus although volume increased for the mills, already weak profit margins declined further. As an example, sales at Shaw Industries—the largest carpet manufacturer in the country—were up 23 percent in the second quarter of 1987 as compared with the same quarter in 1986, but net income barely moved (up about 1 percent). "The learning curve has been expensive for everybody," according to Galaxy Carpet Mills' vice president Dewey French.[41]

Bob Shaw had mixed feelings about the new Stainmaster craze. He believed that it had enhanced sales at a crucial time for the industry, but he questioned the long-term value of the new product. "If we're selling more carpet at lower margins, [then] it detracted [from the industry]," was Shaw's assessment three years after Stainmaster's introduction. "We can talk about how it cost us a lot of money as an industry. We had to resample. We had manufacturing learning curves to go through. But I'd be the last to tell you what would have happened if stain-resistant hadn't come along."[42]

Shaw faced some cost problems associated with the introduction of Stainmaster but was better equipped to handle the temporary crunch than most companies. Indeed, WestPoint Pepperell, parent company of Cabin Crafts, experienced a 70 percent decline in earnings for its carpet and rug division in 1986, mainly attributed to the Stratton acquisition and the start-up costs for Stainmaster. By the fall of 1987, WestPoint's carpet and rug division was a buyout target.[43]

Shaw Industries moved to acquire WestPoint's carpet unit in late September 1987. The two companies negotiated an agreement, but it fell through in early November. Shaw had planned to issue new stock to help pay for the purchase. The stock market crash in October torpedoed that plan. A few weeks later, according to *Forbes,* Bob Shaw decide to go "full speed ahead and damn the stock market." Shaw went ahead with the deal, purchasing WestPoint's carpet division for an estimated $140 million.[44] The acquisition of Cabin Crafts and the rest of WestPoint's carpet division boosted Shaw's annual revenues to $1.2 billion, making Shaw the world's largest carpet manufacturer. The deal also boosted Shaw's presence in market areas in which the company had been weak: high-end plush carpets, commercial carpets, and custom rugs.[45]

WestPoint management had "no regrets" on the sale of Cabin Crafts. In a March 1988 interview, WestPoint CEO Joseph L. Lanier Jr. told *Textile World* that while Cabin Crafts had made good money for West-Point in the early years, the explosion of tufting in the 1950s and 1960s had ruined the Cabin Crafts brand name. Lanier ruefully noted that brand names "mean very little to the ultimate consumer." Consumers bought "carpet once every seven or eight years, names come and go." Lanier underscored the lesson recently learned by Shaw Industries and other carpet manufacturers: "If God's truth is known right now, Du Pont's Stainmaster probably means more to the consumer than any particular brand name or even the store in which they bought [their carpet]."[46]

Shaw's acquisition of Cabin Crafts not only established the company as the top volume producer in the U.S. carpet industry, but it also gave Shaw Industries a market share unmatched by a single carpet company since the pretufting era. Shaw's billion-dollar sales almost doubled those of the company's closest rival, Burlington/Lees (14.3 percent to 7.5 percent). Moreover, when automotive, area rug, and other miscellaneous sales were factored out, Shaw's market dominance was even more pronounced. Shaw Industries' broadloom carpet sales accounted for 16.6 percent of the U.S. market, while Burlington's sales of the same product amounted to only 5.7 percent. From the late 1950s through the mid-1980s, no single carpet company had managed to acquire as much as a 10 percent market share; the sales volume spread between the top company and the number ten company was rarely much greater than about two to one. Shaw's 1987 market share was more than four times greater than that of the tenth-largest firm in the industry (Galaxy Mills, with a 3.2 percent share).[47]

Less than a year after Shaw's acquisition of Cabin Crafts and Stratton, industry insiders were mulling over "the Shaw factor." In two thoughtful articles in 1988 and 1989, Michael Berns, a California carpet manufacturer and former business professor, considered the current state of the carpet industry. Berns characterized the problems facing the carpet industry in the 1980s as "carpet mill anemia." The industry suffered from three key weaknesses that kept profits low even in times of strong sales growth. One of those weaknesses was the lack of a consumer franchise. Carpet companies all used the same fibers, made by others, and produced very similar products. There was no brand loyalty. Berns argued that lack of brand-name loyalty eliminated a major opportunity to add value to a product. Second, the carpet industry had excess capacity and high barriers to exit. There was a glut of excess equipment, as "the tufting machine is virtually indestructible" and "the great majority of tufting machines ever manufactured are still operable." Individuals wishing to switch resources or get out of the business faced great difficulty getting anything like a reasonable return if they tried to sell. "The tired, marginal producers are unable" to get out, and their mere existence "intensifies price competition," keeping profit margins razor thin. Third, carpet manufacturers were in a weak bargaining position for raw materials in relation to fiber producers, as the "Stainmaster" affair of 1986–87 clearly illustrated. For all these reasons, many carpet companies, large, medium, and small, became "zombie mills," lurching along, unable to merge or get out, forced to struggle with low or nonexistent profit margins, unable therefore to invest adequately in new technology. Shaw Industries had "dramatically altered the carpet industry's way of doing business," making "carpet mill anemia" potentially terminal for many companies. Shaw had forced a greater consciousness of cost to the forefront in the industry. With Shaw's commitment to new technology, other companies were forced to follow suit.[48]

Shaw had also forced the industry to reconsider its definition of competitive pricing. It was Shaw's pricing, "more than any other activity, . . . that [struck] fear into the hearts of carpet mill executives." Although Shaw's price policies were variously described as "cut-throat" or "give-away" policies, Shaw, according to Berns, followed a more complex price policy. Shaw sold only a few products at "ridiculously low prices," with many of its products still selling at or near the average rate. Shaw's position as the industry's low-cost producer allowed the company to cut prices on many items "without damaging its bottom line results." Shaw also had established new standards for service with its regional distribution system. For these reasons, unlike previous carpet giants, Shaw had beaten the odds and had become an attractive stock on Wall Street by 1989, further enhancing the firm's access to financial resources.[49]

Shaw moved to enhance its position as the top carpet producer in the world in December 1989. It acquired the carpet division of Armstrong World Industries, which included the assets of E & B Carpets, one of the industry leaders of the 1960s. When asked about Shaw's recent acquisitions, Bob Shaw insisted that in both the Cabin Crafts and Armstrong cases, his firm was first approached by those companies. "Gobbling is a bad word," Shaw said. "We're not a corporate raider by any means."[50]

Shaw emerged from the 1980s as the carpet industry's top company. According to the *Wall Street Journal,* Shaw Industries "snared nearly *all* the industry's growth during the latter half of the decade, ending up with almost 20% of the U.S. carpet market, up from 14% in 1985." Shaw had accomplished this phenomenal growth "by embracing what many companies shunned or mishandled in the 1980s: debt, and lots of it." Shaw spent more than six hundred million dollars on capital improvements and acquisitions in that same period. Those huge expenditures left Shaw Industries "with long-term debt that represents a chilling 56% of total capital." The money was, however, well spent, helping to establish Shaw as the industry's low-cost producer. And as the company's market share increased, Shaw's sales and cash flow easily kept pace with the debt structure. Shaw's "ability to pay down debt is unmatched in the industry," according to an industry analyst.[51]

The recession of 1990–91, according to Bob Shaw, helped increase the company's market share by eliminating weaker rivals. "It's the natural order of things, isn't it," Shaw contended, "the survival of the fittest." The

Wall Street Journal described Bob Shaw as "all Southern charm on the outside and all George Patton on the inside"; he was a man well equipped for the struggle he described. The struggle for existence that Shaw alluded to had already claimed more than half of the estimated 350 carpet manufacturers in operation in 1980.[52] Shaw continued to "buy" market share and integrate backward with two major acquisitions in 1992. First, Shaw purchased Salem Carpet Mills in February 1992, the previous year's number four company. The merger with Salem was expected to give Shaw about a third of the U.S. carpet market. In July, Shaw acquired Amoco's fiber division. This purchase made Shaw self-sufficient in the production of polypropylene fiber, an inexpensive polyesterlike yarn that was responsible for much of the industry's growth in the 1990s.[53]

Robert E. Shaw built Shaw Industries from "a little $300,000-a-year" company that dyed scatter rugs into the leading carpet manufacturer in the world, a $2 billion, *Fortune* 500 company. He did it with a single-minded determination to be the low-cost producer in the industry. Described as "competitive" by some, he has also been termed "ruthless," even by friends. Though his price-cutting policies have been explained by industry analysts as reasonable, many within the industry still felt that Shaw purposely tried to force competitors out of business by selling below cost. Even some longtime industry insiders and leaders were still unsure, as late as 1993, as to precisely how Shaw could make the profits he did with the prices he charged.[54] There was, however, no denying Shaw's business acumen and determination. The puzzlement expressed by some long-time carpet mill owners and executives about Shaw's cost-control methods and pricing policies revealed more about the changing nature of the industry than about Shaw's actions. The carpet industry entered a new era in the 1980s, and many were unequipped to deal with the demands of slow growth.

Shaw Industries' growth was unparalleled in the carpet industry and reflected changes in the industry as much as Shaw's managerial virtues. Other companies had been large, but never as large as Shaw. Barwick Mills, for example, had been the industry leader in the 1960s. Barwick grew in an era when carpet industry shipments were skyrocketing yearly; Shaw dominated in a period of very slow growth for the industry. Barwick was an innovator who could claim many industry "firsts," including printed carpets. Yet Barwick was unable to survive in the long run, eventually going bankrupt in 1979. Barwick and Shaw, like most other carpet companies large and small, were highly leveraged. But Shaw was better able to manage debt than Barwick. Shaw was also more clearly committed to the industry for the long run. While many of the entrepreneurs who pioneered the tufted carpet industry cashed themselves out in the late 1960s and early 1970s, Bob and J. C. Shaw reinvested substantial portions of the proceeds from stock sales. Shaw's willingness to embrace fully the low-cost production strategy—vertical integration, full usage of productive capacity even in recessionary periods, and wise capital improvements—was the key difference.

As the industry's merger movement continued, a few competitors emerged to whittle away at Shaw's market dominance. The awkwardly named old giant Mohasco also stirred in the late 1980s, and by 1995 it had joined Shaw as the only other carpet firm with annual sales in excess of one billion dollars. David Kolb became the first non-Shuttleworth CEO of the firm in 1981. In 1988, Kolb and other members of Mohasco's management team took the company private in a leveraged buyout. The new owners restored the company's old name, Mohawk, dropping the acronym that had combined "Mohawk" with "Alexander Smith Company." The firm went public again in 1992 and began a series of important acquisitions. By 1995, Mohawk had acquired Spirer's Horizon Industries, American Rug Craftsman, Karastan Bigelow, Aladdin Mills, and Galaxy. Chiefly as a result of these acquisitions, Mohawk's annual sales skyrocketed from $352 million in 1992 to $1.6 billion in 1995. Mohawk, by combining the forces of many of Shaw's old challengers, closed the market share gap between the number one and number two carpet producers from about 3–1 in 1990 to a shade under 2–1 by 1995. Mohawk continued to challenge Shaw through major acquisitions in the late 1990s, including the purchase of Shaheen Shaheen's World Carpets, for which, in exchange for an estimated $150 million worth of Mohawk stock, the Shaheen family and the last of the major founding firms of the Dalton district bowed out of the industry they had helped to create.[55]

The Beaulieu Group began to penetrate the American market in 1977 when chairman Roger DeClerck sent his son-in-law, Carl Bouckaert, to establish a U.S. division for the Belgian manufacturer of woven polypropylene rugs. Beaulieu established its own facility for extruding polypropylene yarns in 1982 and remained a successful but low-profile operation until 1988. Beaulieu built the first independent nylon chip plant in the United States that year. At about the same time, Bouckaert entered into partnership with a group including Ed Ralston, former son-in-law of Gene Barwick and head of commission tufting leader D & W Carpets. The consortium purchased Conquest Carpet Mills, an up-and-coming low-end producer with sales of about $120 million and rising. Conquest immediately became a major customer for Beaulieu's nylon and polypropylene fiber production facilities.[56]

Beaulieu joined the merger movement by trying to acquire Peter Spirer's Horizon Industries in 1990 in a hostile takeover. After Beaulieu bought about 18 percent of Horizon's outstanding stock, the takeover bid "was thwarted by a poison pill stock initiative from Horizon." Horizon later accepted an offer from Mohawk. Bouckaert, determined to gain a stronger foothold in the U.S. industry, then purchased Coronet Carpets, the seventh-ranked company in the industry with 1989 sales of about $300 million. By the mid-1990s, the Beaulieu Group had split into several separate firms; the largest was Carl Bouckaert's newly renamed Beaulieu of America. Beaulieu of America had for a time been the number two company in the U.S carpet industry and ranked third in 1995 with sales of about $920 million. The key elements in Beaulieu's operations were Coronet, Conquest, and its commission tufting affiliates.[57]

Aside from Mohawk, no carpet company grew as rapidly as Queen Carpet in the 1990s. Queen celebrated its fiftieth year in business in 1996. Still a privately held family business, Queen was the classic example of a firm that started out manufacturing small tufted goods and then made the transition to carpet production. Founder Harry Saul chose the company's name because he boasted that the tufted robes he made were "fit for a queen"; later the company became a leader in scatter rug production. In a story reminiscent of the Shaw family history, Harry Saul resisted entry into broadloom carpet production, while his son, Julian, argued in favor of such a move. In the Saul family's case, the son persuaded the father, and Queen entered the carpet market in 1963. Queen began making a serious move toward the top of the industry's rankings in 1979 when the Sauls initiated an ambitious expansion program. Within a decade, Queen was a fully integrated manufacturer, encompassing all phases of the production process from fiber extrusion and yarn processing to dyeing and finishing. Queen embarked on its own acquisition campaign in the early 1990s, and the firm's sales jumped from $390 million in 1992 to $720 million in 1995.[58]

By the end of the 1990s, however, Julian Saul had decided to join forces with Shaw Industries. Queen merged with Shaw in August 1998, adding its market share to that of the industry leader. Shaw Industries agreed to pay more than $470 million in cash and stock to acquire the venerable family-owned Queen. As a result of this acquisition, the Saul family owned about 14 percent of Shaw Industries' stock, only slightly less than the 16 percent held by members of the Shaw family. As the tufted carpet industry approached the millennium, the Saul and Shaw families formed what amounted to a strategic alliance to fend off the challenges of Mohawk and Beaulieu.[59]

Shaw's acquisition of Queen represented something of a comeback for the firm in 1998. During the mid-1990s, Shaw had pushed its vertical integration strategy forward to the retail level. In 1995, the company bought a chain of carpet retailing stores. This move put Shaw Industries into direct competition with other retailers who still sold Shaw carpets, including large chains such as Home Depot. Although Shaw was able to sell its products through several hundred stores owned directly by the company, the manufacturer lost other significant accounts as home furnishings sellers refused to stock products made by a firm that also competed in the retail market. This led to erosion of Shaw's market share as Mohawk and Beaulieu rushed to fill the gap for these disgruntled former Shaw customers. Finally, just prior to the purchase of Queen in the summer of 1998, Shaw sold off most of its interest in the retail stores, admitting defeat for one of the few times in the firm's history. The Queen acquisition marked a return to basics for Shaw Industries: the firm would renew its emphasis on low-cost production. With the Queen acquisition, Shaw Industries restored market dominance, which had eroded slightly in the mid-1990s. Shaw's market share fell from about 33 percent to near 26 percent from 1995 to 1998. The purchase of Queen's market share boosted the industry leader's market share back to approximately 34 percent, nearly double that of its closest rival (Mohawk, at roughly 19 percent).[60]

Entrepreneurs and workers in the northwest Georgia area created a new industry—tufted carpet—that provided jobs and relative prosperity to agricultural communities that might otherwise have become ghost towns. The concentration of the tufted carpet industry in the Dalton area created opportunities for self-employment and wealth accumulation among the region's workers, as well as a labor shortage that kept unemployment rates low and allowed workers substantial freedom of movement. Median household income in Whitfield County, for example, amounted to $31,415 in 1993, slightly higher than either the national ($31,241) or state ($31,148) levels. Whitfield's poverty rate (12.9 percent) was also substantially lower that the state average (16.8 percent).[61]

Conversely, the Dalton district's very reliance on carpet manufacture and lack of economic diversification made the region particularly vulnerable to recession. The downturn of 1974–75 produced an unemployment rate of more than 15 percent in Whitfield County; in 1981–82, that county's unemployment rate reached almost 18 percent. By contrast, Georgia's more diversified urban economies fared better—Columbus had the state's highest urban unemployment rate in March 1982 at just over 10 percent. The state average was about 8 percent.[62] With the number of mills declining rather than increasing after 1980, the bargaining power of individual workers declined as well. Except during the brief Stainmaster miniboom of 1987, it was no longer a simple matter to go down the street and find a new job with a new employer. Charles Bramlett and other community leaders complained about the overreliance of Dalton and surrounding communities on a single industry, but alternatives were difficult to find.

As noted earlier, workers in the Dalton area developed a pronounced tendency to drop out of school and enter the relatively low skill manufacturing labor force. By the 1980s, a process of inertia had set in: the carpet industry was no longer growing by leaps and bounds, but the dominance of the carpet industry in the Dalton district limited the market for new and different skills. As workers faced pressure on jobs from the consolidation of the industry, another complication arose that further eroded the old social contract within Tuftland: immigration.

By 1990, the Census Bureau reported more than 3,500 Mexican immigrants in Whitfield County, up from around 200 in 1980. Unofficial reports placed the number of Mexican immigrants closer to 10,000 by 1994. The census numbers were almost certainly too low, though the 10,000 figure may be a bit high. This wave of immigration began as a trickle, with Mexicans moving to Dalton to work in the local Conagra chicken processing plant. The initial immigrants also found jobs in the carpet industry. As word of relatively high paying jobs in the Dalton carpet industry filtered back to the immigrants' homes in Mexico, more Hispanic workers were attracted to northwest Georgia. The immigrants were generally welcomed by mill owners. The labor shortage in the Dalton area became particularly acute in the late 1980s as the unemployment rate in Whitfield County dropped as low as 3.8 percent in the midst of the Stainmaster boom of 1987. Mexican immigration, both legal and illegal, provided some relief from the regional labor shortage about which carpet executives had complained for decades. The immigrants worked hard and kept a low profile, earning the admiration of their employers.[63]

As the number of immigrant workers increased, though, local workers and other community leaders expressed doubts. Workers particularly feared the immigrants as a threat to their jobs, or more precisely, to the tight labor market in the Dalton area. The bargaining power of workers had already been diminished by consolidation; a perceived flood of illegal immigration now threatened to destroy the remaining opportunity for production workers in the Dalton district. Many local residents complained loudly at city council and county commission meetings and produced a steady flow of letters to the local newspaper. Dalton city officials announced in 1995 that the Immigration and Naturalization Service would open a local office in Dalton. This office would be an agency first: it would be funded by *local* taxes, not the federal government. Community leaders hoped this agreement with the INS would help mend a growing rift between mill owners and workers in the Dalton district.[64]

The Dalton tufting district has begun to break down in other ways as well. In the early 1990s, Diamond Carpet Mills filed an antitrust lawsuit against Du Pont and Shaw Industries, charging that Shaw and Du Pont conspired to try to set a minimum price for Stainmaster carpets and that Shaw Industries sent a representative to Diamond owner Ed Weaver to explore the possibility of setting prices on polypropylene carpet. Shaw countersued, alleging that Diamond had brought the entire industry into disrepute by selling shoddy goods and misleading consumers and retailers about the contents of its carpeting. Both suits attracted the attention of federal regulators. The antitrust suit was settled out of court in 1995, and in December of the same year Diamond pleaded guilty to charges that it had mislabeled the fiber content of its carpets. This judgment carried a heavy fine and probably dealt a fatal blow to Diamond's chances of survival. By July 1997 the Weaver family began to reorganize Diamond under Chapter 11 bankruptcy protection; they sold most of the company's assets to Mohawk and quietly began dividing the remains of the maverick firm among creditors.[65]

The degradation of regional water supplies also continued to plague the Dalton district. By the mid-1990s, it appeared that the celebrated land application filtration system, lauded as an innovative approach in the 1980s, was inadequate for the task of treating carpet waste water. The continuing water-quality problems called into question Dalton Utilities' long-standing policy on industrial waste water treatment. As the *Atlanta Business Chronicle* noted in 1995, "historically, Dalton Utilities has lifted the burden of meeting environmental regulations from its customers. . . . Dalton Utilities handle[d] all the treatment of waste water on its end," thus saving each of its carpet mill customers from the considerable expense of establishing pretreatment facilities. Pretreatment programs could "cost a few hundred thousand dollars or millions of dollars, depending on the size of the operation." By absolving carpet manufacturers and finishers from any responsibility for pretreatment of waste water, Dalton Utilities promoted growth, opportunity, and new firm creation.[66] But there were costs associated with these benefits.

Environmental groups charged that the industry and Dalton Utilities had purposely falsified records and misled regulators about discharges into local rivers and streams. In the mid-1990s, a group called the Conasauga River Alliance—formed by local residents in Tennessee and north Georgia, the Nature Conservancy, and the Department of Agriculture— came together to try to protect the natural beauty of an important regional waterway. The Nature Conservancy was most concerned about the threats to endangered species posed by water pollution in the river; local residents were motivated by simpler concerns for preserving safe, clean places for fishing, swimming, and other recreational activities. The main goal of the alliance was the protection of the upper Conasauga River, the sixty miles or so from its origin in the Cohutta Mountains to the city of Dalton. Jimmie Witherow, an alliance member and vice chair of the Murray County Commission, summed up the motivation of the alliance: "All you have to do is look downstream below Dalton and see what can happen if we don't work to protect the river." The *Atlanta Journal-Constitution* reported in early 1997 that for its first sixty miles, the river was "a treasure trove of endangered fresh water fish." After passing through Dalton, the river's waters took on the appearance of chocolate milk.[67]

The problems of the river were more than aesthetic. In 1996, the investigators for Georgia's Environmental Protection Division documented two "major spills" (ten thousand gallons or more) of raw sewage dumped into the Mill Creek, which flowed into the Conasauga. Not only had the local utility failed to notify the EPD, as required by law, but the investigation also disclosed the existence of overflow structures apparently "put into place to direct overflow sewage into the creek. Someone put those there," observed EPD assistant director David Word. In May 1996, the EPD ordered Dalton Utilities to eliminate the overflow structures and "cease practices in which the sanitary sewer system is manipulated to allow a discharge" of untreated waste water.[68] Industry supporters maintained that the utility had done nothing wrong, and they continued to praise Dalton Utilities for its water policies. John Rhodes, economic director of the Whitfield County–Dalton Chamber of Commerce, acknowledged that the utility had been "a great protectionist of the carpet industry." Rhodes observed that "[the city of] Dalton has borne that burden [of water treatment] to shelter the carpet industry from the federal and state regulations" and promote new business development. Julian Saul, CEO of Queen Carpets, argued that the utility "grew us all. You shut down Dalton utilities and you shut us down." Saul dismissed the calls for more extensive pretreatment programs, funded by the companies themselves. "They [environmental officials] want us to pretreat the effluent before we put it into the sewer. That is impossible with the vast quantities of water we use."[69]

Dalton Utilities bore a great part of the responsibility for the continuing concentration of the carpet industry in the Dalton area. The municipal utility had long socialized the entire cost of combating water pollution in the Dalton district. As the Dalton district approached the end of the first half century of tufted carpet production, it appeared that the region had indeed paid a price in environmental degradation for its industrial progress.

The lawsuits and federal investigation, allegations of price-fixing, social conflict over immigration, the water pollution problems, and the changes associated with the merger movement of the late 1980s and 1990s reflected the changing nature of the Dalton carpet district. From the days of home bedspread tufting through the carpet boom of the 1960s, the Dalton district had accumulated substantial social capital. Catherine Evans Whitener freely taught hand-tufting to her friends and neighbors, and handicraft production flourished in the first decades of the twentieth century. Some innovators of the post–World War II period, like Mose Painter, shared their inventions and ideas just as freely in the 1950s. Equipment manufacturer Lewis Card shared risks with his customers, financing tufting machine sales in-house and allowing purchasers to repay debts on the basis of a percentage of sales. Entrepreneurs like Gene Barwick, Bud Seretean, Said and Shaheen Shaheen, and Peter Spirer moved to the Dalton district to participate in this burst of creative activity; they were joined by local businessmen like Jack Bandy and later Robert and J. C. Shaw. The rise of the tufted carpet industry provided a vehicle for upward mobility for men like Charles Bramlett and Ed Weaver. The contacts, connections, and store of mutual respect and trust acquired by such men enabled them to strike out on their own in an expanding market. The district operated on a blend of cooperation and competition. The new industry also provided Georgia with an example of homegrown economic development. Northwest Georgia's Tuftland region produced about three-fourths of the American carpet industry's $11 billion–plus annual sales volume.

The business climate had certainly changed within the Dalton district. Former mill owners often lamented that the industry was less friendly, less hospitable. Bobby Mosteller, cofounder of Galaxy Mills, recalled that in the 1960s and 1970s the annual trade association meetings were as much social gatherings as anything else. The large number of mills meant a substantial turnout by executives from those companies. At meetings in exotic locales like the Grand Bahamas, at which several hundred enterprising businessmen congratulated themselves for the phenomenal growth of their industry, owners and managers forged a sense of common purpose and shared destiny (at least among management personnel; as we have seen, workers were not included in the cooperative spirit of the district). The expanding market for carpet reduced the need for any firm to profit at another's expense. The maturing market of the late 1970s and 1980s and the end of the international economic golden age combined to reduce opportunities and encourage consolidation. During the merger movement of the 1980s and 1990s, large firms sought to increase their share of a slowly growing market through acquisitions. The number of firms in the industry began to decline during the 1981–82 recession.

Robert E. Shaw probably best exemplified the changing nature of the business environment in the carpet industry and in the Dalton district in the mid-1990s. Shaw had been advised by management consultants during the mid-1980s to move his corporate headquarters to Atlanta. He declined, electing to remain in Dalton. Shaw was primarily responsible for the construction of the magnificent new Presbyterian church in Dalton and made generous contributions to a variety of local charities and the local hospital. Shaw retained an affinity for the Dalton district that had spawned his company and a few hundred others over the course of four decades. He was also a tough competitor whose chief concern was his company's bottom line. Shaw's temperament perhaps made a better fit with the market conditions of the 1990s. In a September 1993 interview, he responded to a question about problems within the carpet industry by crystallizing the emerging ethic of Tuftland. "Problems? What problems does the industry have? I can't worry about anyone else but me. I've been in the top four of the Fortune 500 in terms of return on investment for the last five years. What problems do I have?"[70] In the carpet industry's new slow-growth environment, survival of the fittest was the order of the day.

Conclusion

Dalton's industrial past can be divided into two distinct eras. The first, associated with the cotton mills, was based on mammoth enterprises that developed extensive programs of corporate welfare. Notwithstanding all the boosterism of the late nineteenth century, civic leaders and the founders of Dalton's Crown Cotton Mill shared fundamental assumptions about corporate responsibility. Crown developed a paternalistic system of worker benefits as a response to a labor turnover crisis. Workers embraced this pragmatic program, exerted their own influence in shaping the company's policies, and helped build an industrial community. As private paternalism broke down in the depression years, Crown's workers organized a union to defend their community. Through the 1950s, Dalton's original industrial giant embodied ideas of community, shared responsibility, and common purpose. As one former Crown worker observed, "We lived a full life, no doubt about that. It was hard and we had work, but we had a full life."[1]

The carpet industry that replaced the cotton mills in Dalton represented a second distinct era in the region's industrial history. The new economic engine of northwest Georgia developed from the bottom up. Tufted bedspread manufacture, a handicraft revived by Catherine Evans Whitener and other local women around the turn of the century, encouraged the development of a kind of entrepreneurial spirit in the region. Southerners created a new product—albeit a novelty item—and began exploiting the larger national marketplace. The move to factory production in the 1930s initiated a homegrown industrial revolution. Crown and other local cotton and thread mills provided crucial infrastructure for this entrepreneurial revolution by supplying cheap raw materials—yarn and cotton sheeting—locally.

Entrepreneurs like Spencer Love and the Westcotts opened new textile mills in the South during the 1920s and 1930s to produce cheaper "knock-offs" of more expensive northern goods, like hosiery. The Westcotts shifted their investments from hosiery to factory production of tufted bedspreads in the early 1930s. Hosiery mill mechanics like Albert and Joe Cobble and self-trained welders and mechanics like Mose Painter were also attracted to the new industry. This capital and mechanical expertise played a vital role in the development of mass-production technology for tufted textile goods. The tufting machines produced by Cabin Crafts and Cobble Brothers, in turn, made possible the move to broadloom carpet production. The riches associated with carpet production dwarfed the profits of tufted bedspread, bathrobe, and small rug manufacture. This new southern technology revolutionized the market for floor coverings, cutting prices and making wall-to-wall carpeting available to middle- and working-class consumers for the first time.

The new industrial environment of Dalton was characterized by the rapid multiplication of new firms. Barriers to entry into tufting were low, and opportunities for choosing a place of employment, or self-employment, expanded for a generation. As consumers discovered cheap soft floor coverings in the 1950s and 1960s, the sky appeared to be the limit for Dalton's entrepreneurs. The golden age of mass markets, partially driven by government policies that promoted mass consumption, formed the perfect environment for the evolution of a southern-based national industry. The new industry developed its own forms of cooperation and shared responsibility, similar to those that bound together other industrial districts throughout the world. Cooperation and risk sharing characterized the early tufted carpet district. Boundaries between firms remained porous, and managers who apprenticed at one carpet mill were quite likely to strike out on their own. Technological advances in tufting equipment proved difficult to protect in such an environment. A smaller group of companies shifted from bedspread laundering to carpet finishing. The finishing companies shared risks with the tufting firms, though as carpet manufacturing firms grew larger, they generally sought vertical integration. These new firms also competed for labor in a tight market. Small and medium-sized companies in the district formed a manufacturers association to manage competition. Cooperation among manufacturers played an important role in the emergence of the industry. Cooperation also had a darker side; the trade association coordinated antiunion efforts.

Local government, through the municipally owned utility, played a key role in promoting industrial growth. The Water, Light, and Sinking Fund Commission and Dalton Utilities tailored local power and water policies to the needs of the indigenous industry. Utility chief V. D. Parrott explored every avenue in the search for cheap water and electricity. In facilitating the entrepreneurial dreams of prospective carpet manufacturers, Dalton Utilities pushed regional water resources to, and perhaps beyond, the breaking point. By the end of the 1990s, it remained an open question, in Dalton as in other communities throughout the globe feverishly pursuing growth, whether industrial development could be harmonized with a clean and safe natural environment.

The narrative of the carpet district of northwest Georgia has implications beyond southern history. Tufted carpet manufacture confounds the sometimes facile distinction between "mass" and "flexible" production. In many respects, the tufting and finishing processes exemplified "flexible mass production," enabling manufacturers to mass-produce inexpensive goods in a bewildering array of styles and colors. While some firms chose over time to focus on the mass residential market, competing chiefly on price, others specialized in smaller market segments and developed high-quality, high-margin goods. In terms of both products and markets served, the tufted carpet industry embodied the concept of "endless novelty." The evolution of Dalton's carpet industry fits, therefore, into broader national patterns.[2]

The experience of the Dalton district illustrates the possibilities of a regional approach to economic development. Municipal leaders and a group of talented entrepreneurs sketched the contours of a path toward indigenous industrialization in the 1940s and 1950s. The path chosen by northwest Georgia's economic leaders produced tangible benefits for entrepreneurs and, to a limited extent, even for workers. The South often paid a high price—including low wages and environmental degradation—for its recruitment of outside industry. Indigenous industrialization, too, had its price, measured in similar outcomes.

The Dalton district's workers and owners, in conflict and cooperation, built a modern community of autonomous individuals, each calculating his or her own short- and long-term prospects. For better and worse, this new culture differed significantly from the older culture associated with cotton mills, mill villages, and paternalism.

Though it is a crude oversimplification, Dalton appears to exemplify the economic transformation of the South and the region's integration into the national mainstream. Civic and business leaders made an "industrial resolution" in the 1880s, consciously committing themselves to the encouragement of industrialization. Through a variety of twists and turns, and not always intentionally, managers and millhands created an industrial community. The carpet industry arose on the foundation of that old structure. Entrepreneurship emerged from the bottom up in the Dalton area. In this sense, entrepreneurs and workers in the region played their part in the creation of another "New South" in the postwar years.

Numan V. Bartley has argued that economic development encouraged the transformation of the South's social structure. The older culture, associated with paternalism and stability (whether a reflection of Old South values or the adaptation of New South leaders to national economic conditions), faded, replaced by an "expanding market society" in which "southerners were free to pursue personal self-fulfillment through career and achievement." [3] To Bartley's "career and achievement" other scholars might add consumption. From World War II through the 1970s, an expanding national and world economy opened unprecedented opportunities for the South. Northwest Georgia's tufted textile industrial revolution created a society of greater opportunity. The carpet industry provided the framework, albeit limited, within which many individuals could rise according to their talents, and it generated wealth that made fortunes possible for some and absolute deprivation rarer than in much of the rest of the South.

The Manly family has played an important role in community affairs in Dalton for more than a century. The family business, Manly Steel (formerly Manly Jail Works), developed in the early twentieth century to serve local and regional needs. The Manly firm in Dalton continued to prosper by serving distinctive local markets in structural iron- and steelworks for construction and locks and cells for southern jails. The Manly family operated their business with some of the same paternalistic tendencies exhibited by cotton mill owners, though Manly Steel was always a much smaller affair than a cotton mill.

Judson Manly, a second-generation Georgia Tech–trained engineer in his late sixties, related a family story that spoke volumes about industry and community. As the firm's orders dried up and work became scarce in the early 1930s, the family decided to keep workers on the payroll and accept financial losses in the (hopefully) short run. "The Depression came along in the 1930s, and they had a dirt floor in the plant, which they had been accustomed to in the foundry business. Things got so bad, they couldn't keep everybody working, so the employees dug holes in the dirt and played miniature golf on their own time waiting for work to come in." The widow and son of a depression-era Manly employee elaborated on the story. The company laid off workers briefly, but Judson Manly soon visited the homes of furloughed workers and asked if the families had money for groceries for the weekend. He then told employees to return to work on Monday morning and that "we'll find something for you to do." This story, fondly but clearly remembered by a ninety-three-year-old widow six decades later, gave eloquent testimony to the sense of social obligation and mutual responsibility that represented the best aspects of a paternalistic social and economic order.

The Manly family profited from the emergence of the tufted textile industry in the region. Manly Steel made a variety of ancillary products used by the new tufted carpet mills in the 1950s, including creel racks that fed yarn into the tufting machines. Manly Steel, though, represented a passing economic order in the region. The carpet industry generated sales and profits in the billions, serving larger national markets. The Manly family firm, in the hands of a third generation of Georgia Tech engineering alumni by the 1990s, survived but was dwarfed by the carpet giants around town. Michael Manly captured the ambiguous spirit of the Dalton carpet district in a 1997 interview. When asked what the community of Dalton valued, Manly responded, "This community values money. I don't know how else to say it. Things, possessions, money. It's the driving force. And I think it's been that way for the last thirty or forty years." Manly realized that his family history made it difficult for him to criticize the new orientation. "We were always comfortable," he recalled, "we weren't suffering," so his family did not place as much value on material gain; "it was less important." The Manly family's attitude toward money "had to do with the fact that we were well-established in the community. It's different when you're clawing yourself up from the bottom than when you're already comfortable."[4]

Dalton's industrial system may have unleashed some of the less attractive features of modern life—excessive materialism and environmental danger, for example. But this regional economy also created a field of opportunity for the expression of a regional entrepreneurial spirit. The survival of thousands of what might be termed old fashioned manufacturing jobs in the area provided an above average standard of living for citizens of small southern towns. The homegrown carpet industry offered an opportunity for talented local people to create new businesses and provide for their families without leaving the region.

After World War II, the South clawed its way up from the bottom. Like many developing regions, Dixie and Dalton are now struggling with new challenges, challenges created by successful industrial development.

Notes

Introduction

1. Douglas Flamming, *Creating the Modern South: Millhands and Managers in Dalton, Georgia, 1884–1984* (Chapel Hill: University of North Carolina Press, 1992).

2. Philip Scranton, *Figured Tapestry: Production, Markets, and Power in Philadelphia Textiles, 1885–1941* (Cambridge: Cambridge University Press, 1989), and *Proprietary Capitalism: The Textile Manufacture at Philadelphia, 1800–1885* (Cambridge: Cambridge University Press, 1983). Segments of the old woven carpet industry emerged and prospered in Philadelphia as a part of the larger textile environment. The Philadelphia carpet firms shared the flexibility of their neighbors and differed from their larger, better-capitalized New England counterparts such as Bigelow. John Ingham has written about the smaller, more flexible iron and steel producers of Pittsburgh in *Making Iron and Steel: Independent Mills in Pittsburgh, 1820–1920* (Columbus: Ohio State University Press, 1991). Scranton has more recently expanded his analysis in "Diversity in Diversity: Flexible Production and American Industrialization," *Business History Review* 65 (Spring 1991): 27–90. Scranton concurs with Blackford that much more attention must be devoted to the broader spectrum of manufacturing in American history, which has been dominated by the mass-production model. Blackford's proposed research agenda for small business may be found in Mansel Blackford, *A History of Small Business in America* (New York: Twayne Publishers, 1991), 121–25. Michael Piore and Charles Sabel, *The Second Industrial Divide: Possibilities for Prosperity* (New York: Basic Books, 1984), provides an excellent introduction to the topic of flexible specialization and possesses the added strength of an international perspective. See also Charles Sabel, "Studied Trust: Building New Forms of Cooperation in a Volatile Economy," *Human Relations* 46 (September 1993): 1133–69.

3. The best overview of post–Civil War southern industrial development is James C. Cobb, *Industrialization and Southern Society, 1877–1984* (Lexington: University Press of Kentucky, 1984); Cobb's *The Selling of the South: The Southern Crusade for Industrial Development, 1936–1980* (Baton Rouge: Louisiana State University Press, 1982) is the definitive work on the southern strategy of courting outside investment and its costs in the twentieth century. The options facing the South's political and economic leaders at the end of World War II are nicely summarized in Numan V. Bartley, *The New South, 1945–1980: The Story of the South's Modernization* (Baton Rouge: Louisiana State University Press, 1995), 7–21.

4. Alfred Marshall, *Principles of Economics,* 8th ed. (London: Macmillan, 1920), 271–73.

5. Ibid.

6. Ibid.

7. *Economist* 33 (July 29, 1995): 6–9.

8. See Annalee Saxenian, *Regional Advantage: Culture and Competition in Silicon Valley and Route 128* (Cambridge: Harvard University Press, 1994), and Saxenian, "Lessons from Silicon Valley," *Technology Review* (July 1994): 42–51.

9. Saxenian, "Lessons from Silicon Valley," 50–51. For a recent appraisal of the southern regionalists, see David L. Carlton and Peter A. Coclanis, "Another Great Migration?: From Region to Race in Southern Liberalism, 1938–1945," *Southern Cultures* 3 (Fall 1997): 37–62. Vance and Odum, of course, advocated a broader definition of "region" than Saxenian (the entire southeastern United States, in fact), but Saxenian's work, and the work of others in the field of flexible production, recalls the spirit, if not the letter, of the southern regionalists of the 1930s.

10. Gary Anderson, "Industry Clustering for Economic Development," *Economic Development Review* 12 (Spring 1994): 26–32; Michael Porter, *The Competitive Advantage of Nations* (New York: Basic Books, 1990).

11. Charles Sabel and Jonathan Zeitlin, eds., *World of Possibilities: Flexibility and Mass Production in Western Industrialization* (Cambridge: Cambridge University Press, 1997), 5–6.

Prologue. The First American Carpet Industry

1. Anthony N. Landreau, *America Underfoot: A History of Floor Coverings from Colonial Times to the Present* (Washington, D.C.: Smithsonian Institution Press, 1976), 3. See also Nina Fletcher Little, *Floor Coverings in New England before 1850* (Sturbridge, Mass.: Old Sturbridge Village, 1967), 3–4, and Rodris Roth, *Floor Coverings in Eighteenth-Century America,* United States National Museum Bulletin no. 250 (Washington, D.C.: Smithsonian Institution Press, 1967), 3.

2. Susan H. Anderson, *The Most Splendid Carpet* (Philadelphia: National Park Service, 1978), 3–9, 31–38.

3. Gail Caskey Winkler and Roger W. Moss, *Victorian Interior Decoration: American Interiors, 1830–1900* (New York: Henry Holt and Co., 1986), 32–35.

4. Arthur H. Cole and Harold F. Williamson, *The American Carpet Manufacture: A History and an Analysis* (Cambridge: Harvard University Press, 1941), 11–13; J. R. Kendrick, "The Carpet Industry in Philadelphia," in *Annual Report*

of the Secretary of Internal Affairs of the Commonwealth of Pennsylvania, pt. 3, *Industrial Statistics* (Harrisburg, Pa.: Edwin K. Meyers, 1889), 1D; Cornelia Bateman Faraday, *European and American Carpets and Rugs* (1929; reprint, Woodbridge, Suffolk, England: Antique Collectors' Club, 1990), 400; A. N. Cook, *A Century of Carpet and Rug-Making in America, 1825–1925* (New York: Bigelow-Hartford Carpet Co., 1925), 9, 10.

5. Cole and Williamson, *American Carpet Manufacture*, 11, 22.

6. John S. Ewing and Nancy P. Norton, *Broadlooms and Businessmen: A History of the Bigelow-Sanford Company* (Cambridge: Harvard University Press, 1955), 7–33; Winkler and Moss, *Victorian Interior Decoration*, 85–87.

7. Ewing and Norton, *Broadlooms and Businessmen*, 34–57.

8. *The Manufactories and Manufacturers of Pennsylvania of the Nineteenth Century* (Philadelphia: Galaxy Publishing Co., 1875), 500–501.

9. Cole and Williamson, *American Carpet Manufacture*, 12; Timothy Pitkin, *A Statistical View of the Commerce of the United States of America, Including Also an Account of Banks, Manufacturers, and Internal Trade and Improvements* (New Haven: Durrie & Peck, 1835), 492–93.

10. Cole and Williamson, *American Carpet Manufacture*, 21–22.

11. Ibid., 20; Paul A. David, "Growth of Real Product in the United States before 1840: New Evidence, Controlled Conjectures," *Journal of Economic History* 27 (April 1967): 151–97.

12. Cole and Williamson, *American Carpet Manufacture*, 44–46, 249.

13. Pitkin's list, one of the first real censuses of American manufacturing, perhaps undercounted the numbers of looms and yards produced, but there is no reason to suspect that his overall proportions are wrong. Pitkin's list did not include hand-tufted carpets, although they had been produced in the United States since the beginning: the carpet William Sprague made for the Senate chamber was hand-tufted, for example, and the Lowell Manufacturing Company recorded fifteen hundred tufted rugs in 1832 (Ewing and Norton, *Broadlooms and Businessmen*, 26). But American production was small, no doubt at least partly because of the decided advantage foreign countries enjoyed in this labor-intensive area.

14. Kendrick, "Carpet Industry in Philadelphia," 2D.

15. Quoted in Scranton, *Proprietary Capitalism*, 220–21.

16. Scranton, *Proprietary Capitalism*, 180–81, 225; Ewing and Norton, *Broadlooms and Businessmen*, 21; Cole and Williamson, *American Carpet Manufacture*, 19.

17. Cole and Williamson, *American Carpet Manufacture*, 26–27, 44–45, 53.

18. Scranton, *Proprietary Capitalism*, 415.

19. Nancy Norton, "Labor in the Early New England Carpet Factory," *Bul-*

letin of the Business Historical Society 26 (March 1952): 19–20; Ewing and Norton, *Broadlooms and Businessmen,* 21.

20. U.S. Congress, House of Representatives, *Documents Relative to the Manufactures in the United States, Collected and Transmitted to the House of Representatives, in Compliance with a Resolution of Jan. 19, 1832, by the Secretary of the Treasury,* 22d Cong., 1st sess., 1833, H. Doc. 308, I, 16–17, 328–29, 386–87, 660–61 (hereafter cited as *Manufactures Documents*).

21. Claudia Goldin and Kenneth Sokoloff, "Women, Children, and Industrialization in the Early Republic: Evidence from the Manufacturing Censuses," *Journal of Economic History* 42 (December 1982): 751.

22. Ewing and Norton, *Broadlooms and Businessmen,* 21, 22, 38, 48; Norton, "Labor in the Early New England Carpet Factory," 22; *Manufactures Documents,* 339.

23. Ewing and Norton, *Broadlooms and Businessmen,* 22; Norton, "Labor in the Early New England Carpet Factory," 21.

24. David Henderson, "Rules and Regulations of the Merrimack Carpet Factory," January 2, 1855, photocopy, Museum of American Textile History, North Andover, Mass.

25. Ewing and Norton, *Broadlooms and Businessmen,* 15.

26. Information on Bigelow is from Nehemiah Cleaveland, *A Memoir of Erastus Brigham Bigelow* (Boston: District Committee of the Fourth Congressional District, 1860), 4–9; Ewing and Norton, *Broadlooms and Businessmen,* 15–20; Cole and Williamson, *American Carpet Manufacture,* 54–55.

27. Ewing and Norton, *Broadlooms and Businessmen,* 17, 42–43.

28. Cole and Williamson, *American Carpet Manufacture,* 60–62.

29. Ibid., 62, 65–66; E. B. Bigelow, "The Relations of Labor and Capital," *Atlantic Monthly* (October 1878), quoted in Andrew E. Ford, *History of the Origin of the Town of Clinton, Massachusetts, 1653–1865* (Clinton, Mass.: W. J. Coulter, 1896), 234.

30. Cole and Williamson, *American Carpet Manufacture,* 69–71, 257.

31. F. W. Taussig, *The Tariff History of the United States,* 8th rev. ed. (1931; reprint, New York: Capricorn Books, 1964), 149.

32. Cole and Williamson, *American Carpet Manufacture,* 82, 95. The 1850 census data did not record the number of looms, yardage of carpet produced, or other information that would be useful to our discussion; the 1850 yardage figure is my own extrapolation from the available data. Taussig, *Tariff History,* 148.

33. Cole and Williamson, *American Carpet Manufacture,* 83–89.

34. Ibid., 80. Actually the figure of sixty-one power looms was for the entire state, not just the city, and it is therefore perhaps too generous for Philadelphia.

35. Ibid., 82.

36. Quoted in Winkler and Moss, *Victorian Interior Decoration,* 85, 90.

37. Catherine [*sic*] E. Beecher and Harriet Beecher Stowe, *The American Woman's Home; or, Principles of Domestic Science . . .* (1869; reprint, Hartford: Stowe-Day Foundation, 1975), 85–86.

38. Scranton, *Proprietary Capitalism,* 280, 288, 296.

39. Ewing and Norton, *Broadlooms and Businessmen,* 80, 108–9; Susan Levine, "Their Own Sphere: Women's Work, the Knights of Labor, and the Transformation of the Carpet Trade, 1870–1890" (Ph.D. diss., City University of New York, 1979), 21.

40. Scranton, *Proprietary Capitalism,* 308 (Scranton used the Wholesale Textile Index to factor out monetary fluctuations); Levine, "Their Own Sphere," 21.

41. *The Industries of Pennsylvania: Facts, Figures, and Illustrations, Historical, Descriptive and Biographical . . .* (Philadelphia: Richard Edwards, 1882), 226, 259, 264; Revonah Spinning Mills, *The Histories and Backgrounds of Many of America's Outstanding Carpet Mills* (Hanover, Pa.: Revonah Spinning Mills, 1960), [11], [13]; Oliver Evans Chapter, Society for Industrial Archeology, *Workshop of the World: A Selective Guide to the Industrial Archeology of Philadelphia* (Wallingford, Pa.: Oliver Evans Press, 1990), 5, 23.

42. [Samuel Fay et al.], *The Carpet Manufacture: A Statement of Facts Addressed to the United-States Revenue Commission* (Boston: John Wilson and Son, 1866), 4.

43. Taussig, *Tariff History,* 142–43.

44. National Association of Wool Manufacturers, Records, 1:1, National Association of Wool Manufacturers Papers (hereafter cited as "NAWM Papers"), Museum of American Textile History, North Andover, Mass.

45. National Association of Wool Manufacturers, Treasurer's Journal, 1854–82, NAWM Papers; Taussig, *Tariff History,* 199; Arthur H. Cole, *The American Wool Manufacture* (Cambridge: Harvard University Press, 1926), 2:23; Ewing and Norton, *Broadlooms and Businessmen,* 72–73.

46. [Fay et al.], *Carpet Manufacture,* 8. (This pamphlet, signed by officers of five of the largest carpet manufacturers, was later published by the National Association of Wool Manufacturers in *Memoirs Relating to the Wool Industry,* ed. John L. Hayes [Boston: John Wilson and Son, 1872]); Cole and Williamson, *American Carpet Manufacture,* 5; Ewing and Norton, *Broadlooms and Businessmen,* 72; Taussig, *Tariff History,* 200–212.

47. Taussig, *Tariff History,* 215.

48. National Association of Wool Manufacturers, Board of Directors, Minutes, October 1, 1867, NAWM Papers.

49. Cole, *American Wool Manufacture,* 2:32.

50. Levine, "Their Own Sphere," 40, 116–22; Kendrick, "Carpet Industry of Philadelphia," 34D, 35D; Cole and Williamson, *American Carpet Manufacture,* 197–98.

51. Cole and Williamson, *American Carpet Manufacture,* 95.

52. Ibid., 137; Scranton, *Figured Tapestry,* 38; Ewing and Norton, *Broadlooms and Businessmen,* 142; Kendrick, "Carpet Industry of Philadelphia," 19D. It might be noted that these power looms were usually powered by water or coal-produced steam; a trade journal mentioned a small factory in Lafayette, Indiana, that had ten Crompton looms "run by natural gas." *American Carpet and Upholstery Trade Journal* 9 (January 1891): 34.

53. Cole and Williamson, *American Carpet Manufacture,* 62, 71; Ewing and Norton, *Broadlooms and Businessmen,* 87, 114, 126; Levine, "Their Own Sphere," 18–19; *American Carpet and Upholstery Trade Journal* 9 (September 1891): 786, 796; 11 (May 1893): 65.

54. Kendrick, "Carpet Industry of Philadelphia," 16D; Levine, "Their Own Sphere," 19; *American Carpet and Upholstery Trade Journal* 9 (January 1891): 40.

55. John Gay's Sons Park Carpet Mills, "Daybook, 1876–1916," Historical Society of Pennsylvania, Philadelphia, December 31, 1887, January 9, 1890, February 24, 1893; Scranton, *Figured Tapestry,* 38, 66.

56. Sophie Greenblatt, "The History and Development of the Carpet Industry in Yonkers" (master's thesis, Columbia University, 1937), 11–12; Cole and Williamson, *American Carpet Manufacture,* 72–73.

57. Greenblatt, "Carpet Industry in Yonkers," 16, 24, 25, 28–32, 35–36; Ewing and Norton, *Broadlooms and Businessmen,* 112–14.

58. "The Moquette Loom: Its Inventor, Its Origin, Its Development," *American Carpet and Upholstery Trade* 11 (May 1893): 53. Ewing and Norton, *Broadlooms and Businessmen,* 149, gives the credit to Charles; Greenblatt, "Carpet Industry in Yonkers," 37, gives it to Albert.

59. Ewing and Norton, *Broadlooms and Businessmen,* 112–14, 157, 191; Cole and Williamson, *American Carpet Manufacture,* 130–32; *American Carpet and Upholstery Trade* 14 (July 1896): 32; 15 (March 1897): 42–43. Crompton merged with Knowles, another Worcester loom manufacturer, in 1897. *American Carpet and Upholstery Trade* 15 (March 1897): 42–43.

60. Cole and Williamson, *American Carpet Manufacture,* 99–100.

61. Horace Greeley et al., *Great Industries of the United States: Being an Historical Summary of the Origin, Growth, and Perfection of the Chief Industrial Arts of This Country* (Hartford: J. B. Burr & Hyde, 1872), 839; Helene von Rosenstiel and Gail Caskey Winkler, *Floor Coverings for Historic Buildings:*

A Guide to Selecting Reproductions (Washington, D.C.: Preservation Press, 1988), 42.

62. Quotations from *House Painting and Decorating* 1 (January 1886): 118, and Clarence Cook, *The House Beautiful* (1881), both quoted in Winkler and Moss, *Victorian Interior Decoration,* 145.

63. Cole and Williamson, *American Carpet Manufacture,* 113.

64. Ibid., 109–12.

65. Ewing and Norton, *Broadlooms and Businessmen,* 87; Cole and Williamson, *American Carpet Manufacture,* 120–22, 258; *American Carpet and Upholstery Trade Journal* 18 (October 1900): 40; 33 (June 1915): 58.

66. Scranton, *Figured Tapestry,* 239–40, 299; John Gay's Sons Park Carpet Mills, "Daybook," March 14, May 9, June 30, 1916; *American Carpet and Upholstery Trade Journal* 34 (June 1916): 32.

67. Cole and Williamson, *American Carpet Manufacture,* 164–66, 264.

68. Ibid., 166–70; Kendrick, "Carpet Industry of Philadelphia," 11D; John Gay's Sons Park Carpet Mills, "Daybook," March 8–9, 1879.

69. Cole and Williamson, *American Carpet Manufacture,* 176–77; John Gay's Sons Park Carpet Mills, "Daybook," June 10, 1877, October 5, 1877, February 15, 1878, September 29, 1880, December 4, 1880.

70. John Gay's Sons Park Carpet Mills, "Daybook," November 2, 1877, September [?], 1880, June 25, 1881, October 4, 1888, July 24–November 27, 1893.

71. Cole and Williamson, *American Carpet Manufacture,* 178.

72. Levine, "Their Own Sphere," 41.

73. John Gay's Sons Park Carpet Mills, "Daybook," November 11, 1878, January 21, 1879; Levine, "Their Own Sphere," 89–91, 97–101.

74. Levine, "Their Own Sphere," 116; Susan Levine, "Ladies and Looms: The Social Impact of Machine Power in the American Carpet Industry," in *Dynamos and Virgins Revisited: Women and Technological Change in History,* ed. Martha Moore Trescott (Metuchen, N.J.: Scarecrow Press, 1979), 71.

75. John Gay's Sons Park Carpet Mills, "Daybook," September 30, 1879.

76. Levine, "Their Own Sphere," 108–10.

77. John Gay's Sons Park Carpet Mills, "Daybook," November 19, 1884; Levine, "Their Own Sphere," 121–48; Scranton, *Proprietary Capitalism,* 393. Less than a week before making the formal announcement of the reduction, one of the owners of Park Carpet Mills wrote of "business being very dull all over the country on a/c of Election going Democratic." John Gay's Sons Park Carpet Mills, "Daybook," November 13, 1884.

78. Levine, "Their Own Sphere," 134, 142; Susan Levine, "'Honor Each Noble Maid': Women Workers and the Yonkers Carpet Weavers' Strike of 1885,"

New York History 62 (April 1981): 163–64. Greenblatt, "Carpet Industry in Yonkers," 42–56, offers a narrative of the Smith strike from a more pro-company perspective.

79. Scranton, *Proprietary Capitalism,* 394; Levine, "Their Own Sphere," 150–52.

80. Levine, "'Honor Each Noble Maid,'" 173; Scranton, *Proprietary Capitalism,* 394–95; John Gay's Sons Park Carpet Mills, "Daybook," January 2, 1886. There were also brief strikes at Lowell, Bigelow, Higgins, and other firms during this period. Cole and Williamson, *American Carpet Manufacture,* 91, 130–31, 151–52; *Annual Report of the Secretary of Internal Affairs of the Commonwealth of Pennsylvania,* pt. 3, *Industrial Statistics* (Harrisburg, Pa.: Edwin K. Meyers, 1890), 6C, 8C.

81. Ewing and Norton, *Broadlooms and Businessmen,* 91; Greenblatt, "Carpet Industry in Yonkers," 64, 66; John Gay's Sons Park Carpet Mills, "Daybook," August 11, 1893, November 18, 1893, January 30–August 22, 1895; *American Carpet and Upholstery Trade Journal* 13 (March 1895): 26; 13 (August 1895): 23; Cole and Williamson, *American Carpet Manufacture,* 187.

82. *American Carpet and Upholstery Trade Journal* 13 (September 1895): 24.

83. Scranton, *Proprietary Capitalism,* 356, 365, 370; Ewing and Norton, *Broadlooms and Businessmen,* 96.

84. Ewing and Norton, *Broadlooms and Businessmen,* 163–64; Cole and Williamson, *American Carpet Manufacture,* 206–7; Scranton, *Figured Tapestry,* 72–73.

85. Ewing and Norton, *Broadlooms and Businessmen,* 165–69, 383.

86. Cole and Williamson, *American Carpet Manufacture,* 198.

87. John Gay's Sons Park Carpet Mills, "Daybook," June 10 and 14, 1877. The importance of these commission agents to the industry as a whole can be seen in the remark of a leading trade journal that A. T. Stewart, prior to his death in 1876, had been "for years . . . the foremost carpet man in America." *American Carpet and Upholstery Trade* 14 (September 1896): 73.

88. John Gay's Sons Park Carpet Mills, "Daybook," December 10, 1880. Pray also handled the Lowell Company's sales. Ewing and Norton, *Broadlooms and Businessmen,* 84.

89. *American Carpet and Upholstery Trade* 14 (September 1896): 73.

90. Ewing and Norton, *Broadlooms and Businessmen,* 119.

91. Cole and Williamson, *American Carpet Manufacture,* 198–202.

92. Ewing and Norton, *Broadlooms and Businessmen,* 183; Cole and Williamson, *American Carpet Manufacture,* 210–11.

93. Ewing and Norton, *Broadlooms and Businessmen,* 93–94, 152; *American Carpet and Upholstery Trade Journal* 12 (July 1894): 29.

94. Ewing and Norton, *Broadlooms and Businessmen*, 184–85. Trade journals were promoting advertising a decade before this; for example, "Advertising —A Thing of To-Day," *American Carpet and Upholstery Trade Journal* 14 (February 1896): 56–57.

95. Ewing and Norton, *Broadlooms and Businessmen*, 197, 220–21, 228–29; Cook, *Century of Carpet and Rug-Making in America*.

96. Ewing and Norton, *Broadlooms and Businessmen*, 206; Cole and Williamson, *American Carpet Manufacture*, 253–54.

97. Greenblatt, "Carpet Industry in Yonkers," 75–76; *American Carpet and Upholstery Trade Journal* 35 (July 1917): 24.

98. *American Carpet and Upholstery Trade Journal* 36 (June 1918): 19; Ewing and Norton, *Broadlooms and Businessmen*, 215–16, 377.

99. *American Carpet and Upholstery Trade Journal* 36 (March 1918): 20.

100. *American Carpet and Upholstery Trade Journal* 36 (February 1918): 18.

101. Ewing and Norton, *Broadlooms and Businessmen*, 216–21, 377.

102. Ibid., 221, 227–28, 377–78; Greenblatt, "Carpet Industry in Yonkers," 77; Donald L. Grant, "A Case in Collective Bargaining: The Alexander Smith and Sons Carpet Company, Incorporated, and Local 122 of the Textile Workers Union of America, C.I.O." (master's thesis, Princeton University, 1941), 65; Simon N. Whitney, *Trade Associations and Industrial Control: A Critique of the N.R.A.* (New York: Central Book Co., 1934), 76–77.

103. Ewing and Norton, *Broadlooms and Businessmen*, 238; *American Carpet and Upholstery Trade Journal* 45 (August 1927): 46; Whitney, *Trade Associations and Industrial Control*, 78; "The Heritage of the Carpet and Rug Institute," unidentified clipping in files of Carpet and Rug Institute, Dalton, Ga.

104. George McNeir, "Business *Can* Be Good in 1930," *Mohawk Rug Retailer* 4 (January–February 1930): 1.

105. *American Carpet and Upholstery Trade Journal* 47 (November 1929): 75; 48 (January 1930): 29; 48 (April 1930): 59; 48 (June 1930): 34; 48 (August 1930): 30.

106. *American Carpet and Upholstery Trade Journal* 48 (December 1930): 36; 49 (September 1931): 24; 49 (October 1931): 41.

107. Ewing and Norton, *Broadlooms and Businessmen*, 377; National Recovery Administration, *Code of Fair Competition for the Carpet and Rug Manufacturing Industry* (Washington, D.C.: U.S. Government Printing Office, 1934), 84; Grant, "Case in Collective Bargaining," 24; Cole and Williamson, *American Carpet Manufacture*, 257, 263.

108. *American Carpet and Upholstery Trade Journal* 51 (July 1933): 11; 51 (August 1933): 9; 51 (September 1933): 13; NRA, *Code of Fair Competition for the Carpet and Rug Manufacturing Industry*, 83, 84.

109. National Recovery Administration, *Code of Fair Competition,* 89.

110. *American Carpet and Upholstery Trade Journal* 53 (June 1935): 3, 4; 53 (November 1935): 13.

111. Eugene W. Ong, "Report to Louis K. Liggett, . . . October 30, 1926," box KA-1, Bigelow-Sanford Papers, Baker Library, Harvard University, 74.

112. Grant, "Case in Collective Bargaining," 47–51. The following discussion of Alexander Smith is drawn largely from this work.

113. Ibid., 52–56.

114. Ibid., 57–61; Greenblatt, "Carpet Industry in Yonkers," 90–91.

115. Grant, "Case in Collective Bargaining," 76–78, 85–87, 90–92.

116. Ibid., 100, 118, 120.

117. Ewing and Norton, *Broadlooms and Businessmen,* 269–71, 290–91.

118. Untitled chart, dated May 24, 1944, Overseers meetings, Thompsonville, 1935–45, box K-24, Bigelow-Sanford Papers.

119. Ewing and Norton, *Broadlooms and Businessmen,* 298–99.

120. Ibid., 299.

121. Ibid., 302–3; C. H. Masland & Sons, *A Famous Horseman Goes to War: The Peace-Time and War-Time Story of an American Carpet Manufacturer* (n.p., [1943]).

122. Ewing and Norton, *Broadlooms and Businessmen,* 305–6.

123. Ibid., 340–41.

124. Ibid., 340, 343–46.

125. Ibid., 360.

Chapter 1. Crisis of the Old Order

1. For a discussion of the postwar adjustment period as it affected one major firm, see Ewing and Norton, *Broadlooms and Businessmen,* 319–42.

2. For a discussion of the crisis of American textile manufacturing that focuses on the victory by default of the mass-production model due to increased pressure from retailers and distributors, and other factors, see Philip Scranton, "'Have a Heart for the Manufacturers!': Production, Distribution, and the Decline of American Textile Manufacturing," in Sabel and Zeitlin, *World of Possibilities,* 310–43. Timothy Minchin offers an insightful look at the postwar boom and bust and its impact on labor relations in *"What Do We Need a Union For?": The TWUA in the South, 1945–1955* (Chapel Hill: University of North Carolina Press, 1997), esp. 48–68. On Spencer Love, Burlington Mills, and Love's strategy for prospering in the midst of crisis, see Annette C. Wright, "Strategy and Structure in the Textile Industry: Spencer Love and Burlington Mills, 1923–1962," *Business History Review* 69 (Spring 1995): 42–79.

3. "A Review of the Carpet and Rug Industry," Carpet and Rug Conference, New York City, May 24, 1946, Textile Workers Union of America Papers, State Historical Society of Wisconsin, Madison (hereafter cited as "TWUA Papers"), micro 631.

4. Ibid.

5. Ibid.

6. Carpet and Rug Institute, "The Heritage of the Carpet and Rug Institute," clipping found in Tufted Textile Manufacturers Association Papers, Carpet and Rug Institute, Dalton, Ga. (hereafter cited as "TTMA Papers").

7. Material drawn from Carpet Institute, Inc., "Application for Investigation under Section 7 of the Trade Agreements Extension Act of 1951," June 1958, TTMA Papers.

8. Ibid.

9. *Business Week,* August 18, 1951, 116.

10. *Business Week,* August 18, 1951, 114, 116; William A. Reynolds, *Innovation in the United States Carpet Industry, 1947–1963* (Princeton, N.J.: D. Van Nostrand and Co., 1968), 68–69.

11. Reynolds, *Innovation in the United States Carpet Industry,* 69.

12. *Business Week,* December 24, 1955, 46.

13. *Business Week,* November 6, 1954, 54–55.

14. *Business Week,* October 30, 1954, 54; March 24, 1956, 52; December 1, 1956, 86; November 15, 1968, 74; February 1, 1958, 53.

15. *Business Week,* March 24, 1956, 52.

16. Reynolds, *Innovation,* 87.

17. Ibid.

18. *Business Week,* November 27, 1954, 134.

19. *Business Week,* November 1, 1958, 110.

20. William F. C. Ewing to All Stockholders of Alexander Smith, January 11, 1951, Mohawk Papers, Mohawk Public Relations Office, Atlanta, Ga.

21. Ibid.

22. Jack A. Tupper, "The Impact of the Relocation of the Alexander Smith Carpet Company upon the Municipal Government of the City of Yonkers, New York" (master's thesis, New York University, 1963), 44. The best account of Mississippi's BAWI program is found in Cobb, *Selling of the South.*

23. Tupper, "Impact of the Relocation," 43–44.

24. Ibid.

25. Ewing to Smith Stockholders, January 11, 1951.

26. Ibid., 45.

27. Robert H. Bishop to Sales Staff, Regional Managers, and All Salesmen, July 1, 1954, Mohawk Papers.

28. Ibid., 38–39, and Rosalie Flynn, "The Carpet Shop: A History of the Alexander Smith and Sons Carpet Company in Yonkers, New York" (master's thesis, Manhattanville College, 1986), 38, 48–49.

29. Flynn, "Carpet Shop," 49–51.

30. *Wall Street Journal,* February 9, 1955.

31. Ibid.

32. Ibid.

33. "Economic Notes for Carpet Conference," September 17, 1954, TWUA Papers, micro 631.

34. "Carpet Conference Notes," January 1955, TWUA Papers, micro 631.

35. Ibid.

36. *Forbes,* April 15, 1960, 17; *Barron's,* June 19, 1961, 25–26.

37. Petersen quoted in *Business Week,* December 24, 1955, 46.

38. *Retailing Daily,* December 2, 1955, TTMA clipping file.

39. "Economic Notes, Carpet and Rug Conference," December 4, 1955, TWUA Papers, micro 631.

40. "Carpet Economic Notes," March 20, 1959, TWUA Papers, micro 631.

41. Cobb, *Selling of the South,* 113–15. Gavin Wright offered an insightful analysis of the southern textile industry in *Old South, New South: Revolutions in the Southern Economy since the Civil War* (New York: Basic Books, 1986), esp. chaps. 5–7.

42. Carpet Institute, Inc., "Application for Investigation."

43. Ibid.

44. Ibid.

45. Ibid.

46. Ibid.

47. "Minutes of the Board of Trustees Meeting," Carpet Institute, Inc., November 16, 1955, TTMA Papers (hereafter cited as "Minutes—Trustees," followed by date).

48. "Minutes—Trustees," May 16, 1956.

49. John T. Lees to Paul Jones, September 25, 1957, TTMA Papers.

50. Ibid.

51. "Minutes—Trustees," May 14, 1958.

52. Alexander Smith Annual Report, 1954, Mohawk Papers.

53. *Printer's Ink,* February 28, 1958, 2; *Editor and Publisher,* December 21, 1957, 26; *Advertising Age,* January 26, 1959, 8. The author thanks Laura Bailey for her help in developing this theme.

54. *Advertising Age,* October 20, 1958, 28; *Sponsor,* April 9, 1960, 40; *Printer's Ink,* May 25, 1962, 36.

55. *Printer's Ink,* November 18, 1960, 36–37.

56. Ewing and Norton, *Broadlooms and Businessmen,* 319–26. On the evolution of technology in the carpet industry after World War II, see Reynolds, *Innovation.* A colorful account of the rise of the carpet industry in Dalton, based on extensive oral interviews, is Thomas M. Deaton, *From Bedspreads to Broadloom: The Story of the Tufted Carpet Industry* (Acton, Mass.: Tapestry Press, 1993).

57. Excellent general accounts of the postwar economic "golden age" at both the international and national level may be found in Eric Hobsbawm, *The Age of Extremes: A History of the World, 1914–1991* (New York: Random House, 1995), 257–85, and Robert Heilbroner, *The Economic Transformation of America, 1600–Present,* 3d ed. (New York: Harcourt Brace, 1994), 329–36. Hobsbawm emphasizes the role of government spending and economic controls in producing the prosperity of the mid-twentieth century, and the U.S. carpet industry certainly benefited from government housing programs and other policies that promoted home ownership. Reynolds, *Innovation,* 43–46.

58. Reynolds, *Innovation,* 43–45.

59. Scranton, *Figured Tapestry,* 386–87; Scranton, " 'Have a Heart,' " 340–41; Lewis Card, interview by Bart Threatte, May 11, 1994; Roy and Lewis Card, interview by Bart Threatte, May 18, 1994; Dusty Rhodes, interview by Pat Taylor, December 17, 1993, all from Kennesaw State University (hereafter cited as "KSU") Carpet History Project.

Chapter 2. Tufted Textiles Take the Floor

1. Jack Turner, interview with Randy Patton, November 4, 1994, KSU Carpet History Project. The tufted textile industry that arose in the Dalton district can best be characterized by the term *flexible specialization.* Several scholars in recent years have challenged the traditional view of industrial development that posits rigid product life cycles and assumes that all manufacturing will eventually come to be dominated by very large, vertically integrated industrial organizations. These scholars, including Michael Piore, Charles Sabel, Michael Storper, and Susan Christopherson, have identified numerous exceptions to the concept of a product life cycle and the supposedly inevitable development of integrated large firms, including the "Third Italy." The Tuscany and Emilia-Romagna regions of Italy developed in a quite unexpected way. Networks of small firms continued to thrive in these regions, producing specialty products in the automobile and textile fields, "using skilled labor and short production runs." These networks of firms were more flexible and better able to adapt quickly to changing market conditions. Even firms that guessed wrong on market decisions this year might subsist on

subcontracted work from more successful firms, and this year's losers might be next year's winners. "In such flexibly specialized systems production is organized around the interactions of small firms," according to Michael Storper and Susan Christopherson. "These small firms specialize in batch or custom production of general classes of outputs, whereas mass production firms are committed to the production of specific outputs in large quantities."

Put another way, these small firms "are subcontractors in a system of production that is vertically disintegrated." These networks can form "a regional complex of firms interconnected by their numerous transactions with each other." As industrial agglomerations approach flexible specialization as a mode of production, there is constant tension. Firms are lured toward vertical integration by the promise of greater profit margins and pulled toward disintegration at other times by the risk inherent in becoming too devoted to one particular group of products. The fewer links on the production chain a manufacturer occupies, the greater his or her ability to shift resources. As producers engulf more phases of the production process, from raw material production, market research, and product design to initial processing, final production, and distribution, the greater the stake that producer develops in the continuation of the unceasing manufacture of that particular commodity. Michael Piore and Charles Sabel, *The Second Industrial Divide: Possibilities for Prosperity* (New York: Basic Books, 1984); quotations from Michael Storper and Susan Christopherson, "Flexible Specialization and Regional Agglomerations: The Case of the U.S. Motion Picture Industry," *Annals of the Association of American Geographers* 77 (March 1987): 105–6; Charles Sabel, "Studied Trust: Building New Forms of Cooperation in a Volatile Economy," *Human Relations* 46 (September 1993): 1133–69.

The thesis that the South's regional economy developed as a virtual colony of the industrial North was most forcefully stated in C. Vann Woodward, *Origins of the New South, 1877–1913* (Baton Rouge: Louisiana State University Press, 1951), 291–320. A thoughtful recent reappraisal may be found in Wright, *Old South, New South*, 102–25. Wright argued that while the South's "colonial" status can be debated in political terms, the southern economy certainly behaved like a backward, colonial economy because of the region's isolated labor market.

2. Address by William H. Wilkerson to the Southern Machinery and Metals Exposition, April 25, 1946, reprinted by Higgins-McArthur Company, copy found in Morgan Papers, "Boost Birmingham Club" file, Birmingham Public Library, Birmingham, Ala.

3. Ellis Arnall, *The Shore Dimly Seen* (1946; reprint, New York: Acclaim Publishing Co., 1966), 141–43.

4. *Atlanta Journal,* December 9, 1945; Bartley, *New South,* 19–20. Bartley's first chapter, "World War II and the Postwar South," offers an excellent survey of southern attitudes toward economic development.

5. Bartley, *New South,* 19, and Cobb, *Selling of the South,* 3–63; Cobb, *Industrialization and Southern Society,* 43.

6. Bartley, *New South,* 21.

7. "The Tufted Story," *Tufted Textile Manufacturers Association Directory,* January 1950, 26. TTMA Directories are housed at the Carpet and Rug Institute, Dalton, Ga.

8. Catherine Evans Whitener, "If I Had Been a Man," Oral History, Whitfield-Murray Historical Society, Crown Gardens and Archives, Dalton, Ga.

9. Ibid.

10. Ibid.

11. Ibid.

12. Deaton, *Bedspreads to Broadloom,* 6–7.

13. David L. Carlton, "Revolution from Above: The National Market and the Beginnings of Industrialization in North Carolina," *Journal of American History* 77 (September 1990): 449.

14. R. E. Hamilton, "Bedspread Bonanza," *Reader's Digest* (April 1941): 42, and Deaton, *Bedspreads to Broadloom,* 9–11.

15. "The Tufted Story," 27–28.

16. The information in the preceding paragraphs is drawn from Cobble Division, Spencer Wright Industries, "A Chronology of Significant Tufting Developments," Historical Files of Cobble Division, Dalton, Ga. The author is grateful to Bart Threatte for his useful research paper on the role of Cobble Brothers and Lewis Card.

17. Paul Jolley, interview by Thomas M. Deaton, May 30, 1991, Dalton, Ga., tape in the possession of Deaton; Roy Windham, *The Tufting Machine: A Practical Text of Instruction for Machine Fixers* (Rome, Ga.: Southern Craft Co., 1941), 91.

18. Windham, *Tufting Machine,* 89–117; Jolley interview; Chattanooga Manufacturers Association, "Industrial Chattanooga: Dynamo of Dixie," pamphlet produced by the association, 1925, reprinted by the Chattanooga Gas Company, 1993.

19. *Chattanooga City Directory,* vol. 56 (Chattanooga: Rothberger Directory Co., 1936); Jolley interview; Max M. Beasley, "Cobble: The Name That Is Synonymous with Tufting Machinery," notes for a speech, Historical Files of Cobble Division.

20. Lewis Card, interview by Bart Threatte, May 18, 1994, KSU Carpet History Project; Jolley interview; Kimberly Gavin, "The Tufting Machine: Fifty Years of History," *Dalton Carpet Journal* (February 1987).

21. U.S. Patent and Trademark Office, *Multiple Needle Tufting Machine, Patent Number 2,335,487*, Atlanta, Ga., Patent Depository, Price Gilbert Library, Georgia Institute of Technology, microfilm; Jolley interview; and Lewis Card interview, May 18, 1994.

22. *Multiple Needle Tufting Machine, Patent Number 2,335,487*; Lewis Card interview, May 18, 1994; Gavin, "Tufting Machine."

23. U.S. Patent and Trademark Office, *Apparatus for Making Tufted Pile Fabric, Patent Number 2,935,037*, Atlanta, Ga., Patent Depository, Price Gilbert Library, Georgia Institute of Technology, microfilm.

24. U.S. Patent and Trademark Office, *Apparatus for Making Patterned Tufted Pile Fabric, Patent Number 2,935,037*; *Method and Apparatus for Making Patterned Tufted Pile Fabric, Patent Number 2,966,866*; and *Multiple Needle Skip-Stitch Machine, Patent Number 3,016,029*, Atlanta, Ga., Patent Depository, Price Gilbert Library, Georgia Institute of Technology, microfilm.

25. Lewis Card interview, May 18, 1994.

26. Ibid.

27. Max Beasley, interview by Bart Threatte, May 11, 1994; Lewis Card interview, May 18, 1994.

28. "Cobble Bros. Machinery Building New Chattanooga Plant," *Tennessee Industrial Newsletter*, December 1, 1954, photocopy, Local History Collection, Chattanooga Bicentennial Library.

29. Lewis Card interview, May 18, 1994; *Chattanooga Times*, December 11, 1960.

30. Lewis Card interview, May 18, 1994; *Chattanooga Times*, June 29, 1960.

31. Lewis Card interview, May 18, 1994; *Chattanooga News–Free Press*, September 30, 1977.

32. Beasley, "Cobble: The Name That Is Synonymous with Tufting Machinery"; Lewis Card interview, May 18, 1994.

33. Mary Bell Smith, interview with Randy Patton, October 15, 1993, KSU Carpet History Project; Rhodes interview.

34. Rhodes interview; Turner interview; Smith interview.

35. Rhodes interview.

36. *Textile World* (May 1962): 56–62.

37. Ibid.

38. Mose Painter, as told to Elaine Taylor, *I've Had a Millionaire's Fun* (Dalton, Ga.: Painter and Taylor Manuscript Co., 1982), 1, 5, 33–48.

39. Ibid., 50–52.

40. Ibid., 62–63.

41. Ibid., 64.

42. Ibid., 65–66.

43. Ibid., 73–74.

44. Ibid., 82–84.

45. Robert E. Shaw letter, reprinted in Painter, *Millionaire's Fun,* 123.

46. Ibid., and Peter Spirer, interview by author, May 25, 1994, KSU Carpet History Project.

47. Spirer interview.

48. Ibid.

49. Ibid.

50. Spirer letter in Painter, *Millionaire's Fun,* 120–21.

51. Ibid.

52. Ibid.

53. Spirer interview.

54. Clark M. Jones and W. L. Avrett, "Solving a Flashy Water Problem," *Water Works Engineering,* September 10, 1941, 1140–42.

55. Robert McMath and Bruce Sinclair, "Infrastructure for the New South: Dalton Utilities and the Development of an Industrial City" (paper delivered at the Southern Historical Association annual meeting, New Orleans, November 7, 1995).

56. Buford Talley, former president of Barwick Industries, interview by author, March 8, 1994; Bert Lance, interview by author and Virginia Ingram, January 3, 1994, KSU Carpet History Project.

57. Deaton, *Bedspreads to Broadloom,* 93–94.

58. Ibid.

59. Shaheen Shaheen, *World Carpets: The First Thirty Years* (Dalton, Ga.: Lee Printing Co., 1985), 1–2.

60. Ibid., 4.

61. Ibid.

62. Deaton, *Bedspreads to Broadloom,* 95.

63. Shaheen, *World Carpets,* 5.

64. James B. Flemming, "The Northwest Georgia Carpet Finishing Industry: Its Operation and Financing" (master's thesis, Stonier Graduate School of Banking, Rutgers University, 1974).

65. Ibid., 21–23.

66. Ibid., 28–29.

67. Claudio Pernetti, "Differential Dyeing: Advantages and Dyeing Possibilities in the Production of Carpets," *American Dyestuff Reporter* (June 1972): 44.

68. Flemming, "Northwest Georgia Carpet Finishing Industry," 29.

69. Ibid., 30.

70. *Textile World* (October 1962): 106–7.

71. Ibid.

72. Ibid.

73. Walter Guinan, interview with Randy Patton, September 28, 1993, KSU Carpet History Project.

74. Deaton, *Bedspreads to Broadloom,* 84–85.

75. Ibid.

76. Seretean quoted in *Floor Covering Weekly,* January 10, 1983, 47; *Barron's,* July 6, 1964, 19.

77. In doing so, local area manufacturers repeated a process that had occurred elsewhere. James Soltow described a local manufacturers association in Montgomery County, Pennsylvania, in the first decades of the twentieth century. It was open to all manufacturers in the county. The manufacturers association's aims were not the same as those of the chamber of commerce. Originally formed in 1908 to combat the antibusiness sentiment of the Progressive Era, it evolved into much more. The association began to offer workers' compensation insurance, safety training programs, and management training programs and to gather information on wages, hours, holidays, and benefits. The Montgomery County Manufacturers Association evolved from an organization whose primary emphasis was "opposition to social legislation" (child labor laws, etc.) to one that "stress[ed] the performance of services for member manufacturers." Labor relations became a primary focus of the group. When a Philadelphia textile manufacturer asked the group about establishing a factory in the county in order to avoid union agitation in the big city, the Montgomery County Manufacturing Association associate secretary Walter Lynn responded that Montgomery County "would not be a good location for them to select" because a labor shortage already existed for local manufacturers. James H. Soltow, "Small City Industrialists in the Age of Organization: Case Study of the Manufacturers Association of Montgomery County, Pennsylvania, 1908–1958," *Business History Review* 33 (Summer 1959): 178–89.

78. All these functions are detailed in the *Annual Directory and Yearbook of the Tufted Textile Manufacturers Association,* 1950–68, Carpet and Run Institute Library, Dalton, Ga.

79. Georgia Department of Labor, in cooperation with the Tufted Textile Manufacturers Association, "The Tufted Textile Industry: Job Descriptions," TTMA Papers, Industrial Relations Club File.

80. Ibid.

81. "Job Descriptions," 1953, and "TTMA Payroll Analysis," November 10, 1956, TTMA Papers.

82. "TTMA Payroll Analysis."

83. Ibid.

84. Ibid.

85. Ibid.

86. Shaheen, *World Carpets,* 82.

87. Truitt Lomax, interview with author, May 5, 1995, KSU Carpet History Project.

88. D. F. Holmes, "A History of Du Pont's Textile Fibers Department," 64–66, box 1610, Du Pont Textile Fiber Records, MS 1610, Hagley Museum and Library, Wilmington, Del.

89. Ibid.

90. Ibid., and *Financial World,* January 28, 1959.

91. American Carpet Institute, *Confidential Statistical Handbook,* 1963 ed., 31, Carpet and Rug Institute Library.

92. Ibid.

93. American Carpet Institute, *Statistical Handbook,* 1962 ed., 26–27.

94. *Business Week,* June 16, 1956, 56–57.

Chapter 3. A Favorable Business Climate

1. Zeiger quoted from his "Introduction to Part I," in *Race, Class, and Community in Southern Labor History,* ed. Gary M. Fink and Merl E. Reed (Tuscaloosa: University of Alabama Press, 1994), 6–8. Examples of the voluminous historiography of southern cotton mill workers include David Carlton, *Mill and Town in South Carolina, 1880–1920* (Baton Rouge: Louisiana State University Press, 1982); Jacquelyn Dowd-Hall et al., *Like a Family: The Making of a Southern Cotton Mill World* (Chapel Hill: University of North Carolina Press, 1987); James Hodges, *New Deal Labor Policy and the Southern Cotton Textile Industry, 1933–1941* (Knoxville: University of Tennessee Press, 1986).

2. Zeiger, "Introduction to Part I," 7–8.

3. Michael Goldfield, "The Failure of Operation Dixie," in Fink and Reed, *Race, Class, and Community,* 172–82; Barbara Griffith, *The Crisis of American Labor: Operation Dixie and the Defeat of the CIO* (Philadelphia: Temple University Press, 1988); Douglas Flamming, *Creating the Modern South: Millhands and Managers in Dalton, Georgia, 1884–1984* (Chapel Hill: University of North Carolina Press, 1992). On the union's strategy, see James Hodges, "J. P. Stevens and the Union," in Fink and Reed, *Race, Class, and Community,* 53–64.

4. Minchin, *"What Do We Need a Union For?",* 199–209.

5. Georgia State Employment Service, "Labor Market Reports," December 1954 and February 1970, University of Georgia Libraries.

6. Flamming, *Creating the Modern South,* 333–34.

7. Ibid., 289–90.

8. Ibid.

9. Ibid., 298–303, and Mark Pace, interview by Randy Patton and Tom Scott, October 13, 1993, KSU Carpet History Project.

10. John Chupka, "Tufted Rug and Chenille Industry—Dalton, Georgia, Area," February 6, 1962, TWUA Papers, MS 396, box 627.

11. "Financial Report on Bell Industries," TWUA Papers, MS 396, box 627.

12. Ibid.

13. "Organizers Reports," November 7, 1961, December 15, 1961, April 12, 1962, and September 27, 1962, TWUA Papers, MS 396, box 627.

14. Raymond Roach, interview by author, May 23, 1994, KSU Carpet History Project.

15. Ibid. Sociologist John Shelton Reed has suggested that this individualistic approach to labor relations is a part of southern culture. "When Johnny Paycheck has a complaint about his job," Reed noted in commenting on a popular country music song of the late 1970s, "he doesn't ideologize it and join a union or the Communist Party, he tells off his foreman and quits." Reed, *One South: An Ethnic Approach to Regional Culture* (Baton Rouge: Louisiana State University Press, 1982), 54.

16. Chupka, "Tufted Rug and Chenille Industry."

17. "Notes, Dalton, Ga., Campaign," 1962; Memorandum from Wilbur Samuels to William Pollock, April 8, 1963, TWUA Papers, MS 396, Box 627.

18. TWUA leaflets, distributed at Cabin Craft's Springdale plant, August 26, 1963, TTMA Papers.

19. TWUA leaflet, distributed at Cabin Crafts, July 23, 1962, TTMA Papers.

20. "TWUA Broadcasts," July 10, 19, 24, August 8, 1962, TTMA Papers.

21. Roach interview.

22. Douglas Flamming, "Christian Radicalism, McCarthyism, and the Dilemma of Organized Labor in Dixie," in Fink and Reed, *Race, Class, and Community,* 190–211. The close nature of the relationship between the newspaper and the TTMA during the Belcraft campaign was reflected in a letter from the organization's executive vice president, Henry C. Ball, to TTMA general counsel Frank Constangy, November 17, 1955, TTMA Papers.

23. The Industrial Relations Club file was easily the largest file of material in the TTMA Papers.

24. "Blueprint for Union Organization," circulated by Southern Detectives, Inc., n.d., probably 1962; John B. F. Dillon, vice president of Southern Detectives, to Kenneth C. Posey, Chairman of the Industrial Relations Club, January 27, 1964, TTMA Papers.

25. TTMA "Newsletter," n.d., probably late April or early May 1962; R. E. Hamilton to Merchants and Retail Businessmen of Dalton and Whitfield County, TTMA Papers.

26. The TTMA announced the Boosters' plan in its "Newsletter" of September 18, 1962, TTMA Papers.

27. Dalton Boosters "Newsletter," April 12, 1963, TTMA Papers.

28. Quotations from clippings of Booster newspaper ads found in TTMA Papers.

29. Clipping found in TTMA Papers.

30. Ibid.

31. Ibid.

32. "The Progress of Dalton Depends on You," clipping, TTMA Papers.

33. Ibid.

34. Booster ad clipping, n.d., found in TTMA Papers.

35. *Dalton Daily Citizen,* August 6, 1962.

36. *Dalton Daily Citizen,* October 4, 1962.

37. Hamilton quoted in *Dalton Daily Citizen* September 8, 1961. The ambiguous attitude of local mill owners toward new industry was echoed in several interviews with people close to the industry. David Lance, president of the First National Bank of Calhoun, Georgia, addressed this issue obliquely, arguing that state development officials wrongly believed that the Dalton-Calhoun area resisted new industries. Lance maintained that local boosters wanted new industry but especially wanted industry that "fit in" with existing industries. David Lance, interview with author and Virginia Ingram, January 3, 1994, KSU Carpet History Project.

38. *Calhoun Times,* October 4, 1962.

39. Ibid.

40. *Calhoun Times,* October 18, 1962.

41. Transcript of "A Foot in the Door," written and narrated by Fred Briggs, July 9, 1963, 10:30 P.M. (transcript made by TTMA), TTMA Papers.

42. *Calhoun Times,* November 8, 1962.

43. Ibid.

44. See generally the Industrial Relations Club File of the TTMA Papers. This file is filled with TTMA newsletters and *Daily Citizen* editorial clippings that are virtually identical.

45. *Calhoun Times,* November 15, 1962.

46. Ibid.

47. Ibid.

48. Jimmy Walraven, interview with Randy Patton, March 28, 1995, KSU Carpet History Project; Roach interview. Indeed, both men mentioned the column in-

dependently in separate conversations, without prompting from the interviewer; Roach still had a clipping of the editorial in a scrapbook.

49. TWUA, "Report of Organizing Elections," November 21, 1962, TWUA Papers; Raymond Roach, former president of Local 1592, Dixie Belle Mills, interview with Randy Patton, May 23, 1994, KSU Carpet History Project.

50. *Atlanta Journal,* April 5, 1963, 22.

51. Edward Wynne to William Pollock, "Dixie Belle Negotiations," April 4, 1963, TWUA Papers, MS 396, box 627.

52. Ibid.

53. Ibid.

54. Ibid.

55. *Atlanta Journal,* April 15, 1963.

56. Memorandum for Mr. Pollock's use, "Dixie Belle," April 11, 1963, TWUA Papers, MS 396, box 627. The authorship of the memo is unclear. I have attributed the comments to Solomon Barkin, since they seem to be in keeping with his views on southern organizing, but he may not have been the author.

57. Ibid.

58. *Calhoun Times,* June 13, 1963, and "Contract between Dixie Belle Mills, Inc., and the Textile Workers Union of America," June 10, 1963, copy found in TTMA Papers.

59. Transcript of "A Foot in the Door."

60. "President's Address," Interim Meeting, Tufted Textile Manufacturers Association, November 8, 1962, TTMA Papers.

Chapter 4. A World of Opportunity within the Tufting Empire

1. Transcript of TTMA meeting, July 16, 1963, TTMA Papers.

2. Ibid. The role of union-busting specialists like the Constangy law firm has been largely overlooked in attempts to explain the decline of unionism in the United States since the mid-1950s. For an examination of this theme, see Robert Smith, "Using Knowledge Rather Than Goons," *Michigan Academician* 27 (August 1996): 401–19.

3. Transcript of TTMA meeting.

4. Ibid; Jack Barbash, "The Founders of Industrial Relations Theory," in *Industrial Relations Theory,* ed. Roy Adams and Noah Meltz (Metuchen, N.J.: Rutgers University Press, 1993), 70–71.

5. Transcript of TTMA meeting, TTMA Papers.

6. Ibid.

7. Ibid.

8. Ibid.

9. TTMA Newsletter, March 15, 1963, TTMA Papers.

10. TWUA leaflet, distributed at Cabin Crafts, August 26, 1963, TTMA Papers.

11. "Collins and Aikman Corp. and Textile Workers Union of America," in *Decisions and Orders of the National Labor Relations Board*, vol. 141 (Washington, D.C.: U.S. Government Printing Office, 1964), 20–21.

12. Ibid.

13. Ibid.

14. Ibid.

15. "Fruits of Victory at Dixie Belle," September 5, 1963, leaflet found in TTMA Papers.

16. "Labor Bulletin," September 9, 1963, TTMA Papers.

17. TTMA Papers, IRC File, Notes on Industrial Relations Conference, Callaway Gardens, October 22, 1964.

18. "Aids to Supervisors," n.d.; National Association of Manufacturers pamphlet, "Some Dos and Don'ts for Supervisors," n.d., TTMA Papers, IRC File.

19. *B-Line News* 2, no. 4 (October 1963), found in Barwick file, TTMA Papers.

20. Ibid.

21. *Bell Chimes* (September 1961): 5, TTMA clipping file.

22. *B-Line News* 2, no. 4 (September 1963).

23. Ibid.

24. Edith Langley to William Pollock, August 14, 1964, TWUA Papers, MS 396, box 616.

25. Langley to Pollock, November 17, 1964, MS 396, box 616.

26. Paul Swaity to William Pollock, November 17, 1964, TWUA Papers, MS 396, box 616.

27. Paul Swaity to J. R. Bunch, December 4, 1964, TWUA Papers, MS 396, box 616.

28. Kenneth Sheriff to William Pollock, January 27, 1965, and Pollock to Sheriff, February 15, 1965, TWUA Papers, MS 396, box 616.

29. Interview with Jimmy Walraven, March 28, 1995.

30. Ibid.

31. Ibid.

32. Ibid.

33. William O'Neill to Jimmy Walraven, February 23, 1972, TWUA-GTA Papers, 1866:43, Southern Labor Archives, Georgia State University, Atlanta.

34. O'Neill to Walraven, February 23, 1972, 1866:43.

35. Jimmy Walraven to Raymond Roach, February 24, 1972, TWUA-GTA Papers, 1866:43.

36. Notes prepared by Jimmy Walraven, early March 1972, TWUA-GTA Papers, 1866:43; Roach interview.

37. Notes prepared by Jimmy Walraven.

38. Ibid.

39. Notes of Jimmy Walraven, July 23, 1972, TWUA-GTA Papers, 1866:43.

40. Ibid.

41. Ibid.

42. Joseph A. McDonald, "Textile Workers and Unionization: A Community Study" (Ph.D. diss., University of Tennessee, 1981); "Education Is Essential Foundation, Inc., Project Proposal for the Tennessee Valley Authority," 1993–94, Dalton–Whitfield County Library, Dalton, Ga., Vertical File.

43. U.S. Bureau of the Census, *1963 Census of Manufactures,* vol. 2, 22D-4, and *1977 Census of Manufactures,* vol. 2, 22D-5-7, Washington, D.C.

44. Steven S. Plice, "Manpower and Merger: The Impact of Merger upon Personnel Policies in the Carpet and Furniture Industries," Manpower and Human Resources Study No. 5, Industrial Research Unit, Wharton School, University of Pennsylvania, Philadelphia, 1976, 118–19.

45. Ibid.

46. U.S. Bureau of the Census, *1963 Census of Manufactures,* vol. 3, *Area Statistics,* 11–10 and 11–18.

47. U.S. Bureau of the Census, *1963 Census of Manufactures,* vol. 2, 22D-5, and *1967 Census of Manufactures,* vol. 2, 22D-6.

48. Plice, "Manpower and Merger," 114.

49. Ibid., 115–16.

50. Roach interview.

51. Minchin, *"What Do We Need a Union For?",* 206–9.

52. TWUA Research Department, March 5, 1973, TWUA Papers, micro 631.

53. A chamber of commerce study released in late 1968 showed that Dalton had a "shortage" of approximately 650 workers. *Atlanta Journal,* December 17, 1968.

54. William T. Deyo Jr., "Financing the Tufted Carpet Industry," *Journal of Commercial Bank Lending* 53 (November 1970): 40–41.

55. *Atlanta Constitution,* April 20, 1973.

56. Education Is Essential Foundation, Inc., "Developing Job-Specific Training Materials for the Carpet Industry," Whitfield County–Dalton Chamber of Commerce file, Dalton Public Library, Dalton, Ga.

57. Charles F. Floyd and Thomas M. Springer, "The Georgia Economy," report compiled for the Georgia Department of Transportation, 1988, Kennesaw State University Library. Statistics for the report were drawn from census data.

58. *Atlanta Journal and Constitution,* March 5, 1972.

59. Roach interview.

Chapter 5. New South Boom

1. TTMA *Directory,* 1965, 187–90.

2. Deaton, *Bedspreads to Broadloom,* 55.

3. *Business Week,* January 15, 1955, 72–74.

4. *Business Week,* January 15, 1955, 72–74.

5. Quoted in *Southern Textile News,* October 30, 1954, TTMA clipping file.

6. *Retailing Daily,* April 25, 1955, and June 14, 1955, TTMA clipping file.

7. *Retailing Daily,* March 28, 1956, TTMA clipping file.

8. Ibid., April 11, 1956.

9. E. T. Barwick, interview with Tom Deaton, April 8, 1980; used courtesy of Tom Deaton.

10. *Home Furnishings Daily,* March 24, 1958, TTMA clipping file.

11. *Home Furnishings Daily,* April 10, 1958, TTMA clipping file.

12. *Home Furnishings Daily,* April 22, 1958, and April 28, 1958, TTMA clipping file.

13. Hoff quoted in *Home Furnishings Daily,* April 15, 1958, TTMA clipping file.

14. *Home Furnishings Daily,* September 17, 1959, TTMA clipping file.

15. *Business Week,* December 29, 1956, 92, and *Barron's,* July 6, 1964, 19.

16. *Advertising Age,* August 8, 1960, 86.

17. *Advertising Age,* November 18, 1963, 8.

18. Ibid.

19. Figures found in Reynolds, *Innovations,* 143.

20. Ibid., and *Business Week,* June 16, 1956, 56.

21. *Retailing Daily,* March 12, 1955, and TTMA Wage Survey, April 1956 and November 1956, TTMA Papers.

22. *Home Furnishings Daily,* January 24, 1961, and *B-Line News,* Barwick company newsletter, copy found in TTMA Papers, Barwick file.

23. Barwick interview, and *Home Furnishings Daily,* January 24, 1961.

24. Barwick interview.

25. Barwick to Erwin Mitchell, April 1, 1959; n.d., probably early June 1959; July 22, 1959; and August 3, 1959, Erwin Mitchell Papers, box 17, Richard B. Russell Library, University of Georgia, Athens.

26. Mitchell to Barwick, August 6, 1959, Erwin Mitchell Papers, box 17.

27. Barwick to Mitchell, August 10, 1959, Mitchell Papers, box 17.

28. James B. Carey to Erwin Mitchell, August 18, 1959, Erwin Mitchell Papers, box 17. Interestingly, Mitchell's papers contain no negative correspondence from the TWUA locals in Dalton. Perhaps local union leaders recognized a friend in a tough spot and chose not to complicate Mitchell's political life any further.

29. Robert W. Kirk, "The Carpet Industry: Present Status and Future Prospects," Industrial Research Report prepared for the Wharton School of Finance and Commerce, 1970, 42.

30. Barwick quoted in *Atlanta Constitution,* May 10, 1968.

31. Ibid.

32. *Home Furnishings Daily,* July 5, 1968, Sims clipping file, in his possession, Cartersville, Ga.

33. *Home Furnishings Daily,* March 21, 1969, Sims clipping file.

34. *Home Furnishings Daily,* May 3, 1968, TTMA clipping file.

35. *Floor Covering Weekly,* November 25, 1968.

36. Kirk, "Carpet Industry," 50–52.

37. "Barwick—Still an Industry Giant," interview with E. T. Barwick, *Southwest Floor Covering* (November 1985).

38. Ibid.

39. Carpet and Rug Institute, *Carpet and Rug Industry Review, 1993* (Dalton, Ga.: Carpet and Rug Institute, 1993).

40. Kurt Salmon Associates, "Tufting's Unrealized Profit Potential," *Textile Industries* (May 1969): 55–65.

41. Norris Little, interview by Jim Engstrom, April 19, 1995, KSU Carpet History Project.

42. Plice, "Manpower and Merger," 86–90.

43. U.S. Bureau of the Census, *1982 Census of Manufactures,* "Concentration Ratios in Manufacturing," MC 82, 7–64.

44. Ibid.

45. *Business Week,* May 19, 1975, 58–60.

46. Ibid.; *Atlanta Constitution,* June 11, 1975, and July 18, 1975.

47. Quoted in *Business Week,* May 19, 1975, 60.

48. *Business Week,* November 29, 1976, 81; *Atlanta Constitution,* December 13, 1976.

49. *Atlanta Constitution,* November 23, 1977, 9.

50. *Atlanta Constitution,* October 10, 1978.

51. Barwick interview.

52. *Business Week,* May 19, 1975, 59–60.

Chapter 6. A World of Opportunity II

1. U.S. Bureau of the Census, *1963 Census of Manufactures,* vol. 2, *Industry Statistics,* 1964, 22D-5, and vol. 3, *Area Statistics,* 11–18.

2. "History of E & B Carpet Mills," no author or date, in the personal files of Bobby Mosteller, Chatsworth, Ga.; *Dallas Morning News,* July 10, 1966.

3. *Modern Textiles* (February 1966), from Bobby Mosteller clipping file; *Barron's*, June 27, 1966.

4. Bobby Mosteller, interviewed by author, October 27, 1993, KSU Carpet History Project.

5. Ibid.

6. *Calhoun Times*, June 13, 1963, and Mosteller interview.

7. Mosteller interview, and "New Company Prospectus, April 18, 1968," in "History of Galaxy Carpet Mills," Mosteller clipping file. The "History" is a compilation of documents, memoranda, and clippings detailing Galaxy's corporate past, compiled by Bobby Mosteller.

8. Ibid.

9. Charles Bramlett, interview by author, November 18, 1993, KSU Carpet History Project, and "New Company Prospectus," Mosteller clipping file.

10. Bramlett interview.

11. Ibid.

12. Ibid.

13. Mosteller interview.

14. Ibid.

15. Ibid., and Bramlett interview.

16. "New Company Prospectus," Mosteller clipping file, and Mosteller interview.

17. "New Company Prospectus," Mosteller clipping file.

18. Mosteller and Bramlett interviews.

19. "New Company Prospectus," Mosteller clipping file.

20. Ibid.

21. Mosteller interview.

22. Announcement to Galaxy customers, December 1970, and "Special Announcement," January 15, 1971, Mosteller clipping file.

23. "Some Facts about Galaxy Carpet Mills," leaflet distributed at the grand opening of Galaxy's new headquarters in Elk Grove, October 24, 1971, Mosteller clipping file.

24. *Home Furnishings Daily*, December 17, 1971.

25. Pat Terry, "Reaching for the Stars? Galaxy Plays It Safe," *Home Furnishings Daily*, April 25, 1972.

26. Ibid.

27. Enid G. Colp, "Galaxy Is Adhering to Controlled Growth," *Retailing Home Furnishings*, June 5, 1978.

28. *Floor Covering Weekly*, November 27, 1972; *Home Furnishings Daily*, April 9, 1973; *Floor Covering Weekly*, January 7, 1974, and May 20, 1974.

29. *Floor Covering Weekly*, October 10, 1977.

30. Ibid., and *Carpet and Rug Industry* (March 1978).

31. Colp, "Galaxy Is Adhering to Controlled Growth," and *Western Merchandiser* (Summer 1978).

32. *Seattle Times,* March 24, 1978, and *Chicago Daily Herald,* December 24, 1977.

33. Colp, "Galaxy Is Adhering to Controlled Growth."

34. Barbara Marsh, "Galaxy Shrugs Off Downturn, Cleans Up in Carpet Market," *Crain's Chicago Business,* February 1, 1982.

35. Ibid.

36. *Floor Covering Weekly,* July 5, 1982.

37. *Crain's Chicago Business,* February 20, 1984.

38. Ibid.

39. *Crain's Chicago Business,* September 3, 1984.

40. Ibid.

41. *Crain's Chicago Business,* March 4, 1985.

42. *Chicago Daily Herald,* October 23, 1986.

43. *Crain's Chicago Business,* March 14, 1988.

44. Ibid.

45. Mosteller interview.

46. Ibid., and Bramlett interview.

47. Mosteller interview.

48. *Crain's Chicago Business,* March 6, 1989, and *Chicago Sun-Times,* May 2, 1989.

49. *Chicago Sun-Times,* May 2, 1989, and *Floor Covering Weekly,* May 5, 1989, and April 15, 1989.

50. Bobbie Carmical, "Diamond Starts to Dazzle," *Carpet & Rug Industry* (January 1986): 28, 32, and author's notes from interview with James C. Patton, April 5, 1995.

51. Carmical, "Diamond Starts to Sparkle," 32.

52. Ibid., 34.

53. Ibid.

54. Data from U.S. Bureau of the Census, *Census of Manufactures,* 1963, Industry Series, 22D-7, and 1982, 22D-9.

55. Description drawn from notes of author's interview with James C. Patton, former owner of Chief Vann Carpets, Chatsworth, Georgia.

56. Julian Saul, interview with Randy Patton, August 3, 1993, KSU Carpet History Project.

57. Peggy Whaley, "How a Tufter's Tufter Survives the Competition," *Carpet & Rug Industry* (January 1977): 23–26.

58. Ibid.

59. *Carpet & Rug Industry* (July 1975): 16–18; *Dalton Carpet Journal,* September 16, 1990, 3.

60. Billie J. Walters and James O. Wheeler, "Localization Economies in the American Carpet Industry," *Geographical Review* 74 (Spring 1984): 183–91.

61. Ibid.

62. *Dalton Daily Citizen-News,* June 10, 1971; Spirer letter in Painter, *Millionaire's Fun.*

Chapter 7. Managing Growth

1. *Dalton Daily Citizen-News,* January 29, 1982; *Dalton Daily Citizen-News,* December 3, 1955.

2. *Dalton Citizen,* May 5, 1959.

3. *Dalton Daily Citizen-News,* August 30, 1963; June 25, 1968.

4. *Atlanta Journal,* January 10, 1967.

5. *Atlanta Journal,* December 11, 1969.

6. *Chattanooga Times,* October 30, 1971; *Dalton Daily Citizen-News,* December 10, 1971.

7. Peggy Whaley, "Taking the Novel Approach," *Carpet & Rug Industry* (December 1982): 18–21.

8. Fred Lehman, Prog. Manager, Surface Water Program, to Gene Welsh, Chief Water Protection Branch, March 19, 1979, 88-2-14, box 84, Department of Natural Resources (DNR), Georgia Department of Archives, Atlanta; Marshall Painter, Operations Manager, Dalton Utilities, to Ben Carmichael, Environmental Protection Division, Water Dept., April 24, 1979, 88-2-14, box 55, DNR.

9. Whaley, "Taking the Novel Approach," 19–20; *Dalton Daily Citizen-News,* July 3, 1985.

10. "Associations of the Carpet and Rug Industry in the United States Leading to the Carpet and Rug Institute," n.d., probably 1970, Carpet and Rug Institute Papers, Carpet and Rug Institute, Dalton, Ga.

11. *Wall Street Journal,* September 2, 1970, 6.

12. Carpet and Rug Institute, *The Carpet Specifier's Handbook* (Dalton, Ga.: Carpet and Rug Institute, 1992), 21.

13. Carpet and Rug Institute, *Directory and Report,* 1976, 84.

14. *New York Times,* February 15, 1970, 76.

15. *New York Times,* April 5, 1970, 37.

16. *Wall Street Journal,* September 2, 1970, 6; Lila Shokes, *Contract Carpeting* (New York: Watson-Guptill Publications, 1974), 82.

17. *New York Times,* October 7, 1972, 18, and July 15, 1973, 36.

18. Barry Torrance, interview with Randy Patton, May 10, 1995, KSU Carpet History Project.

19. Ibid.

20. Shaheen, *World Carpets,* 94–95.

21. *Business Week,* November 26, 1966; TTMA annual report, *Tufting Industry Review,* 1967, 144.

22. Shaheen, *World Carpets,* 95.

23. Ibid., 94–95.

24. CRI Executive Committee "Minutes," July 23, 1970, Carpet and Rug Institute Papers (hereafter cited as "CRI Papers").

25. Ibid.

26. CRI Executive Committee "Minutes," December 23, 1970, CRI Papers.

27. CRI Executive Committee "Minutes," March 18, 1971, CRI Papers.

28. Ibid.

29. CRI Executive Committee "Minutes," May 19, 1971, CRI Papers.

30. Ibid.

31. Shaheen, *World Carpets,* 97–98.

32. *New York Times,* February 27, 1975, 38; Shaheen, *World Carpets,* 96.

33. Shaheen, *World Carpets,* 98–99.

34. Richard Eldredge to CRI Board of Directors, February 19, 1979.

35. CRI Executive Committee "Minutes," 1979–80, CRI Papers.

36. Hobsbawm, *Age of Extremes,* 286; Carpet and Rug Institute, *Industry Review,* 1993, 8–9; U.S. Dept. of Labor, Bureau of Labor Statistics, *Employment, Hours, and Earnings, 1909–1994,* vol. 1 (Washington, D.C.: U.S. Government Printing Office, 1995).

37. Spirer interview.

38. Ibid.

39. Memorandum from Ann S. Foster, CRI Comptroller, to Truitt Lomax and Richard Eldredge, March 9, 1979, CRI Executive Committee File, 1979–80, CRI Papers.

40. Spirer interview.

41. *Dalton Carpet Journal,* November 18, 1990; Jane Osborne, executive director of Carpet Manufacturers Marketing Association, interview with Kitty Kelly, July 27, 1994, KSU Carpet History Project.

42. *Carpet & Rug Industry* (January 1980): 16–17.

43. Reported in *Carpet & Rug Industry* (January 1984): 17–18, (January 1985): 36–37, (May 1986): 41.

44. *Atlanta Constitution,* July 6, 1986.

45. *Atlanta Constitution,* January 14, 1987; January 21, 1987.

46. *Atlanta Constitution,* February 14, 1987, and November 18, 1987; *Carpet & Rug Industry* (November 1991): 16–18.

Chapter 8. Survival of the Fittest

1. *Wall Street Journal,* March 31, 1998, 15.

2. Anderson quoted in *Atlanta Journal and Constitution,* December 22, 1986; Bramlett interview.

3. J. C. Shaw, interview with Randy Patton, April 11, 1998, KSU Carpet History Project.

4. Ibid.

5. *Dalton Daily Citizen-News,* May 13, 1985. Shaw was interviewed for this story and was quoted at length.

6. *Atlanta Journal and Constitution,* March 17, 1985, and "Shaw Industries, Inc. Inter-office Memorandum," March 22, 1993, provided by Warren Sims.

7. Shaw interview.

8. *Textile World* (October 1962): 106–7.

9. Shaw interview.

10. "Shaw Memorandum," March 22, 1993, copy provided by Warren Sims.

11. Arthur Andersen & Co. Financial Report on Philadelphia Carpet Co., August 4, 1967, Sims clipping file.

12. Ibid.; "Shaw Industries, Inc.: J. C. Bradford & Co. Regional Research Report," January 17, 1972, Sims clipping file; and *Floor Covering Weekly,* January 1, 1968.

13. "Prospectus" for Shaw Industries, prepared by Drexel Firestone, October 14, 1971, Sims clipping file.

14. Bob Shaw quoted in *Dalton Daily Citizen-News,* May 13, 1985; *Moody's Industrial Manual,* 1976, 3895.

15. *Daily Citizen-News,* May 13, 1985.

16. Ibid.

17. "Progress Report," August 1972, by Drexel Firestone, Sims clipping file.

18. Enid G. Colp, "Shaw Changes Marketing with Command Post Switch," *Retailing Home Furnishings,* January 2, 1978; Robert E. Shaw quoted in *Atlanta Journal and Constitution,* March 17, 1985.

19. Colp, "Shaw Changes Marketing."

20. Margaret Vogel and Frank O'Neill, "The Top 25 Manufacturers of Carpet and Rugs in the United States—1982," *Carpet & Rug Industry* (June 1983): 6–10.

21. *Merrill Lynch Market Review,* December 5, 1983. Similar assessments came from Wheat First Securities, reported in the *Miami Herald,* September 7, 1984; and Walter Mintz, reported in *Barron's,* January 14, 1985.

22. Warren Sims, interview with Randy Patton, August 15, 1994, KSU Carpet History Project; Chuck Reece, "Carpet King," *Georgia Trend* (August 1990).

23. Observations drawn from a presentation at Kennesaw State University by Reg Burnett of Reg Burnett International, a carpet industry consulting firm, April 5, 1994; Lusk quoted in *Textile World* (June 1985).

24. Observations gleaned from Burnett presentation.

25. *Textile World* (June 1985).

26. *Atlanta Journal and Constitution,* March 17, 1985, and Reg Burnett presentation.

27. *Atlanta Journal and Constitution,* March 17, 1985.

28. Ibid.; *Daily Citizen-News,* May 13, 1985.

29. *Daily Citizen-News,* May 13, 1985.

30. *Floor Covering Weekly,* April 29, 1985.

31. *Textile World* (June 1985), and Dan Alalmo, "Robert Shaw's Terms of Controversy," *Flooring* (February 1989).

32. Frank O'Neill, "The Top 25," *Carpet & Rug Industry* (June 1987).

33. Ibid.

34. This discussion of Du Pont is based on "Case C-1: Du Pont 'Stainmaster,'" in O. C. Ferrell, George H. Lucas, and David J. Luck, *Marketing Strategy and Plans,* 3d ed. (Englewood Hills, N.J.: Prentice Hall, 1989), 315–19.

35. *Carpet and Rug Industry Review, 1993,* 7.

36. Bette Collins, "Stainmaster," case study, Graduate School of Business Administration, University of Virginia, 1989, 2–3. This study was prepared with the assistance of Du Pont.

37. Ibid., 6.

38. Ibid.

39. *Textile World* (January 1987): 75, and *Flooring* (July 1987): 8.

40. Frank O'Neill, "Has the American Carpet Industry Entered into a New Era of Consumer Marketing?" *Carpet & Rug Industry* (October 1987): 7–8.

41. *Atlanta Constitution,* August 10, 1987.

42. Quoted in Alalmo, "Robert Shaw's Terms of Controversy."

43. *Wall Street Journal,* September 30, 1987.

44. Ibid., and Kerry Hannon, "Full Speed Ahead and Damn the Stock Market," *Forbes,* January 25, 1988.

45. Hannon, "Full Speed Ahead."

46. *Textile World* (March 1988): 12.

47. Frank O'Neill, "The Top 25," *Carpet & Rug Industry* (June 1988): 12–14.

48. Michael Berns, "Carpet Mill Anemia," *Carpet & Rug Industry* (January 1989), and Berns, "The Shaw Factor," *Carpet & Rug Industry* (October 1989).

49. Berns, "Shaw Factor."

50. "Shaw Inter-Office Memorandum," March 22, 1993; Shaw quoted in *Atlanta Journal,* May 16, 1990.

51. *Wall Street Journal,* June 12, 1991, and Chuck Reece, "Carpet King."

52. *Wall Street Journal,* June 12, 1991.

53. Janet Herlihy and Janice Kirby, "The World's Top 50 Carpet and Rug Manufacturers," *Carpet & Rug Industry* (November 1992).

54. David Lance and Charles Bramlett interviews; Burnett presentation.

55. *Atlanta Constitution,* March 14, 1995, and *Carpet & Rug Industry* (April 1996): 20–22; DowJones Online News, October 22, 1998.

56. *Carpet & Rug Industry* (June 1991): 16–17; (April 1996): 23.

57. *Carpet & Rug Industry* (April 1996): 23.

58. Julian Saul interview; *Carpet & Rug Industry* (April 1996): 25.

59. *Wall Street Journal,* August 19, 1998, B4.

60. Ibid.

61. Data obtained from the U.S. Census Bureau, County Estimates for Median Household Income and Poverty Rates, Table C93-13, http://www.census.gov/hhes/www/saipe93/estimate/c93_13.htm and *Census of Manufactures,* 1992, Area Statistics.

62. *Atlanta Journal and Constitution,* March 21, 1982, 8-A.

63. Kitty Kelley, "Blue Collar Jobs and Brown Workers: Immigration in a Southern Mill Town" (paper presented at the Southern Historical Association Annual Meeting, New Orleans, November 9, 1995); Julian Saul interview; *Atlanta Constitution,* August 24, 1987, 8-D.

64. Kelley, "Blue Collar Jobs and Brown Workers."

65. Lindsey Kelly, "Is Shaw Industries Too Big?" *Georgia Trend* (September 1993): 33–34; *Atlanta Constitution,* December 14, 1995; *Atlanta Constitution,* December 13, 1995, 1E; American Lawyer Media, L.P., "Fulton County Daily Report," July 16, 1997, http://web.lexis-nexis.com/universe.

66. *Atlanta Business Chronicle,* October 20, 1995.

67. *Atlanta Journal and Constitution,* February 2, 1997.

68. *Atlanta Business Chronicle,* May 24, 1996.

69. Rhodes and Saul quoted in *Atlanta Business Chronicle,* October 20, 1995.

70. Shaw quoted in Kelly, "Is Shaw Industries Too Big?" 31.

Conclusion

1. Flamming, *Creating the Modern South*, 328–34.

2. Philip Scranton, *Endless Novelty* (Princeton: Princeton University Press, 1997).

3. Bartley, *New South*, 469–70.

4. Martha Nelson interviews with Judson Manly, November 2, 1997, and Michael Manly, November 13, 1997. Nelson conducted these interviews for a project called "Family Stories," and the transcripts and tapes are available at the Dalton Regional Library. The "elaboration" on the story was given informally to the author by a widow and son of a Manly employee following a public program based on Nelson's interviews in Dalton, Georgia, February 5, 1998.

Bibliography

Manuscript Collections and Other Unpublished Material

American Carpet Institute Papers. Carpet and Rug Institute, Dalton, Ga.

Bigelow-Sanford Papers. Baker Library, Harvard University.

Carpet and Rug Institute Papers. Carpet and Rug Institute, Dalton, Ga.

Cobble Division, Spencer Wright Industries. Historical Files of Cobble Division, Dalton, Ga.

Du Pont Textile Fibers Department Records. Hagley Museum and Library, Wilmington, Del.

Erwin Mitchell Papers. Richard B. Russell Library, University of Georgia, Athens.

Mohawk Papers. Mohawk Public Relations Office, Atlanta, Ga.

Morgan Papers. Birmingham Public Library, Birmingham, Alabama.

National Association of Wool Manufacturers Papers. Museum of American Textile History, North Andover, Mass.

Textile Workers Union of America Papers. State Historical Society of Wisconsin, Madison.

Tufted Textile Manufacturers Association Papers. Carpet and Rug Institute, Dalton, Ga.

TWUA-GTA Joint Board Papers. Southern Labor Archives, Georgia State University, Atlanta.

Oral Histories

Evans Whitener, Catherine. "If I Had Been a Man." Whitfield-Murray Historical Society, Crown Gardens and Archives, Dalton, Ga.

Most of the following interviews were conducted by KSU faculty and students as part of the Kennesaw State University Carpet History Project, Oral History Series, and transcripts can be found at the Sturgis Library, Kennesaw State University, Kennesaw, Ga. As indicated, some interviews were conducted by Tom Deaton and are used with his permission.

Tina Adame, Jan. 30, 1994, interviewed by Kitty Kelly.

Ruth Aikens, Apr. 12, 1996, interviewed by Linda Williams.

Jim Baird, Jan. 30, 1994, interviewed by Kitty Kelley.

Jack Bandy, Mar. 4, 1994, interviewed by Randy Patton.

Jack Bandy, Oct. 10, 1995, interviewed by Jim Engstrom.

E. T. Barwick, Apr. 8, 1980, interviewed by Tom Deaton.

Max Beasley, May 11, 1994, interviewed by Bart Threatte.

Paul Bradley, Nov. 16, 1995, interviewed by Jim Engstrom.

Charles Bramlett, Nov. 18, 1993, interviewed by Randy Patton.

Pat Brock, Apr. 5, 1996, interviewed by Linda Williams.

James Brown, Mar. 8, 1994, interviewed by Randy Patton.

James Brown, May 18, 1995, interviewed by Jim Engstrom.

Norman Burkett, Aug. 10, 1995, interviewed by Jim Engstrom.

Lewis Card, May 21, 1979, interviewed by Tom Deaton.

Lewis Card, May 11, 1994, interviewed by Bart Threatte.

Roy Card, May 11, 1994, interviewed by Bart Threatte.

Roy and Lewis Card, Apr. 15, 1994, interviewed by Bart Threatte.

Roy and Lewis Card, May 18, 1994, interviewed by Bart Threatte.

Charles Carmical, Jan. 7, 1994, interviewed by Tom Scott.

Patsy Cooper, Apr. 10, 1996, interviewed by Linda Williams.

Tom Durkan, Feb. 24, 1994, interviewed by Randy Patton.

Smith Foster, May 1, 1995, interviewed by Jim Engstrom.

Linda Freeman, Aug. 9, 1994, interviewed by Kitty Kelley.

James Gamblin, Mar. 29, 1995, interviewed by Jim Engstrom.

Ann Gentry, Apr. 20, 1996, interviewed by Linda Williams.

Walter Guinan, Sept. 28, 1993, interviewed by Randy Patton.

David Hamilton, Nov. 28, 1996, interviewed by Jim Engstrom.

Willie Hicks, Apr. 17, 1996, interviewed by Linda Williams.

Lois Johnson, Apr. 29, 1996, interviewed by Linda Williams.

Jim Jolly, Sept. 23, 1993, interviewed by Jill Good.

Jim Jolly, July 27, 1995, interviewed by Jim Engstrom.

Katherine Kerr, Mary Lou Bankston, Nov. 17, 1993, interviewed by Randy Patton.

Glynn King, Apr. 5, 1996, interviewed by Linda Williams.

Bert Lance, Jan. 3, 1994, interviewed by Randy Patton and Virginia Ingram.

David Lance, Jan. 3, 1994, interviewed by Randy Patton and Virginia Ingram.

Addison Layson, July 13, 1994, interviewed by Randy Patton.

Norris Little, Apr. 19, 1995, interviewed by Jim Engstrom.

Truett Lomax, May 5, 1995, interviewed by Randy Patton.

Jean Manly, Sept. 30, 1993, interviewed by Bill Davidson.

Judson Manly, Feb. 25, 1994, interviewed by Bart Threatte.

Randall Maret, June 15, 1995, interviewed by Jim Engstrom.

Jim Middleton, Apr. 12, 1995, interviewed by Jim Engstrom.

Erwin Mitchell, Dec. 15, 1994, interviewed by Randy Patton.

Bobby Mosteller, Oct. 27, 1993, interviewed by Randy Patton.
John Neal, July 6, 1995, interviewed by Jim Engstrom.
Jane Osborne, July 27, 1994, interviewed by Kitty Kelley.
Mark Pace, Oct. 13, 1993, interviewed by Randy Patton and Tom Scott.
Lynne Peer, Nov. 14, 1995, interviewed by Jim Engstrom.
Dusty Rhodes, Dec. 17, 1993, interviewed by Pat Taylor.
Raymond Roach, May 23, 1994, interviewed by Randy Patton.
Derrell Roberts, Nov. 14, 1995, interviewed by Jim Engstrom.
Leonard Rollins, May 10, 1998, interviewed by Randy Patton.
Butch Sanders, Apr. 12, 1995, interviewed by Jim Engstrom.
Julian Saul, May 10, 1983, interviewed by Tom Deaton.
Julian Saul, Aug. 3, 1993, interviewed by Randy Patton.
Shaheen Shaheen, May 26, 1994, interviewed by Tom Deaton.
J. C. Shaw, Apr. 11, 1998, interviewed by Randy Patton.
Warren Sims, Aug. 8, 1994, interviewed by Randy Patton.
Donald Sloan, July 8, 1994, interviewed by Randy Patton and Tom Scott.
Mary Bell Smith, Oct. 15, 1993, interviewed by Randy Patton.
Mary Bell Smith, Aug. 8, 1994, interviewed by Randy Patton.
Peter Spirer, May 25, 1994, interviewed by Randy Patton.
Joe Stubbs, July 6, 1995, interviewed by Jim Engstrom.
Buford Talley, Mar. 8, 1994, interviewed by Randy Patton.
Charles Thomas, Mar. 29, 1995, interviewed by Jim Engstrom.
John J. Todd, Dec. 17, 1993, interviewed by Steve Hall.
Barry Torrance, May 10, 1995, interviewed by Randy Patton.
Jack Turner, Nov. 4, 1994, interviewed by Randy Patton.
Jack Turner, Jan. 8, 1995, interviewed by Jim Engstrom.
Ron Van Gelderen, Jan. 17, 1995, interviewed by Jim Engstrom.
Jimmy Walraven, Mar. 28, 1995, interviewed by Randy Patton.
Lulu Westcott, Jan. 20, 1994, interviewed by Kitty Kelley.

Government Documents

Decisions and Orders of the National Labor Relations Board. Washington, D.C.: U.S. Government Printing Office, 1961–65.
Patent Depository. Price Gilbert Library, Georgia Institute of Technology. Microfilm.
U.S. Bureau of the Census. *Census of Manufactures.* Washington, D.C., 1947–92.
U.S. Congress. House of Representatives. *Documents Relative to the Manufactures in the United States, Collected and Transmitted to the House of Repre-*

sentatives, in Compliance with a Resolution of Jan. 19, 1832, by the Secretary of the Treasury. 22d Cong., 1st sess., 1833, H. Doc. 308, I, 16–17, 328–29, 386–87, 660–61.

U.S. Department of Labor. Bureau of Labor Statistics. *Employment, Hours, and Earnings, 1909–1994*. Vol. 1. Washington, D.C.: U.S. Government Printing Office, 1995.

Newspapers and Periodicals

Advertising Age
American Carpet and Upholstery Trade Journal
Atlanta Journal and Constitution
Barron's
Business Week
Calhoun Times
Carpet & Rug Industry
Chattanooga News–Free Press
Chattanooga Times
Crain's Chicago Business
Daily Citizen-News
Dalton Citizen
Dalton Daily News
Editor and Publisher
Floor Covering Weekly
Fortune
Georgia Trend
Home Furnishings Daily
New York Times
Printer's Ink
Retailing Daily
Textile World
Wall Street Journal
Water Works Engineering

Primary and Secondary Sources

Adams, Roy, and Noah Meltz, eds. *Industrial Relations Theory*. Metuchen, N.J.: Rutgers University Press, 1993.

American Carpet Institute. *Basic Facts about the Carpet and Rug Industry.* 1968.

Anderson, Gary. "Industry Clustering for Economic Development." *Economic Development Review* 12 (Spring 1994): 26–32.

Anderson, Susan H. *The Most Splendid Carpet.* Philadelphia: National Park Service, 1978.

Archer, Earnest R. "A Study of Managerial Decision-Making in a Social Responsibility Area." Ph.D. diss., University of Georgia, 1971.

Arnall, Ellis. *The Shore Dimly Seen.* 1946. Reprint, New York: Acclaim Publishing Co., 1966.

Bartley, Numan V. *The New South, 1945–1980: The Story of the South's Modernization.* Baton Rouge: Louisiana State University Press, 1995.

Beecher, Catherine [*sic*] E., and Harriet Beecher Stowe. *The American Woman's Home; or, Principles of Domestic Science. . . .* 1869. Reprint, Hartford: Stowe-Day Foundation, 1975.

Blackford, Mansel. *A History of Small Business in America.* New York: Twayne Publishers, 1991.

Brandt, Harry. "Tufted Textiles." Federal Reserve Bank of Atlanta Economic Studies, no. 2., 1955.

Carlton, David L. *Mill and Town in South Carolina, 1880–1920.* Baton Rouge: Louisiana State University Press, 1982.

———. "The Revolution from Above: The National Market and the Beginnings of Industrialization in North Carolina." *Journal of American History* 77 (September 1990): 445–75.

Carlton, David L., and Peter A. Coclanis. "Another Great Migration?: From Region to Race in Southern Liberalism, 1938–1945." *Southern Cultures* 3 (Fall 1997): 37–62.

Carpet and Rug Institute. *Carpet and Rug Industry Review.* 1993.

Carpet & Rug Institute Directory and Report. 1970.

Cleaveland, Nehemiah. *A Memoir of Erastus Brigham Bigelow.* Boston: District Committee of the Fourth Congressional District, 1860.

Cobb, James C. *Industrialization and Southern Society, 1877–1984.* Lexington: University Press of Kentucky, 1984.

———. *The Selling of the South: The Southern Crusade for Industrial Development, 1936–1990.* Baton Rouge: Louisiana State University Press, 1982.

Cole, Arthur H. *The American Wool Manufacture.* 2 vols. Cambridge: Harvard University Press, 1926.

Cole, Arthur H., and Harold F. Williamson. *The American Carpet Manufacture: A History and an Analysis.* 2 vols. Cambridge: Harvard University Press, 1941.

Collins, Bette. "Stainmaster." Case study, Graduate School of Business Administration, University of Virginia, 1989. This study was prepared with the assistance of Du Pont.

Cook, A. N. *A Century of Carpet and Rug-Making in America, 1825–1925.* New York: Bigelow-Hartford Carpet Co., 1925.

David, Paul A. "Growth of Real Product in the United States before 1840: New Evidence, Controlled Conjectures." *Journal of Economic History* 27 (Fall 1967): 151–97.

Deaton, Thomas M. *From Bedspreads to Broadloom: The Story of the Tufted Carpet Industry.* Acton, Mass.: Tapestry Press, 1993.

Dowd-Hall, Jacquelyn, Robert Korstad, James Leloudis, Mary Murphy, Lu Ann Jones, and Christopher Daly. *Like a Family: The Making of a Southern Cotton Mill World.* Chapel Hill: University of North Carolina Press, 1987.

Ewing, John S., and Nancy P. Norton. *Broadlooms and Businessmen: A History of the Bigelow-Sanford Company.* Cambridge: Harvard University Press, 1955.

Faraday, Cornelia Bateman. *European and American Carpets and Rugs.* 1929. Reprint, Woodbridge, Suffolk, England: Antique Collectors' Club, 1990.

[Fay, Samuel, et al.]. *The Carpet Manufacture: A Statement of Facts Addressed to the United-States Revenue Commission.* Boston: John Wilson and Son, 1866.

Fink, Gary M., and Merl E. Reed, eds. *Race, Class, and Community in Southern Labor History.* Tuscaloosa: University of Alabama Press, 1994.

Flamming, Douglas. *Creating the Modern South: Millhands and Managers in Dalton, Georgia, 1884–1984.* Chapel Hill: University of North Carolina Press, 1992.

Flynn, Rosalie. "The Carpet Shop: A History of the Alexander Smith and Sons Carpet Company in Yonkers, New York." Master's thesis, Manhattanville College, 1986.

Ford, Andrew E. *History of the Origin of the Town of Clinton, Massachusetts, 1653–1865.* Clinton, Mass.: W. J. Coulter, 1896.

Goldin, Claudia, and Kenneth Sokoloff. "Women, Children, and Industrialization in the Early Republic: Evidence from the Manufacturing Censuses." *Journal of Economic History* 42 (December 1982): 741–74.

Grant, Donald L. "A Case in Collective Bargaining: The Alexander Smith and Sons Carpet Company, Incorporated, and Local 122 of the Textile Workers Union of America, C.I.O." Master's thesis, Princeton University, 1941.

Greeley, Horace, et al. *Great Industries of the United States: Being an Historical Summary of the Origin, Growth, and Perfection of the Chief Industrial Arts of This Country.* Hartford: J. B. Burr & Hyde, 1872.

Greenblatt, Sophie. "The History and Development of the Carpet Industry in Yonkers." Master's thesis, Columbia University, 1937.

Griffith, Barbara. *The Crisis of American Labor: Operation Dixie and the Defeat of the CIO.* Philadelphia: Temple University Press, 1988.

Heilbroner, Robert. *The Economic Transformation of America, 1600–Present.* 3d ed. New York: Harcourt Brace, 1994.

Henderson, David. "Rules and Regulations of the Merrimack Carpet Factory." January 2, 1855. Photocopy. Museum of American Textile History, North Andover, Mass.

Hobsbawm, Eric. *The Age of Extremes: A History of the World, 1914–1991.* New York: Random House, 1995.

Hodges, James. *New Deal Labor Policy and the Southern Cotton Textile Industry, 1933–1941.* Knoxville: University of Tennessee Press, 1986.

The Industries of Pennsylvania: Facts, Figures, and Illustrations, Historical, Descriptive and Biographical. . . . Philadelphia: Richard Edwards, 1882.

Ingham, John. *Making Iron and Steel: Independent Mills in Pittsburgh, 1820–1920.* Columbus: Ohio State University Press, 1991.

Kendrick, J. R. "The Carpet Industry in Philadelphia." In *Annual Report of the Secretary of Internal Affairs of the Commonwealth of Pennsylvania.* Pt. 3, *Industrial Statistics.* Harrisburg. Pa.: Edwin K. Meyers, 1889.

Kirk, Robert W. "The Carpet Industry: Present Status and Future Prospects." Wharton School of Finance and Commerce, Industrial research report no. 17, University of Pennsylvania. 1970.

Landreau, Anthony N. *America Underfoot: A History of Floor Coverings from Colonial Times to the Present.* Washington, D.C.: Smithsonian Institution Press, 1976.

Levine, Susan. "'Honor Each Noble Maid': Women Workers and the Yonkers Carpet Weavers' Strike of 1885." *New York History* 62 (April 1981): 153–76.

———. "Ladies and Looms: The Social Impact of Machine Power in the American Carpet Industry." In *Dynamos and Virgins Revisited: Women and Technological Change in History,* edited by Martha Moore Trescott, 67–76. Metuchen, N.J.: Scarecrow Press, 1979.

———. "Their Own Sphere: Women's Work, the Knights of Labor, and the Transformation of the Carpet Trade, 1870–1890." Ph.D. diss., City University of New York, 1979.

Lewis, W. David. *Sloss Furnaces and the Rise of the Birmingham District: An Industrial Epic.* Tuscaloosa: University of Alabama Press, 1994.

Little, Nina Fletcher. *Floor Coverings in New England before 1850.* Sturbridge, Mass.: Old Sturbridge Village, 1967.

The Manufactories and Manufacturers of Pennsylvania of the Nineteenth Century. Philadelphia: Galaxy Publishing Co., 1875.

Marshall, Alfred. *Principles of Economics.* 8th ed. London: Macmillan, 1920.

Masland, C. H., & Sons. *A Famous Horseman Goes to War: The Peace-Time and War-Time Story of an American Carpet Manufacturer.* N.p., 1943.

McDonald, Joseph A. "Textile Workers and Unionization: A Community Study." Ph.D. diss., University of Tennessee, 1981.

Minchin, Timothy J. *"What Do We Need a Union For?": The TWUA in the South, 1945–1955.* Chapel Hill: University of North Carolina Press, 1997.

National Recovery Administration. *Code of Fair Competition for the Carpet and Rug Manufacturing Industry.* Washington, D.C.: U.S. Government Printing Office, 1934.

Norton, Nancy. "Labor in the Early New England Carpet Factory." *Bulletin of the Business Historical Society* 26 (March 1952): 19–20.

Oliver Evans Chapter, Society for Industrial Archeology. *Workshop of the World: A Selective Guide to the Industrial Archeology of Philadelphia.* Wallingford, Pa.: Oliver Evans Press, 1990.

Painter, Mose, as told to Elaine Taylor. *I've Had a Millionaire's Fun.* Dalton, Ga.: Painter and Taylor Manuscript Co., 1982.

Piore, Michael, and Charles Sabel. *The Second Industrial Divide: Possibilities for Prosperity.* New York: Basic Books, 1984.

Pitkin, Timothy. *A Statistical View of the Commerce of the United States of America, Including Also an Account of Banks, Manufacturers, and Internal Trade and Improvements.* New Haven: Durrie & Peck, 1835.

Porter, Michael. *The Competitive Advantage of Nations.* New York: Basic Books, 1990.

Reed, John Shelton. *One South: An Ethnic Approach to Regional Culture* (Baton Rouge: Louisiana State University Press, 1982.

Revonah Spinning Mills. *The Histories and Backgrounds of Many of America's Outstanding Carpet Mills.* Hanover, Pa.: Revonah Spinning Mills, 1960.

Reynolds, William A. *Innovation in the United States Carpet Industry, 1947–1963.* Princeton, N.J.: D. Van Nostrand and Co., 1968.

Roth, Rodris. *Floor Coverings in Eighteenth-Century America.* United States National Museum Bulletin no. 250. Washington, D.C.: Smithsonian Institution Press, 1967.

Sabel, Charles. "Studied Trust: Building New Forms of Cooperation in a Volatile Economy." *Human Relations* 46 (September 1993): 1133–69.

Sabel, Charles, and Jonathan Zeitlin, eds. *World of Possibilities: Flexibility and Mass Production in Western Industrialization.* Cambridge: Cambridge University Press, 1997.

Saxenian, Annalee. "Lessons from Silicon Valley." *Technology Review* (July 1994): 42–51.

———. *Regional Advantage: Culture and Competition in Silicon Valley and Route 128*. Cambridge: Harvard University Press, 1994.

Scranton, Philip. "Diversity in Diversity: Flexible Production and American Industrialization." *Business History Review* 65 (Spring 1991): 27–90.

———. *Endless Novelty*. Princeton: Princeton University Press, 1997.

———. *Figured Tapestry: Production, Markets, and Power in Philadelphia Textiles, 1885–1941*. Cambridge: Cambridge University Press, 1989.

———. *Proprietary Capitalism: The Textile Manufacture at Philadelphia, 1800–1885*. Cambridge: Cambridge University Press, 1983.

Shaheen, Shaheen. *World Carpets: The First Thirty Years*. Dalton, Ga.: Lee Printing Co., 1985.

Shokes, Lila. *Contract Carpeting*. New York: Watson-Guptill Publications, 1974.

Storper, Michael, and Susan Christopherson. "Flexible Specialization and Regional Agglomerations: The Case of the U.S. Motion Picture Industry." *Annals of the Association of American Geographers* 77 (March 1987): 104–17.

Taussig, F. W. *The Tariff History of the United States*. 8th rev. ed. 1931. Reprint, New York: Capricorn Books, 1964.

Tupper, Jack A. "The Impact of the Relocation of the Alexander Smith Carpet Company upon the Municipal Government of the City of Yonkers, New York." Master's thesis, New York University, 1963.

von Rosenstiel, Helene, and Gail Caskey Winkler. *Floor Coverings for Historic Buildings: A Guide to Selecting Reproductions*. Washington, D.C.: Preservation Press, 1988.

Walters, Billie J., and James O. Wheeler. "Localization Economies in the American Carpet Industry." *Geographical Review* 74 (Spring 1984): 183–91.

Whitney, Simon N. *Trade Associations and Industrial Control: A Critique of the N.R.A.*. New York: Central Book Co., 1934.

Windham, Roy. *The Tufting Machine: A Practical Text of Instruction for Machine Fixers*. Rome, Ga.: Southern Craft Co., 1941.

Winkler, Gail Caskey, and Roger W. Moss. *Victorian Interior Decoration: American Interiors, 1830–1900*. New York: Henry Holt and Co., 1986.

Woodward, C. Vann. *Origins of the New South, 1877–1913*. Baton Rouge: Louisiana State University Press, 1951.

Wright, Annette C. "Strategy and Structure in the Textile Industry: Spencer Love and Burlington Mills, 1923–1962." *Business History Review* 69 (Spring 1995): 42–79.

Wright, Gavin. *Old South, New South: Revolutions in the Southern Economy since the Civil War*. New York: Basic Books, 1986.

Index